Little Women Abroad

Little Women Abroad

THE ALCOTT SISTERS'

LETTERS FROM EUROPE,

1870–1871

Louisa May Alcott and May Alcott

Edited by Daniel Shealy

The University of Georgia Press

ATHENS & LONDON

Designed by Erin Kirk New

Set in Minion by Graphic Composition, Inc.

Printed and bound by Thomson-Shore

The paper in this book meets the guidelines for
permanence and durability of the Committee on
Production Guidelines for Book Longevity of the
Council on Library Resources.

Printed in the United States of America

08   09   10   11   12   C   5   4   3   2   1

Library of Congress Cataloging-in-Publication Data

Alcott, Louisa May, 1832–1888.

[Correspondence. Selections]

Little women abroad : the Alcott sisters' letters from
Europe, 1870–1871 / edited by Daniel Shealy

p.   cm.

Includes bibliographical references and index.

ISBN-13: 978-0-8203-3009-9 (hardcover : alk. paper)

ISBN-10: 0-8203-3009-4 (hardcover : alk. paper)

1. Alcott, Louisa May, 1832–1888—Correspondence.

2. Alcott, Louisa May, 1832–1888—Travel—Europe.

3. Alcott, May, 1840–1879—Correspondence. 4. Alcott,
May, 1840–1879—Travel—Europe. 5. Authors, American—
19th century—Correspondence. 6. Europe—Description
and travel. I. Alcott, May, 1840–1879. II. Shealy, Daniel.
III. Title.

PS1018.A44 2008

813'.4—dc22 [B]

2007039027

British Library Cataloging-in-Publication Data available

Contents

List of Illustrations

vii

Acknowledgments

xi

Abbreviations of Works Cited

xiii

Introduction

xv

Notes on the Text

lxxv

Chronology

lxxviii

The Letters

1

Index

271

Illustrations

1. Louisa May Alcott (ca. 1870) xvi
2. May Alcott (ca. 1870) xix
3. Elizabeth Sewall Alcott (mid-1850s) xxii
4. Anna Alcott Pratt (ca. 1870) xxiii
5. Abigail May Alcott (ca. 1870) xxvii
6. Alice Bartlett (ca. 1870) xxxii
7. Amos Bronson Alcott (ca. early 1870s) xxxiii
8. John Bridge Pratt (late 1860s) lv
9. Fred and John Pratt (late 1860s) lvii
10. "A Seasick Nun" aboard the *Lafayette* (April 1870), by May Alcott 5
11. "Polly," frontispiece to *An Old-Fashioned Girl* (1870) 6
12. The Tower of St. Melanie, Morlaix, France (April 1870),
    by May Alcott 11
13. Madame Coste's pension (1999) 14
14. Dinan, France (17 April 1870), by May Alcott 18
15. Dinan, France (22 April 1870), by May Alcott 18
16. "Polly's Sermon," *An Old-Fashioned Girl* (1870) 21
17. Dinan, France (1999) 24
18. Gateway into Dinan, France (7 June 1870), by May Alcott 25
19. La Chapelle des Beaumanoirs, Lehon, France (1870),
    by May Alcott 31
20. Frontispiece to *Moods* (1865) 33
21. Madame Coste (ca. 1870), by May Alcott 34
22. Madame Coste's pension (1870), by May Alcott 37
23. Street Archway, Dinan, France (1870), by May Alcott 38
24. Dinan, France (1870), by May Alcott 40
25. Chateau de la Garaye, near Dinan, France (1870), by May Alcott 42

26. "Hawthorne's Seat," from *Concord Sketches* (1869), by May Alcott 53

27. "Notre salon chez Mdlle Coste," Dinan, France (1870), by May Alcott 55

28. Alice Bartlett (1870), by May Alcott 59

29. St. Malo Cathedral, near Dinan, France (28 April 1870), by May Alcott 61

30. Orchard House, home of the Alcotts (ca. 1870), Concord, Massachusetts 66

31. A servant at Madame Coste's pension (1870), by May Alcott 70

32. "Our Sleeping Room," Madame Coste's pension (1870), by May Alcott 71

33. Alice Bartlett and Gaston Forney, Dinan, France (1870) 74

34. "Mlle Kane," Dinan, France (1870), by May Alcott 80

35. Madame Coste, Dinan, France (ca. 1870) 81

36. William Niles, London (May 1871), by May Alcott 83

37. Louisa May Alcott, by E. L. Allen, Boston (ca. 1870) 85

38. Gaston Forney, Dinan, France (1870), by May Alcott 90

39. Madame Forney, Dinan, France (1870), by May Alcott 91

40. Alice Bartlett (ca. 1870) 99

41. Alice Bartlett and May Alcott (1870–71?) 100

42. Franklin B. Sanborn 109

43. Alice Bartlett (1870–71?), by May Alcott 117

44. Franklin B. Sanborn, Orchard House (1869–70?), by May Alcott 127

45. The dogs of St. Bernard Hospice (ca. 1870) 136

46. "Our Little Invalid," Emma Warren, Bex, Switzerland (1870), by May Alcott 148

47. Alfred Tidey, Bex, Switzerland (1870), by May Alcott 152

48. One of the Tidey boys, Bex, Switzerland (1870), by May Alcott 152

49. Lena Warren with her dog, Bex, Switzerland (1870), by May Alcott 154

50. Louisa May Alcott, engraving, *Hearth and Home* (1870) 156

51. Frontispiece to *Little Women, Part One* (1868), by May Alcott 157

52. Bronson Alcott in his study, Orchard House (1869–70?), by May Alcott 164

53. "The Golden Goose," Louisa May Alcott, Bex, Switzerland (1870), by May Alcott 172

54. Thomas Niles 180

55. "Pension Paradis," Vevey, Switzerland (1870), by May Alcott 182

56. "Americans Leaving Paris" (17 December 1870) 187

57. Orchard House, Concord, Massachusetts (with Bronson Alcott and grandson) 197

58. Bronson Alcott, from Caroline Hildreth's crayon portrait (1857) 203

59. Bois de Boulogne in Paris Cut Down (22 February 1871) 207

60. "Tom and Polly" (20 August 1870) 212

61. Herbert J. Pratt, Vevey, Switzerland (1870), by May Alcott 216

62. Strasbourgh Cathedral (19 November 1870) 219

63. "Flight of French Peasants" (5 November 1870) 220

64. Herbert J. Pratt, Vevey, Switzerland (1870), by May Alcott 223

65. Anna Alcott Pratt (ca. early 1860s) 225

66. Orchard House, Concord, Massachusetts (1870s) 230

67. "Crossing the Simplon" (3 October 1870), by May Alcott 234

68. Monte Rosa, Switzerland (5 October 1870), by May Alcott 235

69. Lake Lugano, Italy, by May Alcott 241

70. May Alcott to Bronson Alcott (30 October 1870) 244

71. John Bridge Pratt with son (mid-1860s?), by May Alcott 252

72. "Recent Flooding in Rome" (11 February 1871) 254

73. Army Guards, Rome, Italy (winter 1871), by May Alcott 255

74. Alice Bartlett, Rome, Italy (March 1871), by May Alcott 259

75. Advertising poster for *Little Men* (1871) 260

76. Frontispiece for *Little Men* (1871) 261

77. John Bridge Pratt in theatrical costume (1860s) 266

78. Orchard House, with removable winter doorway (1870s) 268

Acknowledgments

In preparing this volume, I have incurred many debts of gratitude. I am grateful to the following libraries for assistance in using their collections: Boston Public Library; Concord Free Public Library; Columbia University Library; Harvard University Libraries (Houghton and Pussey); Fruitlands Museums; New England Historic Genealogical Society; New York Public Library (Henry W. and Albert A. Berg Collections and Manuscripts Division); North Carolina State University Library; Orchard House, Home of the Alcotts; University of North Carolina Charlotte (Atkins Library).

The Alcott sisters' letters are published with the permission of Charles Pratt, Frederick Pratt, and John Pratt. I greatly appreciate the generosity and help of the Pratt family over the years.

I am grateful to the following institutions for permission to publish material from their collections: Columbia University Library; Houghton Library, Harvard University; Fruitlands Museums; New York Public Library (Astor, Lenox, and Tilden Foundations, Henry W. and Albert A. Berg Collections, and Rare Books and Manuscripts Division); Orchard House, Home of the Alcotts; University of North Carolina at Charlotte (Atkins Library).

Among the number of people who helped me, I would especially like to thank Ronald A. Bosco, Abigail Gordon, Jayne Gordon, Jenny Gratz, Herman Hunt, Sandy Petrulionis, Alan Rauch, Katherine Stephenson, John Matteson, Jan Rieman, Catherine Rivard, Stephanie Upton, Mark West, and Greg Wickliff.

This work was supported in part by funds from the Foundation of the University of North Carolina at Charlotte and from the State of North Carolina. A Reassignment of Duties provided me time to research material for this volume. Small grants from the College of Arts and Sciences and from the Department of English's Center for Writing, Language, and Literacy also helped fund travel to archives. I would like to acknowledge the support of Nancy A. Gutierrez, dean of the College of Arts and Sciences, and Malin Pereira, chair of the Department of English at UNC Charlotte.

Jan Turnquist, executive director of Orchard House, Home of the Alcotts, provided her usual generosity by allowing use of archival material from the Louisa May Alcott Memorial Association collection, and Maria Powers, executive assistant, gave generously of her time in preparing digital images of the material. For more information about Orchard House and the Alcotts, please visit their website at www.louisamayalcott.org.

Leslie Wilson, head of Special Collections at the Concord Free Public Library, shared her vast knowledge of Concord history and families. Joel Myerson, who listened to numerous questions and stories about the Alcott sisters' European adventures, provided good counsel in textual editing matters. I am also grateful to Nancy Grayson for the opportunity to publish this book.

This book is dedicated to Luke and Hannah, whose love makes all the work worthwhile.

Abbreviations of Works Cited

Cheney. Ednah Dow Cheney. *Louisa May Alcott: Her Life, Letters, and Journals*. Boston: Roberts Brothers, 1889.

Handbook (1870). John Murray. *A Handbook for Travellers in France*. 11th ed. London: John Murray, 1870.

Journals. Louisa May Alcott. *The Journals of Louisa May Alcott*. Eds. Joel Myerson, Daniel Shealy, Madeleine B. Stern. Athens: University of Georgia Press, 1997.

Journals of BA. Bronson Alcott. *The Journals of Bronson Alcott*. Ed. Odell Shepard. Boston: Little, Brown, 1938.

Letters of ABA. A. Bronson Alcott. *The Letters of A. Bronson Alcott*. Ed. Richard L. Herrnstadt. Ames: Iowa State University Press, 1969.

Selected Letters. Louisa May Alcott. *The Selected Letters of Louisa May Alcott*. Eds. Joel Myerson, Daniel Shealy, Madeleine B. Stern. Athens: University of Georgia Press, 1995.

Shawl-Straps. Louisa May Alcott. *Aunt Jo's Scrap-Bag*. Volume 2. *Shawl-Straps*. Boston: Roberts Brothers, 1872.

Switzerland. Karl Baedeker. *Switzerland and the Adjacent Portions of Italy, Savoy, and Tyrol. Handbook for Travellers*. 4th ed. Leipzig: Karl Baedeker, 1869.

Ticknor. Caroline Ticknor. *May Alcott: A Memoir*. Boston: Little, Brown, 1928.

Introduction

In the "Preface" to *Shawl-Straps* (1872), Louisa May Alcott's account of her grand European tour with her sister May and their friend Alice Bartlett in 1870–71, Alcott complains that "there is nothing new to tell, and that nobody wants to read the worn-out story. . . . The only way in which this affliction may be lightened to a long-suffering public is to make the work as cheerful and as short as possible." Therefore, she declares at the onset, she "has abstained from giving the dimensions of any church, the population of any city, or description of famous places . . . but confined herself to the personal haps and mishaps, adventures and experiences, of her wanderers" (v). True to her word, Louisa's narrative focuses on the "adventures and experiences" of the three women. But she did not write primarily from memory. Instead, she turned to letters written to her family while abroad to recount "the personal haps and mishaps" of the travelers. For it was in these often lengthy and descriptive personal letters that Louisa and her sister May first told the events found in *Shawl-Straps*. Of course, using her own letters to form the basis of her literary work was not new to Louisa. In 1863, her letters home to family had formed the basis for her first successful book, *Hospital Sketches*.

The same year that Louisa published her travel narrative, her father, A. Bronson Alcott, wrote in his *Concord Days* (1872): "A lifelong correspondence were a biography of the correspondents. Preserve your letters till time define their value. Some secret charm forbids committing them to the flame. . . . Letters . . . better represent life than any form in literature" (123–24). Such a declaration directly contrasts with the thoughts of Alcott's most famous daughter, Louisa May, who, late in her life, penned the following in her 1885 journal: "Sorted old letters & burned many. Not wise to keep for curious eyes to read, & gossip-lovers to print by & by" (*Journals*

FIGURE 1. Louisa May
Alcott (ca. 1870). *Louisa
May Alcott's Orchard
House/L. M. A. Memorial
Association.*

262). Fortunately, Bronson Alcott thought the letters that Louisa and May
had written to him; his wife, Abigail; and his oldest daughter, Anna Alcott
Pratt, were worth preserving, and he carefully transcribed the majority of
the letters that Louisa and May wrote home while on their 1870–71 tour,
providing future "curious eyes" a remarkable inside narrative of the Alcott
sisters' odyssey. These letters indeed form a brief biography of the Alcott
sisters during two remarkable years in their lives.

The women were certainly different types of letter writers—Louisa's
epistles clearly bearing the mark of a professional author. "I mean to keep
a letter on hand all the time," Louisa wrote to her mother on 14 April 1870,
"and send them off as fast as they are done." The two "American innocents,"

as Louisa's editor Thomas Niles called them, absorbed and reported to Concord all the colorful sights. Louisa's comment on seeing a humorous priest, "I shall put him in a story," shows that she was ever alert for the potential of turning her experiences into fiction (25 May). If Louisa's letters reveal a writer's eye for stories, then the letters of the artist May demonstrate an eye for color, detail, and composition. Her purpose in writing was to fill her letters "with the power of delineating the enchanting views and objects" (30 May). When at a loss for words, she resorted to art and sketched pen-and-ink drawings to include. The Alcott sisters' correspondence home gives us an interesting viewpoint of two independent women on the grand tour of Europe. While these letters reveal much about the European scene, they also tell us about the relationship between the two Alcott sisters. The sisters' European correspondence, however, has importance beyond the scope of Alcott studies. Not only does it tell much about the sisters' lives, but it also reveals much about how Americans viewed Europe in the late nineteenth century.

In her 1880 novel *Salvage*, Elizabeth Wormeley Latimer writes: "The leading interests of daily life in America are connected with the Atlantic Ocean. There it is regarded as a link. . . . The ocean is the highway which brings everything most delightful to an American's home. . . . An American's news, letters, books, clothes, primma donnas, fashions, ancestors, and church associations, all come . . . from across seas" (12). The transatlantic experience became such a common occurrence in the nineteenth century that an unsigned article titled "Going Abroad," which appeared in *Putnam's Magazine* in 1868—the same year that Louisa published *Little Women*—stated that "[i]f the social history of the world is ever written, the era in which we live will be called the nomadic period. With the advent of ocean steam navigation and the railway system, began a traveling mania which has gradually increased until half of the earth's inhabitants, or at least half of its civilized portion, are on the move" (530–31). Emerson's words that "[t]raveling is a fool's paradise" were met with deaf ears as more and more Americans—including Emerson himself—left behind their quiet shade-covered villages and bustling, growing towns for the ancient splendors of Europe (81). As William W. Stowe notes in his 1994 study *Going Abroad*, "Americans from Emerson to Adams used European travel as an occasion for establishing a relation to historical and cultural authority, to the 'noble,' the 'high,' the 'artful,' the 'beautiful,' the 'venerable'" (126). For Louisa Alcott and her sister May, Europe had always possessed that air of enchantment.

As children, growing up in Boston and Concord, the Alcott sisters, especially Louisa, reveled in the fiction of Charles Dickens, Sir Walter Scott, Charlotte Bronte, and Johann Wolfgang von Goethe. Louisa penned adolescent tales filled with exotic European characters and settings. Her first novel, *The Inheritance*, written when she was only seventeen, was set on an estate in England with an Italian orphan as a heroine, and Italy itself had also served as the setting for several early stories. For her youngest sister, May, who had studied art in Boston and had taught art classes in Concord (she gave the famous American sculptor, Daniel Chester French, his first sculpting tools and lessons), Europe, especially France and Italy, was the land of the great masters, the mecca of the art world. As the artistic Amy, nicknamed "Little Raphael," declares in *Little Women*: "I have ever so many wishes; but the pet one is to be an artist, and go to Rome, and do fine pictures, and be the best artist in the world" (161). The chance to visit firsthand the great cathedrals and to view the famous paintings and sculptures was May's lifelong dream and was not to be missed. Thus, when the opportunity arose, the two Alcott sisters left behind the sleepy village of Concord, a place Louisa had called "one of the dullest little towns in Massachusetts" (*Selected Letters* 127), and set forth on a European odyssey.

Although Louisa was eight years older than May, both women had long endured the economic hardships of what Louisa called "the Pathetic Family" (*Journals* 85). Louisa, born in 1832, in Germantown, Pennsylvania, was two years old when Bronson Alcott started his Temple School in Boston. With her sister Anna, nineteen months her senior, Louisa often visited the school taught by her father. The once-successful school closed in March 1839, however, and a year later the family (which now included Elizabeth Sewall Alcott, born in 1835) moved to the village of Concord, where Bronson could be near his new friend Ralph Waldo Emerson.

There, on 26 July 1840, the fourth Alcott daughter was born to Bronson and Abigail. Named for her mother, the new baby, Abby May, was seen as special. Bronson wrote in his journal: "'A new life has arrived to us. She was born with the dawn, and is a proud little Queen, not deigning to give us

FIGURE 2. May Alcott
(ca. 1870). *Louisa
May Alcott's Orchard
House/L. M. A. Memorial
Association.*

the light of her royal presence, but persists in sleeping all the time, without notice of the broad world of ourselves'" (qtd. in Ticknor 6). That Christmas Eve, Bronson composed a poem for his new daughter, in which he called her "Concordia's Queen."

Abby May was not quite three when the Alcotts moved on 1 June 1843, to rural Harvard, Massachusetts, where her father, along with his British friend and reformer Charles Lane, planned to establish a new American Eden named Fruitlands. The utopian community, however, collapsed by the end of the year, and Bronson's dreams were crushed. Eleven-year-old Louisa recorded the sad times in her childhood journal: "I was very unhappy. Anna and I cried in bed, and I prayed to God to keep us together" (47). Bronson was devastated, but with some financial help from Emerson, as well as the inheritance gained by Abigail on the death of her father, the

Alcotts moved back to Concord in 1845 and purchased a house they named Hillside. Here the family remained for two years, surrounded by Bronson's friends—Emerson, Henry David Thoreau, and Nathaniel Hawthorne. Bronson was unable to secure reliable employment, however, and the family was once again forced to relocate—this time back to Boston. Louisa later recalled those teenage years in Concord as "the happiest of my life," and she must have been reluctant to leave and "to move to Boston and try our fate again after some years in the wilderness." Hurt by the news of the move, she ran to her favorite place near Hillside—an old cartwheel almost hidden in the tall grass. She stared out at the dull November landscape with barren trees outlined against the gray sky and shook her defiant fist at the universe: "I *will* do something by-and-by. Don't care what, teach, sew, act, write, anything to help the family; and I'll be rich and famous and happy before I die, see if I won't!'" ("Recollections" 261).

To help the family, Anna and Louisa taught school while their mother opened an intelligence office for the poor, a type of employment office. In the city, Louisa began to focus more on writing, completing an unpublished novel, *The Inheritance*, and selling her first story, "The Rival Painters: A Tale of Rome," to the *Boston Olive Branch* in 1852, for which she was paid five dollars. Louisa's entry in her "Notes and Memoranda" for 1852 succinctly sums up the year: "Father idle, mother at work in the office, Nan & I governessing. Lizzie in the kitchen, Ab doing nothing but grow[ing]. Hard times for all" (*Journals* 68).

On 5 January 1853, the twelve-year-old Abby May entered the Bowdoin Grammar School; it was, according to Bronson, "her first admission to the Boston Public Schools" (*Diary for 1853* 19). The other children had been taught primarily at home by Bronson, and Abigail Alcott had hopes that a more structured education would prepare Abby May for employment and that she would continue there "untill She is well qualified for teaching in the elementary or primary departments of our Schools. She bears the drill of the formal education better than the other girls would have done" (n.d., diary, Houghton Library, Harvard University). By the end of 1854, Louisa would note her sister's budding artistic talents: "Ab at school getting prizes for drawing" (*Journals* 72).

In December 1854, Louisa published her first book, *Flower Fables*, peaceful nature fairy tales she once had told to Ellen Emerson, Ralph Waldo Emerson's daughter, in the old Hillside barn. Although the collection earned only about thirty-five dollars for her, the young author was hopeful: "My book came out; and people began to think that topsey-turvey Louisa would amount to something after all, since she could do so well as house-maid, teacher, seamstress, and story-teller. Perhaps she may" (*Journals* 73). Two years later, Abby May, now seventeen, also showed promise of talent. In the fall of 1857, studying art with a Mrs. Murdock in Boston, she completed a crayon drawing of Abigail's head, a drawing that Louisa proclaimed was "a very good likeness. All of us proud as peacocks of our 'little Raphael'" (*Journals* 84).

By the fall of 1857, the family once again planned a return to Concord, and with money from Abigail, they purchased an old eighteenth-century house on Lexington Road—just next door to their former Hillside home, now owned by Nathaniel Hawthorne, and less than half a mile from Ralph Waldo Emerson. As Louisa declared, her father was "never happy far from Emerson, the one true friend who loves and understands and helps him" (*Journals* 85). Because of the numerous apple trees planted by Bronson, the property was aptly named Orchard House. Louisa would more than often refer to it, however, as Apple Slump. But before Bronson could finish repairs on the structure and move the family into their new home, Elizabeth Alcott died on 15 March 1858, never fully recovering from the scarlet fever she had contracted in the summer of 1856. Louisa poignantly recorded her death, a scene that she would later re-create in her fiction: "Tuesday she lay in Father's arms, and called us round her, smiling contentedly as she said, 'All here!' I think she bid us good-by then, as she held our hands and kissed us tenderly" (*Journals* 88).

A few weeks later, on 7 April 1858, Anna announced her engagement to John Bridge Pratt, son of Concord farmer Minot Pratt. The two would later marry in 1860. Louisa felt she had now lost a second sister. As she confessed to her journal: "[S]o another sister is gone. J. is a model son and brother,— a true man, full of fine possibilities, but so modest one does not see it at once. . . . I moaned in private over my great loss, and said I'd never forgive

FIGURE 3. Elizabeth
Sewall Alcott (mid-1850s).
*Louisa May Alcott's
Orchard House/L. M. A.
Memorial Association.*

J. for taking Anna from me, but I shall if he makes her happy, and turn to little May for my comfort" (*Journals* 89).

Writing to her good friend Alfred Whitman on 27 October 1858, Louisa told him: "Abby is getting her plumage in order for a flight to town where the long talked of drawing lessons will come off. She is very well & in great spirits about her winters work & play—has many engagements for skating dancing & 'larking' parties already made & intends to do & enjoy more this winter than any young woman ever did before" (*Selected Letters* 37). On 29 November, Louisa's twenty-sixth birthday, John and Anna sent Louisa a ring of their hair "as a peace-offering" (*Journals* 91). In December, Abby May came to stay with Louisa at 98 Chestnut Street, where she was boarding at the home of their relative Thomas Sewall. May was to study art at the School of Design under the Boston artist Stephen Salisbury Tuckerman (1830–1904), who, years ago, had been a student at Bronson's Temple

FIGURE 4. Anna Alcott Pratt (ca. 1870). *Louisa May Alcott's Orchard House/L. M. A. Memorial Association.*

School. The School of Design, which operated from 1851 to 1860, was Boston's main opportunity for women to obtain an art education; its emphasis, however, was on the more practical use of design for manufacturing (Hoppin 18). May stayed until April 1859, and Louisa wrote: "May went home after a happy winter at the School of Design, where she did finely, and was pronounced full of promise. Mr. T. said good things of her, and we were very proud. No doubt now what she is to be, if we can only keep her along" (*Journals* 94).

In March 1860, Louisa noted: "Made my first ball dress for May, and she was the finest girl at the party. My tall, blond, graceful girl! I was proud of her" (*Journals* 98). In November, a family friend sent May thirty dollars to study art in Boston with David Claypoole Johnston. Louisa claimed May "is one of the fortunate ones, and gets what she wants easily. I have to grub for my help, or go without it. Good for me, doubtless, or it would n't be so; so cheer up, Louisa, and grind away!" (*Journals* 100). Already established as an important American cartoonist, David Claypoole Johnston (1799–1865), born in Philadelphia, began his career as an engraver and was quickly known for his caricatures. Later he turned to drawing and book illustrations and was popular as a lithographer. From 1830 to 1849, he published an annual of humorous sketches entitled *Scraps*, an undertaking that earned him the reputation as the American Cruikshank.

After May had completed her art lessons with Johnston in Boston, she was invited to accept a position as a drawing teacher and pianist in Dr. Hervey B. Wilbur's asylum in Syracuse, New York. That month, December 1860, Louisa again noted: "More luck for May. She wanted to go to Syracuse and teach, and Dr. W[ilbur]. sends for her. . . . I sew like a steam-engine for a week, and get her ready. On the 17th go to B[oston]. and see our youngest start on her first little flight alone into the world, full of hope and courage. May all go well with her" (*Journals* 100). May Alcott worked in Syracuse until the summer of 1861, when Louisa noted that her younger sister would not go back to work in Syracuse but come home to Concord, "and being a lucky puss, just as she wants something to do, F. B. S[anborn]. needs a drawing teacher in his school and offers her the place" (*Journals* 105). Franklin B. Sanborn, a fervent abolitionist and Harvard graduate, had moved to Concord in the mid-1850s and became active on the political, social, and philosophical scene there. He operated a private academy in the village from 1855 to 1863, teaching the children of many of the town's leading citizens. Once again Louisa deemed May the fortunate one.

But Louisa herself also began to experience some success during the early 1860s. Her story "Love and Self-Love" appeared in the March 1860 *Atlantic Monthly*, one of the most prestigious literary magazines in the country. In December 1862, her sensational story "Pauline's Passion and Punishment" won a hundred-dollar prize offered by *Frank Leslie's Illustrated Newspaper*, securing her a ready market over the next five years for blood-and-thunder tales that she wrote anonymously for Leslie's various publications.

In December 1862, with the Civil War raging, Louisa volunteered as a nurse at Union Hotel Hospital in Georgetown, D.C. As the new year began, she recorded her thoughts in her journal: "I never began the year in a stranger place than this; five hundred miles from home, alone among strangers, doing painful duties all day long, & leading a life of constant excitement in this greathouse surrounded by 3 or 4 hundred men in all stages of suffering, disease & death" (113). Within a few weeks, however, she contracted typhoid fever, and Bronson arrived to bring her home. At the doctor's order her hair was shaved off, and she was unable to leave her room at Orchard House until late March 1863. But as soon as she was well again, Louisa was back at her writing desk. She took her experiences, recorded in letters home to her family, and published them in F. B. Sanborn's *Boston Commonwealth*. They were so well received that the abolitionist James Redpath agreed to publish them as a book. In late August 1863, *Hospital Sketches* appeared, a work that helped establish a regional reputation for Alcott. In October, she noted with some pride: "A year ago I had no publisher & went begging with my wares, now three have asked me for something, several papers are ready to print my contributions & F. B. S[anborn]. says 'any publisher this side Baltimore would be glad to get a book.' There is a sudden hoist for a meek & lowly scribbler who . . . never had a literary friend to lend a helping hand! Fifteen years of hard grubbing may be coming to something after all, & I may yet 'pay all the debts, fix the house, send May to Italy & keep the old folks cosy,' as I've said I would so long yet so hopelessly" (*Journals* 121).

That same month she also reported that "May began to take anatomical drawing lessons of Rimmer. I was very glad to be able to pay her expenses up & down & clothe her neatly" (121). William Rimmer (1816–79), who gave talks on anatomy and drawing at the Boston School of Design from 1861 to 1866, had already made a name for himself as a sculptor with such works as the head of *St. Stephen* (1860) and the *Falling Gladiator* (1861). His lectures on anatomy in Boston, New York, and other cities were extremely popular, and in 1864 he published *Elements of Design*. Although an accomplished sculptor (he completed a statue of Alexander Hamilton for the city of Boston in 1865) and painter, he was more influential as a teacher, and his *Art Anatomy* (1877) was hailed as an important work in anatomical drawing.

Later, Rimmer would go on to teach at the Cooper Union School of Design for Women in New York and at the Boston Museum of Fine Arts.

May's good fortune was to continue. In February 1864, Louisa revealed that Mary E. Stearns, wife of the antislavery reformer George Luther Stearns, "takes a great fancy to May, sends her flowers, offers to pay for her to go to the new Art School, & arranges everything delightfully for her. She is a fortunate girl, & always finds some one to help her as she wants to be helped. Wish I could do the same, but suppose as I never do that it is best for me to work & wait & do all for myself" (*Journals* 128).

On Christmas Eve 1864, Louisa herself had more cause to celebrate—the appearance of *Moods*, her first novel. Published by A. K. Loring, the book, however, drew mixed reviews. As Louisa herself noted: "People seem to think the book finely written, very promising, wise & interesting, but some fear it is n't moral because it speaks freely of marriage." Some of the criticism was so sharp that by May 1865, she would declare that her "next book shall have no *ideas* in it, only facts, & the people shall be as ordinary as possible, then critics will say its all right" (*Journals* 139–40).

In July 1865, Louisa, now thirty-two years old, saw one of her lifelong dreams realized as she was asked by the Boston shipping merchant William Fletcher Weld to accompany his invalid daughter Anna, three years Louisa's junior, and her half brother George to Europe. The trip would last for a year—from July 1865 to July 1866—and take her to Germany, Switzerland, France, and England. The journey was, as Louisa later noted, "Hard work . . . but I enjoyed much" (*Journals* 148). One of the highlights of her trip abroad was meeting a young Pole, Ladislas Wisniewski, in Vevey, Switzerland. With "Laddie," as Louisa called her new friend, she would sail on Lake Geneva and have "[p]leasant walks & talks with him in the chateau garden & about Vevey" (*Journals* 145). After completing her chaperone duties and leaving Anna Weld in Nice, France, on the first of May 1866, Louisa set off alone for Paris, where she was met by Laddie, who escorted her about the French capital for two weeks. Laddie would not be soon forgotten, and he would serve as partial inspiration for the character of Laurie in *Little Women*. The last seven weeks of her trip would take her to London, where she would spend time with the reformer and coeditor of the *Boston Commonwealth*, Moncure Daniel Conway, and his

FIGURE 5. Abigail May Alcott (ca. 1870). *Louisa May Alcott's Orchard House/L. M. A. Memorial Association.*

wife, Ellen, at their home on Wimbledon Common. She was also invited to stay at Aubrey House at Notting Hill Gate, Kensington, the mansion of Peter Alfred Taylor, an MP for Leicester. The Taylors were champions of many radical causes, including women's suffrage. When she sailed to America, she found John Bridge Pratt on the wharf, waiting to escort her home. Arriving in Concord, she discovered "Mother looking old, sick & tired. Father as placid as ever. Nan poorly but blest in her babies. May full of plans as usual." In a few weeks, she would write: "Soon fell to work on some stories for things were, as I expected, behind hand when the money-maker was away" (*Journals* 152).

For the first six months of 1867, Louisa was ill and unable to write; by June, however, she was back to work "for bills accumulate & worry me. I dread debt more than the devil" (*Journals* 158). In September, she agreed to edit the children's magazine *Merry's Museum* for Horace B. Fuller for five hundred dollars a year. She also recorded a now-famous passage in her journal: "Niles, partner of Roberts, asked me to write a girls book. Said I'd try" (*Journals* 158). In order to complete her work without being worried by family obligations, Louisa rented a room in Boston that October. The next month, May started teaching art in Boston, commuting from Concord but coming to see Louisa each day. As 1868 began, Louisa wrote: "May busy with her drawing classes, of which she has five or six, and the prospect of earning $150 a quarter. . . . I am in my little room, spending busy, happy days, because I have quiet, freedom, work enough, and strength to do it" (*Journals* 162). In fact, she was so occupied with editing *Merry's Museum* and writing sensational tales for Frank Leslie that she was unable to begin the girls' book for Roberts Brothers until May 1868: "Marmee, Anna, and May all approve my plan. So I plod away, though I don't enjoy this sort of thing. Never liked girls or knew many, except my sisters, but our queer plays and experiences may prove interesting, though I doubt it." Later in life, when rereading her journal, Louisa inserted her reaction—"Good joke" (*Journals* 166).

Despite Louisa's misgivings about the novel's popularity, *Little Women, Part One* was published in October 1868 to critical and commercial success. May Alcott contributed four illustrations for the novel, including the frontispiece, the now-famous tableau of the March sisters gathered around Marmee as she reads Mr. March's letter home to her four daughters. Louisa's editor, Thomas Niles, wisely encouraged her to keep the copyright rather than sell it outright to Roberts Brothers. Niles also contracted with Louisa for a sequel, and she immediately fell to work on *Little Women, Part Two* on the first of November: "I can do a chapter a day, and in a month I mean to be done. A little success is so inspiring that I now find my 'Marches' sober, nice people, and as I can launch into the future, my fancy has more play." She also complained that girls "write to ask who the little women marry, as if that was the only end and aim of a woman's life." She vowed: "I *won't* marry Jo to Laurie to please anyone" (*Journals* 167). On New Year's Day, she sent the completed novel to Roberts Brothers and noted: "My dream is beginning to come true; and if my head holds out I'll do all I once hoped to do" (*Journals* 171).

As 1869 began, she wrote to Ellen Conway, the wife of Moncure Daniel Conway, on 9 February, that "May & I are having a jolly winter boarding in Boston, she teaching drawing & studying the same with Wm Hunt, I writing, editing and poking about in my usual style" (*Selected Letters* 123). May was indeed fortunate to study with William Morris Hunt (1824–79), brother of the famous architect Richard Morris Hunt, and he may have played a role in helping to foster her desire to study art in Europe, especially France. Hunt, born in Vermont, traveled to Europe in the 1840s, where he studied with the French artist Thomas Couture. In France, he met Jean-Francois Millet with whom he studied and by whom he was greatly influenced. Hunt, among his many accomplishments, is credited with introducing the Barbizon school of painters to an American audience. After returning to the United States in 1855, he painted such Millet-influenced works as *Girl at the Fountain* (1857) and *Hurdy-Gurdy Boy* (1857) as well as portraits of prominent people. According to Martha J. Hoppin, Hunt, unlike William Rimmer with whom May had studied anatomical drawing earlier, desired "spontaneity and originality" from his students (19). Truman Bartlett, who had known both William Rimmer and Hunt, argued that "Rimmer taught that the constructive character of an object was the first thing to learn, and the acquisition of knowledge of the first importance," but William Morris Hunt believed in "the expression of the essential quality of an object as an artistic effect of the first importance, with the understanding that the knowledge of art, anatomy, perspective, ethnology and the rest would follow with the pupil's progress as a conscious necessity" (80). As Daniel Chester French said, the two men "saw nature with different eyes, Doctor Rimmer chiefly interested in line; Mr. Hunt in masses of light and shade and color; they both were great artists and May Alcott seems to have reconciled their conflicting methods in her own work" (xx).

While May enjoyed her study and teaching, Louisa was soon exhausted with her constant writing, and the two sisters gave up their room in Boston in March 1869 and went home to Orchard House. The second part of *Little Women*, published on 15 April, was even more successful than the first, and Louisa soon found the high price of fame: "People begin to come and stare at the Alcotts. Reporters haunt the place to look at the authoress, who dodges into the woods à la Hawthorne, and won't be even a very small lion" (*Journals* 171). Hoping to find a respite from weariness and a haven from celebrity seekers, she spent July in Quebec, Canada, with her relative O. B. Frothingham and his family, and in August, Louisa and May retreated to the island of Mt. Desert, Maine, for relaxation. While she was away, Roberts Brothers was busy capitalizing on their new bestselling author. Niles purchased the copyright for Louisa's narrative of her wartime hospital experiences, and, with eight additional stories, the company issued *Hospital Sketches and Camp and Fireside Stories* in August 1869. Two thousand copies were sold in the first week alone (*Journals* 172).

By October, Louisa and May were back in Boston, boarding at 43 Pinckney Street, where Louisa, at the urgings of Roberts Brothers, was hard at work on a new book, this time revising a serial "An Old-Fashioned Girl," which she had written that year for *Merry's Museum*. May happily resumed giving art lessons to thirty students. She herself was also working on a book—a series of drawings depicting various Concord scenes, including Orchard House, Hillside (or Wayside, as Hawthorne renamed it), Emerson's home, and the Old Manse. In all, she completed twelve sketches, each with an accompanying motto or quote from various authors, such as Emerson, Thoreau, Ellery Channing, and Daniel Ricketson. The drawings were then photographed by Edward F. Smith of Boston, and in late November, *Concord Sketches Consisting of Twelve Photographs from Original Drawings* was published by Fields, Osgood and Company. Louisa contributed a brief preface to the volume. Louisa, however, could not do much else. Ill, with hardly any voice, she visited a doctor "every day to have my windpipe burnt with a caustic" (*Journals* 172). On Christmas, Roberts Brothers sent her royalties in the amount of twenty-five hundred dollars—money, Louisa wrote to them—that "made my Christmas an unusually merry one" (*Selected Letters* 129).

The year 1870 saw the promise of change in Louisa's health and the fulfillment of May's dream. In her "Notes and Memoranda" for 1870, Louisa briefly reported that "Alice Bartlett invites May to go abroad with her for a year, & I decide to go as duenna, hoping to get better" (*Journals* 175). Alice Amelia Bartlett, born on 21 December 1844, was the daughter of Dr. George and Catherine Amelia Greenwood Bartlett of Boston. Her father, born in 1807 to Captain Zaccheus and Hannah Jackson Bartlett of Plymouth, graduated from Harvard College in 1827 and received his medical degree in 1830.

When Alice was not quite twenty years old, Dr. Bartlett, however, died from epilepsy on 24 September 1864 at the age of fifty-seven.

Tragically, Alice's only sibling, her older brother William Pitt Greenwood Bartlett, died less than four months later at age twenty-eight. Born on 27 October 1837, her brother had entered Harvard College with William Fitzhugh Lee, son of Robert E. Lee, who left the college during the second term of his junior year. William Bartlett, whose health was never very good, graduated from Harvard in 1858 and was immediately employed as an assistant computer in the Nautical Almanac office, Cambridge. In the summer of 1860, he had accompanied Benjamin P. Pierce, professor of mathematics at Harvard, to Paris and London to attend several scientific meetings. Elected to the American Academy of Sciences, William was a proctor at Harvard from 1859 to 1861 and contributed articles to the *Mathematical Monthly*. Immediately after his father's death, the Bartlett family moved from their Boston home to Cambridge in October 1864, and William died, unmarried, at his mother's house on 13 January 1865 ("William Pitt Greenwood Bartlett" 12).

Sadly, Alice's mother, Catherine, survived her son by just under three years. Born in Boston on 24 March 1810, Catherine was the daughter of Dr. William Pitt and Mary Langdon Greenwood. Evidently, she had suffered greatly since her husband's death in the autumn of 1864, as she died on 20 October 1867, from "disease of the brain," which had lasted for two years (MA Vital Records). Her mother fortunately provided for Alice, leaving her half of her estate, which was placed in a trust to be paid quarterly for the duration of Alice's life.

Not yet twenty-three years old at the time of her mother's death, Alice Bartlett, having lost all of her three immediate family members during the past three years, must have welcomed the opportunity to go abroad in the spring of 1870. She had been to Europe before and could speak French and Italian well, an advantage that would help the Alcott sisters in the coming year. Promising to pay May Alcott's main expenses—ship passage, meals, hotels—Alice would be a perfect traveling companion—experienced, knowledgeable, fun loving, and a Bostonian. May excitedly agreed to the proposition, but only if her older sister would accompany them. Louisa assented, realizing she was about to help one of her sister's dreams come true at last.

FIGURE 6. Alice Bartlett
(ca. 1870). *Louisa
May Alcott's Orchard
House/L. M. A. Memorial
Association.*

The three women's European sojourn would last fourteen months and take them to France, Switzerland, Italy, Germany, and England. Louisa must have thought back to her first transatlantic trip and how all was different now. Louisa May Alcott's life had indeed changed forever in those five intervening years since 1865. Now, in 1870, the author of *Little Women* was the literary lion on grand tour. Her first European journey had been a benchmark in her life; this trip, however, offered a chance to relax—to rest from the hard years of toiling to support herself and her family, to rest from the onslaught of public acclaim, to rest from the illness and weariness that had plagued her since 1863. As Amanda, Alice's thinly fictionalized character in *Shawl-Straps*, advises Lavinia, Louisa's alter ego: "Just the thing for you, my poor old dear. Think of the balmy airs of Sicily, the oranges, the flowers. Then a delicious month or two at Sorrento, with no east winds, no

FIGURE 7. Amos Bronson Alcott (ca. early 1870s). *Louisa May Alcott's Orchard House/L. M. A. Memorial Association.*

slosh, no spring cleaning. We shall be as merry as grigs, and get as buxom as dairy-maids in a month" (2).

The Alcott sisters left to rendezvous with Alice Bartlett in New York on 1 April 1870—April Fools' Day. The timing was not lost on Louisa, who noted in her journal: "fit day for my undertaking" (174). Three days earlier, Bronson had written a friend: "I wish Louisa were in better health and spirits, but am consoled in the hope that she is under weigh to find them in a foreign climate. May takes both along with her, with happy expectations—the fulfilment of long cherished dreams" (*Letters of ABA* 509). Their fellow boarders at Boston's 43 Pinckney Street gave them a farewell party, and they received thirty gifts from well-wishers, including a case of champagne from Edward Emerson, Ralph Waldo Emerson's son. As friends said goodbye to them at the train station, Louisa thought of her parents, especially her beloved Marmee, who had spent the previous day with May and her, helping them pack trunks and greet sixteen callers: "But I remember only Father and Mother as they went away the day before, leaving the two ambitious daughters to sail away, perhaps forever." She observed that her mother "kept up bravely, and nodded and smiled; but at the corner I saw a white handkerchief go up to her eyes, after being gayly waved to us. May and I broke down, and said, 'We won't go;' but next day we set forth, as young birds will, and left the nest empty for a year" (*Journals* 174). Bronson, who had presented May a mirror and Louisa a pocketbook for their journey, recorded the departure in his journal: "We bid them farewell with fear and hope. Deserving girls! they are now being rewarded for their toils and sacrifices in childhood and early womanhood. If Louisa can recover lost health and nerves, and May gratify her thirst for art—then God be praised, and our cup will overflow" (*Diary for 1870* 180–81).

Accompanied by John Bridge Pratt as their escort, the sisters departed Boston by rail to meet Alice in New York City. Even on the train, Louisa could not escape her ever-growing fame. A boy selling reading material put a copy of the just-published *An Old-Fashioned Girl* in her lap, but Louisa declined: "'Bully book, ma'am! Sell a lot; better have it.' John told him I wrote it; and his chuckle, stare, and astonished 'No!' was great fun" (*Journals* 174). In the late afternoon of 2 April, John Bridge Pratt telegrammed Anna: "'All on Board. Safe. Well and happy.'" Abigail Alcott recorded the day in her journal: "Let me gratefully acknowledge the propitious weather which prevails for my darlings—especially the poor invalid—Louisa—calm, bright, warm, Spring odors in the air; cheerfulness on every aspect" (1870, diary, Houghton Library, Harvard Library). The Alcott sisters' European journey was underway.

A week out of port, both women reported home in their first letters. "Tomorrow we come to our long journeys end, . . . thank the Lord!" declared Louisa Alcott on 12 April 1870. The beginning of the journey, which took approximately twelve days, was, according to May, "rough and stormy" (9–12 April). Louisa, already a sight for the curious celebrity spotters, usually remained sequestered in her cabin. As she told her mother: "I never go up for meals. . . . I lie and peck all sorts of funny messes and receive calls in my den. People seem to think we are 'guns,' and want to know us; but as they are not interesting, we are on the reserve and it has a fine effect" (9 April). Not yet able to escape her fame, Louisa wrote in her journal that girls, with their copies of *An Old-Fashioned Girl*, suddenly appeared at her cabin "in a party to call on me, very seasick in my berth, done up like a mummy" (174). Her sister also reported that passengers were "principally New Yorkers, but everyone is reading 'Old Fashioned Girl,' and of course there is some interest taken in the 'Alcott sisters'" (9–12 April).

May, who, like Louisa, could not speak a foreign language, now found herself aboard a French steamer, and she remained, at first, below with her sister during the dinner hours, "dreading the French waiters." Instead, the women preferred to sit on the lower deck every day and "take in the warm breezes," which, to May, appeared to be "the first taste of foreign lands; for there is a peculiar softness even when the wind is strong, that is enchanting" (9–12 April). But soon May also began to enjoy the social atmosphere on ship: "We shall however be quite Parisian by the time we return, and I already begin to quick my fingers and make bright speeches at table, so much so, that I am considered quite the star of the dining salon, happening to have told a joke that convulsed the whole table the other day" (9–12 April). Unlike her sister and Alice Bartlett, both of whom had traveled abroad, May Alcott was the one most transfixed by the idea of Europe. As she wrote her mother: "I long to see the first glimpses of foreign shores, for I can't form an idea of how things are to look to us" (9–12 April).

On 14 April, the ship anchored in Brest, France, and the three women traveled to Morlaix, a flourishing port of over fourteen thousand inhabitants. Quickly heading for the fourteen-mile trip to Dinan, the women experienced, as Louisa recounted to her mother, the first of many adventures: "[I]nstead of a big diligence we found only a queer ramshackle thing, like an insane carry all, with a wooden boot and queer perch for the driver. Our four big trunks were piled on behind and tied with old ropes, our bags stowed in a wooden box on top, and ourselves inside with a fat Frenchman. The humpbacked driver, 'ya hooped' to the horses, and away we clattered at a wild pace, all feeling dead sure that something would happen, for the old thing bounced and swayed awfully, the trunks were in danger of falling off, and to our dismay we soon discovered that the big Frenchman was tipsy." Already seeming to play the role of duenna, Louisa noted: "He gabbled to

Alice as only a tipsy Frenchman could, quoted poetry, said he was Victor Hugo's best friend, and a child of Nature, that English ladies were all divine, but too cold, for when he pressed Alice's hand, she told him it was not allowed in England, and he was overwhelmed with remorse, bowed, sighed, rolled [his] eyes, told her that he drank much ale, because it flew to his head and gave him 'Commercial Ideas.'" Despite the impropriety of the passenger, Louisa, who would later re-create the scene for *Shawl-Straps*, clearly saw the humor in the whole event:

> You ought to have seen us and our turnout, tearing over the road at a breakneck pace, pitching, creaking, and rattling. The funny driver, hooting at the horses, who had their tales done up . . . blue harness and strings of bells. The drunken man warbling, exhorting, and languishing at us all by turns, while Alice headed him off with great skill. I sat a mass of English dignity and coolness suffering alternate agonies of anxiety and amusement, and May, who tied her head up in a bundle, looked like a wooden image. It was rich, and when we took up first a peasant woman in wooden shoes and fly-away cap, and then a red-nosed priest smoking a long pipe, we were a superb spectacle. In this style, we banged into Dinan. (17 April)

The European odyssey had officially begun; the Alcotts were not in Concord any longer.

The women's *Handbook for Travellers in France*, published by John Murray, declared that Dinan was "perhaps the most beautiful [country] in Brittany. The situation of the town is very romantic, on the crown and slopes of a hill of granite, overlooking the deep and narrow valley of the Rance" (148). The Alcotts and Bartlett settled into the pension of Madame Coste on the Place St. Louis, renting their own salon with an adjoining small room for Alice and a large bedroom upstairs with a view looking out over the verdant river valley. Louisa bragged: "Everything is very cheap, board $6 a week, wine 25 cts a bottle, washing a franc a dozen, &c. People live so simply that little money goes a great way, which suits us nicely for Miss B[artlett]. pays Mays expenses and I my own, and we find we can indulge in donkeys, flowers, gloves &c. without getting bankrupt" (24 April).

Of course, adapting to the French customs would take some getting used to—especially the food. Even on board the ship, May Alcott found the meals dreadful: "The French messes we have . . . nearly kill me, and I shall never learn to like the horrid soups; but there is plenty of fruit, and some simple things that I make my dinner of, after sitting two hours at table" (9–12 April). Now on shore, the Alcotts were still not impressed. Madame Coste's meals did not fare well with the younger Alcott as Louisa noted: "May was a little upset by some of the new messes and kept quiet all day leaving 'nater' to right her self" (20 April). Louisa told her mother that the sustenance was not quite the Concord fare: "We have . . . had fun about the queer food, as we don't like brains, liver, &c. &c. A[lice]. does, and when we eat some mess, not knowing what it is, and find it is bowels or sheep's tails or eels, she exults over us and writes poems" (25 May). She confessed to her sister Anna, "I would give more for a cup of cream and good home-made brew than all the french messes for the special purpose of ruining the coats of our stomach" (30 May).

Not only did they find the French food different, but many of the people they also found amusing. Louisa wrote to her cousin: "[E]very thing is so funny that we shall soon laugh ourselves fat. They offer us at table dishes of snails, which they pick with pins and eat like ants; and other messes equally inviting—they call each other pet names that convulse us—'my little pig,' my 'sweet hen,' 'my cabbage,' and, 'my tom-cat'. A french lady with her son and daughter board here, and their ways amuse us mightily. The girl is to be married next week to a man she has seen twice and never talked to but an hour [in] her life" (24 April). The girl's fiancé, Jules Clomadoc, Louisa reported, was "a tiny man in uniform with a red face, big moustache and blue eyes. He thinks he talks English and makes such very funny mistakes. He asked us if we had been to 'promenade on monkeys,' meaning donkeys, and called the Casino 'the establishment of dance'" (24 April). Clomadoc, who Louisa would remember clearly in *Shawl-Straps*, "posed on the rug, raving about the 'loves of his young past,' while Madame and Coste and the fiance's girl wept and applauded, and we did'nt dare to look at each other, it was so absurd" (29 April).

Despite the funny escapades, the Alcotts were still outsiders, both women unable to speak French. Louisa wailed: "No one speaks English in the house but Alice, and she threatens to talk only French to us, which will be awful but useful. Two pleasant half English ladies live near, and I shall rush to them when I'm exhausted by 'the babytalk,' as I call French" (17 April). She also told her mother on 17 April: "After dinner we were borne to the great salon, where a fire, lights and a piano appeared. Every one sat round and gabbled except the Alcotts, who looked and laughed. Mademoiselle Forney played, and then May convulsed them by singing some 'Chants Amerique' which they thought lively and droll . . . Alice told them I was a celebrated authoress, and May a very fine artist, and we were beamed at more than ever." Determined to learn the language, at least enough to communicate, May confessed to her sister Anna: "I . . . have got quite attached to the French tongue, for now the first time in many years, having plenty of time, I dig away at exercises and verbs pretty constantly, and can make quite long sentences, though I can't talk readily yet" (19 May). Three months later, the Alcotts were still having trouble and hired a French governess to help them. Louisa admitted: "We must speak the language for it is so disgraceful to be so stupid, so we have set to work and mean to be able to *parley-vous* or die. . . . Alice is tired of fussing with us, and we are tired of being perfect noodles" (29 August).

Even though the food appeared "queer," the people amusing, and the language difficult, the Alcotts were still awed by the culture and landscape of Europe. Walking just over a mile to the little village of Lehon, Louisa declared: "It was a very picturesque sight, for the white-capped women, sitting on the green hillsides, looked like flowers, and the blue blouzes of the men and wide brimmed hats, added to the effect. The little street was lined with booths where they sold nuts, queer cakes, hot sausages, and pan cakes, toys, &c. . . . We also indulged in nuts and sat on our camp-stools in a shady place and ate them boldly in the public mart, while en-joying the lively scene" (20 April). "May is in a state of unutterable like bliss, and keeps flying out with her big sketch book and coming back in despair, for every thing is so pictureseque she don't know where to begin," Louisa wrote her mother. She added, "This is a good chance for her in every way" (17 April). May herself realized her dream was now a reality: "I am in such perfect bliss. . . . We sit with open windows and wear spring clothes, are out the greater part of the day, seeing such enchanting old ruins, picturesque towns, churches, and crumbling fortifications, that it seems almost like a dream, and if I did n't see Lu admiring the landscape, I should often doubt if I am myself" (20 April). Impressed by the contrast of her surroundings when compared to life in America, May told her mother: "Everything is made of stone in this part of the world, and it has a very rich look to me after our wooden buildings. . . . I am constantly delighted with the arched doors, and pretty picturesque windows, always carved, (never like our plain carpenter's work at home) and having quantities of ivy running in every direction. I enjoy every minute of my life here" (29 April).

Clutching her sketch book, May Alcott, after a late breakfast at ten o'clock, would "wander forth, perching about, on my pretty little camp stool Alice has given me, whenever anything strikes me as especially lovely." She noted that except for Rome, Dinan "is as old as anything [I] ever shall see, and 'Murray' says 'affords as much for the painter's pencil and brush as anything on the continent,' and I am only troubled as to where to begin with such perfect richness on every side" (20 April). For May, Europe represented a chance not just to see antiquities but to explore her own artistic ability:

> Yesterday we went to some lovely gardens surrounding the most beautiful gothic church, old and gray with vines clinging about the stone ornament and running over the great roof—almost to the top of the spire, and see this on a level with the principal part of the town, the whole being built on very high ground with fortifications and a moat which in old times made Dinan almost impregnable, but now the crumbling gray walls are overhung with the most luxuriant ivy and clinging vines of all sorts; even the stone archways to the town have little verdant plateaus on top, and women with immaculate caps sit about looking so picturesque that I long to make pictures on every hand, but get extremely discouraged when I try, as it needs all the surroundings to make the scene complete. (20 April)

As she sent sketches of churches and chateaus home, she also felt that "ruined castles, bell towers, and churches, are so lovely, it seems absurd to try to draw them, and I long to use color for the pretty flowers, ferns and trailing ivy running over the gray stones all about is truly enchanting, and is nothing done with pencil" (29 April). A month later she complained to her sister Anna that "everything looks so very flat on paper; it gives me no satisfaction. If I could only use colors easily all would go well, but never having *painted* from nature, I am timid about beginning" (30 May).

May also admitted to Anna that Europe was all that she had thought it would be: "You ask, if after dreaming of foreign parts for so many years, I am not a little disappointed in reality. But I can truly say that every thing so far has been quite as picturesque, new, and lovely as I expected; and what rather surprises me is that many things should be so nearly what I thought to find them. I cannot describe to you the strange sensation that took possession of me, when, after leaving Brest, we travelled by cars to Morlaix. . . . Then I really began to feel how very strange and very different it all was from America." She knew, however, that this feeling would be a once-in-a-lifetime sensation: "The queer gabled houses, stone crosses, and white-capped peasants . . . all delighted me, and I never again expected to feel the real *foreign* thrill that came over me in full force when I first entered Morlaix" (30 May). To May, Brittany was like stepping back in time. She felt she had "learned a good deal of old ways and customs, for everything seems hundreds of years behind the times, and I never enter Lehon . . . without being greatly impressed by its great antiquity and feeling quite sure it has always been exactly so ever since the world began." But May's letters also revealed that America would never be quite the same for her again: "I very much admire the primitive, simple manners and customs of the people here, so much so, that our life at home begins to seem a little artificial and unattractive to me" (30 May).

Louisa too believed that the grand tour proved a good experience for her artistic sister. As they visited places along the Cher River, she told her mother that "the best thing I saw was May's rapturous face opposite me as she sat silently enjoying *everything*, too happy to talk." The sights, she felt, were "a good lesson for her, and she will be ready to read up now, for she knows very little, and begins to find it out; as I do" (20–21 June). May herself confessed to Bronson: "I do feel, as mother predicted, that I have read very little, and know very little, but now that I have the time, I study and do what I can to improve my mind" (30 May). By the end of July 1870, she believed that "there is nothing like travel for bringing out one's character and improving one's mind" (26 July). On her thirtieth birthday, she declared to her parents: "I feel quite sure that within the last year or two my views and opinions about things in general, and a womans life in particular have been getting right and that my real life was beginning, and think when I come home, father will find I have grown a little near him and we shall have some good talks together" (26 July).

While May absorbed the new experiences and sketched the people and scenes, Louisa rested, hardly writing anything beside letters. She was, however, keeping check with her business affairs, corresponding regularly with her editor, Thomas Niles. Just a few days after reaching France, she wrote her parents: "Yesterday I got a letter from Niles, beginning 'Dear Jo,' I'd better reply, 'Dear Tom', only he will go and publish it, so I won't. He put in some notices, and very glowing accounts of 'Old Fashioned Girl'—18,000 sold &c. I am glad, for money *must* come, and it makes things easy all round" (20 April). Nine days later, she learned that A. K. Loring had reissued *Moods*, her 1865 novel, hoping to capitalize on the popularity of *Little Women* and *An Old-Fashioned Girl*. Alcott had never felt that the book was what she had intended because she had made so many changes at the publisher's request: "I have the copyright and don't wish the book sold as it is" (29 April). By the first of June, she was so disgusted with her former publisher that she vented her frustrations to her parents: "I am so mad at Lorings doings. . . . The dreadful man says that *he has a right to print as many editions as [he] likes for fourteen years*! What rights has an author then I beg to know? and where does 'the courtesy' of a publisher come in? He has sent me a book and if you hear I'm dead, you may know that a sight of the *picters* slew me, for I expect to have fits when I behold Sylvia with a top-knot, Moore with mutton chop whiskers, and Adam in the inevitable checkered trousers which all modern kinds wear. If the law gives over an author and her work to such slaverey as L[oring]. says, I shall write no more books but take in washing, and say adieu to glory." Several days later, she once again wrote home to Anna, fearing that more old material would be resurrected: "Dont have 'Flower Fables' printed for God's sake, or any other old thing—and if Loring writes lies about '*Moods*,' put a notice in the *Transcript* contradicting him. I have fears [Horace B.] Fuller will 'bust' out, so keep an eye on him. I forbid any book of little tales, and have a *right* to do it Niles says. O dear, what a bother fame is, aint it?" (9 June).

Despite her objections, a part of Alcott liked the attention she and her works were receiving. As she confessed to her family: "Tom is rather— 'ahem'—but at this distance I don't mind; it is rather fun to get his letters and notices, and Alice twits me about my rival publishers, for Loring writes long and elaborate letters to 'my friend, Miss Alcott'" (17 June). Niles also sent Alcott her fan letters, which continued to pour into Roberts Brothers' office on Washington Street, Boston. Mindful that she had to pay for forwarding the letters from England, however, she told Niles in August 1870 to "please send all letters to me that come to your care to my family at Concord. . . . Most of them are enthusiastic little bursts from boys and girls who want auto- or photographs which I can't send them; so they may as well go to Concord and be kept for future settlement. . . . [T]he dears must wait till I come back, or take it out in looking at the damp and earwigly, 'Home of the great American authoress'" (10 August).

Louisa May Alcott was also now beginning to control the image that people had of her as the first biographical piece of any note was being prepared for publication in a July 1870 issue of *Hearth and Home*. Franklin B. Sanborn (whom she often referred to as "Bun," a play on the New England pronunciation of the name), a family friend, was writing the front-page article about the author of *Little Women*. Alcott herself, however, seemed to shun the publicity: "About 'Hearth and Home'. I don't wish any notice, but suppose I must, so Pa can give a few facts, when born and where, and just the most interesting bits of my life." She was careful too about which photograph appeared: "Allens picture or none. Thank Marshall for keeping his word. His pictures are vile" (4 June). On 1 July, Bronson brought home proofs of the *Hearth and Home* article and recorded its appearance: "It is gracefully written and should give her pleasure. Sanborn has been a good friend of hers from his first acquaintance and is better acquainted with her history than any one not of our family" (*Diary for 1870* 417).

Even in Europe, Louisa could not escape her fame. She wrote to her family that they had "let little bits of news leak out about us, and they think we are dukes and duchesses in Amerique, and pronounce us 'tres spirituelle, tres charmmante, tres seductive femmes.' We grin in private and are now used to having the entire company rise when we enter and embrace us with ardor, listen with uplifted hands and shrieks of 'Mon Dieu,' 'grand ciel' &c. to all our remarks and point us out in public as 'Les dames Amercaine.' Such is fame!" (1 June). Later, in Bex, Switzerland, May reported that "Lu's fame follows her even here, in this out of the way little town; for yesterday a New

York lady and her two stylish daughters were quite excited on looking over the hotel-book to see Miss Alcotts name, and immediately enquired if it was the Miss Alcott who wrote 'Little Women,' and were much impressed when they found it was the lion" (17 July). In Vevey, Louisa wrote that "Benda, the crack book and picture man here asked May, 'if she was the Miss Alcott who wrote the popular books,' for he said he had many calls for them, and wished to know where they could be found. We told him at London and felt puffed up" (10 September).

Back home in Concord, the Alcott family also was still coping with Louisa's fame, receiving letters for autograph requests and finding visitors on the doorsteps of Orchard House. Louisa wrote Anna in late July: "I hope the 'Jo Worshippers' were not regaled with my papers. Has the old box ever been nailed up? I squirm to think of my very old scribble being trotted out" (24–27 July). Admirers and lion hunters, as Louisa often called her fans, could wait until she returned. As she adamantly wrote Thomas Niles: "Dont give my address to any one. I don't want the young ladies notes. They can send them to Concord and I shall get them next year" (23 August). When she heard that her family was besieged by people seeking her out, Louisa became outraged. She defiantly told Anna that "when we read of the strangers swarming round, I *fairly panted for my garden hose and a good chance to blaz away at 'em. Is'nt it dreadful? and am I not glad I am safe?"* (11 September).

Despite Louisa's desire for privacy, her life in Europe was finding its way into American papers. She wrote, tongue-in-cheek, to her family: "I will only add a line to give you the last news of the health of her Highness Princess Louisa. She is such a public character now-a-days that even her bones are not her own, and her wails of woe, cannot be kept from long ears of the world—Old Donkey as it is!" (30 May). As she noted in July:

Niles sent me a notice in the gossipy old Republican telling about my "good old English Dr and my legs, and my grief for Dickens (dont care a pin) and all my plans and ails &c." I suppose [Ellery] Channing or Bun wrote it, and I should like to knock their heads off for meddling with what dont concern them old tattle tails!—Another notice said I wrote diaries at 6, plays at 10, went out to service at 15, and was governess and dragged a baby round the

Common. I recognized Pa's nice derangement of dates here, and fancy it was written by some of his admirers. I suppose I ought to like it, but I dont. (Oh aint Lu cross?). (8 July)

Even her royalties seemed to be a topic for public consumption: "As my 'ten thousand income' has got into the papers, the tax men will know just how much to charge me. Does my being absent free me from taxes?" (20 July). Worried that some of the more personal information was coming, in fact, from her own letters home, she often marked certain paragraphs "private" and warned Anna: "Dont read this stuff aloud. I dont write for the public now" (11 September).

The sisters' letters clearly were relished back at Orchard House. In his diary entry for 6 May 1870, Bronson reported that Abigail, after receiving one of the early letters from Dinan, "was made 16 by the intelligence" (*Diary for 1870* 257). The letters also provided a source of entertainment for friends as they were read aloud. Ellen Emerson wrote her sister, Edith, on 19 May 1870 that she and her mother "went in the carryall to see Mrs Alcott and hear the letters. Unhappily Mrs Alcott couldn't believe we were interested in the letters, but they were just what we wanted to hear" (555). In late May, Bronson purchased *Harper's Hand Book for Travellers in Europe and the East*, noting: "While the girls are travelling we shall enjoy looking out their routes on the map, and reading descriptions of places they stop" (*Diary for 1870* 279). By 5 June, he began copying the letters because "Anna sometimes likes to have the originals for perusal at her leisure" (329). Two months later, 4 August, he began numbering the letters, possibly already with the idea of preserving the correspondence as a volume: "I copy the letters, these numbering 33 & 34 of the series" (494). At the beginning of October, he noted: "Copy girl's letters—now numbering 55" (647). By the time the women reached Italy, Bronson reported: "Louisa and May's letters are sprightly and full of descriptions and experiences amusing to read" (5 March 184).

While Louisa used the grand tour to rest and not work on her writing, she gradually grew healthier. By 13 May, she could write home that she was "much better": "My leg lets me sleep, and I eat and feel quite chipper again. The weather has been cold, and I tried to walk too much, and so had a bad time. . . . We are all growing fat and Alice sasses me about it. . . . May sleeps like a boa constrictor, and is in clover generally. We laugh so much we ought to [be] plump as porpoises." On 25 May, she had seen a British physician in Dinan and reported that "I am now better, thanks to the English Dr Kane. . . . He only told me to keep warm and still and take . . . a little opium to get sleep. I did so and perked up at once. . . . I . . . drink wine, eat like a pig . . . and the girls [say] I'm growing fat and rosy. I look heaps better and feel so. . . . I believe this trip is going to fit up the old ruin." Less than a week later, May wrote to her family that "Louisa is up and down according to the weather. . . . The climate will do more than medicine [the Dr.] thinks, and if she can get natural sleep, that all must be left to time. So if she gets strong through the warm weather, and has a respite from pain, then with a winter in some warm place in Italy, she will begin to regain some of the strength she has wasted in overwork" (30 May). In mid-June, May would tell her family that Louisa "looks and eats better than she has for several years, growing fat and rosy, and losing that drawn tired look which worried us before she left home" (17 June).

By the middle of July, however, Louisa bemoaned to Anna: "You ask if I am not in bliss? No. I find that I've lost the power of enjoying as I used to, and though I like the fine scenes, I get tired of it very soon, and want to rest and be still. If I could have had a party like this four years ago I should have enjoyed it with great relish. Now I feel so old and stupid and wimbly, I don't deserve to be in the way of such things and you should be here in my place" (24 July). The weariness was felt even as she looked back at her success: "It is droll, But I cant make the fortunate Miss A. seem me, and only remember the weary years, the work, the waiting and disappointment—all that is forth in my mind; the other don't belong to me, and is a mistake somehow. Perhaps it will come real when I get used to rest and comfort, and not feeling as if 'the hounds were after me'" (24 July). May wrote to her father on 30 July that "Louisa is so well, sleeping naturally without narcotics, having no pain and growing so strong and well, that it would be too bad if she was obliged to winter in England, or by any possibility return to America, as the change of climate must do its work thoroughly to prevent the horrors of last winter from being repeated." But by the beginning of August 1870, Louisa felt even better: "I am so tickled to wake every morning after a long sound sleep that I can't believe it is me. . . . I can walk and ride and begin to feel as if a chain of heavy aches had fallen off and left me free. If this goes on without any break down for a month or so I shall feel as if my trip was a brilliant success" (31 July–2 August).

After two restful months in the quiet town of Dinan, the three women said their farewells to Madame Coste and traveled across France to Switzerland, stopping along the route in Le Mans, Tours, Amboise, Blois, Orleans, Bourges, Moulins, and Lyon to visit, as Louisa put it, "fresh 'chateaux and churches new'" (20 June). For the first time May was seeing some of the grand architectural structures of Europe and was impressed again and again: "At Le Mans we saw the most enchanting cathedral, in all France I thought then, but having just seen the one here [Tours], I can't say so now, for of all superb buildings I ever imagined this is the most so, and my second sensation since leaving America, I felt this morning when, turning a sharp corner suddenly we found ourselves in a large square and before us this grand church. . . . I was certainly breathless at the sight. . . . But the immensity of both the Le Mans and this one strike me with awe, and it seems disrespectful to enter without falling on ones knees" (17 June).

Always the writer, Louisa seemed to be more enchanted with people she would see rather than the grand architecture. In Tours, she also wrote about visiting the cathedral, but her focus was not on the building: "We wandered about it the other evening till moonrise and it was very interesting to see people scattered here and there at their prayers, some kneeling before St. Martin's shrine, some in a flowery little nook dedicated to the infant Christ, and one, a dark corner with a single candle lighting up a fine picture of the Mater Dolorosa, where a widow all in her weeds sat alone crying and praying." Fascinated by the human drama unfolding before her, Louisa had an eye for highlighting tragedy and comedy together. "In another a sick old man sat while his wife knelt by him praying with all her might to St. Gratien, (the patron saint of the church) for her dear old invalid. Nuns and priests glided about, and it was all very poetical and fine till I came to an imposing priest in a first class chapel who was taking snuff and gaping, instead of piously praying" (20 June).

By the end of June, the party reached Geneva, where Louisa had stayed in 1865. She wrote her mother: "It seems almost like getting home again to be here where I never thought to come again when I went away five years ago with my Weld incumbrances. We are at the Metripole Hotel right on the Lake with a glimpse of Mount Blanc from our windows. It is rather fine after the grimy little Inns of Brittany, and we enjoy a sip of luxury and put on our best gowns with feminine satisfaction after living in old travelling suits for a fortnight" (29 June).

Geneva was also along the grand route of Europe, and the three women soon met up with relatives, which included Alice Bartlett's uncle and aunt, Richard and Angelina Greenwood Warren and their children, one of whom—Henry Warren—would become Alice's husband in a few years. On June 29, the Alcotts themselves were surprised by a knock on their hotel door. They opened it to discover their cousin Sophy Bond, the daughter of their aunt and uncle George W. and Louisa Carolina Greenwood Bond: "We howled and flew at her, and she told us Aunty and Mr. B. were below, so down we rushed and have had a good pow-wow." A few weeks later in Bex, May wrote her mother that Alice's first cousin Herbert J. Pratt, a graduate of Harvard Medical College and a past acquaintance of the Alcott sisters, "surprised us the other night and it really is very entertaining to hear about his adventures, for he tells them well, and as he went to Tunis and Constantinople where every thing was exceedingly foreign, it sounds like a romance. We have good times sketching and walking together. . . . He is handsomer and more manly than formerly" (5 September). May had first met Herbert J. Pratt in August 1863 at Clarks Island, near Plymouth, Massachusetts, and he had visited her in Concord a number of times during that year. Louisa had commented on him in her journal during one of those 1863 visits, observing that Pratt "sings well but seems a silly youth though amiable" (121). Now, seven years later, Louisa noted, "We have had lively times since he came, for he has traveled far and wide, and can tell his adventures well. . . . He dances wild dances for us, sings songs in many languages. We had a moonlight ball in the road the other night coming from the Warrens—fine affair. He is much improved and quite appals us by talking Arabic, French, German, Italian, and Armenian in one grand burst" (10 September).

Early July 1870 saw the three women comfortably settled for a month into a pension in Bex, Switzerland, "a rambling old Hotel all balconies and steps and trees and funny nooks." Once again, Louisa showed by her descriptions that she was always observing the characters around her: "A few English are here and a Polish Countess with her four servants, governess, two children, and her lover. The Count is in Paris and Madame flirts in a calm, cool way which rather amazes the Yankees." But none of the memorable characters or events spurred her into writing: "Such a lazy life I lead lying round reading novels from morning till night, without an idea in my head or any desire for one. I'm afraid Niles will have to wait a long time for any new work from me" (8 July).

In early August 1870, the Alcotts and Bartlett reached Vevey, a town that certainly held many fond memories for Louisa. Staying at the Pension Paradis, they had, as Louisa declared to her editor Thomas Niles, "French counts and Spanish grandees to play croquet with us, boats to go paddling in and three or four ex kings and queens to stare at us when we take our walks abroad" (10 August). She wrote her family on 10 September: "Our house is brim full and we have funny times. The sick Russian lady and her old ma make a great fuss if a breath of air comes in at meal times, and expect twenty people to sit shut tight in a smallish room for an hour on a hot day. We protested, and Madame put them in the parlor where they glower as we pass and lock the door when they can . . . The Polish General, a little crooked, is very droll and bursts out in the middle of the general chat with stories about transparent apples and golden horses." Just over a week later, she would note: "We have a French family now, a funny fat old lady with a white beard and a vast purple bonnet in which she lives day and night apparently, and her married daughter, a handsome shrill blonde, who dresses in as delicate violet and white, and picks her teeth at table with a hairpin! I thought Alice and H[erbert]. J. P[ratt]. would have fainted at the full spectacle; but we are fast getting used to the little peculiarities of foreigners and I trust they will forgive us many sins in return" (19 September).

Despite the colorful characters and spectacular sights, Louisa was not writing anything besides letters, and she reported this inactivity to Niles: "I am glad the books continue to go well since I am doing nothing now. I am afraid I shall not write till I get home, for all I do is scribble odds and ends as notes, and dawdle round without an idea in my head." She had, however, composed "The Lay of a Golden Goose," a poem that humorously told how people and publishers had not believed in her talents years ago but now were clamoring after her, wanting to meet her, to find out information about her, to publish anything she wrote. Thomas Niles thought the poem too direct and suggested it not be published. Bronson acknowledged the same on 29 August, writing that Louisa had sent the poem to Niles but that it was "too personal to publish, yet too characteristic to be lost. They [the verses] will tell becomingly by and by" (*Diary for 1870* 535). Unwilling to push for publication, Louisa replied to Niles: "I don't think the printing of the 'Lay of the Golden Goose' would do us any harm, but I don't care any thing about it either way, so you can let it pass." She was now more concerned with rest and relaxation than writing: "Alice says no one does anything in Italy, so after six months of idleness, I may get back and go to work" (20 September).

But all was not peaceful, and the trip itself was not without trouble. Rumors of war between France and Prussia had been in the air for months. On 15 July 1870, Emperor Napoleon III declared war on Prussia, but the three women believed Switzerland to be a safe haven. Louisa reassured her anxious parents: "Dont be worried if you don't hear regularly, or think us in danger. Switzerland is out of the mess, and if she gets in, we can skip over into Italy, and be as cosy as possible" (18 July). Just a week later, the Franco-Prussian War was raging, and Louisa wrote: "The war along the Rhine is sending troops of travellers to Switzerland for refuge, and all the large towns are brimful of people flying from Germany" (24–27 July). Several days later, however, May warned Bronson: "I fear this war is going to be more of an inconvenience than we at first imagined, for if Italy joins in it, or does not remain entirely neutral as she now declares herself to be, we cannot go there in September. . . . What do the papers say in America?—for it is impossible to get any news here, and you hear everything sooner than we do" (30 July). Ten days later, May reported to her mother: "Just now everything looks rather bleak for the French. McMahon having just lost this last battle and it being thought necessary to fortify Paris, it seems as if the Emperor had underrated the strength of the Prussians. It seems such a silly war that it makes it all the more provoking to have our plans so upset just be cause one man wants a little more territory" (10 August). The next day, Louisa noted that the newspapers "tell us that the French have lost two big battles, the Prussians are in Strasbourg, and Paris in a state of siege. The papers are also full of theatrical messages from the French to the people asking them to come up and be slaughtered for 'La Patrie,' and sober cool reports from the Prussians. I side with the Prussians, for they sympathized with us in our war and old Nap. did'nt. I guess he is going to get a good thrashing, and he deserves it. Hooray for old Pruss!" (11 August). Vevey, Louisa confided to her parents, "is full of Spaniards who are gathered round the Ex-Queen Isabella and Don Carlos, all plotting and planning some mad revolution. Mysterious little brown men come and take the Count out from his meals to jabber darkly in corners and then vanish as mysteriously as they came" (21 August).

On 2 September 1870, Emperor Napoleon III surrendered to the Prussians, and three days later, in Paris, the empire was declared over and the new republic of France began. May wrote to Abigail on 5 September that the "war news of course is the great subject of conversation and Napoleon's surrender caused quite a panic to the French here in the house. I dont see how there can be much more fighting, and you need not be surprised if our next letters are dated Stresa which you know is on Lake Maggiore." A few days later, still safely ensconced in Vevey, Louisa told her parents that "all Europe seems to be going to destruction" (10 September). She declared that the war, however, was not going to spoil all their plans: "We mean to skip over the Alps next week if weather and war permit, for we are bound to see Milan and the lakes, even if we have to turn and come back without a glimpse of Rome." Vevey was still filled with refugees from France, and Louisa noted that ten families alone had asked the day before if Pension Paradis had rooms for them. Her dislike of Napoleon III increased as she witnessed the tragic effects of war: "It is awful to think of the misery that wretch Nap has made, and I don't wonder his people curse him after he got them into such a war, and then slipt out like a coward. Hope his ills will increase, and every inch of him will suffer for such a shameful act" (10 September). By the next day, however, their plans of leaving, Louisa told Anna, were dampened by learning that the Italian government had ordered its army to take the city of Rome, a separate Papal State, ruled by the pope: "We are thrown aback to day by the news that Italy is getting under arms just where we want to go. Russia and England must hurry and make peace or Europe will be in a general toss, and we shall have to go to England" (11 September).

Feeling that the threat of war was over, the three women finally departed Vevey on 6 October 1870 and headed to Italy. They arrived by diligence that evening in Brieg, Switzerland, but set out early at four o'clock the next morning. Louisa, as only a writer could, gave a detailed description of the journey to her mother a few days later:

> Our start in the dawn from Brieg, with two diligences, a carriage, and a cart, was something between a funeral and a caravan: first an immense diligence with seven horses, then a smaller one with four, then our *calèche* with two, and finally the carrier's cart with one. It was very exciting,—the general gathering of sleepy travellers in the dark square, the tramping of horses, the packing in, the grand stir of getting off; then the slow winding up, up, up out of the valley toward the sun, which came slowly over the great hills, rising as we never saw it rise before. The still, damp pine-forests kept us in shadow a long time after the white mountain-tops began to shine. Little by little we wound through a great gorge, and then the sun came dazzling between these grand hills, showing us a new world. Peak after peak of the Bernese Oberland rose behind us, and great white glaciers lay before us; while the road crept like a narrow line, in and out, over chasms that made us dizzy to look at, under tunnels, and through stone galleries with windows over which dashed waterfalls from glaciers above. Here and there were refuges, a hospice, and a few *châlets*, where shepherds live their wild, lonely lives. (6 October)

May herself, as she too related the experience to her mother, was in awe during the trip across the Simplon Pass: "I tingled with delight when Monte Rosa opened before us with its dazzling white snow against a perfectly clear blue sky and behind us the Bernese Alps and the glaciers. This was something to have lived for and as we climbed still higher while white peak after white peak showed itself in the direction of Brieg and over the valley we had left so far below us" (8 October). Then after dinner in Simplon, the party started in their caleche down the Alps towards Italy. May wrote: "I nearly stood on my head with delight at the intense beauty of the valley of Gondo for any thing wilder and more picturesque cannot be imagined. Then this wonderful road which we had traversed so far in safety led along the edge of precipices, through tunnels and over cataracts." They entered the town of

Domo D'Ossola as the sun set, and by the moon's glow headed into Stresa. As May told her mother: "This I consider making a Pass successfully for its not every traveller who sees sunrise in the Alps, an Italian sunset and first sight of Lago Maggiore by moonlight all in one day" (8 October).

After visiting the Isola Bella in the Borromean Islands the next morning, where, according to Louisa, they "felt like butterflies after a frost, and fluttered about, enjoying the sunshine" (8 October), the three women boarded a steamboat to Luini and from there they took a diligence to Lugano. May, clearly filled with exuberance, related to Abigail the details of the once-in-a-lifetime journey: "[H]ere among the jeers and shouts of an Italian crowd, Alice and I mounted to the very top of a high diligence and sat with perfect complacency amid the baggage while Louisa from the coupe begged us to come down and the inside passengers craned their necks to see of what nation the insane travellers could be who preferred to view the landscape from that great elevation. But I wouldn't have missed the enjoyment of the next few hours for all the ridicule in the world." Not only was May awed by the view from atop, she was also impressed by their driver: "We had a last glimpse of Lago Maggiore and Monte Rosa by sunset and following the shores of the lake drove into Lugano by moonlight with our superb cocker playing a festive tune on a Robin Hood's horn which hung by gilt bands at his side, putting on two brakes, driving four horses and making himself agreeable to us all at the same time. I consider this man, a person of mind for he spoke three languages easily, and did everything with such a superior air that I felt intensely honored to have him lift me down in his great arms when we reached the Hotel Washington and stopped in a crowded square" (8 October).

As the memorable day ended, the Alcotts discovered that they could look out their hotel room window onto the stage of an opera house, where Verdi's *La Traviata* was being performed. Louisa, who many years earlier had composed and performed melodramatic plays with her sister Anna, wrote: "My Nan can imagine with what rapture I stared at the scenes going on below me, and how I longed for her as I stood wrapped in my yellow bed-quilt, and saw gallant knights in armor warble sweetly to plump ladies in masks, or pretty peasants fly wildly from ardent lovers in red tights; also a dishevelled maid who tore her hair in a forest while a man aloft made thunder and lightening,—and *I saw him do it!*" (8 October). May noted that the performance "reminded me so much of the old days when Annie dressed in the velvet puffs and everlasting yellow top boots sang baritone to Lu's soprano and brought down the house in every act" (8 October).

The following day, the travelers headed up Lake Lugano on a steamer to Porlezza, where they took a carriage to Menaggio, located on the west bank of Lake Como. From there, it was only a short sail to Cadenabbia, where they rested for several days before departing for Milan. May reported: "Como is charming but I must repeat nothing equals the beauty of Lugano to me. . . . [N]ow more than ever I am convinced we travel under a lucky star" (8 October). "All looks well," wrote Louisa, "and if the winter goes on rapidly and pleasantly as the summer we shall soon be thinking of home, unless one of us decides to stay" (8 October).

During the last half of October, the women made their way to Milan, then on to Parma, Pisa, Bologna, and, by the end of the month, Florence. Here, they found themselves amid a circle of American expatriate artists. The painter and sculptor Thomas Ball, whose equestrian statue of General George Washington had been unveiled in the Boston Public Garden the previous year, held a party in the Alcotts' honor. The sculptors Hiram Powers and Joel Tanner Hart invited them to their studios, Hart even encouraging May to model a bust of Louisa because, as May told her father, "he thinks I could clear a few hundreds by the sale of it, as her reputation seems spreading so rapidly" (30 October). May confided: "It seems 'Little Women' is as well known here as in Boston and has made many friends for Louisa. She was showered with compliments from the distinguished people here . . . and several ladies from Rome . . . were full of kind offers about apartments &c." (30 October).

May spent her time studying the great works of art at Florence's famous Uffizi and Pitti museums. She was captivated by the paintings of Andrea del Sarto, Correggio, Giotto, and Fra Angelico. Titian's reclining nude Venus and Raphael's bare-breasted *Fornarina*, however, were not to her tastes. There can be no doubt that May was quite taken by the city—by its current artists and their bohemian lives and by its past artistic glories: "I cant be reconciled to this city so full of history, and so connected with remarkable people looking so modern and new that it might be New York or any flourishing American city" (30 October). Louisa appeared less impressed, confessing in her journal: "Disappointed in some things, but found Nature always lovely and wonderful, so did n't mind faded pictures, damp rooms, and the cold winds of 'sunny Italy'" (175).

Their stay in Florence was short, however. As they bought furs there to prepare for the coming winter, the three began, as May wrote, "our march to Rome" (30 October), and by 10 November, they found themselves in the Eternal City. They paid sixty dollars a month for six rooms on the Piazza Barbarini, and an extra six dollars for a girl who cooked and cleaned. The initial weeks were cold and rainy, however, and Louisa noted that her "first view most of the time was the poor Triton with an icicle on his nose" (*Journals* 175). Louisa wrote in her journal that she "felt as if I had been there before and knew all about it. Always oppressed with a sense of sin, dirt, and general decay of all things. Not well, so saw things through blue glasses" (175).

Her sister, on the other hand, was enjoying the new experience: "May in bliss with lessons, sketching, and her dreams" (175). The younger Alcott was now taking lessons from the Boston-born Frederic Crowninshield (1845–1918), five years May's junior. Crowninshield had graduated from Harvard in 1866 and the following year began to study in watercolors with Thomas Charles Rowbotham in London. He had been in Europe four years, working primarily in landscapes, when May began her study with him. He would remain on the continent until 1879, when he returned to Boston and taught art in the Museum of Fine Arts. Louisa told Bronson that May would usually spend her mornings in the studio on the Via Margutta working with Crowninshield, whom Louisa pronounced "an excellent artist," and in the afternoons she and her sister would drive on the Campagna or tour the art museums. She stated, with a hint of satisfaction, that May "takes Rome very calmly and has raptures over but few of the famous things. Her own tastes are so decided that the general opinion affects her very little, and we indulge in our naughty criticisms like a pair of Goths and Vandals as we are" (20 November).

On 29 November, Louisa celebrated her thirty-eighth birthday in Rome, with May presenting her a sketch and Alice a nosegay of flowers. That holiday season, however, was soon saddened. Louisa recorded a brief entry in

FIGURE 8. John Bridge
Pratt (late 1860s),
husband of Anna Alcott
Pratt. *Louisa May Alcott's
Orchard House/L. M. A.
Memorial Association.*

her "Notes and Memoranda" for 1870: "Dec. 23rd saw John's death in a pa-
per & soon learned it was a fact. Sad time" (*Journals* 176). John Bridge Pratt,
Anna's husband, who had so happily greeted Louisa on her return from
Europe in 1866, had died at their home in Maplewood, Massachusetts, on
November 27. His body was brought back to Concord, and he was buried
in Sleepy Hollow Cemetery on 29 November—Louisa's birthday. Ellen Emerson, writing to her sister, called the death "sudden & sad," and she noted:
"It was a heart-breaking funeral, all the more so for the calmness of poor
Annie & Mrs Pratt. Freddy sat at his mamma's feet. Mrs. Alcott didn't come,
and kept Johnny at home with her. Mr Pratt was only sick a week, it was a
heavy cold and pneumonia set in" (572). Grieving, Louisa wrote home to
his bereaved widow: "You need not to be told what he was to me, or how
I mourn for him, for no born brother was ever dearer, & each year I loved
& respected & admired him more & more. He did more to make us trust

& respect men than any one I know & with him I lose the one young man whom I sincerely honored in my heart. Good bye my dear, honest, tender, noble John!" (December [?]). Her letter to her cousin Lizzie Wells conveyed her distress at being so far from home and unable to offer personal comfort to her older sister: "Annie bears her loss so beautifully that it makes it possible to stay away now in order that I may be more useful by & by. But *you* know how hard it is for me to be even in Rome when my heart is at home & every day a burden till I can come." She implored her cousin to "*fill my place a little till I come.*" Greatly saddened by Anna's and her nephews' loss, Louisa confessed to Lizzie that she was also concerned about Abigail: "My heart is very anxious about mother & I ache to go to her, but winter, distance, health, & my duty to Alice hold me till April. I think God will keep my Marmee for me because I couldn't bear to miss my Good bye & the keeping of my promise to close her dear eyes. Annie says she is not well & so I dread another loss before I have learned to bear the last" (9 January).

With the thoughts of John Bridge Pratt in her mind, Louisa set about to recapture the more glorious times as she began her new novel—*Little Men.* She noted in her journal: "Begin to write a new book . . . that John's death may not leave A. and the dear little boys in want. John took care that they should have enough while the boys are young, and worked very hard to have a little sum to leave, without a debt anywhere" (177). Recalling memories of her father's Temple School, she started to spin out the tale of Plumfield and the further adventures of Jo March—this time for her nephews John and Fred Pratt, to whom she would dedicate the novel. She wrote: "In writing and thinking of the little lads, to whom I must be a father now, I found comfort for my sorrow" (*Journals* 177). As she told her faithful readers in a public letter: "But I now have a motive for work stronger than before, and if the book can be written, it shall be, for the good of the two dear little men now left to my care, for long ago I promised to try and fill John's place if they were left fatherless" (1 January).

As this sad Christmas season closed, Louisa's grief may have been lessened or briefly forgotten with new excitement in Rome. On 28 December, the women's maid, Lavinia, rushed into their apartment "with the news that the Tiber had overflowed its banks and inundated the lower part of the city, that people just outside the walls were drowned, others in the Ghetto were

FIGURE 9. Fred and
John Pratt, the sons of
Anna and John Pratt
(late 1860s). *Louisa
May Alcott's Orchard
House/L. M. A. Memorial
Association.*

washed out of their houses, the Corso was under water, and the world generally coming to an end" (29 December). The Tiber had risen to its highest
level since 1805, because of the rains and the melting mountain snows. The
Jewish Ghetto, with its overcrowding and proximity to the river, seemed
to fare the worst. Louisa reported that a friend had observed "a man and
woman pushing a mattress before them as they waded nearly to their waists
in water, and on the mattress were their little children—all they could save"
(29 December). Louisa, always watching through a writer's eyes, noted:
"One old woman who had lost everything but her life besought the rescuers to bring her a little snuff for the love of heaven. . . . One poor man,
in trying to save his wife and children in a cart, upset them, and the little
ones were drowned at their own door. Tragedy and comedy, side by side"
(29 December).

As the new year 1871 dawned and the waters of the Tiber began to recede, Rome was astir with new excitement—the arrival of Victor Emmanuel, king of Italy, who came to offer aid and comfort to the flood victims. With the September 1870 defeat of the Emperor Napoleon III, who had been the sovereign of Rome for almost twenty years, the French could no longer offer protection for Pope Pius IX's Papal State, and the Italian people wanted their government to seize control of Rome. The Italian army, under the leadership of General Cadorna, finally made a slow advance on Rome, reaching the Aurelian Walls on 19 September 1870. With light resistance put up by the pope's Zouaves, the Italian army fired their cannons for several hours on 20 September before finally breaching the walls at Porta Pia and marching into Rome. Refusing to accept the legitimacy of King Victor Emmanuel's right to rule the city, the pope retreated to the Vatican, where he said he was a prisoner. Pope Pius was certainly free to go about Rome, but clearly the citizens of Rome welcomed rule by the kingdom of Italy, and in early 1871, the capital of Italy was moved from Florence to Rome. Although the king was due to arrive in a grand procession on 10 January, he had unexpectedly arrived at four in the morning on New Year's Day 1871, much to the approval of the Roman population. Caught up in the excitement of the times, the three American travelers joined the well-wishers atop the Quirinal hill to see and cheer the king. Louisa reported to readers of the *Boston Daily Evening Transcript*: "There was a great flurry among the officials, and splendid creatures in new uniforms flew about in all directions. Grand carriages arrived, bringing the high and mighty to welcome the King" (1 January). After standing for an hour in the rain, Louisa's health forced her to retire to their apartment while May and Alice "took a carriage and chased the King all over the city, till they caught him at the Capitol. They had a fine view of him as he came down the steps of the Capitol, through a mass of people cheering frantically and whitening the streets with waving handkerchiefs" (1 January).

Alice Bartlett, perhaps inspired by Louisa's burst of creativity, also took up her pen in Rome, writing a humorous article about the three women's search for an apartment in the city, with advice to tourists wishing to do the same. Louisa liked the piece enough to send it to Thomas Niles to see if he could place it. Niles replied on 13 January 1871, saying that Miss Bartlett was "clever with the quill for a novice." But he thought Alcott's "praise was perhaps too generous"; however, he added that "those who have read it do not follow much behind you." He offered the article to the editor of the *Saturday Evening Gazette*, a paper that had published many of Louisa's early tales, but the "'immense' sum" that Alcott had suggested "dampened his ardor." The *Boston Transcript* agreed to publish it but not pay for it, and Niles was "despairing of success" when he gave it to Edward Everett Hale, minister, author, and cofounder in 1869 of the monthly magazine *Old and New*. Hale responded the next day: "[A]fter you left we all listened to the reading of 'Apartment in Rome' with real pleasure; I take it at once for 'Old & New.'" He told Niles that he had not "'seen anything so fresh & clever for a long while—it's capital.'" Advising Alice Bartlett to accept the terms and publish the article under her own name, Niles wrote: "The *pay* is not large, but the chance for *fame* will compensate for this; I consider it a good long feather in Miss Bartlett's hat" (ALS: Houghton Library, Harvard University). Alice agreed and "Our Apartment. A Practical Guide to Those Intending to Spend a Winter in Rome" was published in two parts in the April and June issues of *Old and New*. The thinly fictionalized account presents the trials and delights of the three travelers' time in Rome, painting a portrait of the women that would be much like the one Alcott herself would compose for *Shawl-Straps* in 1872. Bartlett ends her article, warning that the climate of Rome may not be suitable to all: "To all invalids intending to come to Rome, I would say, consult some very competent physician before you decide to do it, and do not think that you will be able to see the great works of art unless you are quite as strong as average mortals." Louisa's character (Sophia) cries out: "'Tell them to stay at home'" (663).

As the winter wore on, Louisa noted in her journal that she went to the Capitol often, looking at the paintings and the statues, but once again, it was not the artwork that greatly impressed her: "But a better sight to me was the crowd of poor people going to get bread and money sent by the king; and the splendid snow-covered hills were finer than the marble beauty inside. Art tires. Nature never" (177). By February, work progressed on *Little Men* and Louisa seemed a bit cheered: "A gay month in Rome, with the carnival, artists' fancy ball, and many parties, and much calling" (*Journals* 177). A. K. Loring sent her seven hundred dollars from the sales of *Moods*, which certainly must have helped to lift her spirits. With this royalty check and the one thousand dollars coming for the new novel, she felt she had enough money to spare for May to spend more time in Europe as she herself went home to care for Anna and her parents: "Decided to leave May for another year . . . so she may be happy and free to follow her talent" (*Journals* 177).

On 12 April, Bronson noted that in a recent letter from May in Rome, she had written that the eminent portrait painter George Peter Alexander Healy (1808–94) had "asked to paint Louisa's head, and that she had consented to sit to him. Healy has a wide reputation and should get a likeness" (242). Healy, born in Chicago, indeed, had a "wide reputation." After studying art in the United States as a teenager, he had left America for Europe in 1834, where he studied with Baron Gros and was influenced by Couture. Although he briefly came home to Chicago in 1855, he had returned to Europe by 1869, where he painted primarily in Rome and Paris for the next twenty-one years. By the end of his career, he had painted more portraits than any American artist; his subjects included most of the prominent people of his lifetime. Among his works are portraits of Daniel Webster, Nathaniel Hawthorne, Henry W. Longfellow, Abraham Lincoln, and Ulysses S. Grant. Louisa must have been flattered by the request and May honored to watch the artist work at his studio on the Via S. Nicola di Tolentino. By 2 May, Bronson had received letters from Louisa noting that the portrait was finished "and thought a fair likeness" (259). While she sat for Healy, Louisa, dressed in a black dress with white lace around the collar and a simple black ribbon adorning her hair, was perhaps unaware that the great painter's daughter was an aspiring novelist. As he presented the completed painting to her as a gift, Louisa later recollected: "'I wondered . . . what was going to come next; when one day Mr. Healy's daughter appeared with a novel in manuscript which she wished I would give an opinion of. I found it to be good and sent it to my London publisher, who happily published it for her'" (Stearns 87). Thomas Niles must have also agreed as Mary Healy's novel, *A Summer's Romance*, was published by Roberts Brothers in 1872.

Before leaving Italy, however, the three women departed Rome in mid-March for the rest of the month in Albano. Louisa wrote in her journal:

"A lovely place. Walk, write, and rest. A troop of handsome officers from Turin, who clatter by, casting soft glances at my two blond signorinas, who enjoy it very much. . . . May sketches, I write, and so we go on" (178). After the relaxing time at Albano, the travelers moved on to Venice for a fort-night: "Floated about for two weeks seeing sights. A lovely city for a short visit. Not enough going on to suit brisk Americans. May painted, A[lice]. hunted up old jewelry, and friends, and I dawdled after them" (*Journals* 178). Bronson reported on 24 April that he had received letters from Louisa and May, who were in Venice; the two, he wrote, were "charmed with the city of bridges and gondolas, and write in the best of spirits. Louisa sends Anna a chapter of her new book. It is concerning John Brooks's last days, and to be inserted if Anna judges it best" (250). In mid-April, the group headed to England, via Germany. They traveled over the Brenner Pass and across Germany, stopping briefly in Munich and Cologne, and finally reach-ing Antwerp, Belgium, where they set sail for England. By the first of May, they were in London.

As the sisters secured lodgings on Brompton Road in London, Louisa was happy to show May her "favorite places and people." She took her to see old friends Moncure Daniel Conway and his wife, Ellen, with whom she had stayed on her trip abroad in 1865. Aubrey House on Notting Hill once again welcomed Louisa, and she introduced May to the Taylors. William Niles, Thomas Niles's brother and Roberts Brothers' representative in Lon-don, arrived to advise Louisa about the upcoming novel—and to serve as the women's escort around the city. The weeks there were, as Louisa noted, a "busy month" (*Journals* 178). She oversaw the British edition of *Little Men* by Sampson Low on 15 May 1871, hoping to secure British copyright by printing the novel first in England and physically being in the country at the time of publication.

May too was busy taking art lessons from the noted watercolor painter Thomas Charles Leeson Rowbotham (1823–75). Born in Dublin, Ireland, he was the son of Thomas Leeson Rowbotham (1782–1853), also a well-known watercolor artist. Often called T. L. Rowbotham Jr., he started painting seri-ously in 1844 and was probably influenced by the work of J. M. W. Turner. He produced, with his father, *The Art of Painting in Watercolours* (1850). Known primarily as a landscape painter, his work was praised by John

Ruskin. Rowbotham, also skilled as a lithographer, illustrated many books and was professor of drawing at the Royal Naval School, New Cross, London. Once again, May had been fortunate in finding a skilled artist to help her further her knowledge and skill.

On 10 May 1871, Bronson recorded that Louisa had written and confirmed that she and Alice Bartlett would be leaving soon, but that May would stay on and probably study art. Alice Bartlett departed for the United States on 11 May, leaving behind the two Alcott sisters. Louisa wrote that she was "glad to know her, for she is true and very interesting" (*Journals* 178). The three had shared many experiences and would not forget their time together. Their paths would occasionally cross again, but never would they be so close as they had been during the past year. Alice would go back abroad several times throughout the 1870s. She became friends with Henry James, who once said of her, "I esteem her rather a good fellow than a lively woman. I couldn't love her" (*A Life in Letters* 90). In 1873, James would ride on the Campagna in Rome with Alice and read poetry with her. According to the master novelist, Alice Bartlett was the one who provided him with the germ of the story that inspired *Daisy Miller*, published in 1878 (Edel 214). In Florence in March 1873, Ralph Waldo Emerson and his daughter Ellen would also encounter Henry James and Bartlett, who then was traveling with Alice Mason Sumner, who was awaiting the finalization of her divorce from Massachusetts Senator Charles Sumner. Alice and Mrs. Sumner were, according to Ellen Emerson, "our sole delight & home in the city" (60). Alice continued to write about her travels in Europe for *Old and New*, publishing "Some Pros and Cons of Travel Abroad" for the October 1871 issue and "The French Provinces" in March 1873. On 31 October 1878, she would marry her first cousin, Henry Edward Warren, age thirty-five, a banker then living in Weatherford, Texas. Alice Bartlett Warren died of paralysis of the heart in Plymouth, where she was wintering, on 17 December 1912, just five days shy of her sixty-ninth birthday, and was buried in Mount Auburn Cemetery in Cambridge, Massachusetts, next to the graves of her father, mother, and brother.

Alice Bartlett was never forgotten by the Alcotts. Louisa spent a week in June 1882 with her in Mattapoiset, a Massachusetts coastal town and a popular summering home for the wealthy. The two enjoyed the time "driving about or talking over our year in Europe" (*Journals* 234). In March 1885 Alice visited Louisa for several days at her Chestnut Street residence in Boston, where the author was undergoing mind-cure treatments for exhaustion. When Louisa composed *Shawl-Straps* in 1872, Alice found herself as Amanda, a major character in a work by one of America's most beloved authors. Forever would she be thus immortalized. Louisa, in her narrative, wrote about the departure of their traveling companion and cohort for many adventures: "Amanda hurried home with friends to enjoy a festive summer among the verdant plains of Cape Cod. With deep regret did her mates bid her adieu, and nothing but the certainty of soon embracing her again would have reconciled Livy [Louisa] to the parting; for in Amanda she found that rare and precious treasure, a friend. . . . Livy had searched long years for a friend to her mind, and got one at last" (223).

After Alice left the two sisters, Louisa, knowing that duty to Anna and her parents was calling her home, made plans for departure: "I decided to go home on the 25th, as I am needed. A very pleasant year in spite of the constant pain, John's death, and home anxieties. Very glad I came, for May's sake. It has been a very useful year for her" (*Journals* 178). Bronson had noted a month earlier: "It will be hard for the sisters to part in a foreign land. But May has the courage and perseverance to carry out her plans, against any fortune, however adverse for the moment. She loves her art too well to lose an opportunity like the present" (*Diary for 1871* 265).

Louisa left her sister and sailed for America aboard the steamer *Malta* on 25 May 1871. The journey home proved to be a fearful one, however, as Louisa noted in her journal: "After an anxious passage of twelve days, got safely home. Small-pox on board, and my room-mate . . . very ill. I escaped, but had a sober time lying next door to her, waiting to see if my turn was to come" (178). While her sick roommate was left on one of the harbor islands, Thomas Russell, collector of the Boston Custom House, carried Louisa and some other passengers safely into Boston harbor in his tugboat on 6 June 1870. This time John Bridge Pratt, who had been there to escort her home in 1866 after her first European trip, was not there to greet her. Instead Bronson Alcott and Thomas Niles arrived in a carriage bedecked with a poster announcing the publication of *Little Men*—fifty thousand copies having been sold in advance.

After spending the night in Boston and taking precautions against small-pox, Louisa and her father returned to Orchard House. There, Louisa found her upstairs bedroom refurnished with the monies earned from her father's latest Conversations. While her nephews, John and Fred, were "tall, bright lads, devoted to Marmee, and the life of the house," her sister Anna was changed: "Nan well and calm, but under her sweet serenity is a very sad soul, and she mourns for her mate like a tender turtle-dove." Abigail, Louisa's beloved Marmee, however, seemed the one who had suffered most during her daughter's absence: "Mother feeble and much aged by this year of trouble. I shall never go far away from her again." During June, visitors arrived at the house on Lexington Road, as well as many letters, all bearing happy wishes and welcomes for Louisa. She too was delighted to be back with her family: "A happy month, for I felt well for the first time in two years. I knew it would n't last, but enjoyed it heartily while it did, and was grateful for rest from pain and a touch of the old cheerfulness. It was much needed at home" (*Journals* 178–79).

Louisa had brought home G. P. A. Healy's portrait of her, and it now hung in Orchard House, a reminder of those days in Rome. Bronson, however, thought that it "rather disappointing." Noting that it was painted in Italy while she "was suffering from neuralgia," Louisa's father observed: "The artist has not painted out the pains and weariness as became his art. It was an unpropitious moment for his project and himself, but the portrait may grow upon us, as we look from day to day. Now the flesh is haggard and the features too elongated for a true lifelike likeness" (*Diary for 1871* 313). Perhaps Healy had captured the real Louisa May Alcott with his oils as her health continued to decline year after year.

May would stay on in England throughout the summer and fall, spending her time seeing the sights of London, often with William Niles as escort, visiting the museums and galleries, and working on her own art, especially copying the paintings of J. M. W. Turner. But May certainly felt the pull of home as Louisa's health was again failing—and realized that it was Louisa's earnings that allowed her to remain. In Louisa's journal entry for the months of July, August, and September, she simply noted: "Sick. Holiday soon over. Too much company and care and change of climate upset the poor nerves again" (179). By October, she had hired two girls to help her parents and left

Concord for a room on Beacon Street as Concord was "so hard for me, with its dampness and worry" (179).

By November 1871, May had decided to come home "as she feels she is needed." Louisa wrote: "Marmee is feeble, Nan has her boys and her sorrow, and one strong head and hand is wanted at home." Perhaps feeling guilty that her own ill health was the reason May was returning, Louisa rationalized: "A year and a half of holiday is a good deal, and duty comes first always. Sorry to call her back, but her eyes are troublesome, and housework will rest them and set her up. Then she can go again when I am better." Louisa, who had worked hard and long for her success, seemed to want the fortunate May to struggle—if only just a bit—to achieve her dreams: "I don't want her to be thwarted in her work more than just enough to make her want it very much" (*Journals* 179).

May Alcott arrived home on 19 November 1871, bringing "[p]iles of pictures, merry adventures, and interesting tales of the fine London lovers." Louisa and her family rejoiced, "enjoying the cheerful element she always brings into the house" (*Journals* 179). Abigail too was overjoyed: "May arrives—Thank God for these special mercies—My girls *all* home" (20 November, diary, Houghton Library, Harvard University). Ten days later, 29 November, Louisa and Bronson celebrated their shared birthday, she thirty-nine and he seventy-two. On Thanksgiving Day, the Alcott family gathered at the farm of Minot Pratt in order to help ease the loss of John for both Anna and the Pratts. In her journal, Louisa marked the day: "All well and all together. Much to give thanks for" (179).

The "Pathetic Family" indeed had much for which to be thankful. Louisa's success now had provided them all a comfortable life. But the money would never buy Louisa the health she so desired. In late 1872, Louisa would turn her grand European tour with May and Alice Bartlett into a book, something that Niles had encouraged all along. As early as 30 August 1870, he had written to Louisa, asking her to "give me 'Jo's Letters from Abroad to the March's at Home' as talked about between us before you sailed" (ALS: Houghton Library, Harvard University). Louisa would take Niles's advice as she clearly used her European letters to form the basis for her semiautobiographical account of the trip—the book *Shawl-Straps*, first serialized in the *Christian Union* during March and April 1872 and published by Roberts Brothers in November 1872 as the second volume in the *Aunt Jo's Scrap Bag* series. As Louisa noted in her journal that spring: "All is fish that comes to the literary net. Goethe puts his joys and sorrows into poems; I turn my adventures into bread and butter" (182). Obviously rereading her European correspondence as she worked, Louisa would now recall for readers the journey aboard the *Lafayette*, the marriage of Jules Clomadoc to Mrs. Forney's daughter, the Byronic poses of Gaston, the visit to Chenonceaux, the mysterious ex-royalty of Spain in Vevey, the drive across the Simplon Pass, the flood of Rome, and much more. This work, with thinly fictionalized characters representing the three women, at times borrows word-for-word from Alcott's own letters. With the publication of her European account, Alcott added to the ever-growing list of travel books. In fact, Harold F. Smith's *American Travellers Abroad: A Bibliography of Accounts Published Before 1900* contains 1,822 books published by Americans documenting their trips abroad.

Louisa's fame and fortune would continue to grow, and the lion hunters and Jo worshippers would continue, much to Louisa's dismay, to seek out the author of *Little Women*: "I can't entertain a dozen a day, and write the tales they demand also. . . . Reporters sit on the wall and take notes; artists sketch me as I pick pears in the garden; and strange women interview Johnny as he plays in the orchard" (*Journals* 183). Even though her own health declined, she would continue to publish novels: *Work* (1873), *Eight Cousins* (1875), *Rose in Bloom* (1876), *A Modern Mephistopheles* (1877), *Under the Lilacs* (1878), and the final book in the March family trilogy, *Jo's Boys* (1882). Tale after tale would appear in the most popular periodicals of the day and then be gathered for short-story collections: *Aunt Jo's Scrap-Bag*, six volumes (1872–82); *Proverb Stories* (1882); *Spinning Wheel Stories* (1884).

For May, the grand tour of 1870–71 began a love affair with Europe. With a one-thousand-dollar gift from Louisa, she left for London on 26 April 1873 and once again set about copying the works of Turner at the National Gallery. Her excellent copies brought about her acquaintance with the critic John Ruskin, who publicly commended her work (Ticknor 109). After a year's study, she returned to Concord in March 1874 and once again took up her duties at home. In June 1875, she helped establish Concord's first Art

Center in the Masonic Hall on the village square, providing material, supplies, and art books. But the lure of Europe was pulling at her desire to be a successful artist, and she departed home again in September 1876—never to return.

May traveled first to London, but soon found her way to France, eventually settling in Paris, where she studied with Edouard Krug. She also established a friendship with an American artist from Philadelphia, Mary Cassatt. May wrote often to her family in Concord, telling them of her doings, and Louisa noted: "May's letters our delight. She is so earnest she will not stop for pleasure, rest, or society, but works away like a Trojan. Her work admired by masters and mates for its vigor and character" (*Journals* 204). On 18 April 1877, May's greatest success to date arrived when one of her still lifes was selected for the Paris Salon exhibition. Of the 8,500 works submitted, only 2,000 were selected for such an honor, among them Rodin's famous *Man of the Bronze Age* sculpture. As Louisa wrote: "The little picture is accepted, well hung, and praised by the judges. No friend at court, and the modest work stood on its own merits. She is very proud to see her six months' hard work bear fruit" (*Journals* 204). Despite May's many accomplishments in 1877, they, unfortunately, would be overshadowed by sad news from home that autumn—the death of her mother.

Abigail May Alcott had been ill since the spring but worsened as autumn began, and Louisa spent much of her time watching over her, even while writing. Anna was busy preparing to move into the old Thoreau house on Main Street in Concord, which Louisa had helped her purchase by paying $2,500 of the $4,000 cost. When Anna and her two boys moved into the large home on 14 November 1877, Abigail was so ill she had to be carried upstairs in her chair. On 25 November, all of her family knew the end was at hand. Louisa wrote that her mother "was very happy all day, thinking herself a girl again, with parents and sisters round her. . . . Looked often at the little picture of May and waved her hand to it, 'Good-by, little May, good-by!'" (*Journals* 206). She died peacefully with Louisa at her side. That evening Louisa wrote to her sister in Europe with words of comfort and encouragement: "Our Marmee is at rest. . . . I took off your ring today, & gave her a good bye kiss for you. . . . I wish I was with my darling for I know how hard it will be to bear alone this sorrow, but dont think of it much till time makes it easier & never mourn that you didn't come. All is well & your work was a joy to Marmee" (*Selected Letters* 225). Two days later—seven years to the date of John Bridge Pratt's death, Abigail was buried in a private ceremony at Sleepy Hollow, Louisa noting that "we left her at sunset beside dear Lizzie's dust,—alone so long" (*Journals* 206). May wrote back that she was "'with you in spirit I know, as I feel sure, *she has come to me*, as I did not go to her. . . . I get through the days by painting busily, but at night it is hard not to have a good cry, though I look out at a bright star that twinkles in at my window and feel it is Marmee smiling at me'" (qtd. in Ticknor 250).

May's sadness was soon comforted by love. Much to the surprise of her family in Concord, May, in February 1878, announced her engagement to Ernst Nieriker, a Swiss businessman, fourteen years her junior. They were married on 22 March 1878 in London, and May appeared happy with her work and her husband as they settled into a small suburb, Meudon, just outside of Paris.

The following year, 1879, promised to be a good one for the youngest Alcott sister. Her painting *Negresse* was exhibited at the Paris Salon exhibition that spring, and her guide for American artists in Europe, *Studying Art Abroad and How to Do It Cheaply*, was published by Roberts Brothers. On 8 November 1879, her daughter Louisa May Nieriker, named after her literary sister, was born in Paris. Unfortunately, the happiness would not continue. As the year was drawing to a close, May Alcott, "Concordia's Queen," died in Paris on 29 December.

The cause of May's death has never been firmly established. Louisa noted in her journal that she had endured "three weeks of fever & stupor." On New Year's Eve, a telegram from Ernst in Paris was sent to Ralph Waldo Emerson. When Emerson had gone over to Orchard House to inform the family of the sad news, he discovered Louisa was alone for Anna had gone in to Boston and Bronson to the post office, expecting news from Europe about the new baby and May's health. Louisa wrote in her journal: "I found him looking at May's portrait, pale & tearful with the paper in his hand. 'My child, I *wish* I could prepare you, but alas, alas!' there his voice failed & he gave me the telegram." Louisa read the message, looked sadly at Emerson, and replied, "'I *am* prepared.'" Louisa forever regretted not going to Paris to see her ailing sister, claiming: "If I had lived to see her & help her die, or save her, I should have been content" (*Journals* 218). Now, the Alcotts' "midsummer girl," as Louisa once called May, was gone forever (*Journals* 191).

Bronson Alcott, who had recently lost his wife and now his second daughter, wrote a moving private tribute to May that January, saying, "Her temperament was elastic, susceptible. She had a lively fancy, a clear understanding." He noted that "[i]ndependence was a marked trait. . . . She held her fortunes in her hands, and failure was a word unknown in her vocabulary of effort." Remembering her departure for Europe in September 1876, he wrote: "When last seen by me, she was standing on the steamer's deck and waved her handkerchief till lost in the distance. Her active career has now closed in the night of happiness and fame and she has passed into a future of fuller opportunities and holier engagements" (*Journals of BA* 515–16).

On 10 January 1880, Alice Bartlett wrote Louisa from Weatherford, Texas, telling her that she "was very much shocked when I learned by a letter . . . that May was dead." She admitted that "I could not at all take it in, and even now I do not believe it entirely. . . . My poor old Louisa, what can I say to you. I can only say that I, who lived so long in intimacy with you both, know how terrible the blow is to you, and that my heart goes out to you." Alice asked her friend to write her when she could and tell her about May's death as she was aware of "nothing but the bare fact." She ended by saying that "I can not tell you how sad it seems to me, coming so almost *with* your letter to me telling of the birth of the baby. . . . [H]old up your brave old heart" (ALS: Houghton Library, Harvard University).

But Louisa could not long dwell on her sister's death as she soon had other obligations to the living. May had requested that her baby be sent to Massachusetts to be raised, and on 19 September 1880, ten-month-old Louisa May Nieriker (nicknamed "Lulu"), blue eyed and blond haired like her mother, arrived in Boston to live with her aunt and her family. Louisa, who took her new responsibility seriously, continued to write—when health allowed—even compiling a short-story collection named after her niece, *Lulu's Library's*, three volumes (1886–89). Trying to find peaceful surroundings in which to work, she moved about from Concord to Boston, with many summer months in Nonquitt, located on the Massachusetts coast. Her father suffered a stroke in late October 1882, giving Louisa a new care. Now, she helped to support Anna and her two sons, her invalid father, and her young niece.

On 1 March 1888, Louisa, then living in Roxbury, a suburb outside Boston, in a convalescent home and under the care of the homeopathic physician Dr. Rhoda Lawrence, visited her dying father in Boston. She knelt at his bed, held his hands, and said: "'Father, here is your Louy, what are you thinking of as you lie so happily?'" Grasping her hand, he pointed heavenward, declaring, "'I am going *up. Come with me.*'" Louisa responded, "'Oh, I wish I could'" (*Selected Letters* 337). Leaving behind her wrap, she left for the carriage ride back to Roxbury in the brisk March air. By the time she got home, she was ill. She fell into a fever and did not learn that her father, with whom she had shared the birth date of 29 November, had died in his sleep on 4 March. Just two days afterward, Louisa May Alcott died on 6 March 1888. She was laid to rest beside her mother, father, and younger sister, Elizabeth, in Concord's Sleepy Hollow Cemetery.

At her death, Louisa May Alcott was one of the most popular authors in America. She had published over two dozen books and over three hundred articles or stories in periodicals. During the years 1868–86, she earned, on book publications only, royalties of approximately $103,375, equivalent to over $2,250,000 today. This did not include payments for poetry, stories, serials, or European editions of her works. These earnings are impressive figures for someone who once ironically referred to herself as "'a shiftless Alcott'" (*Selected Letters* 121). The Goose had certainly laid golden eggs.

The European tour of 1870–71 in many ways can be seen as a pivotal point in the lives of both Alcott sisters. The journey marked a division in Louisa's life and literary career. Eighteen years before her April 1870 departure for Europe, Louisa had published her first story. When she returned in May 1871, she would continue to write for seventeen years. The trip, in many ways, also divided the pre–*Little Women* years, when she had struggled to support herself and her family, and the post–*Little Women* years, when she was the celebrated authoress. Trying to regain her health in Europe, she had felt that perhaps her best days were behind her.

But she had been the literary lion on the grand tour—wrote about, sought after, fawned over—even in Europe. *An Old-Fashioned Girl*, published the day of her departure, announced the beginning of her European adventure, and the publication of *Little Men* heralded her return to America. Most of all, she had helped realize part of her sister May's dream of studying art abroad, and all the weariness and pain of travel had been worth that effort.

The European tour had made May Alcott more mature, more independent. As May wrote her sister Anna on 25 July 1870, from Bex, Switzerland: "I am quite hardened now, and think nothing of poking round strange cities alone." The independence she asserted is evident throughout both Louisa's and May's letters home. Louisa herself, in the conclusion of *Shawl-Straps*, told her readers the significance of the journey: "One point was satisfactorily proved by the successful issue of this partnership; for, in spite of many prophecies to the contrary, three women, utterly unlike in every respect, had . . . travelled unprotected safely over land and sea, had experienced two revolutions, an earthquake, an eclipse, and a flood, yet met with no loss, no mishap, no quarrel, and no disappointment worth mentioning." Furthermore, she encouraged her female readers to follow suit: "With this triumphant statement as a moral to our tale, we would respectfully advise all timid sisters now lingering doubtfully on shore, to strap up their bundles in light marching order, and push boldly off. They will need no protector but their own courage, no guide but their own good sense and Yankee wit, and no interpreter if that woman's best gift, the tongue, has a little French polish on it. Wait for no man, but take your little store and invest it in something far better than Paris finery, Geneva jewelry, or Roman relics." Alcott essentially wants her female readers to return to America as *new* women, ones who will help build a better country: "Bring home empty trunks, if you will, but heads full of new and larger ideas, hearts richer in the sympathy that makes the whole world kin, hands readier to help on the great work God gives humanity, and souls elevated by the wonders of art and diviner miracles of nature. Leave . . . discontent, frivolity and feebleness among the ruins of the old world, and bring home to the new the grace, the culture, and the health which will make American women what they just fail of being, the bravest, brightest, happiest, and handsomest women in the world" (225–26). May Alcott put it more simply and more directly when she declared in May 1870 that "all America seems to be abroad" (19 May).

WORKS CITED

Alcott, A. Bronson. *Concord Days*. Boston: Roberts Brothers, 1872.

———. *Diary for 1853*. MS: Houghton Library, Harvard University. MS Am 1130.12 (23).

———. *Diary for 1870*. MS: Houghton Library, Harvard University. MS Am 1130.12 (40).

———. *Diary for 1871*. MS: Houghton Library, Harvard University. MS Am 1130.12(41).

———. *The Journals of Bronson Alcott*. Ed. Odell Shepard. Boston: Little, Brown, 1938.

———. *The Letters of A. Bronson Alcott*. Ed. Richard L. Herrnstadt. Ames: Iowa State University Press, 1969.

Alcott, Abigail May. Diary. MS: Houghton Library, Harvard University. MS Am 1130.14(1).

Alcott, Louisa May. *Aunt Jo's Scrap-Bag. Volume 2. Shawl Straps*. Boston: Roberts Brothers, 1872.

———. *The Journals of Louisa May Alcott*. Eds. Joel Myerson, Daniel Shealy, Madeleine B. Stern. Athens: University of Georgia Press, 1997.

———. *Little Women*. 1868. Boston: Roberts Brothers, 1890.

———. "Recollections of My Childhood." *The Youth's Companion* 61 (21 May 1888): 261.

———. *The Selected Letters of Louisa May Alcott*. Eds. Joel Myerson, Daniel Shealy, Madeleine B. Stern. Athens: University of Georgia Press, 1995.

Bartlett, Alice A. "Our Apartment. A Practical Guide to Those Intending to Spend a Winter in Rome." *Old and New* 3 (April, June 1871): 399–407, 663–71.

———. To Louisa May Alcott. 10 January 1880. ALS: Houghton Library, Harvard University. bMs Am 800.23(231).

Bartlett, Truman H. *The Art Life of William Rimmer*. Boston: James R. Osgood, 1882.

Edel, Leon. *Henry James: A Life*. New York: Harper and Row, 1985.

Emerson, Ellen. *The Letters of Ellen Tucker Emerson*. Vol. 2. Ed. Edith E. W. Gregg. Kent, Ohio: Kent State University Press, 1982.

Emerson, Ralph Waldo. "Self-Reliance." *Essays: First Series*. Boston: Houghton Mifflin, 1904. 43–90.

French, Daniel Chester. "Prelude." *May Alcott: A Memoir*. By Caroline Ticknor. Boston: Little, Brown, 1928. xv–xxi.

"Going Abroad." *Putnam's Magazine* n. s. 1 (1868): 530–38.

Hoppin, Martha J. "Women Artists in Boston, 1870–1900: The Pupils of William Morris Hunt." *The American Art Journal* 13 (Winter 1981): 17–46.

James, Henry. *Henry James: A Life in Letters*. Ed. Philip Horne. New York: Viking, 1999.

Latimer, Elizabeth Wormeley. *Salvage*. Boston: Roberts Brothers, 1880.

MA Vital Records. Deaths. Vol. 203–4. 1867.

Murray, John. *A Handbook for Travellers in France*. 11th ed. London: John Murray, 1870.

Niles, Thomas. ALS: Houghton Library, Harvard University. MS Am 1130.8.

Smith, Harold F. *American Travellers Abroad: A Bibliography of Accounts Published Before 1900*. Carbondale-Edwardsville: Library of Southern Illinois University, 1969.

Stearns, Frank Preston. *Sketches from Concord and Appledore*. New York: Putnam's, 1895.

Stowe, William W. *Going Abroad: European Travel in Nineteenth-Century American Culture*. Princeton, N.J.: Princeton University Press, 1994.

Ticknor, Caroline. *May Alcott: A Memoir*. Boston: Little, Brown, 1928.

"William Pitt Greenwood Bartlett." *Harvard College. Class of 1858. Report of Class Secretary. 1868*. Cambridge, Mass.: John Wilson and Son, 1868.

Notes on the Text

Little Women Abroad: The Alcott Sisters' Letters from Europe prints in their entirety the seventy-one letters for which I have discovered either the extant manuscript, a copy of the manuscript, or a printed text. With this edition, fifty-eight of these letters are being published for the first time in their entirety.

The publishing history of the Alcotts' letters from Europe is quickly told. *The Selected Letters of Louisa May Alcott* (1986), edited by Joel Myerson and myself, with Madeleine B. Stern as associate editor, printed eleven of Louisa's letters from Europe. Ednah Dow Cheney in her *Louisa May Alcott: Her Life, Letters, and Journals* (1889) partially printed twenty-eight of Louisa's letters. Caroline Ticknor in her *May Alcott: A Memoir* (1929) partially printed five of May's letters, most in the form of three- or four-paragraph excerpts. The *Boston Daily Evening Transcript* printed one of May's letters in 1870 and one of Louisa's letters in 1871. Only the texts in the *Selected Letters* are accurate and complete.

The majority of the texts for the Alcott sisters' letters from Europe are based on copies of the originals made by Bronson Alcott and bound in a one-half leather volume with marble-paper-covered boards and measuring 5.2 by 8.2 inches. Stamped in gold on the spine is the following: "Letters from Louisa & May 1870." The volume is in the Alcott collection at the Houghton Library, Harvard University (MS Am 1130.9[23]). Two original manuscript letters by May Alcott are bound into the end of the volume. No original letters for which Bronson has made copies have been located.

As for the fate of original manuscript letters, one can only speculate. May Alcott often sketched small illustrations on her letters, and these were duly noted by her father in his copies. Some of the sketches exist at Harvard and at Orchard House, revealing on the reverse portions fragments of the original manuscript letter. Thus, a number of her letters were cut up and sketches preserved. At various times in Louisa's career, most noticeably after her mother's death in 1877 and the family's move from Concord to Boston in 1885, Louisa went through her papers and destroyed letters and journals to ensure privacy after her death. Thus, she may have intentionally destroyed her letters from Europe. She also clearly used these letters for her 1872 travel narrative *Shawl-Straps* and may have revised the original manuscript letters so they would serve as printer's copy for the book publication, in which case they would have been discarded once composition was completed. It is also clear from reading the letters that the actual manuscripts were passed around by the family (Anna Alcott Pratt was living in Maplewood, Massachusetts, during the time; Abigail and Bronson primarily in Concord), to each other and to friends. Letters were possibly lost this way. Bronson's manuscript journals reveal, however, that he was methodical about recording and copying the letters, and it appears that he copied all that reached him—at least those written in 1870. This also accounts for the fact that the few surviving extant manuscript letters from Louisa were not to her immediate family.

Why do Bronson's copies end in October 1870? And why have so few later manuscript letters been located? Bronson clearly indicates in his manuscript *Diary for 1871* that he received letters from Louisa and May while they were in Rome, Albano, Venice, and London. One possibility is that after the sisters left Rome in mid-April 1871, they may have written fewer letters as they were traveling through Germany to Belgium, not appearing to stop anywhere for long periods of time. Another possibility is that Bronson was occupied with his own work. He left home on 26 October 1870 for his western tour of Conversations and did not return to Concord until 3 March 1871. Thus while traveling he would have had little time to copy letters. Perhaps a better possibility is that Bronson bound his volume at the end of the year, as he regularly would do for his annual journals. (The title he used for the bound volume clearly indicates the year 1870.) Thus, those letters written later were not included and subsequently perhaps destroyed.

In editing the Alcott sisters' letters, I have tried to present a text faithful to the writers, yet readable for a modern audience. Because neither May nor Louisa spoke or wrote foreign languages well, they regularly misspelled proper names of people and places. Many times, they would have different spellings for the same people (for example, Gaston's last name is spelled both "Forney" or "Fournier"). I have kept their original spellings and have not regularized them. I have let stand their other misspellings (LMA, for example, had particular trouble with "ie" and "ei" words, as in "thier"), contractions such as "dont" and "does n't," punctuation placed outside of closing quotation marks, and the use of an apostrophe to form plurals (chateau's). I have silently made the following changes: regularized paragraphing and the alignment of datelines, salutations, and closings; and supplied opening or closing paired quotation marks or parentheses, commas in a series when the meaning would otherwise be unclear, and missing final punctuation. In addition, when the only available text was a printed one, I have silently turned large and small capitals into capitals and lower case letters and corrected obvious typographical errors. Periods and commas were often indeterminate in both the manuscript copies by Bronson and in the few surviving manuscripts of the sisters; I have given them the benefit of the doubt according to the context. Incomplete words or confusing abbreviations have been filled out in brackets. The letters contain few cancellations or insertions; I have printed the final text of the letter, reporting significant revisions in the notes. Someone, most likely Louisa, reread Bronson's copies at a later date and occasionally revised them by striking through words and inserting others or making brief notes. I have mentioned significant revisions or annotations in my notes. Several times in Bronson's copies of the letters, he wrote "Sketch" at the top of the page, indicating that a small pen and ink sketch by May Alcott was at the top of the original letter. I have noted these instances in brackets. All letters are printed in full, and if ellipses are present, it is because they are in the original text (always a printed one in the absence of a manuscript).

I have used the following standard abbreviations in my notes describing the texts I am using: ALS for autograph letter, signed with name or initial(s); AL for autograph letter, unsigned; and MS for manuscript. In the notes I have consistently used the abbreviations LMA for Louisa May Alcott and ABA for Amos Bronson Alcott. In addition, I have used, in both my introduction and notes, the Alcott sisters' first names (Anna, Louisa, May) so as to avoid any confusion with the surnames "May" or "Alcott."

Chronology

1870

1 April	*An Old-Fashioned Girl* published by Roberts Brothers
2 April	Alcott sisters depart New York aboard the *Lafayette*
12 April	Arrive in Brest, France; travel to Morlaix, France
15 April	Travel to Dinan, France; remain at Madame Coste's pension for two months
15 June	Sail down the Rance to St. Malo; rail to Le Mans, France
16 June	Travel to Tours, France
20 June	Travel to Ambois, France
22 June	Travel to Blois, France
24 June	Travel to Orleans, France
25 June	Travel to Bourges, France
26 June	Travel to Moulins, France
27 June	Travel to Lyons, France
28 June	Arrive in Geneva, Switzerland
30 June	Sail Lake Geneva to Vevey, Switzerland
8 July	In Bex, Switzerland
8–10 July	May Alcott and Lena Warren travel to Mount St. Bernard
26 July	May Alcott's thirtieth birthday
10 August	In Vevey, Switzerland, at the Pension Paradis for two months
3 October	Depart Vevey; arrive Brieg, Switzerland
4 October	Travel to Domodossola, Italy; arrive Stresa, Italy
5 October	Travel to Isola Bella and Luino, Italy; arrive Lugano, Italy
6 October	Travel to Porlezza and Menaggio; arrive in Cadenabbia, Italy

10 October	Depart for Milan, Italy
Mid-October	In Parma, Pisa, and Bologna, Italy
30 October	In Florence, Italy
10 November	In Rome, Italy
27 November	John Bridge Pratt dies in Maplewood, Massachusetts
29 November	John Bridge Pratt buried at Sleepy Hollow Cemetery, Concord; Louisa May Alcott's thirty-eighth birthday

1871

15 March	Depart Rome
Early April	In Albano, Italy
Mid-April	In Venice, Italy, for two weeks
April–May	Travel over Brenner Pass; visit Munich and Cologne, Germany; sail from the port of Antwerp, Belgium, to London, England
Early May	In London
11 May	Alice Bartlett departs London for home
15 May	*Little Men* published by Sampson Low and Marston in England
25 May	LMA departs London on the *Malta*, leaving May to study art
5 June	*Little Men* published by Roberts Brothers in America
6 June	LMA arrives in Boston, Massachusetts
19 November	May arrives from England
29 November	Louisa and Bronson celebrate shared birthday at Orchard House
Late November	Alcott family celebrates Thanksgiving at the Pratt farm, Concord

15°   0°   15°

NORWAY
and
SWEDEN

Baltic Sea

55°

ATLANTIC OCEAN

UNITED

KINGDOM

33

PRUSSIA

NETHERLANDS

LUXEMBOURG

BELGIUM

DENMARK

GERMANY

PRUSSIA

32   31

30   AUSTRIA

45°

FRANCE

1 2
     4
3

5 6 8
   7
      9
10
      11

13
14 15
16   19
17 18 20
      21
      22 23
            25
      24 26
            27

HUNGARY

29

ITALY

28

SWITZERLAND

SPAIN

PORTUGAL

35°

Mediterranean

OTTOMAN

SCALE OF MILES

0   250   500

15°   0°   15°

The Alcott Sisters' European Travel Itinerary 1870—1871

1. Brest, France, 12 April 1870
2. Morlaix, France, 12 April 1870
3. Dinan, France, 15 April 1870
4. Le Mans, France, 15 June 1870
5. Tours, France, 16 June 1870
6. Amboise, France, 20 June 1870
7. Blois, France, 22 June 1870
8. Orleans, France, 24 June 1870
9. Bourges, France, 25 June 1870
10. Moulins, France, 26 June 1870
11. Lyons, France, 27 June 1870
12. Geneva, Switzerland, 28 June 1870
13. Vevey, Switzerland, 30 June 1870
14. Bex, Switzerland, 8 July 1870
13. Vevey, Switzerland, 10 August 1870
15. Brig, Switzerland, 3 October 1870
16. Domodossola, Italy, 4 October 1870
17. Stresa, Italy, 4 October 1870
18. Isola Bella and Luino, Italy, 5 October 1870
19. Lugano, Italy, 5 October 1870
20. Porlezza and Menaggio, Italy, 6 October 1870
21. Cadenabbia, Italy, 6 October 1870
22. Milan, Italy, 10 October 1870
23. Parma, Italy, mid-October 1870
24. Pisa, Italy, mid-October 1870
25. Bologna, Italy, mid-October 1870
26. Florence, Italy, 30 October 1870
27. Rome, Italy, 10 November 1870
28. Albano, Italy, early April 1871
29. Venice, Italy, mid-April 1871
30. Munich, Germany, late April 1871
31. Cologne, Germany, late April 1871
32. Antwerp, Belgium, early May 1871
33. London, England, early May 1871

Note: Prussia and Germany were unified as the German Empire in 1871.

The Letters

Louisa May Alcott to Abigail Alcott

Ship Lafayette,[1]
April 9 1870.

Dearest Marme,

To-morrow we come to our long journeys end, (Brest, France[2]) thank the Lord! It has been a good one on the whole, and I have got along as well as I expected. But it is tiresome to be day after day doing nothing; for my head will not let me read. May has done well, and been very kind to me and good, and is the life of the table, I guess. I never go up to meals; for Marie takes such good care of me.[3] I lie and peck all sorts of funny messes, and receive calls in my den. People seem to think we are "guns," and want to know us; but as they are not interesting, we are on the reserve and it has a fine effect.

About 3000 miles away does not seem possible in such a little while. How do you all get along, Marmee, the Feature, the Laddies, my Lass, and dear old John?[4] He was so good and kind all the way I had no care or worry, but just lopped round and let him do all the work, bless the dear!

I shall despatch a good long letter as soon as we arrive and have something to tell. We send this to ease your mind. Letters here are not prepaid, so pay for mine out of my money. Don't forget to tell the Postmaster in Boston about my letters.

Bless you all says,
Your Lu.

MS: Unlocated; copy by ABA at Houghton Library, Harvard University. Partially printed: Cheney 211–12.

1. LMA, May Alcott, and Alice Bartlett had left New York aboard the French steamer *Lafayette* on 2 April 1870 and arrived in Brest, France, on 14 April.

2. Brest, a large town located in northwest France, is the chief naval port for the country.

3. Marie was the French stewardess who waited on LMA.

4. "Marmee" is the Alcott sisters' pet name for their mother, Abigail May Alcott (Abba); John and Fred Pratt ("the laddies") are the two children of Anna Alcott ("my lass") and John Bridge Pratt. John had accompanied the three women to New York. "The Feature" refers to Bronson Alcott, who at the time was giving a series of Conversations, talks on various topics, where the participants were encouraged to engage in discussion.

May Alcott to Abigail Alcott and Anna Alcott Pratt

[ABA wrote "(From May)" at the top of the page.]

Steamer Lafayette.
Saturday 9th April 1870

Dear Marmee and Nan,[1]

Just a week to day we left New York, and I am now writing aboard the steamer, though every thing dances about, and it is impossible to make the words straight, but I know you will so delight to get a line, even if you cannot read it, that I shall scribble away.

The first two days out it was rough and stormy, and every one was sick—I among the rest. But after a good "spring cleaning"[2] which I really needed, I got my bearings and was fully able to go on deck to meals but put off doing the latter, dreading the French waiters, and enjoying the nice things better below with Lu. She has'nt been as sick as before, and gets onto the lower deck every pleasant day, and takes in the warm breezes which seem to me the first taste of foreign lands; for there is a peculiar softness even when the wind is strong, that is enchanting. We expect to get into Brest next Wednesday morning, and then as soon as we have had a bath, we mean to write you a good letter and after resting to go onto Morlaix[3] a lovely picturesque place about 30 miles from Brest, according to "Murray."[4] The last day or two have been lovely, with only little showers instead of the constant drizzle we had at first, and the evenings on deck are very jolly, as it is moonlight, and now I know many pleasant people it is bearable.

We played whist[5] last night, it being too windy to stay on deck, and put

FIGURE 10.
"A Seasick Nun" aboard the *Lafayette* (April 1870), by May Alcott. *Louisa May Alcott's Orchard House/ L. M. A. Memorial Association.*

FIGURE 11. "Polly," frontispiece to *An Old-Fashioned Girl* (1870). *Rare Book Collection, University of North Carolina at Charlotte Library.*

champagne up as stakes, for Lu and I are so tired of it that we can't get rid of it, and it will only be a bother when we land. It is the right kind and a very handsome present from Edward E.[6] John has probably told you how we were met by relays of friends along, beginning with the Whieldon's with many presents and Sanborn at Springfield with more.[7] Brown was to have surprised us the morning of sailing but did'nt get there; for which I was sorry, as he probably had something of price for me.[8] We opened Marmee's little notes when four days out and had a little weep over them, though they were very cheerful.

People on board are principally New Yorkers, but everyone is reading "Old Fashioned Girl,"[9] and of course there is some interest taken in the

"Alcott sisters." Alice and the Howes[10] are pleasant, and Lu sits much in the air in an easy chair, and will send you a long account of her adventures. But precious little happens on board a steamer to tell, as we only eat five times a day, and that seems to be all. I shall write some more at Brest. ·

April 12th. [1870]

Dear People,

As we have had head winds and lots of rain, we shall not get into Brest till Wednesday night instead of morning, so I shall scribble a line more as it may get to you sooner than the long jolly one Lu intends writing from Brest; but she is not quite up to the mark yet, though she has composed a funny poem dedicated to our stewardess who is lovely and kind, and has been dutifully devoted to us all the way. Mrs Howe who is bright, and Alice, are to add something and issue a paper to come out after we leave the steamer, as there has been a silly one written by the gentlemen which don't amount to anything, and we wish to show them what ladies can do.[11]

Lu, on the whole, has been pretty well, and I think when she gets to shore and gets her poize, will be quite chipper. The French messes we have on board nearly kill me, and I shall never learn to like the horrid soups; but there is plenty of fruit, and some simple things that I make my dinner of, after sitting two hours at table. We shall however be quite Parisian by the time we return, and I already begin to quick my fingers[12] and make bright speeches at table, so much so, that I am considered quite the star of the dining salon, happening to have told a joke that convulsed the whole table the other day. Every now and then I read mother's letter over and think I have got the best one in the world. I showed it to Alice, who thought it lovely and sends her regards to Marmee. She improves on acquaintance; is quite independent and will be of great importance to us in travelling as she speaks French and Italian easily and will smooth many difficulties on the way. There is a pleasant little couple just married—Mr and Mrs Tiffany from Worcester,[13] he being a graduate of Harvard, we can compare notes about many friends, and I am to sketch him in several attitudes. Lu calls them the little boy and girl couple in Dicken's "Boots at the Inn",[14] and it is fresh to hear them "My dear" one another.

I long to see the first glimpse of foreign shores, for I can't form an idea of how things are to look to us. Alice means to buy a horse as, (they are very cheap,) and we shall careen over the country in some kind of little basket-carriage, and make a regular pic-nic of it—in fact, live just the kind of life I enjoy.

John was such a dear, and took lovely care of us to New York, and then gave me his precious seal ring, which I shall wear with care till I get back; and Lu says she kisses her little diamond every night in memory of her Sairy.[15] We shall prepay our letter, as you will have only to pay over again for them. I don't think you have to prepay yours to us, but father can find out at the office in Boston.

Lu has left all the business of selling her photographs' in Prescott Baker's hands,[16] who has a friend in Doll's picture store,[17] who knows all about such matters, and will do it to the best advantage and father need'nt bother about it at all, but when there is some money for him Baker will send it to him.

This is a mean letter but absolutely nothing happens aboard a steamer.

I write French exercises every chance I get and Alice helps me talk.

I hope Marmee won't go to Concord yet as there is a dreadful chill about [the] house so early, and May will be time enough for the little painting we shall want done. I hope she won't buy a new carpet for Pa's room, as the house will be open so little while, it seems a pity, and we should so like the fun of selecting one—a pretty crimson and black to match his red things.

Goodbye, dear people, and as soon as we know our direction we will send it; though if you direct to "Munroe and Co." Paris,[18] it will reach us.

May.

MS: Unlocated; copy by ABA at Houghton Library, Harvard University.

1. Nan is Anna Alcott Pratt's nickname.

2. Quotation marks were added in different ink.

3. Morlaix, in northern France, located about four miles from the English Channel, is, according to Murray's *Handbook* (1870), "a flourishing port" of just over fourteen thousand inhabitants and is "picturesquely seated in a valley wide enough for the tidal river or creek which runs up to it" (135).

4. John Murray, located at Albemarle Street, London, published a series of "handbooks" for European travelers.

5. Whist is a card game usually played by four people, with the persons opposite each other being partners. Each is dealt thirteen of the fifty-two cards, with the last card dealt

turned face upward. The suit of that card is known as "trumps." Each player then follows, laying down a card of the suit led or discarding; a rotation of the four players thus constitutes a "trick." Points are scored by the number of "tricks" won. Various forms of the game exist.

6. Edward Emerson, the son of Ralph Waldo Emerson, gave the Alcott sisters a case of champagne as a departure gift.

7. Probably the family of William Wilder Wheildon (1805–92), who moved to Concord in 1846. The Wheildons had four girls and two boys, several close in age to May. Franklin Benjamin Sanborn (1831–1917), editor, author, abolitionist, was a good friend of ABA, having first met him in 1853. He grew close to the Alcott family, even serving as pallbearer for Elizabeth Alcott's funeral in 1858. He had published LMA's "Hospital Sketches" in his *Boston Commonwealth* during 1863. ABA left a blank space in the manuscript at the end of the sentence and "more" was added in pencil.

8. Before the name "Brown," ABA had written "Quincy" then crossed it out. Probably T. Quincey Browne, of Boston, who married W. W. Wheildon's daughter Juliet Frances Wheildon. ABA originally wrote "he" in the sentence but it was later amended with pencil to read "they."

9. *An Old-Fashioned Girl* was published by Roberts Brothers of Boston in April 1870.

10. Dr. and Mrs. Estes Howe; Dr. Howe was treasurer of the Cambridge Gas Light Company.

11. In *Shawl-Straps*, LMA writes: "A little newspaper was concocted, replete with wit and spirit, by these secluded ladies, and called the 'Sherald,' to distinguish it from the 'Herald' got up by sundry gentlemen whose shining hours were devoted to flirtation, cards, and wine" (10).

12. "Quick" means to sharpen to a point.

13. Dexter Tiffany (1846–1921), from Worcester, Massachusetts, graduated from Harvard in 1869 and was chosen poet of his class. Apparently he and his wife, Annie Hathoway Shepley, married on 29 March 1870, were on their honeymoon. Tiffany, a lawyer, later moved to St. Louis.

14. "The Holly Tree Inn" first published in December 1855 and later reprinted in *Christmas Stories* (1871) featured the character Boots. In the story, eight-year-old Harry Walmer Jr. runs away "to marry" his love, seven-year-old Norah.

15. In their theatricals, LMA played Sairey Gamp to Anna's Betsey Prig, both characters from Charles Dickens's *Martin Chuzzlewit* (1844). LMA often addressed herself as "Sairy" or "Sairey" in her letters, especially those to Anna. At times, she would refer to Anna as "Sairy" also.

16. A. Prescott Baker (age twenty-six), a Boston physician and friend of the Alcotts, was the son of Amos Baker, a U.S. assistant assessor, and his wife, Matilda. Prescott Baker was handling the sale of LMA's carte de vistas. Evidently, LMA was using a photograph by E. L. Allen, but Doll was in charge of the production of the carte de vistas.

17. In 1870, Hendrickson, Doll, and Richards was located at 28 Summer Street in Boston. By the following year, Doll and Richards had opened a store at 145 Tremont Street.

18. Messrs. Munroe and Company, located at No. 7, Rue Scribe in Paris, served as LMA's banker while she was in Europe.

Louisa May Alcott to Abigail Alcott

Morlaix April 14th 1870

Dearest Marmee,

Having got our "poise" a bit by a day and night on land, I begin at once to scribble to you, as I mean to keep a letter on hand all the time, and send them off as fast as they are done.

We had a twelve day's passage owing to a double screw which they were trying and which delayed us, though it is safer than one. The weather was cold and rainy, and the sea rough, so I only went up once or twice, and kept warm in my den most of the time. After the first two days I didn't feel sick, except my head as usual. I slept, ate, ruminated and counted the hours. May poked about more, and was liked by all. There were no beaux except fast N Y men, so she had no flirtations. Alice was not sick at all and very kind to us, as were the Howes.

We got to Brest about noon Wednesday. Alice and I got our trunks through the Custom House, and after some squabbling with the men got all aboard for Morlaix which is a curious old place worth seeing. It was a lovely day, warm as our June, and we had a charming trip of three hours through a country already green and flowery. We reached our Hotel all right, and after a nice dinner had baths and went to bed. May's room being some way from mine, she came and bunked in with me in my little bed and we slept.

FIGURE 12. The Tower of St. Melanie, Morlaix, France (April 1870), by May Alcott. *Louisa May Alcott's Orchard House/L. M. A. Memorial Association.*

To-day is lovely, warm, and I am sitting at an open window looking on the square, enjoying the queer sights and sounds, for the air resounds with the rattle of many wooden shoes on the stones. Market women sit all about selling queer things, among which are snails: they buy them by the pint, pick them out with a pin like nuts and seem to relish them mightily.

We went out this A.M. after breakfast and took a stroll over the queer town. May was in heaven and kept having raptures over the gables, the

turrets with storks on them, the fountains, people and churches. She is now sketching the tower of St Melanie,[1] with a crowd of small boys round her enjoying the sight and criticising the work [see figure 12]. It don't seem very new to me, but I enjoy it, and feel pretty well. My bones only ache at night, and then not badly. May is very well, and Alice kind and pleasant. We are to study French every day when we settle, and I am to do the mending &c for Alice, who is to talk for us, and make our bargains. So far we go well together, and I think shall have no trouble, for A. is [a] true lady, and my other A. was not.[2]

Tomorrow we go onto Lamballe[3] where we take the diligence to Dinan[4] fourteen miles further, and there settle for some weeks—I wish the boys could see the funny children here in little wooden shoes like boats, the girls in blue cloth caps, aprons, and shawls just like the women, and the boys in funny hats and sheepskin jackets.

Now I must go and get May who can't speak a word of French, and has a panic if any one speaks to her. The beggars afflict her, and she wants to give them money on all occassions.

This P.M. we go for a drive to see all there is, as neither Alice nor I are great walkers. "Adoo" till by and by. I wish I could send you this balmy day.

Dinan, Sunday, 17th April [1870]

Here we are all settled at our first neat stopping place and are in clover as you will see when I tell you how plummy and lovely it is.

We left Morlaix Friday at 8 A.M. and were so amazed at the small bill presented us that we could'nt praise the town enough. You can judge of the cheapness of things, when I say that my share of the expenses from Brest here, including two days at a Hotel, car, 'bus, and diligence[5] fare, fees and everything, was $8.00. The day was divine, and we had a fine little journey to Lamballe where the fun began; for instead of a big diligence we found only a queer ramshackle thing, like an insane carry all, with a wooden boot and queer perch for the driver. Our four trunks were piled on behind and tied on with old ropes, our bags stowed in a wooden box on top, and ourselves inside with a fat Frenchman. The humpbacked driver, "ya hooped" to the horses, and away we clattered at a wild pace, all feeling dead sure that something would happen, for the old thing bounced and swayed awfully, the trunks were in danger of tumbling off, and to our dismay we soon discovered that the big Frenchman was tipsy. He gabbled to Alice as only a tipsy Frenchman could, quoted poetry, said he was Victor Hugo's[6] best friend, and a child of nature, that English ladies were all divine, but too cold, for when he pressed Alice's hand, she told him it was not allowed in England, and he was overwhelmed with remorse, bowed, sighed, rolled his eyes, and told her that he drank much ale, because it flew to his head and gave him "Commercial Ideas." I never saw any thing so perfectly absurd, as it was, and after we got used to it we laughed ourselves sick over the lark. You ought to have seen us and our turnout, tearing over the road at a break-neck pace, pitching, creaking, and rattling. The funny driver, hooting at the horses, who had their tails done up in chignons,[7] blue harness and strings of bells. The drunken man warbling, exhorting, and languishing at us all by turns, while Alice headed him off with great skill. I sat a mass of English dignity and coolness suffering alternate agonies of anxiety and amusement, and May, who tied her head up in a bundle, and looked like a wooden image. It was rich, and when we took up first a peasant woman in wooden shoes and a fly-away cap,[8] and then a red-nosed priest smoking a long pipe, we were a supurb spectacle. In this style, we banged into Dinan, stopped at the gate, and were dumped, bag and baggage in the Square. Finding Madame Coste's man was not [there] for us we hired a man to bring our trunks up for us. To our great amazement an oldish woman, who was greasing the wheels of a diligence, came, and catching up our big trunks, whisked them into two broad carts, and taking one, trotted down the street at a fine pace followed by the man with the other. That was the finishing touch, and we went laughing after them through the great arched gate into the quaintest, prettiest, most romantic town I ever saw. Narrow streets with overhanging gables, distracting roofs, windows and porches, carved beams, and every sort of richness. The strong old lady beat the man, and finally landed us close by another old gate at a charming house fronting the south, overlooking a lovely green valley, full of gardens, blooming plum and peach trees, windmills, and a ruined castle, at sight of which we all skipped. Madame Costé[9] recieved us with rapture, for Alice brought a letter from Mrs Lodge[10] who stayed here, and was the joy of the old lady's soul. We were in great luck, for being early in the season, she had three rooms left and

FIGURE 13. Madame Coste's pension (1999). *Photograph by Abigail Gordon.*

we nabbed them at once. A salon with old oak walls and wardrobes, blue damask furniture, a fireplace, sunny windows and quaint furniture. A little room out of it for Alice, and upstairs a larger room for May and me, with two beds draped in green chintz and carved big wardrobe &c. and best of all, a sunny window toward the valley. For these rooms and our board we each pay $1,00 a day, and I call that cheap. It would be worth that to get the sun and air alone, for it is like June, and we sit about with open windows, flowers in the fields, birds singing and every thing lovely and spring like.

We took possession at once and dressed for dinner at six. We were then presented to our fellow boarders, Madame Forney, a buxom widow, her son Gaston, a handsome Frenchy youth of 23, and her daughter, a homely girl of 20, who is to be married here on the 3rd May.[11] After a great bowing and scraping, we had a funny fish dinner, it being Good Friday. When they found we did'nt speak French they were "desolated," and begged us to learn at once, which we solemnly vowed to do. Gaston knew English, so May at once began to teach him more, and the ice being broken we got gay and friendly at once. I could understand them pretty well, but cant talk, and Alice told them that I was forbidden to say much on account of my throat.

This will give me a chance to get a fair start. May pegs away at her grammar, and with that and the elegant Gaston, she will soon begin to "parleyvoo."

After dinner we were borne to the great salon, where a fire, lights and a piano appeared. Every one sat round and gabbled except the Alcotts, who looked and laughed. Mademoiselle Forney played, and then May convulsed them by singing some "Chants Amerique" which they thought very lively and droll. They were all attention and devotion to Madame Coste, a tall old lady with whiskers, [who] kept embracing Alice and beaming at us in her great content at being friends of "Chere Madame Lodge". Alice told them that I was a celebrated authoress, and May a very fine artist, and we were beamed at more than ever.—Being tired, we turned in early, after a jolly time in our own little salon, eating chocolate and laying plans.

Saturday, we had coffee in bed at 8, walked on the ramparts and in the Park under the old tavern till 10 when we had breakfast; then till dinner at 6, we rampaged about having raptures about every thing. I can't tell you how lovely it is! The climate *must* cure me for they say throat and lung invalids always get well here. The air is dry and soft, the town lies high, and we are in the sunny country part. Shall live cheaply, learn French, enjoy my life, and grow fat and strong. D.V.[12]

Private

I think this is to be one of our lucky years, and this trip a success if things go on as well as they have begun, for not a single hitch have we had from the time we left Boston. It don't seem possible that a fortnight could do so much, and put us in such an entirely new scene.

May is in a state of unutterable like bliss, and keeps flying out with her big sketch book and coming back in despair, for every thing is so picturesque she don't know where to begin. This is a good chance for her in every way. No one speaks English in the house but Alice, and she threatens to talk only French to us, which will be awful but useful. Two pleasant half English ladies live near, and I shall rush to them when I'm exhausted by "the baby talk," as I call French.

Our house is on the walk close to the great tower of Anne of Brittanny, and the public walk which is made on what used to be the moat.[13] Ask some one to lend you a "Murray's Guide" and you can read all about the place. There are a good many English here and we shall come to know some of them, I don't doubt, which will complete our task and give a relish. Tomorrow Gaston is to escort us to the mineral waters on donkeys, and we shall be an imposing sight as you may suppose.

Direct your letters to me, "Care of Mademoiselle Coste, place St. Louis, Dinan," for the present. It will save a postage and we shall stay a month at least.

Goodbye, God bless you all, May sends lots of love and so does

Your Lu.

MS: Unlocated; manuscript copy by ABA at Houghton Library, Harvard University. Printed: *Selected Letters* 129–34 (*Selected Letters* printed this letter as two separate letters); partially printed: Cheney 212–17.

1. The church of St. Melanie, constructed in 1550, is located near the Place Theirs in Morlaix. Its tower was completed in 1574. See figure 12 for May's sketch of the church tower.

2. Anna Weld was the daughter of Boston merchant and shipbuilder William Fletcher Weld and his wife, Elizabeth. LMA had accompanied Anna and her half brother George on a European trip in 1865–66. She recorded in her journal: "Hard work with a fretful invalid, but I enjoyed much" (*Journals* 148).

3. Lambelle, a small town of 4,151 inhabitants in 1870, approximately fifty miles from Rennes, France, is situated on the slope of a small hill, atop which sits the gothic Church of Notre Dame.

4. Dinan, a small town in northern France, lies on the left bank of the Rance River. Murray's *Handbook* (1870) claims: "The country in which Dinan is placed is perhaps the most beautiful in Brittany. The situation of the town (8510 Inhab.) is very romantic, on the crown and slopes of a hill of granite, overlooking the deep and narrow valley of the Rance, flowing 250 ft. below it. The sides of the hill are excessively steep; but, notwithstanding, houses and streets have been built along the face of it to the water's edge" (148).

5. A diligence, a term most often used in Europe, was a public stagecoach. Murray's *Handbook* (1870) notes: "The diligence of the present day is composed of a *Coupé*, like a chariot, in front, with 3 places, and an *Intérieur* behind with 4 or 6 places, entered from behind. There is a *Banquette*, or outside seat, on the top. It affords a comfortable and roomy seat by the side of the conductor, with the advantages of fresh air and the best view of the country" (xx).

6. Victor Hugo (1802–85), French novelist, playwright, and statesman, best known for his novels *Notre-Dame de Paris* (1831), translated into English as *The Hunchback of*

Notre-Dame, and *Les Misérables* (1862). When Napoleon III declared himself emperor of France in 1851, Hugo publicly attacked him. He fled the country and settled on the island of Guernsey, where he stayed until 1870, continuing his attacks upon Napoleon III, calling him "Napoleon the Little." After Napoleon III's defeat during the Franco-Prussian War and the establishment of the Third Republic, Hugo returned to France and was elected to the National Assembly and the Senate.

7. Chignons were made by folding the horses' tail hair into large coils.

8. A fly-away cap, a traditional form of headwear in parts of Brittany, were lace coiffes, which fit close to the back, top, and side of the head, with large winglike sides.

9. Possibly Mrs. Mary Langdon Greenwood Lodge (1829–89), Alice Bartlett's first cousin, once removed, whose husband James Lodge (b. 1820) had died in 1865. Senator Henry Cabot Lodge was their nephew.

10. Madame Coste owned the pension on the Place St. Louis in Dinan where the three stayed.

11. Gaston Forney, his mother, and his sister were fellow boarders in Madame Coste's pension in Dinan. In *Shawl-Straps*, LMA writes: "Sometimes [Gaston] was lost in fits of Byronic gloom, when he frowned over his coffee, sighed gustily, and clutched his brow, regardless of the curls, usually in ambrosial order. . . . Dear, dandified, vain Gaston. His great desire was to go to Paris, and when the war came he had his wish; but found sterner work to do than to dress and dance and languish at the feet of ladies" (37, 39).

12. "Deo volente" (God willing).

13. Anne of Brittany (1477–1514) was the daughter of Francis II, Duke of Brittany, and Margaret of Foix. After her father's death in 1488, she became Duchess of Brittany. She was married (by proxy) to Roman Emperor Maximilian I in 1490. Charles VIII, king of France, invaded Brittany in 1491, however, and forced Anne to marry him. On the death of Charles VIII, Anne married, in 1499, his cousin, Louis XII, the next in line to the throne. After Anne's death in 1514, the duchy of Brittany no longer had independence from the French throne. Anne of Brittany's tower (often called the castle of Dinan), near Porte St. Louis, constructed about 1300, was originally a castle; it was occupied only once by Anne of Brittany and later converted into a prison. It lies on the edge of a ravine near the end of town. The Rue Theirs leads to the large promenade called Grands-Fossés.

FIGURE 14. Dinan, France (17 April 1870), by May Alcott. *Louisa May Alcott's Orchard House/ L. M. A. Memorial Association.*

FIGURE 15. Dinan, France (22 April 1870), by May Alcott. *Louisa May Alcott's Orchard House/ L. M. A. Memorial Association.*

Louisa May Alcott to the Alcott Family

Dinan, Brittany, April 20 1870.

Dearest People.

Nothing very astonishing has happened, but as I mean to keep Journal Letters, I'll ramble on and give the pleasant bits out of our new day to amuse you.

The lovely weather alone is constant delight, so warm and clear and bright, with a pleasant fresh air from the sea, and every thing in its loveliest spring dress. I am glad we came early, for a month later it would be full summer, and the first freshness all gone.

Monday, we sent a lot of letters home, and told Munroe our address.

May was a little upset by some of the new messes and kept quiet all day leaving "nater" to right her self, which she did very soon. Alice and I went shopping. A. got a gay little bird to enliven our parlor—a sort of sparrow, gray with a red head and a lively song. We named him Bernard du Guesclin (the hero of the town)[1] and call him Bernie. I got some nice gloves for 3 francs, (60 cents) and a white sun umbrella for May, for 40 cents. She needs it when she sketches and as there is always a crowd of children round her to watch and admire, she gives one of them a sous[2] to hold the umbrella and so gets on nicely.

In the P.M. A. and I went to the little village of Lahon[3] in the valley, where the ruined castle is, to a fair. It was a very picturesque sight, for the white-capped women, sitting about on the green hillsides, looked like flowers, and the blue blouzes of the men and wide brimmed hats, added to the effect. The little street was lined with booths where they sold nuts, queer cakes, hot sausages, and pan cakes, toys, &c. I got a funny cake just the size and shape of a deep pie-dish, and A. a jack knife, for a sous. We also indulged in nuts and sat on our camp-stools in a shady place and ate them boldly in the public mart, while enjoying the lively scene. French and English people went by in droll parties, and we coolly sat and stared at them.

May is going to sketch the castle so I wont waste paper describing the pretty place with the ruined church full of rooks, the old mill with the water wheel housed in vines, or the winding river, and meadows full of blue hyacinths and rosy daisies.

Yesterday, A. and I had to return the call of Mad[lle] Mervaille[4] and as she speaks English I got on very well. The stairs to her apartment were so steep that we held on by a velvet-covered rope as we climbed up.

In the P.M. we had fun, for we took two donkey carriages and went to the mineral spring. Gaston was sick and could'nt go as we had planned, so May drove herself in one, and A. and I in the other. I wish the boys could have seen us, it was so funny. The carriages were Bath-chairs[5] with a wee donkey harnessed to each, so small, so meek and looking so venerable with thin long ears and bits of feet, that I felt as if I was driving my grandmother. May was a very imposing sight, alone in her chair under her new umbrella, in her grey suit, with bright gloves and a big whip, driving a grey rat who would n't trot unless pounded and banged and howled at in the maddest way. Our steed was bigger but the most pigheaded old scamp you ever saw, for it took two big women to make him go. I drove, and A. thrashed away with all her might. Our joint efforts only producing occasional short trots which enraged us dreadfully. We laughed till we were sick, it was so very absurd, while May trundled serenely along enjoying the fine views regardless of her rat, who paced along at his ease, waggling his ears and meditating. We had a nice trip, but did'nt drink the water as iron don't suit us.[6] Coming home, we passed the home of the donkeys, and they at once turned in, and were with much difficulty persuaded to go on by two short girls in caps and short gowns,[7] who ran and shouted, E! E! ja oui! and punched sticks into the poor asses, rattling us over the stones till our eyes danced in our heads. We found it rather hard work, and A. means to buy a horse and straw-pony chaise, so we can drive ourselves in peace where we like.

Thursday A.M.

Yesterday I got a letter from Niles, beginning "Dear Jo," Ahem![8] I'd better reply, "Dear Tom", only he will go and publish it, so I won't.[9] He put in some notices, and very glowing accounts of "Old Fashioned Girl"—18,000 sold &c. I am glad, for money *must* come, and it makes things easy all round. Send me Buns' notice in the Springfield Republican.[10] He said he had a long

FIGURE 16. "Polly's Sermon," *An Old-Fashioned Girl* (1870). *Rare Book Collection, University of North Carolina at Charlotte Library.*

one, and I'd like to see it. Today Munroe has sent me my letter of credit for £300, or $600, so I can use it *anywhere* if I need it. But I shan't for a long time yet, everything is so cheap.

Alice is bargaining for a horse which an Englishman wishes to sell for $50 including harness and cart. We can't hire horses for less than $2.00 a drive, and donkeys are vile, so it is cheaper to buy and sell when we go away, and so drive as much as we like. Alice knows about such things and takes all the responsibility.

I dont remember whether I told you to put "Britaiyne" on your letters. If not, do it while we are here. I long to get news from you. Alice has had six letters and we only two.

To-morrow we go on a little excursion in the steamboat down the river, and return a-la-donkey with the English ladies, who have returned our call and are very friendly.

Please forward this little note in an envelope to its address. The child wrote me a pretty letter which Niles sent, and the Pa said I would'nt answer, the child said, "I know she will she is so nice", so I do.

Best love to every one. Don't go home too soon. I shall write to Fred and Jack next time.[11]

Good bye,

Lu.

MS: Unlocated; manuscript copy by ABA at Houghton Library, Harvard University. Partially printed: Cheney 217–19.

1. Bertrand du Guesclin (1320?–1380), constable of France under Charles V and a Breton soldier during the Hundred Years War, recaptured Dinan from the English in 1359, by defeating in single combat an English knight, called "Sir Thomas of Cantorbery" by Breton chroniclers.

2. In 1870, a sou was worth half a pence or 1.165 U.S. cents.

3. Lehon, approximately one and a quarter miles south of Dinan. Murray's *Handbook* (1870) says the village is "prettily situated in the bottom of a dell, through which a streamlet falls into the Rance" (149).

4. Mervaille was probably one of the "half English" neighbors LMA referred to in her 14–17 April letter.

5. A bath-chair carriage, often found waiting for steamer arrivals, is a large chair on wheels, used primarily for invalids.

6. The region was known for its mineral waters and baths.

7. The "s" in "shorts" was later deleted and "gowns" inserted in pencil.

8. "Ahem" was later struck through in pencil.

9. Thomas Niles's letter, dated 5 April 1870, is located at the Houghton Library, Harvard University (bMS Am1130.8).

10. F. B. Sanborn reviewed LMA's recently published novel *An Old-Fashioned Girl* in the 4 April 1870 *Springfield Daily Republican*. Calling the book "hastily written," he does praise LMA for her ability "to select artistically from the every day details of New England life" and claims that the work is "as good as" *Little Women* (2).

11. Frederick Alcott Pratt (1863–1910) and John Sewall Pratt (1865–1923) were the sons of John Bridge and Anna Alcott Pratt. They served as the models for Demi and Daisy in *Little Women*.

May Alcott to Abigail Alcott
and Anna Alcott Pratt

Dinan April 20th 1870.

Dearest Marmee & Nan,

I am in such perfect bliss that I must write and tell you all about things here and our goings on generally, that you may see why I am so happy. In the first place air soft and lovely like early June at home. We sit with open windows and wear spring clothes, are out the greater part of the day, seeing such enchanting old ruins, picturesque towns, churches, and crumbling fortifications, that it seems almost like a dream, and if I did'nt see Lu admiring the landscape, I should often doubt if I am myself. It seems impossible that less than three weeks has transported us here, after seeing Morlaix and doing so much, beside being so settled and comfortable in this funny Frenchy family, and feeling quite at home, only having been here six days. This air makes me very sleepy all the time, so I don't get up as early as I should like to; but get dressed before coffee is brought up to us, then do some French exercises, and study verbs, (for it is such a chance to get a good knowledge of French that I am determined to make the most of it) till ten, when we have breakfast. Then I take my big sketch book and wander forth, perching about, on my pretty little camp stool Alice has given me, whenever anything strikes me as especially lovely. With the exception of Ancient Rome, this town is as old as anything [I] ever shall see, and "Murray" says "affords as much for the painter's pencil and brush as anything on the continent,"[1] and I am only troubled as to where to begin with such perfect richness on every side. We drive in the P.M. and then dine at six— which amazement did not suit my Yankee stomach at first, but as it gives such long uninterrupted hours, from ten to six, for work or play, I am at last reconciled to it. We have a pretty room with two little curtain beds and a cosy little salon down one flight, out of which is Alice's chamber. The family of Fourniss who are the only other boarders are very kind and help us about our French, as Gaston, the sick son, 22 years old, draws, sculps, paints and

FIGURE 17. Dinan, France (1999). *Photograph by Abigail Gordon.*

is generally very artistic, also desirous of speaking English, which I try to do, and think under these circumstances, I shall learn French rapidly, don't you? Tell the Dr. that he is handsome, rich and of noble family, and I shall take decided steps without delay as a crest would look well on the wedding silver, but the slight difference in age is bad. I hope the Dr. is settled in Concord by this time with immense practice to encourage his staying.[2] I spoke to Mrs. Cheney[3] and several Concord people about him when they came to say goodbye to us, and they seemed to think it a great chance for him, and were delighted at the prospect of such an addition to the society there.

FIGURE 18. Gateway into Dinan, France (7 June 1870), by May Alcott. *Houghton Library, Harvard University.*

Yesterday we went to some lovely gardens surrounding the most beautiful gothic church, old and gray with vines clinging about the stone ornaments and running over the great roof—almost to the top of the spire, and see this on a level with the principal part of the town, the whole being built on very high ground with fortifications and a moat which in old times made Dinan almost impregnable, but now the crumbling gray walls are overhung with

May Alcott —

Dinan June [...]

the most luxuriant ivy and clinging vines of all sorts; even the stone arch-
ways to the town have little verdant plateaus on top, and women with im-
maculate caps sit about looking so picturesque that I long to make pictures
on every hand, but get extremely discouraged when I try, as it needs all the
surroundings to make the scence [i.e., scene] complete.

I was entirely captivated by some antique things I saw in a store yesterday
and could'nt get out of it till I had bought a lovely ring with a liquid violet
stone inlaid with a pansy in pearls, and all this in a pretty velvet lined box
for $6.00. It would have cost in America anywhere from $30 to 60. and Alice thought it pretty and a great bargain. Lu is longing to buy some elegant
ones that she saw there, and as she had a nice letter from Niles yesterday
full of the success of "O. F. G." I encourage her doing anything she likes and
revelling with perfect freedom for once in her hard life.

Alice is sweet and kind, fond of us both, and on all occasions a *perfect
lady*, talks French remarkably well, is finely educated, and very well read,
independent, and has opinions of her own. She means to buy a horse so we
can drive off and see places that would be impossible to us otherwise, and
it is expensive hiring donkeys which are stupid beasts and dreadfully slow,
taking a whole day to get anywhere with them.

We have had enchanting weather ever since we came, and they say that
we have very little that is unpleasant at any season.

Why don't we get some letters from you? for if you have directed to Monroe & Co. they ought to have reached us before now. Give my love and a kiss
to John, the lovies, & papa.

I was waked this morning by such a braying of donkeys, squaling of pigs,
and noise generally, that I rose and looked out to find that it was Thursday, the usual weekly pig market was beginning right in front of the house
which will be quite interesting to watch from our windows, as people from
the outer districts come to it in funny costumes.

I wish I could send Nan some of the pretty gloves we can get here for
60 cts a pair, very handsome kid ones all sorts of pretty colors, such as we
should pay $2.25 for at home. I shall get alot of them while I am away.

Again, love to all

from

May.

MS: Unlocated; manuscript copy by ABA at Houghton Library, Harvard University. Partially printed: Ticknor 73–74.

1. Murray's *Handbook* (1870) says that "no spot in Brittany is better fitted to exercise the artist's pencil" (149).

2. Dr. Arthur Ricketson (1835–1912), eldest son of Daniel (friend and admirer of Thoreau) and Louisa Ricketson, graduated from Harvard Medical College in 1860 and enlisted in the U.S. Navy, serving until 1863. He married Louise Dolben Bliss in 1864. After the Civil War, he rented and then purchased a home at 50 Monument Street in Concord. He practiced medicine in Concord until he sold his home in 1874 to Edward Emerson, who had just graduated from Harvard Medical College and was beginning his own practice in Concord.

3. Ednah Dow Cheney (1824–1904), widow of the Boston artist Seth Cheney and good friends with the Alcotts, had first met Bronson in 1848. Writer, reformer, abolitionist, suffragist, Cheney would eventually write *Louisa May Alcott: Her Life, Letters, and Journals* (1889), the standard edition of LMA's private writings for almost a century.

Louisa May Alcott to the Alcott Family

Dinan April 24ᵗʰ 1870

My Dearest People.

No letters yet; but I hope for some every mail, for you *must* have got one or two of ours by this time.

I enclose a note to Tommy[1] which Pa can put in an envelope and leave some day. Also one to Mary Sewall,[2] to which Nan may like to add a line. I ought to have written to Polly before I left, but dare say she will like one from foreign parts better. Pay postage of all our letters out of my cash. They go better from and to us *unpaid*. If there is any trouble let us know at once.

April 27ᵗʰ [1870]

I left my letter to drive to another ruined Chateau, which we went all over, as a part is inhabited by a farmer who keeps his hog in the great banqueting hall, his grain in the chapel, and his hens in the lady's chamber. It was very picturesque, the old rooms with ivy coming in at the windows, choking up the well, and climbing up the broken towers. The lady of the chateau was starved to death by her cruel brothers, and buried in the moat where her bones were found long afterward, and her ghost still haunts the place they say. Here we had cider, tell Pa.

Coming home we saw a dolemn [i.e., dolmen], one of the Druidical remains.[3] It stood in a grove of old pines, a great post of gray stone, some 25 feet high, and very big round. It leaned as if falling, and had queer holes in it. Brittany is full of these relics which no one can explain, and I was glad to see the mysterious things.

Yesterday, we took a little trip down the river in a tiny steamer going through a lock, and skimming along between the green banks of the narrow river,[4] to Miss Marvaile's country house, where we had new milk, and laid on the grass for an hour or so. Then May and Miss M. walked home, and Alice and I went in a donkey cart.

Today, the girls have gone to La Garaye[5] with Gaston on donkeys. My bones ache, so I'm at home with a fire in our little salon. The weather has been cold for a day or two with easterly winds. So I feel it at once, and keep warm. It is very unusual at this time, but comes I suppose because I've travelled hundreds of miles to get rid of 'em. It wont last long and then we shall be hot enough. We lead such quiet lazy lives that I really have nothing to tell.

Oh, yes, the fiance of Mademoiselle has arrived and amuses us very much. He is a tiny man in uniform with a red face, big moustache and blue eyes. He thinks he talks English and makes such very funny mistakes. He asked us if we had been to "promenade on monkeys," meaning donkeys, and called the Casino "the establishment of dance." He addresses all his attentions to the Ma, and only bows to his future wife who admires her diamonds and is contented. We are going away on the day of the wedding as it is private.

The girls have just returned in great spirits, for Alice's donkey kept lying down, and it took all three to get him up again. They sat in a sort of chairs and looked very funny with the four little legs under them and long ears flopping before. I shall go to Garaye some fine day and will tell you about it.

May is well and jolly. Alice much better, and I hope to stop aching soon.

None of us are homesick yet but I often long for my marmee in the night when I fuss over my poor bones,

Adieu. Love to all.

Your

Lu.

MS: Unlocated; copy by ABA at Houghton Library, Harvard University. Partially printed: Cheney 219–21.

1. "Tommy" was later cancelled and in a different hand "T. N." was inserted.

2. Mary K. Sewall ("Polly") was the daughter of Thomas Sewall (Samuel E. Sewall's brother) of Boston. After her father's death in September 1864, Mary decided the following year to move to St. Paul, Minnesota. LMA noted in her journal for 1865: "M. K. S. breaks up housekeeping & goes to St. Paul" (*Journals* 146). Thomas Sewall's family had helped the Alcotts a number of times during the 1850s and 1860s, even allowing LMA to stay with them in December 1855, while she supported herself in Boston.

3. A dolmen (called a cromlech by the English) is a prehistoric stone monument in the shape of an altar or table made from a large flat stone supported by two smaller stones.

4. The lock of Le Châtelier, located in Dinan, allows boats to enter the Rance River from the sea and sail up as far as Dinan.

5. La Garaye, located outside of Dinan near Lehon, is the chateau once owned by Claude Toussaint Comte de la Garaye and his wife. Known for their charity and self-sacrifice, both studied medicine and surgery; she became a well-known oculist and they converted the mansion into a hospital. Their story is told in the 1866 poem "Lady of Garaye" by the British writer Caroline Sheridan Norton. The word "grange" was later inserted in pencil next to "Garaye."

Louisa May Alcott to Mary Sewall

Dinan, Brittany. April 24th 1870.

My Dear Faraway Polly,

I meant to have written to you before I left, but was so poorly and so hurried that I did'nt, and now fancy you'd like a letter from over the sea, quite as well as from old Pinckney Street.[1]

Here we are, May and I and our pleasant friend Alice Bartlett, in this quaint old town where Bernard du Guesclin lived and died, surrounded by ruined chateaus, churches, castles, and convents, for here are some of the oldest relics left in France. We are living, en pension, with a nice old lady just on the walls of the town with Anne of Brittanys round tower on the one hand, the Porte of St Louis on the other, and a lovely promenade made in the old moat just before the door.[2] The beautiful valley of the Rance[3] lies below full of blooming trees and gardens, windmills, little towns, and the ruined Chateau De Lahon.[4] [See figure 19.] It is summer weather here and my poor bones rejoice in continual sunshine. May sketches frantically and we all three live out of doors like gypsies. Every thing is very cheap, board $6 a week, wine 25 cts a bottle, washing a franc a dozen, &c. People live so simply that little money goes a great way, which suits us nicely for Miss B. pays Mays expenses and I my own, and we find we can indulge in donkeys, flowers, gloves &c. without getting bankrupt.

Our plan is to stay about these old French towns by the sea till September, then go to Italy for the winter. And if we like it and can afford it, stay two years, seeing all we can in an economical, leisurely way. This is better for me than paying doctors at home, and for May it is a good chance in every way. I wish you and Nan were here too, would'nt we have larks. Every thing is so funny that we shall soon laugh ourselves fat. They offer us at table dishes of snails, which they pick with pins and eat like ants; and other messes equally inviting—they call each other pet names that convulse us—"my little pig," my "sweet hen," "my cabbage," and, "my tom-cat". A French lady with her son and daughter board here, and their ways amuse us mightily. The girl is to be married next week to a man whom she has seen twice and never talked to but an hour [in] her life. She writes to him what her mother dictates and says she should be ashamed to love him before they were married. Her wedding clothes absorb her entire mind and her Jules will get a pretty doll when he takes Mademoiselle Alice Fornier[?] to wife. Gaston, the son, puts on blazé airs, though only 22, and languishes at May, for they can't talk as he don't know English, nor she French.

I hope you will come East this summer and manage to give Marmee and Nan a good visit. I'm afraid they will be rather lonely unless Nan is with Ma a good deal, so visits from friends will be a comfort to both. I pine for my boys who will be big lads when I get back but they wont forget old Aunt

FIGURE 19.
La Chapelle des Beaumanoirs, Lehon, France (1870), by May Alcott. *Louisa May Alcott's Orchard House/L. M. A. Memorial Association.*

Weedy.[5] Your flock of little girls must be very dear to you, so you'll understand my feelings. If Mary Joe comes with you and brings some of her babies,[6] you and Nan can have the long talked-of-confabulation. Wish I could be there to see and "'jine' in."

Now goodbye, my dear,—write to us and don't think that I ever forget the kindest of Pollys though oceans roll between.

May joins in much love to all the St Paulians.

Affectionately yours,

L. M. Alcott.

MS: Unlocated; copy by ABA at Houghton Library, Harvard University. Partially printed: Cheney 219–21. Cheney prints part of only the first paragraph of the letter to Sewall; the rest is part of the 24–27 April letter to LMA's family (see previous letter). ABA wrote at the top of page 1: "'Louisa's letter to Mary Sewall, at St. Pauls, Min.'"

1. LMA and May boarded at 43 Pinckney Street, Boston, in October 1869 and remained there until they departed for Europe.

2. Porte St. Louis is one of the four main gateways leading into Dinan.

3. The Rance River begins in the Landes du Mené, a range of hills in northwestern France, and flows for sixty miles, emptying into the English Channel between Dinard and St. Malo. The Rance, before it forms the estuary on the coast, flows past Dinan.

4. The ruined abbey, La Chapelle des Beaumanoirs, in Lehon, was the burial place of the Beaumanoirs family. See figure 19 for May's sketch of Beaumanoirs.

5. Her nephews' pet name for LMA, "Aunt Weedy," perhaps derived from the nickname, "Lu-Weedy," that ABA gave LMA when she was a girl because she grew as fast as a weed.

6. Probably Mary Sewall, the wife of Mary ("Polly") Sewall's brother Joseph S. Sewall.

Louisa May Alcott to the Alcott Family

All well.

Dinan April 29th 1870

My Precious People,

Your first letter has just come to our great joy, and I hope you have one or more of the *three* I have sent. So glad to hear that all are well, and such good news of "O. F. G." Stow away the $3000 when it comes and live

FIGURE 20. Frontispiece to *Moods* (1865). *Rare Book Collection, University of North Carolina at Charlotte Library.*

on it as cosily as you can.[1] Don't scrimp, Marmee; have clothes and good food[2] and be as jolly as possible. Then I shant[3] feel as if I was the only one who was spending money.

I see by a Transcript that Niles sent, that Loring is selling "Moods" again.[4] I told him not to do it, and he said he would'nt, for there was no call for it. I won't have it; for it is not *my Book*. So I wish Pa would see if it can't be stopped. Niles will know if I hav'nt the right to do it. I have the copy right and don't wish the book sold as it is.

The storm you speak of didn't do us any harm; we knew nothing of it except that the first day was rather rough. So don't be scared, for the ocean is a big place, and hurricanes dont seem to matter much.[5]

The cold snap here holds on and it is like our spring this last week. We

FIGURE 21. Madame
Coste (ca. 1870), by
May Alcott. *Houghton
Library, Harvard
University.*

have an open wood fire over which I simmer for my leg and arm begins to
ache the moment the east wind comes. Old Coste is very funny and kind,
and talks about my "*atrocious* suffering," is obsessed "with anguish" that I
don't sleep well and cossets me up with hot wine and funny messes.

Alice told[6] her about my good news from home, my new book, &c. and
the good old soul said, "She must embrace me" and did so with tears in her
eyes. Madame Fournier presented her compliments at breakfast, and A.
and M. kissed me heartily. Jules Clamadoc the fiance talked about "Poesee,"
and recited a poem of his own in a way which convulsed us. The little red-
faced man with China blue eyes, big moustache, and dirty hands posed[7]
on the rug, raving about the "loves of his young past," while Madame and
Costé and the fiance's girl wept and applauded, and we did'nt dare look at
each other, it was so absurd.

I have written to the Bartons.[8] Read them bits, if you like, they were so
good to us, I'd like to please them any way.

I wish you'd send your notices also. Niles' first paper never has come to hand and he has'nt sent the "Republican notice." Any others like the "Fireside Companion," Pa can answer by saying I'm away and don't wish to write.[9] I mean to send Ford something soon, and he will hand over $15 or 20 to Pa.[10] Get a copy for me if you can—"Youth's Companion, Daniel Ford."

Fetcher has dash but nothing more and is too Frenchy for me.[11]

I shall write to the dear boys a letter all to their little selves, and you must read it to 'em. It made me laugh right out to think how Donny used to come down on Fred and check mate him, and old Fred look so amazed, and Donny so tickled, Gramima so grand. Bless the dears! I often look at my locket and wear it all the time. I am glad you aint going to Concord till its' really warm.

Pa, if you talk about Jo in public, I won't write "the Cost of an Idea."[12] Say *I* forbid it, and don't cluck like an old hen over your ugly duckling.

Lu.

MS: Unlocated; copy by ABA at Houghton Library, Harvard University.

1. Niles had written LMA on 5 April 1870, including a recent advertisement and reporting on the sales of the book: "It won't discompose you half so much as the storm which blew you off did to have me report what the advt. tells you viz that we have nearly 18,000 O. F. Girls ordered by booksellers and have only been able to supply 12,000; we hope to deliver 3000 more on the 6th & 7th & balance a few days later, by wh. time let us pray that 6000 more may be ordered" (ALS: Houghton Library, Harvard University).

2. The word "food" has been written in a different ink over an indecipherable word.

3. The word "not" was inserted in different ink after "shant."

4. A. K. Loring of Boston had published LMA's first novel *Moods* in December 1864. The *Boston Daily Evening Transcript* for 15 April 1870 published the following ad: "We want every one who has read Miss Alcott's 'L. W.' and 'The Old Fashioned Girl,' to read her first novel, MOODS. One chapter alone, 'The Golden Wedding' at a Farm House, is worth the price of the book. With the author this is her favorite book, added to all the Libraries, sold at all the Bookstores. Loring, Publisher, Boston" (3).

5. The *Boston Daily Evening Transcript* for 9 April 1870 noted the following under the heading "ROUGH AT SEA": "New York, 9th. All the vessels that arrived at this port from the southward and eastward during the past three days, reported exceedingly rough weather" (2).

6. The word "told" was inserted in a different ink.

7. The word "pounced" was crossed out and "posed" inserted in a different ink.

8. Edward Henry Barton and his wife had also boarded at 43 Pinckney Street in Boston while May and LMA lived there.

9. *The Fireside Companion*, a weekly family magazine, was first published in New York in 1867 by George Munro.

10. Daniel Sharp Ford was editor of the *Youth's Companion*. "Mother's Trial" appeared in the *Youth's Companion* 43.26 (26 May 1870). LMA's next contribution would not appear for two years; "Grandma's Team" was published in the *Youth's Companion* 45.48 (28 November 1872).

11. London-born actor Charles Albert Fetcher (1824–79) gained recognition, first in France and then England, for his radical interpretations of Hamlet, Othello, and Iago. He came to America in January 1870 and was well received in Boston in February 1870. In September 1870, he returned to Boston to be manager of the Globe Theater. LMA may have seen him perform in February 1870 before sailing to Europe. She did see him act again in *Camille* on 9 December 1875. She wrote ABA about the performance: "This was in French & F. did the lover well but has grown fat & I never ca[re] to see him again" (*Selected Letters* 206).

12. "The Cost of an Idea," LMA's attempt at depicting her father's boyhood, was never finished. She noted in 1872: "Got hints for my novel, 'The Cost of an Idea,' if I ever find time to write it" (*Journals* 183). She again unsuccessfully tried the same idea in "An Old-Fashioned Boy." See LMA to Mary Mapes Dodge, 29 May [1880] (*Selected Letters* 248).

May Alcott to Abigail Alcott and Anna Alcott Pratt

[May's sketch appeared here in the original letter]

Dinan
29th April '70.

Dear Marmee and Nan,

Here I have sketched in the roughest way our abiding place for the present, just to give mother an idea of the most modern house in Dinan, from the upper window of which, she will see Lu nodding at her, as that is our little salon, furnished prettily with blue damask and looking quite homelike with our pictures and books about [see figure 22].

This last week we have had remarkably cold weather for this region and

FIGURE 22. Madame
Coste's pension
(1870), by May Alcott.
Houghton Library,
Harvard University.

the East winds have brought back a severe attack of Lu's rheumatism; but
Madam Coste and Alice and I have [been] devoted to her, and everything
is done that can be, but as you know there really is nothing that will essentially help her, but the change of weather, which the people say will be
settled and lovely after this "cold snap" as they call it, but we should hardly
consider it so at home. There is an English Library here, so Lu has books
which are always a comfort to her you know, and yesterday your letters, the
first we have had, came to cheer her up, as her leg ached all day. She has a
pretty ring like a pansy for herself as jewelry is very cheap here, and when
we begin to move again, we shall hardly stop at any place for long between
this and Spezia.[1] Alice is much better since she came and thinks this fine air
has done wonders for her, and I think it must do Lu good if she can once get
relief from this constant ache in her bones.

Dinan stands very high, and is only five miles from the sea, and is generally considered a very perfect climate. I am growing very fat, and do nothing but eat and sleep, the bracing airs making me dozy at all hours. I study
my French Verbs every day, and sketch a little, but the ruined castles, bell
towers, and churches, are so lovely, it seems absurd to try to draw them,

FIGURE 23. Street Archway, Dinan, France (1870), by May Alcott. *Louisa May Alcott's Orchard House/L. M. A. Memorial Association.*

and I long to use color for the pretty flowers, ferns and trailing ivy running over the gray stones all about is truly enchanting, and is nothing done with pencil. Monsieur Gaston Forneier has given me a charming photograph of St. Sauveur, the most interesting church here, and I have also got quite a satisfactory sketch of it, but the very old stone gate ways delight me, for they are so large that gardens are planted on top and the flowering shrubs add a great deal to the general effect.[2] Yesterday we went down the oldest street in town, (where in spite of the steepness, Queen Ann's carriage is said to have trundled over it), to the river which runs at the foot.[3] The houses overhang the street in funny little gabled stories almost shutting out all light from above, and it being very narrow & extremely steep, you can see it was quite a sensation to have explored it. I have just finished[4] a large sketch of the swell Church of the place—that of St. Malo,[5] and long to do a painting of a fine row of arches in a subdued light that makes the effect very beautiful, but don't dare sit long in these dreadfully damp places, for when one enters from the outside air, it is like going into a refrigerate[r] and sends a dreadful chill to one's bones. I can't understand how old women I see kneeling on the cold stone for hours can stand it, though such real devotion makes an impression on me.

Love to John, Papa, and the babies, also the Richardsons,[6] and write soon to

your loving May.

I will try and send a little sketch everytime to please mamma.

MS: Unlocated; copy by ABA at Houghton Library, Harvard University. Partially printed: Ticknor 76–77.

1. La Spezia, a major military and commercial harbor in northern Italy at the head of the La Spezia Gulf, lies at the foot of beautiful hills. Its mild Mediterranean climate made the town a popular winter residence for the English and an attractive sea-bathing summer resort for Italians.

2. Church of St. Sauveur in Dinan was originally a Romanesque-style edifice, part of which was constructed as early as the eleventh or twelfth century, but a Gothic chapel was added in the fifteenth century. Bertrand du Guesclin's heart was supposedly buried in the north transept; May's sketch of St. Sauveur has not been located.

3. Probably the Rue de Jerzual, which Murray's *Handbook* (1870) says is "so precipitous as to be scarcely practicable except on foot . . . yet this originally formed the only approach to the town on the side of St. Malo" (148).

4. ABA originally wrote "purchased" then deleted it and inserted "finished."

5. Church of St. Malo, a large structure, was constructed in the fifteenth century. For May's sketch of St. Malo, see figure 29.

6. Possibly Caroline Richardson (age forty-eight) and her four children, who lived near the Alcotts.

FIGURE 24. Dinan, France (1870), by
May Alcott. *Louisa May Alcott's Orchard
House/L. M. A. Memorial Association.*

May Alcott to Abigail Alcott

Chateau de la Garaye
[May's sketch appeared here in the original letter]

Dear Mother,

I have tried to sketch from memory a lovely old ruin, where we spent the day yesterday; but can only give you a very indefinite notion of the gray old tower with ivy clinging to it in all directions, the rear walls having all crumbled away [see figure 25]. The blue sky shone through the little ornamental windows in a way that was quite enchanting. It is only about two miles from Dinan and a pretty walk through the woods to the moat and great embattled walls, which surround the chateau.

Alice and I walked, while Lu went in a donkey carriage. I had fits all the way over the old stone walls, bridges, and queer great crosses, that are very common in all directions. We found a large party of English people all ready at the castle sketching it with pencil in colors. We eat [i.e., ate] our luncheon in a great stone building formerly used as the stables to the grand mansion, but now used as a house by the peasants who keep the place. They had their beds made in great stone alcoves, and several polished foreign looking wardrobes and clock's ornamented with brass hinges, figures and jewells would have delighted father's heart. If it would'nt cost a fortune to get it home, I should certainly buy one of them, as we have three perfectly elegant old polished mahogony ones with a great deal of brass ornament shining so that one can see his face in it, in our rooms here; and they are very common in the smallest huts. Everything is made of stone in this part of the world, and it has a very rich look to me after our wooden buildings. I am constantly delighted with the arched doors, and pretty picturesque windows, always carved, (never like our plain carpenter's work at home) and having quantities of ivy running in every direction. I enjoy every minute of my life here, and if Louisa could only feel quite well and bright again, I should have nothing to wish for.

Château de la Garaye.

FIGURE 25. Chateau de la Garaye, near Dinan, France (1870), by May Alcott. *Houghton Library, Harvard University.*

Alice and I were weighed to day and great was my surprise that in all my thick things I only come up to 122 lbs—just the same as Alice who seems so much smaller. It is less than I have ever weighed before—the smallest within a year or two, being 139. However I suppose the voyage took off a good deal of flesh, though I was'nt sick but two days. We go off on expeditions almost every day, and now the weather is beginning to be a little warmer, I hope Lu wont suffer so much at night as she has done while the east winds prevailed. Alice is very kind and attentive and very patient with me about my French verbs, which are enough to try men's souls, and are particularly hard to me as it is so long since I committed anything to memory.

We are expecting Herbert Pratt[1] here anyday, though Alice has'nt heard from him since she came, but rather twits me about him, calling me "her future cousin &c."

Today we are going over to Queen Anne's great stone fortress, which is now a prison, being surrounded by a moat, and is only connected with a high street by a little bridge. From the top of her tower is the most superb view all over the country, and I am expecting great things in going to see it.

Niles tells Lu not to worry about funds as there is plenty in store from "Old Fashioned Girl." The papers seem to think it as good as "Little Women".

Goodbye, dear family, and write soon to your, loving May.

MS: Unlocated; copy by ABA at Houghton Library, Harvard University. This letter is undated. In her 27 April letter to Abigail Alcott, LMA mentions that May and Alice had gone to the Chateau de la Garaye that day and she had stayed at the pension. May's letter indicates that LMA accompanied her in a donkey carriage; therefore, this particular trip must have occurred after 27 April.

1. Herbert J. Pratt, Alice's first cousin, would not meet up with the Alcotts until Vevey, Switzerland. Pratt had accompanied May on many social outings during 1863–65.

Louisa May Alcott to the Alcott Family

Dinan May 6th 1870.

Dear People,

I have just got a fat letter full of notices from Niles, all good, and news generally pleasant, except that Loring is going to get out a new lot of "*Moods*," which disgusts me and I think it is mean.[1] Do stop it if you can.

The great event of the season is over, and Miss Forney is Mrs. Cloponadene.[2] It was a funny scene, for they had a breakfast the day before, then on Tuesday the wedding. We did not go, as the church is like a tomb, but we saw the bride in white satin, pearls, orange flowers and lace, very pretty and like other brides. Her ma in purple moire[3] and black lace was fine to see, and the little groom in full regmentals with a sabre as long as himself, was very funny. A lot of people came in carriages to escort them to church, and our little square was full of queer turn outs, smartly dressed people, and a great bustle. We looked out of window and enjoyed the fun. There was some mistake about the bride's carriage, and it did'nt drive up in time, so she stood on the steps till it came as near as it could, and then she trotted out to it on Gaston's arm with her maid holding up her satin train. Uncle, Ma, bride and brother drove off, but the groom's carriage was delayed by [the] breaking of a trace,[4] and there he sat, with his fat Pa and Ma, after everyone had gone, fuming, and poking his little cocked hat out of window, while the man mended the harness and every one looked on with breathless interest.

We went to Dinan with Costé in the P.M., and had a fine view of the sea and San Malo.[5] We did'nt like Dinard[?], and wont go there. When we got home about 8 P.M. the wedding dinner was in full blast, and I caught a glimpse of the happy pair at the head of the table, surrounded by a lot of rigged-up ladies and fine men, all gabbling and gobbling as only French folk can. The couple are still here, resting and getting acquainted before they go to Lamballe for a week of festivity. A French wedding is a very funny thing, and I wish you could have seen it.

The Marvales are very pleasant neighbors, and I am trying some baths which did Miss Fanny[6] great good when she had rheumatism. I have bad nights still and suffer much as at home. I hope warm days (if they *ever* come again) will help me; but I get discouraged sometimes, my wretched bones spoil every thing, and never stop aching.

The dry season continues and the people have processions and masses to pray for rain. One short flurry of hail is all we have had, and the cold winds still blow. When our month is out, we shall go somewhere near the sea, if it is at all warm. Nothing could be kinder than dear old Costé, and I could'nt be in a better place to be poorly in than this. She coddles me like a mother, and is so grieved that I don't get better.

May is well and jolly and very good to her cranky old sister. Alice is kind and funny, and we rub on as nicely as can be. If I can only get my bones right all will be so nice and pleasant.

We have had but one letter from you written just after we sailed, and it is time we had more. Tell any one who will to write; it is so jolly to get them, and I've got used to having lots, and miss it.

I send Ma a bit of gorse flower with which the fields are now yellow.[7]

Your Lu.

MS: Unlocated; copy by ABA at Houghton Library, Harvard University. Partially printed: Cheney 221–22.

1. Niles's letter "full of notices" has not been located.

2. The wedding of Col. Jules Clomadoc to Mademoiselle Pelagie F. is recounted in LMA's "Pelagie's Wedding," published in the 6 June 1872 issue of the *Independent* and included in *Shawl-Straps* (45–54). LMA also writes in *Shawl-Straps* that Coste received a letter in the spring of 1871 informing her that Col. Clomadoc had been killed in his first battle during the Franco-Prussian War and that Pelagie and her new son were living with Madame F. (55).

3. Moire is a fabric that has a rippled look due to pressure or heat that has been applied to it after it has been weaved.

4. A trace is the leather strap, rope, or chain that connects to the collar of a horse's harness, allowing the horse to pull a carriage or wagon.

5. St. Malo, in northern France, is a fortified seaport built on a rock between the harbor and the mouth of the Rance. On its left is the town of St. Servan; it faces Dinard on the right bank. Dinard was a popular tourist town because of its beaches and mild climate.

6. Miss Fanny is unidentified.

7. Gorse, often called furze, is a shrub (a variety of the genus *Ulex*) with fragrant yellow flowers and thorns.

Louisa May Alcott to the Alcott Family

May 13th [1870] Dinan.

Dearest folks,

No letters yet, and as I get letters from T. N. and [A. Prescot] Baker, I don't see where yours are. I think the direction has puzzled some of the stupid Postmasters, and that you had better direct to Munroe and Co. no. 7 Rue Scribe, Paris, for all the letters so directed come right. I *know* you have written, and it breaks my heart to think of my letters stowed away somewhere. I'd rather pay lots of extra postage than not have my lawful letters.

I have but two bits of news: one is I've got a new dress, gray silk, costing 90 cts per yard, thick, silvery, and very pretty in the piece. Alice and I got ours together in a very nice way. Finding that there was a Paris dressmaker here, and that we could send to a Paris house for patterns and get silks cheap, we did so. And having selected our dresses they were sent us Express free, and are to be made up next week in walking suits all so fine. I wish I could send you and Nan each one like it.

My other bit of news is, that I have got a Dr.[1] My poor old leg was so bad, I couldn't bear it any longer. After two weeks of misery, and hearing and hearing there was an excellent English Dr. here, I rushed off to him one day, and asked for something to make me sleep. I found Dr. Kane a handsome hearty grayheaded Englishman who was very sensible in his ideas, and gave me some good advice about diet, wine &c. He said as all the Drs. have done that it was rhuematism of the membrane next the bone, and that it was more painful than dangerous. He gave me quieting pill, and some Iodine of Potash, recommended sleep and mattress, a little wine, and lots of sleep. Not to walk at all, but to drive a good deal, and get up my strength without medicine, if possible. This is a good healthy plan, he says, and we like it, so I guess we shall stay another month. Dr. K. is very kind and jolly, and said when he found I'd been a army nurse, that he should esteem it an honor to cure me. He is a rich bachelor and the girls call him my beau, and plague me about him. Mad[lle] Coste knows him and his niece, and has asked them here to breakfast next week.

But the point of the joke is that I'm much better. My leg lets me sleep, and I eat and feel quite chipper again. The weather has been cold, and I tried to walk too much, and so had a bad time. Now I drive and, as Alice goes halves it is cheap for us both.

We drove to Guildo[2] yesterday to see if we should like it for July. It is a queer little town on the sea shore, with ruins near by, bright houses and lots of boats. Rooms a franc a day, and food very cheap. The man of the house, a big brown Peggotty sailor,[3] has a sloop and promised the girls as much sailing as they liked. We may go, but our plans are very vague, and one day we say we will go to one place and the next to another and shall probably end by staying where we are.

We are all growing fat and Alice sasses me about it. She is much better, and her deaf ear is well. May sleeps like a boa constrictor, and is in clover generally. We laugh so much we ought to [be] plump as porpoises.

I had a letter from P. Baker saying he was to be married the 9th May, and go at once to Germany.[4] He said he had written to John about the photographs but got no reply. If there is any fuss, or it is not profitable, just stop the whole thing and let Allen howl.[5]

Niles is devoted in sending me notices and bits of news about my works. If people knew how O. F. G. was written, in what a hurry and pain and woe, they would wonder that there was any grammar at all.[6] I'll get M. R. Sewall[7] to read the next M.S. and then every morsel will be right.

I havn't written a thing as yet and don't feel as if I ever should. Ive got so lazy and sozzle round all day and don't do a thing. If that is what I need, I'm in a fair way to get enough of it. The girls are ever so good to me, and Alice confided to May that she liked me very much. May and she are great cronies and I make [a] fine duenna[8] for I let them do as they like in everything. Alice sends a fine pen and ink sketch of me as I now appear; for the minute, my legs behave, I pick up and we train like mad. Alice is very funny and has just grabbed May, and cut off a bit of her hair. A. is the strongest and she whacks May round like a doll, "for exercise therapy" she says. Dr. Kane is to lend me a boat and then they can let of [i.e., off] their steam in that way.

Sat. May 14th [1870] 11 A.M.

I have nothing to say, so must scribble off a few odds and ends and dispatch the letter. I shall pay the postage so that there can be no mistake. Let me hear if you have to pay it over again, and if you have got four or five from us.

Dr Kane and his neice are coming to breakfast in an hour, and Coste is flying round getting up all sorts of funny messes. May is primping and A. is putting on her silk dress. The handsome old Dr. is to be fascinated by some of us; it don't matter much which, and then we can travel in style with an M.D. in our train.

We had the first rain for a month yesterday and now every thing looks lovely.

Lu

MS: Unlocated; manuscript copy by ABA at Houghton Library, Harvard University. Printed: *Selected Letters* 134–37; partially printed: Cheney 223.

1. Dr. William Kane, a former British military physician in India, attended LMA while

his younger brother Dr. John Kane, who apparently practiced medicine in Dinan, was away in England. When John Kane returned, he assumed care of LMA's health.

2. The picturesque old town of Le Guildo is a small seaport and bathing resort near St. Jacut de la mer; the ruins of Le Guildo Castle, dating from the late Middle Ages, are nearby on the Arguenon River.

3. LMA is referring to characters from Charles Dickens's *David Copperfield* (1850), one of her favorite novels. Both Daniel Peggotty, the brother of Clara Peggotty (servant to the Copperfields and David's lifelong companion, who later marries Mr. Barkis), and Ham Peggotty, his nephew, whom he takes into his custody, are sailors.

4. A. Prescott Baker married Ellen T. Smith on 9 May 1870 and boarded the steamer *Saxonia* in New York en route to Hamburg, Germany, for their honeymoon in Europe.

5. Allen's photographic studio was located at 24 Temple Place in Boston.

6. A number of reviews for *An Old-Fashioned Girl* criticized LMA's use of slang and incorrect grammar even though she addressed the issue in the novel, saying she was trying to depict these characters realistically. The *Springfield Daily Union* for 9 April 1870 wrote: "We might criticise the use of slang words and phrases, but the author claims that without these she should not have been true to life in describing fast Young America. But she in some instances puts these phrases into the mouths of those who should have been better taught" (6). The *New York Tribune* for 22 April 1870 declared: "We have much more serious fault to find with Miss Alcott's grammar. Trifling violations of the rules of Murray we can bear, for they only make the dialogue more natural; but phrases such as 'Each pays what *they* can,' are too much for critical endurance" (1).

7. M. K. Sewall is unidentified.

8. A duenna is a chaperon.

May Alcott to the Alcott Family

[13 May 1870]

Lu has probably written you a detailed account of everything,[1] and I can only add that our life goes on about the same here, one day being very much like the other—a little sketching, studying, and driving, with a great [deal] of eating at all times,[2] occupies me through the short session from ten A.M. to ten P.M. So you see I get sleep enough, for one can't get up early here, for there is no breakfast till 10½, and as Lu gets most of her sleep towards morning, I find it particularly enticing to lie in bed also. She is much better since the English Dr. here has attended her, and the air must be doing her good in spite of want of sleep, for she looks a heap better than she did, and has an excellent appetite.

I have sent to Paris for a new black silk for a street suit, which is to be made here as Alice and Lu are to have their grey silks done here, and if we go to the Italian Lakes in September, we shall probably meet many nice people, and I shall want a nice dress in Rome anyway, so we decided to get our things here, and now clothes will absorb us for some time.

Dr. Kane, who is unmarried, has offered us a boat, so we shall have a good row every day. We joke Lu about her grey bearded Dr. who comes to breakfast this morning at 12.

(Sketch of St. Serves)[3]

Alice says this picture looks more like [the] Concord meetinghouse than our lovely St. Serves, but L. is hurrying me to get it in before the mail closes, so I must let this horrid sketch go, but dont show it to anyone.

Good bye,

May.

MS: Unlocated; copy by ABA at Houghton Library, Harvard University.

1. At the top of the page, ABA has written "From May, same date." Therefore the letter was written on 13 May 1870.

2. ABA inserted the word "hours" above "times." However, he did not cross out "times."

3. May's sketch of St. Sauveur church appeared here in the original letter. May's sketch of the church has not been located.

Louisa May Alcott to the Alcott Family

Dinan May 17th 1870.

Dear People,

No letters yet! I wait and wonder, and meantime keep writing, so that you may not be disappointed as we are. I imagine you are thinking about Concord, if the weather is anyway decent. I wish you had such days as we now enjoy; regular June days, hot and fine, with a balmy wind, and every thing growing like mad. We have at last got into our summer clothes, and feel quite airey. I hope it will last, for my old bones need it. Thanks to Dr. Kane's   I have very little pain now, and can walk quite easily.[1]

The last joke is nails. Alice cuts hers in points and polishes them with little brushes and files, and they look very stylish. May has got at hers, and now sits filing and rubbing at her aristocratic fingers.

It is a devine day, and being Thursday, pigs are out in full force, and the town full of folks come to market. A woman has just gone by with a baby, a distaff, a whip, a basket, a pig, two black sheep, three cows, a donkey and a dog. How she managed them all was a miracle; but she seemed to be very comfortable, and looked like Mrs Noah just out of the Ark.

I have no news to tell for we lead such quiet lazy lives, the days go by, and we do nothing. We run out and do errands in the cool before breakfast, at 10. Then we write, sew, read, and lark round till 4 when we go to drive. May and I in the cherry-bounce[2] with M. Harmon to drive us, and Alice on horseback, for after endless fuss, she has at last evoked a horse out of chaos, and comes galloping gaily after us, as we drive about the lovely roads, with the gallant hotel-keeper, Adolph Harmon. We are getting satiated with ruins and Chateaux, and plan a trip by water to Nantes,[3] for the way they do it, is to hire a big boat and be towed by a horse in the most luxurious manner.

We have decided to stay here till June 15th when our second month will expire. It is so comfortable and pleasant and wholesome. We are all getting rosy and fat, and lazy, as well as we may be, for we do nothing but eat, sleep, loaf, and laugh. If utter and entire laziness is what we need, I ought to be a marvel of strength in a few months for I don't do a blessed thing all day. It is awful and I shall go at something soon in self defense for idleness is very tiresome. Alice is writing a thrilling tale for fun, and I am to begin one soon which I can give Leslie when I get home.[4] May pegs away at her French like a Trojan, but don't talk much yet.

Tommy sends me papers devotedly. I got a Transcript of April 2nd today with a notice of my departure and a fine little paragram after it.[5]

Adieu for today. I am going out now to find a photograph for you.

Lu.

MS: Unlocated; copy by ABA at Houghton Library, Harvard University. Partially printed: Cheney 223.

1. ABA leaves a blank space in the sentence.

2. A cherry-bounce is probably LMA's phonetic pronunciation for a char à banc, a type of light country carriage, often with wooden benches.

3. Nantes, France, is approximately forty miles from the coast and lies on the right bank of the Loire at the influx from the north of the Erdre River. This large commercial town was once the ancient residence for the dukes of Brittany.

4. The last-known thrillers that LMA wrote for Frank Leslie, "Betrayed by a Buckle" and "La Belle Bayadère," were composed in 1869 and published in the February 1870 issue of *Frank Leslie's Lady's Magazine*. No later thrillers by LMA have been located.

5. The *Boston Daily Evening Transcript* for 2 April 1870 published a two-paragraph notice of LMA's departure and the publication of *An Old-Fashioned Girl*, writing that she "sails today for Europe, accompanied by her sister and friend. . . . It will be the fervent hope of multitudes whom she has delighted and instructed, that Miss Alcott may be as successful in regaining the health and strength she seeks, as she has been in sending the purest pleasure and genial counsel into households almost numberless all over the land" (2).

May Alcott to Abigail Alcott and Anna Alcott Pratt

May 19th. [1870]

Dear Marmee and Nan,

As Lu says there is very little to write about, as our days are spent in just about the same way, very pleasant and lazy with the only difference of going to drive in the P.M. or staying at home. Alice and I had a nice row on the river here the other P.M. for as we walked along the bank looking lovingly at a very nobby little boat (belonging to a very cross Englishman who does not use it himself nor will he let it to any one else) we came across a fat old woman, quite imposing in appearance, with a striking cap on and her hands in the large pockets of an immense apron, who said she owned a boat in which we could go up the river, with a man to row us. So off we started in a great wind-scow and a very heavy pair of oars, which, however, Alice and I insisted on using much to the surprise of our gondalier, who found it quite pleasant to lie in state, and let us work, but it really was refreshing *to do something*, after so many days of laziness. It was about 6 when we got underway, and a more enchanting river I never beheld, with lovely groves on each side over which, high up, we could see the old walls of the city covered with ivy, and many chateaux belonging to the rich people here. Alice wants a boat to use the rest of our stay in Dinan but we can't buy one, and if we have one made, we shall have to wait long months before getting leave from the Sous-Prefit to put on their precious river. There are regular ships papers made out, and kept in a tinbox for every craft, even a wherry,[1] which seems so very absurd that we have lost all patience about it.

To day a great event happened, for my black silk for a walking suit came from Paris, and, as there are five French dressmakers here, I shall have it made immediately. If we go to the Italian Lakes in the fall, we shall want a rag or two, as it is on the grand route of all travellers, and probably we shall meet every friend we ever had, for all America seems to be abroad.

Dr. Kane, who has helped Lu so wonderfully is very nice, and yesterday he made us a long call, talking of America and our authors; being a great admirer of Hawthorne I gave him the photograph of "the Seat" [see figure 26] which he liked exceedingly, and is going to have it copied and reduced. If I go to England I shall regret not having brought all the pictures connected with Hawthorne and Emerson, as I might have them copied, and sell them to some profit perhaps there where people know them.[2]

To-day is very hot and even quite thin clothes are oppressive. They tell us we shall have strawberries soon and rhubarb, both of which you [know] I am very fond of. We decided not to buy a horse as every thing seemed at that time so uncertain. But Alice has found a good one for the saddle, which I am to ride whenever the spirit moves. In short, I have everything that [my] heart could desire, and have got quite attached to the French tongue, for now the first time for many years, having plenty of time, I dig away at exercises and verbs pretty constantly, and can make quite long sentences, though I can't talk readily yet.

What can be the reason we have received no letters? Do direct to "Monroe and Co. No. 7 Rue Scribe, Paris," as all sent to them have come, though

FIGURE 26. "Hawthorne's Seat," from *Concord Sketches* (1869), by May Alcott. *Louisa May Alcott's Orchard House/L. M. A. Memorial Association.*

it costs a little more. We are dying to know if Ma and Pa have gone to Concord, and of everything that has happened since we left. We had so many letters in Pinckney Street, that we miss them very much, so do tell us how you directed yours.

May.

MS: Unlocated; copy by ABA at Houghton Library, Harvard University.

    1. A wherry is a small rowing vessel used to carry both passengers and goods on a river.

    2. "Hawthorne's Seat" (see figure 26) is one of the illustrations May Alcott drew for *Concord Sketches Consisting of Twelve Photographs from Original Drawings* (Boston: Fields, Osgood and Co., 1869). Among the other illustrations were Emerson's house, Hawthorne's home (Wayside), and the Old Manse. LMA wrote the preface to the volume.

Louisa May Alcott to the Alcott Family

Saturday May 21st [1870]

[May's sketch appeared here in the original letter.]

May has drawn our salon, for you with Alice on the sofa and me reading by the fire [see figure 27]. It is very good, only it gives the idea of a larger room than it is. The dark oak panels are very effective, and the bird cage in the window introduces little Dribble, the bird, who is a funny mite and a great pet of ours.

Tommy sent me a nice notice yesterday, and a pretty note from a lame girl in Vermont who wants "a picter." But no letters from home and we are raging. It is maddening to have the postman leave two or three letters for Alice everyday, and none for us. Where the dickens are they? I read over the one letter we have had and try to be patient, but it is hard work. I do so want to know what is going on.

In the letter, you say S. E. S. reports $350 income from the invested money.[1] That is'nt enough for you and Pa. So when T. Niles pays up in July, take out $1000, and let S. E. S. keep it for you to draw upon till the next settlement in January. He can invest all the rest, and before January, I shall

know if I want more money. Don't go poor, for heaven's sake, or I shan't feel as if I had any right to be here so idle and cosy. I'm better; and this hot weather is just what I need.

    Bless you all, and good bye.

Your Lu.

FIGURE 27. "Notre salon chez Mdlle Coste," Dinan, France (1870), by May Alcott. *Houghton Library, Harvard University.*

MS: Unlocated; copy by ABA at Houghton Library, Harvard University.

    1. Samuel E. Sewall, whose family was related to the Alcotts by marriage, oversaw LMA's finances and made investments for her after the success of *Little Women*.

Louisa May Alcott to Moncure Daniel Conway

Dinan May 21st [1870]

My Dear Mr Conway[1]

    Here we are, May & myself with a Boston friend, out on our travels for a year or more, & this is our first halt in Brittany. Were you ever here? It is the oldest, quaintest, loveliest place I ever saw, & we are revelling in hot weather after American East winds & much snow.

I longed to come to England first but April was too early for my miserable neuralgia[2] so we landed at Brest, & after a little tour about the most interesting parts of France we mean to go to Italy for the winter.

May is studying & sketching in a rapturous state, Alice Bartlett devotes herself to Italian & horses, while I play duenna & try to get well that I may go to work again, for I have done nothing for a long time.

I have some short tales by me & it occurred to me that it would be cheaper to send them to London than to Boston *if* I can get as much for them there as at home. I remembe[r] you kindly offered to say a word for me to some news paper man when I was in London once upon a time.

Is it worth trying? Sampson & Low[3] will take books, but I'm not going to write any more just yet, & prefer to do little tales for the present.

If you are very busy pray dont trouble yourself about my small concerns; if you have a spare minute to give me a line I shall be very glad of the address of one or two story taking papers, after which I can do the business myself.[4]

I hope Mrs Conway & the little people are well.[5] I have heard of them from time to time through Sanborn & Mrs Taylor[6] who still writes to me. Please remember me to them, & tell Mrs C. that I wrote last, but getting no answer didn't worry her with any more letters. Never the less I have never forgotten her great kindness to

Yours truly,

L. M. Alcott.

Address me care Munroe & Co 7 Rue Scribe Paris & it will be forwarded. Best regards to Mrs Taylor & Mrs Malleson[7] when you see them.

.

ALS: Moncure D. Conway Papers, Rare Book and Manuscript Library, Columbia University. At the top of page four, possibly in another hand, is "23 Norfolk St Strand".

1. Moncure Daniel Conway (1832–1907), minister, abolitionist, reformer, and coeditor with F. B. Sanborn of the *Boston Commonwealth*. Conway, originally from Virginia, had been living abroad, primarily in London, since 1863. LMA had stayed "a fortnight at a

lovely old place on Wimbledon Common with the Conways" while in London in May 1866 (*Journals* 151).

2. Neuralgia is a burning or sharp pain in an area near a nerve.

3. Sampson Low and Marston had already published *Little Women* and *An Old-Fashioned Girl*. LMA often called the firm "Sampson and Low," mistakenly thinking they were two different individuals.

4. No stories written by LMA during this time period have been located in British periodicals.

5. Ellen Davis Dana Conway (1833–97), wife of Moncure D. Conway; the couple had a daughter, Mildred, and two sons, Eustace and Dana. Another son, Emerson, had died in 1864.

6. Clementia Taylor (1810–1908), wife of Peter Alfred Taylor (1819–91) of Aubrey House on Notting Hill in England (LMA had spent ten days with them in June 1866). She was an active participant in various radical movements, including abolition and women's suffrage.

7. Probably Elizabeth Whitehead Malleson (1828–1916), wife of Frank Rodbard Malleson (d. 1903) and daughter-in-law to Rev. J. P. Malleson (1796–1869). The Unitarian minister J. P. Malleson ran a school in West Hove, Sussex, which Peter Alfred Taylor attended and where he met his future wife Clementia, who was a governess for the Malleson children. Elizabeth and Frank Malleson founded the Working Women's College in 1864, and Elizabeth later published notes on the *Early Training of Children* (1884).

Louisa May Alcott to Anna Alcott Pratt

Dinan May 25, 1870

All well.

My Precious Betsey.[1]

Your letter dated May 7th has just come, the only one we have got except that which you wrote just after we sailed. You say you have only got *two* of ours, one written on the steamer, and one dated 20th April. Now I have written a long letter every *week*, and May has put in a little sketch now and then. I sent them all to Concord as mother asked me to, that there might be no confusion. But I will send this to John, so you can have first skim.[2]

You don't know how glad I was to hear at last. I've waited so long, and every day been so disappointed. To-day May came bounding up with a letter and a paper from Tommy who sends one very often. I hope the British will like my "Old Fashioned Girl" as the notice was good.[3]

I am glad Marmee is all settled in C. and hope _____ will turn out well.[4] The things in my old trunk in the closet are for Ma's private picking, so don't let other folks crib 'em. We thought of you on the 23rd, and imagined you were having some sort of a revel. This miss sends her best love and many 'isses' to that dear Miss on her *tin wedding*, and wishes she could send her a collender, or a spice-box, or a *biler* in honor of the day.[5] Many happy returns!

Now I'll answer your questions as I find them. My health I have told you about in my last letters. But will say again, after a pretty tough spell with my leg, which ached for three weeks, and broke out in little sores, I am now better, thanks to the English Dr. Kane, to whom I went in despair. He only told me to keep warm and still and take Iodine of Potash, and a little opium to get sleep. I did so and picked up at once. The fine weather helped me, for after a cold snap it came very warm, and I felt that my bones liked it. Dr. K. said this was an old trouble, it would take some time to cure it entirely, but the cure had begun, and change of air, food, and rest would be all that was needed. So I take my potash three times a day, drink wine, eat like a pig, and ride when I go out, for it hurts me to walk, and will till the little knobs are gone. I begin to sleep without opium, and the girls [say] I'm growing fat and rosy. I look heaps better and feel so, therefore be at rest, my dear, for I believe this trip is going to fit up the old ruin.

May eats, sleeps, dawdles, and gets so fat she can hardly walk. She is also growing a moustache, as it is the fashion here, for most of the women have 'em and some wear full beards. Alice and I are budding. I think its the wine. Ha! ha! We get on nicely with Alice, who is jolly, kind, and awful clever. She calls me "dear Granny," and is ever so good to me. She sends you one of her poems which needs a word of explanation. Alice has [been] teasing us to let our nails grow and cut them in points, and we wouldn't. But at last May began to [be] so fascinated with the process of polishing with powder, files &c. that she is now the possessor of ten long glossy claws, gracefully rounded, which much improves her hands. I have lately done the same for

FIGURE 28. Alice Bartlett (1870), by May Alcott. *Houghton Library, Harvard University.*

lack of amusement, and my nails beat all the rest. Alice thinks my hands very handsome, also my nose, and goads me to keep all three with great care. We have also had fun about the queer food, as we don't like brains, liver, &c. &c. A. does, and when we eat some mess, not knowing what it is, and find it is bowels or sheep's tails or eels, she exults over us and writes poems.[6]

I wander dreadfully, but the girls are racketting, Birdie singing like mad, and nine horses neighing to one another in the place, so my ideas do not flow as clearly as they should. Besides I expect Gaston to come in every minute to show us his rig, for he is going to pic-nic in Breton costume; a very French affair, for the party are to march two and two with fiddlers in front, and donkeys bearing the feast in the rear. Such larks!

Yesterday we had a funny time. We went to drive in a basket chaz,[7] very fine, with a perch behind and a smart harness, but most of the horses here are stallions and act like time. Ours went very well at first, but in the town took to cutting up, and suddenly pounced onto a pile of brush, and stuck his head into a bakeshop. We tried to get him out, but he only danced and neighed, and all the horses in town seemed to reply. A man came and led him on a bit, but he did'nt mean to go, and whisked over to the other side where he tangled us and himself up with a long string of team horses. I flew out and May soon followed. Alice was driving and kept in while the man led the critter back to the stable. I declined my drive with the insane beast, and so we left him and bundled home in the most ignominious style. All the animals are very queer here, and unlike ours, especially pigs.

We went to a ruin one day, and were about to explore the castle, when a sow with her family of twelve charged through the gateway at us so fiercely that we fled in dismay, for pigs are not nice when they attack, as we don't know where to bone 'em, and I saw a woman one day whose nose had been bitten off by an angry pig. I flew over a hedge; May tried to follow but stuck and lay with her long legs up and her head in a ditch howling for me to save her, as the sow was charging in the rear, and a dog, two cows, and a boy looking on. I pulled her over head first, and we tumbled into the tower, like a routed garrison. It was'nt a nice ruin, but we were bound to see it, having suffered so much. And we did see it in spite of the pigs, who waylaid us on all sides, and squealed in triumph when we left, dusty, torn and tired. The ugly things wander at their own sweet will, and are tall, round-backed, thin wretches who run like race horses and are no respecters of persons.

Sunday was a great day here, for the children were confirmed. It was a pretty sight to see the long procession of little girls in white gowns and veils, winding through the flowery garden and the antique square into the old church, with their happy mothers following, and the boys in their church robes singing as they went. The old priest was too ill to perform the service, but the young one who did, announced afterward that if the children would pass the house, the old man would bless them from his bed. So all marched away down the narrow street with crosses and candles; and it was very touching to see the feeble old man stretch out his hands above them as the little white brides passed by with bended heads, while the fresh boyish voices chanted the responses. This old priest is a very interesting man, for he is [a] regular Saint, helping every one, keeping his house as a refuge for poor and old priests, settling quarrels among the people, and watching over the young people as if they were his own. I shall put him in a story.[8]

May don't seem disappointed in anything, but very happy, and has told her raptures in the letters which are *somewhere*. If you don't get 'em, she will repeat, but is now doing a charcoal sketch of St. Malo church, and is in bliss [see figure 29].

FIGURE 29. St. Malo Cathedral, near
Dinan, France (28 April 1870), by May
Alcott. *Louisa May Alcott's Orchard
House/L. M. A. Memorial Association.*

Viola! Gaston has just come in rigged in a white embroidered jacket with the Dinan coat of arms worked in scarlet and yellow silk on it fore and aft, a funny hat with streamers and a belt with a knife, horn, &c. He is handsome, and as fond of finery as a girl. I'll send you his picture next time, and one of Dinan.[9]

Our new silk gowns are being made. Alice's is nearly done, very simple but handsome. I sent you a pattern of the stuff. I have also got a plain black silk; A's and mine are very alike. I have also got a black jacket worked in colors to wear with thin dresses, for I have to bundle more or less even in warm weather. The work is famous, and a jacket costs here $5,00, in America $20.—so it is a good chance to get a pretty useful thing cheap. I don't mean to buy much, for as I have to ride and my Dr.s to pay, I must be careful. I also have May's washing to pay, and little things unexpected, for her small store won't last long, and I want her to have a good time.

You will see that Marmee has all she needs, and a girl, and as much money as she wants for being cosy and comfortable. S. E. S. will let her have all she wants and make her take it. I'm sorry the chapel $100 did n't come, for she likes to feel that she has some of her very own.

I have written to Conway and Mrs. Taylor, so that if we decide to take a run to England before we go to Italy, the way will be open. Mrs. Howe (A's cousin) is going to Caen,[10] and if it is cheap and pleasant, we are to join her bye and bye. But Dinan is so healthy and cozy that we shall linger till the heat makes us long for the sea. Roses, cherries, strawberries, and early vegetables are come (a month late they say) and we are in clover. Dear old Costé broods over us like a motherly hen, and just now desired me to give her affectionate and respectful compliments to my "bon mere."

Now I'm spun out, so "adoo," my darling Nan. Write often and I will keep sending trusting that you will get them in time.

Kisses all round.
Your Lu.

Direct to Munroe and put on "Via Liverpool or Havre." There has been a fuss about postage, the government wont pay the steamers for taking the mails, so they go off to Germany and get here anyhow.

MS: Unlocated; copy by ABA at Houghton Library, Harvard University. Partially printed: Cheney 223–26.

1. Betsey Prig, from Charles Dickens's *Martin Chuzzlewit* (1844). LMA often addressed Anna as "Betsey" in her letters.

2. Anna and John Bridge Pratt were currently living in Maplewood, Massachusetts, a small town about six miles north of Boston.

3. *An Old-Fashioned Girl* was published in England by Sampson Low and Marston in April 1870.

4. ABA and Abigail returned from Boston and settled in Concord for the summer on 16 April 1870. ABA and Anna had spent the previous two weekends preparing Orchard House (see ABA's *Diary for 1870* 195, 203–4). ABA drew a blank line in his copy of the letter.

5. Anna and John Bridge Pratt were married at Orchard House on 23 May 1860 (Emerson and Thoreau were in attendance). Exactly thirty years earlier (23 May 1830), ABA and Abigail were married at King's Chapel, Boston. An item made of tin is the traditional gift for a couple's tenth anniversary.

6. Alice Bartlett's poem is included in *Shawl-Straps* (1872). Titled "The Downward Road," the poem details how the Alcott sisters, "[t]wo Yankee maids of simple mien," initially despise French food and customs. Matilda (May) is the first to succumb to French cuisine and then "promised for one little week / To let her nails grow long." Lavinia (LMA) soon follows suit, declaring American food to be plain in comparison. The poem ends: "Morning and noon and night they sit / And polish up their nails. / Then if in one short fatal month, / A change like this appears, / Oh, what will be the net result / When they have stayed for years?" (109–11).

7. A basket chaise is a lightweight, open pleasure carriage for one or two people.

8. No story with this character has been located.

9. No individual photograph of Gaston, nor one of Dinan, has been located.

10. Mrs. and Dr. Estes Howe had traveled to Europe aboard the *Lafayette* with the three women. Caen, in northern France, is located on the Orne River, about nine miles from the coast. ABA had written in parentheses after "Caen" the word "Cazinne" then cancelled it.

Louisa May Alcott to the Alcott Family

Dinan May 30th 1870

Dear Folks,

May has made up such a big letter that I will only add a line to give you the last news of the health of her Highness Princess Louisa. She is such a public character now-a-days that even her bones are not her own, and her wails of woe, cannot be kept from long ears of the world—Old Donkey as it is! Dr. Kane who was army surgeon in India, and Dr in England for forty years, says, my leg trouble and many of my other woes, come from the calomel they gave me in Washington.[1] He has been through the same thing with an Indian-Jungle-fever, and has never got the calomel out of him. The bunches on my leg are owing to that, for the mercury lies round in a body and don't do much harm till a weak spot appears when it goes there and makes trouble. I dont know anything about it, only [my] leg is the curse of my life. But I think Dr. K's Iodine of Potash will cure it in the end as it did his arms, after taking it for three months. It is simple, pleasant, and seems to do something to the bones that gives them ease, so I shall sip away and give it a good trial.

We are now revelling in big strawberries, green peas, early potatos, and other nice things, on which we shall grow fat as pigs.

We are beginning to think of a trip into Normandy[2] where the Howes are. Direct to Munroe and Co. and no one else, then we shall get them without delay.

Love to all. XX By, by.

Your loving Lu.

P. S.
I sent a letter to Nan last week.

MS: Unlocated; manuscript copy by ABA at Houghton Library, Harvard University. Printed: *Selected Letters* 137; partially printed: Cheney 226–27, who adds two final paragraphs, not in ABA's transcription, from a later letter.

1. LMA volunteered as a nurse during the Civil War, and reported to the Union Hotel Hospital in Georgetown, District of Columbia, on 13 December 1862; however, she soon fell severely ill with typhoid fever. Bronson arrived on 16 January and returned with her to Concord on 24 January 1863. On doctor's orders, her head was shaved and she wore a wig for some time. On 22 March 1863, she was finally able to leave her room for the first time. While ill she was prescribed calomel, a form of mercurous chloride.

2. Normandy, the region in northwest France along the English Channel, was formerly an independent duchy.

May Alcott to Abigail and A. Bronson Alcott

Dinan May 30th, 1870

Dear Mother and Father,

After your letters of the 6th, we imagine you settled again in Concord, among the apple blossoms, birds and squirrels. What wonders you must have wrought in a few days, to have put that old house to right between Tuesday and Saturday; and though I know how cosily it must be looking, yet I am not in the least homesick, but very, very happy, and thank the good Lord every day that I have the health and spirits to enjoy every thing as it comes along. I do feel, as mother predicted, that I have read very little, and know very little, but now that I have the time, I study and do what I can to improve my mind, though it is rather late in the day. But if one can't be blessed with strong eyes, I don't see any thing for it, but to make the best of being a dolt.

I am delighted that you have such a nice person as Mrs. Conant,[1] and it must make it pleasant having the Ricketson's in Concord. Give them my best love, also remember me to Mr. Channing,[2] and ask him to write me the gossip of Concord, for he is the only person up in interesting items.—Did father see Mrs. Stearns? and how are matters settled in that quarter?[3] We had a letter from Prescott Baker about his marriage, and perhaps we may meet him if he comes to Italy. But that is off the usual line of travel and few strangers come here, though there is nothing on the continent more interesting to be seen than these most ancient of all ancient towns.

Louisa is up and down according to the weather. Now, we are having very warm days she is comfortable, but the Dr. thinks it is more than neuralgia

FIGURE 30. Orchard House, home of the Alcotts (ca. 1870), Concord, Massachusetts. *Louisa May Alcott's Orchard House/L. M. A. Memorial Association*

or rheumatism; that the membrane next [to] the bone is inflamed, and makes it so painful to bear, and which it will take an entire rebuilding of her general system to remove. The climate will do more than medicine, he thinks, and, if she can get natural sleep, that all must be left to time. So if she gets strong through the warm weather, and has a respite from pain, then with a winter in some warm place in Italy, she will begin to regain some of the strength she has wasted in overwork. She is sweet and amiable all the time whether her leg aches or not, and Miss Bartlett is very much attached to her; Besides being a great admirer of her Genius, she takes great interest in all the notices that come and everything relating to Lu's literary success. We like Alice more and more everyday and the whole party seem to pull together excellently thus far. There is hardly a person I know, who would stand the test of being together as we are, every day and all day, as well as she does. And I have never before met a person of her age, who proved so highly cultivated, refined, well educated, and always interesting. The Nation[4] comes regularly to her, and Niles is constant in his devotion to Lu, sending notices, Transcripts, and little notes constantly to keep the run of things at home.

I should not be surprised if we left here June 15th, as it is getting warm and I have twice been tempted to put on muslins. Mrs Howe who came out with us is to be with her husband and brother in-law at some watering place near, and Alice wants to be with her. We shall probably leave when our second month ends here. I am quite reluctant to leave as I have not accomplished all the sketching I hoped to, and also think it hardly possible for us to find another such comfortable home for Lu; in case of an attack of rheumatism she wont hardly find a hotel satisfactory. But I think she is a little tired of this place, and perhaps changes will be better for her, though I cant imagine more perfect air than this. There is never much sickness here, we are told, and Alice and I grow perceptably fat from day to day.

Did John make any arrangement with Baker about the photographs? If not, Mr. Chase, a young man with glasses, at 'Doll & Hendersons', Summer Street, can tell him all about it, as he and Baker were to do it together and agree with Allen, who, P. B. wrote made a very fair offer of per centage. Somebody is going to make something out of it, and why should it [not] be ourselves instead of Allen? Do look into it because it is easy to forbid Allen's printing any, unless he comes to terms.

Lu and Alice have been to the horse fair here, and now have gone for a turn in a donkey wagon, as Lu must'nt walk much for fear of making her leg ache; and it is such enchanting air that she cannot stay at home. We have got the dearest little bird, which I shall [be] sorry to leave when we go, as we cant take him along very well; and so must give him to Mad^{lle} Costé. He is a bright yellow brown and red, and sings beautifully. We have had delcious strawberries this last week and nice sweet peas and new potatoes.

Do put the old piece of cousin Lu's[5] red piano cloth up at my low studio window over the green one, behind fathers bust, as it looks frightfully without the red behind. When you see Mr. or Mrs. French ask them if they received a good bye note from me containing one of Lu's autographs for Miss Sally.[6] I wrote one from Pinckney Street, but it disappeared in a mysterious manner from my bureau and I never felt certain that it got to the P. Office.

Direct to Munroe as it is safer now we shall be changing about so soon, and he will always have our directions.

Your loving May.

MS: Unlocated; copy by ABA at Houghton Library, Harvard University.

1. ABA and Abigail had hired fifty-two-year-old Mary B. Conant from Massachusetts to cook for them at Orchard House. ABA notes on 4 May in his manuscript *Diary for 1870* that "Mrs. Conant, a sensible woman, comes to assist my wife about her housekeeping" (255).

2. Ellery Channing (1817–1901), poet, biographer, and close friend to Thoreau (he is "the poet" mentioned in *Walden*). Nephew to the elder William Ellery Channing (1780–1842), the famous Unitarian minister, he was also a friend to ABA and often visited Orchard House.

3. In July 1870, Bronson paid three hundred dollars to Mrs. Mary Preston Stearns, wife of the antislavery reformer George Luther Stearns from Medford, Massachusetts (*Letters of ABA* 520). Mrs. Stearns had been a financial angel to the Alcotts, underwriting the publication of ABA's *Emerson* (1865) and helping May attend art school. In his manuscript *Diary of 1870*, ABA writes that he had borrowed the money "for repairing my house in 186_[.] Both Mr and Mrs Stearns have befriended us in times past, and one likes to pay debts in coin as well as thanks. Louisa advises the payment out of her funds. And now that she is in receipt of a considerable sum, there seems to be a fitness in returning the money" (432).

4. The *Nation: A Weekly Journal Devoted to Politics, Literature, Science, and Art*, a New York publication, founded in 1865 and edited by English journalist E. L. Godkin, competed for the *Atlantic*'s intellectual readers.

5. Probably Louisa Wells, the daughter of Elizabeth Sewall Willis Wells, whom the Alcott sisters often addressed as "Lu."

6. Henry French was an attorney in Concord. He and his wife, Pamela, had two children, Sarah ("Sally"), who was twenty-three in 1870, and the future noted sculptor Daniel Chester French, who was twenty.

May Alcott to Anna Alcott Pratt

Dear Anna,

 We have just received your last letter dated May 6th which gave us great joy, after waiting so long for news from home.

You ask, if after dreaming of foreign parts for so many years, I am not a little disappointed in the reality. But I can truly say that every thing so far has been quite as picturesque, new, and lovely as I expected; and what rather surprises me is that many things should be so nearly what I thought to find them. I cannot describe to you the strange sensation that took possession of me, when, after leaving Brest, we travelled by cars to Morlaix, and getting into a funny little omnibus, wound down through the steep streets to the Hotel de Europe.[1] Then I really began to feel how very strange and very different it all was from America, and could hardly believe there were still stranger things in store for me. The grand viaduct which, according to Murray, is about the finest in the world, fairly took away my breath, and I could'nt understand how human ingenuity ever planned and carried out, with such perfect success, so wonderful a scheme.[2] The queer gabled houses, stone crosses, and white-capped peasants with their noisy sabots,[3] all delighted me, and I never again expected to feel the real *foreign* thrill that came over me in full force when I first entered Morlaix.[4] Now I am quite accustomed to wonders of any kind, and can you believe it? am even a little tired of seeing ruined castles, and ivy covered chateaux, and yet very angry with myself for not having the power of dilineating the enchanting views and objects which interest you all so much.[5] But every thing looks so very flat on paper; it gives me no satisfaction. If I could only use colors easily all would go well, but never having *painted* from nature, I am timid about beginning; but think I must come to it, and plunge along the best I can, going on the principle of its being better to try and fail than not to try at all. As we have been off pretty regularly every other day on excursions to neighboring places of interest, we now feel as if we had made good use of our time, and learned a good deal of old ways and customs, for everything seems

FIGURE 31. A servant at Madame Coste's pension (1870), by May Alcott. *Houghton Library, Harvard University.*

hundreds of years behind the times, and I never enter Lehon, (a little village twenty minutes walk down a long stone staircase, from Dinan,) without being greatly impressed by its great antiquity and feeling quite sure it has always been exactly so ever since the world began. I very much admire the primitive, simple manners and customs of the people here, so much so, that our life at home begins to seem a little artificial and unattractive to me. The peasants seem to have perfect confidence in one another, and Mad[lle] Costé says they are perfectly honest, there never having been a robbery in Dinan; and I have noticed with surprise how horses carriages and loaded express wagons are left in the streets all night without any guards.—I never spent such lazy days in all my life, and do very little besides eat, sleep, draw, and study French. Today, being tired after a long excursion yesterday, I am in bed and beside my coffee and toast at eight oclock, Francoise has just brought me, an inviting waiter of breakfast (it is now 10½) consisting of omulette, such as only the French can make, cold meat chops, toast, tea, and oatmeal pudding, which Mad[lle] Coste furnishes for our special benefit. We

have every comfort and lots of fun, all for five francs a day, which is a great satisfaction, don't you think so? In fact I am so happy I often say to myself, "If this be I, as I think it be, I have a little dog at home and he'll know me," to make me quite sure it is not all a dream, and I shall not wake up to find myself in my own little room at "Apple Slump."[6]

We thought of you all on the 23rd, and Lu wrote her last letter to you on that day, sending you in the same envelope a little photograph of Dinan, which, if Father will mount on one of the old photograph cards, which he will find on the shelves in my chamber, you will then get some idea of this enchanting place. I have made little rough pen and ink sketches on some of the last letters to please mother, who likes to *locate* us, and will draw our sleeping room with its two little curtained beds, so little in fact is mine that

FIGURE 32. "Our Sleeping Room," Madame Coste's pension (1870), by May Alcott. *Houghton Library, Harvard University.*

five feet eight has to lie diagonally across it or not at all [see figure 32]; but it *looks* pretty, so that makes up for the trifling discomfort.—I so wish that the lace curtain to my bed might be whitened and put up again. Do be sure and tell me how the pictures are hung.

I think Lu seems decidedly better, looks better, eats heartily, and is jolly and more like herself than I have seen her for a great while. The Dr. thinks her troubles arise from the calomel she took at the Hospital.

Now, dear Nanny, do write me long letters, as all the home items seem of immense importance and we have only had two letters since we arrived. How funny that we should have a cousin of the S's as cook.[7] I hope she will prove all mother wants, and the dear old couple will fatten and flourish on Parker House rolls[8] and gingersnaps.

I would give more for a cup of cream and good home-made bread than all the rich french messes for the special purpose of ruining the coats of our stomachs.

Your loving sister

May.

MS: Unlocated; copy by ABA at Houghton Library, Harvard University. Most of this letter is also copied in ABA's *Diary for 1870* (352–55) with little change.

1. Murray's *Handbook* (1870) ranks the Hotel de Europe as "good" with "'excellent rooms'" (135–36).

2. The grand viaduct, which runs between the Place Theirs and the Place Cornic, is 310 yards long and 190 feet high.

3. Sabots, the traditional footwear of Brittany, are wooden shoes, each usually carved from one block of wood.

4. Murray's *Handbook* (1870) notes how Morlaix may enchant first-time visitors: "To the stranger its chief attraction will be the picturesque air of antiquity which it retains in its older quarters . . . and the thoroughly Breton character of its street architecture and houses overhanging the footway, each story, fronted with an apron of slates, more nearly approaching its neighbor on the opposite side of the way, until the inmates of the garret may shake hands" (136).

5. Murray's *Handbook* (1870) notes that "the grotesquely carved corner posts, ornamented with the figures of kings, priests, saints, monsters, and bagpipers, the Gothic doorways, the sculptured cornices, would enrich an artist's sketch-book, and furnish employment for many days" (136).

6. "Apple Slump" is the desultory name LMA often gave to Orchard House.

7. Mary B. Conant possibly may have been related to the Sewall family. On 10 August, ABA would note that he and his wife "have been most fortunate in securing an efficient and tidy housekeeper, competent to take charge of all matters, besides being an agreeable companion for my wife, and who comprehends the habits of an engaged scholar like myself. I have never known [since?] the head of a family another whose accomplishments met our needs so faithfully and with so little to remind us of her relations to us. She is one of us and agreeably servicable" (*Diary for 1870* 499).

8. The Parker House, a five-story hotel and dining room established in 1855 by Harvey D. Parker at the corner of School and Tremont streets, Boston, was the gathering place for the Saturday Club, whose members included Emerson, Longfellow, Holmes, and Lowell among others. It was known for its moist, crustless rolls, first created by an in-house German baker named Ward. Parker House, the oldest continuously operating hotel in the United States, still serves Parker House rolls today.

Louisa May Alcott to the Alcott Family

Dinan June 1st, 1870.

My dearest People,

I am so mad at Lorings doings and letter that I must begin a new budget to you, by way of frothing my wrath. The dreadful man says that he has a *right to print as many editions as [he] likes for fourteen years!* What rights has an author then I beg to know? and where does "the *courtesy*" of a publisher come in? He has sent me a book and if you hear I'm dead, you may know that a sight of the *picters* slew me, for I expect to have fits when I behold Sylvia with a top-knot, Moore with mutton chop whiskers, and Adam in the inevitable checkered trousers which all modern kinds wear.[1] If the law gives over an author and her work to such slaverey, as L. says, I shall write no more books but take in washing, and say adieu to glory.

Now having let off steam, I will close this portion of my discourse, only adding that my family and friends will deeply oblige me by stating from the house-tops, on all occassions, that I don't consent or approve, and am an injured party ever more.

We are now in great excitement over Gaston, who has lately become so very amiable that we don't know him. We began by letting the spoilt child severely alone. This treatment worked well, and now he offers us things at

FIGURE 33. Alice Bartlett
and Gaston Forney,
Dinan, France (1870).
*Louisa May Alcott's
Orchard House/L. M. A.
Memorial Association.*

table, bows when we enter, and today presented us with green tulips, violet shrubs and queer medals all round. We have let little bits of news leak out about us, and they think we are dukes and duchesses in Amerique, and pronounce us "tres spirituelle, tres charmmante, tres seductive femmes." We grin[2] in private and are now used to having the entire company rise when we enter and embrace us with ardor, listen with uplifted hands and shrieks of "Mon Dieu," "grand ciel" &c. to all our remarks and point us out in public as "Les dames Amercaine." Such is fame!

An English lady arrived to day, a Mrs Braxton, dressed with English taste in a little green skirt, pink calico waist, a large crumpled frill, her hair in a tight knot, one front tooth sticking straight out, and a golden oriole in a large cage. She is about forty, very meek and "pursy," and the old ladies have been sitting in a heap since breakfast, talking like mad.

May has *sack* on the brain just now and Alice has *hose* on the brain, and at this moment they are both gabbling wildly, one saying, "I shall trim it with blue and have it pinked," the other shrieking "My *hose* must be red with little dragons in black all over it like small pox" and the bird flies to her upper perch in dismay at the riot, while I sit and laugh with an occasional duennaish: "Young ladies, less noise if you please."

It rained last eve, and we are waiting for it to dry before going out in the donkey chaz to buy a warm bun and some strawberries for lunch, to be eaten as we parade the town and drink ale at intervals.

I have lost my dear old Dr. It seems that *William* only took his brother's place while he went to England, and when *John* returned, old Billy washed his hands of the patients, put on *knickerbockers* and begin to disport himself. Imagine my feelings when I beheld his manly form in loose grey knee breeches, long hose and hightops! I was fond of *William*, for he had assuaged my woe, and I was so deeply grateful that the girls advised me to pay my bill by offering him those fossil remains known as my affections. I was thinking seriously of it, but the *knickerbockers* gave me such a shock that I abandoned the idea feeling that I really *could* not walk to the alter beside the worthy man whose "*figger*" was like the enclosed sketch. Alice calls me "Lucretria Borgia," and did the accompanying gem.[3]

The brother M.D. comes now, but I don't like him. He is a handsomish widower with two daughters, and you know, I have Welleresque horror of widowers.[4] He dresses very richly, has a military moustache, and fine manners. I prefer dear, simple, jolly old Billy, who troops by often as brisk and gay as a stout grey headed boy, and leaves pictures for us, and nods and attitudinizes with his well developed legs, of which I suspect he is triple proud, and well he may be, for Colonel May's were not more imposing![5]

I am better, and feel as if steadily improving on my one medicine, and plenty of good food and wine *ad libatim*.

Ma and Pa's letters came this morning and were highly satisfactory, though why they did'nt put the two in one envelope was not clear to our minds. We did not write from Morlaix where we spent only two days. Don't forget to tell us how many letters you have got.

I am glad Pa is made over as good as new, and Ma is *sixteen*, Bless 'em both! I don't think I shall need Dr. Smedley, but hope he will cure dear Nan.[6] If you could see us eat, you would feel that "getting pink" was an impossibility in France. I look fat and May plumps up "wisibly afore my werry eyes." Alice gets strong and brown, seldom coughs, and is a trump of the finest water. We live like three turtle doves all coo and no peck. Dear old Coste is desolated at [the] thought of our leaving and cannot do enough for the "chere damoiselles."

X X X[7]

I don't think we shall meet Baker unless we go to Germany. Do tell me how things are about my pictures. I see they are advertised, and if they sell I want my share of the profits. Chase at Doll's knows about it—I think. Send one of those that are in the market after taking off the heavy card.

Now that our letters begin to go right, I hope you have got all ours. We mailed last Friday, another Monday and today Thursday June 2nd. We send off this for Saturday's steamer.

Love to all and the best of luck.

Ever Your Lu.[8]

MS: Unlocated; copy by ABA at Houghton Library, Harvard University. Partially printed: Cheney 227–29. Cheney incorrectly includes a portion of this letter in another letter dated 4 June 1870 to Anna A. Pratt.

1. Sylvia Yule, Geoffrey Moore, and Adam Warwick are the main characters in *Moods*. Loring had commissioned new illustrations for his 1870 edition. LMA evidently did not own the copyright to *Moods* because when Loring was closing his publishing business, he sold LMA the rights to *Moods*, along with the printing plates (see Loring to LMA, 19 August 1881, Barett Collection, University of Virginia). LMA revised *Moods* and Roberts Brothers printed the new edition in January 1882.

2. The word "grin" was crossed out and "laugh" inserted in pencil.

3. Alice Bartlett's sketch is located at the Houghton Library, Harvard University (*59M-314). At the top is written "Sweet William"; at the bottom is "Lucretia Borgia."

4. LMA's reference is to chapter 20 of Charles Dickens's *The Posthumous Papers of the Pickwick Club* (1836–37). She paraphrases Tony Weller, who tells his son, Sam Weller, to be wary of "widders": "Take example by your father, my boy, and be wery careful o' widders all your life." *The Pickwick Papers* (New York: Penguin, 1999): 267.

5. Col. Joseph May (1760–1841), Abigail's father, was a Boston merchant. He had served as commander of Boston's Cadet Corps during the Revolution, thus obtaining the honorary title of "Colonel."

6. Dr. Alvin H. Smedley was the principal physician at the Tremont Eye and Ear Institute, located at 129 Tremont Street in Boston. He was treating ABA for hearing problems. Anna also had hearing problems; by the time she was middle-aged, her hearing loss was acute. In his manuscript diary entry for 6 May 1870, Bronson wrote that Abigail, after receiving one of the early letters from Dinan, "was made 16 by the intelligence" (*Diary for 1870* 257). This news was probably conveyed to the sisters in a recent letter from home.

7. The X's appear in ABA's manuscript. They could symbolize "kisses," or they could indicate that ABA cut material out of LMA's original letter. They could also serve as a break in the letter, perhaps separating the more personal comments about the sale of LMA's photographs (a comment she probably would not want read aloud) from the rest of the letter. It is not apparent what LMA or ABA meant by the X's.

8. After the closing, ABA adds the following: "A note to Freddie and Johny not copied in this collection."

May Alcott to Abigail Alcott

Dinan June 1st 1870.

Dear Mother,

As I sent the last envelope full of sketches and notes, I shall leave this for Lu to fill, and only tell you how much better she looks and seems. For example; last night she took no pill, but had quite a fair amount of sleep without it, and her limb pains her much less than it did. She eats well, and enjoys the fresh potatoes, peas, and immense strawberries which we are having now, very much. I must sketch the size of one of them which I eat this morning, as at home we never have such large ones.

[May's sketches of three strawberries go across the page with
the following captions]

the Ideal	the True berry	the Real
by Alcott	by L.M.A.	by Bartlett

I know you will be delighted with the very characteristic sketches on the opposite page, but really mine is none too large for many that I have eaten last week. Lu has just returned from taking a bath, and having eaten a luncheon of a plummy bun, bread and butter, with a glass of strong brandy and water, and now feeling rather chipper insists on drawing the *thin* strawberry for your amusement. It seems so funny to have to go out of the house for one's bath, as all the water being brought from the fountains some way off, by maids, it is impossible to have enough for a bath in the house without great trouble, and a *warm* one is entirely out of the question, there being no way of warming a large quantity of their funny little cooking things. So the French people said some time ago, that a dreadful drought they had here was certainly owing to the English using so much water for their baths. When we want a weekly scrub, we trot to the neat little houses in a funny nook, and there lie and soak, drinking something spirituous afterwards to keep us from getting colds.

Alice has given me a lovely long trail white skirt with a wide frill round the bottom to wear with a nice dress. She is very generous, and gives away her things right and left, having already given me a nice thick black poplin dress, a cloak and white saque,[1] all of which I am very grateful for. I only wish we had left some of our thick jackets and outside things at home for you and Nan, as we have'nt used many of them, and gave several of them to the stewardess, as we can't lug them around with us. If Nan wants that thick tight fitting blue outside sacque I left at home, she is welcome to it, as I shall never want it again.

Gaston Fournier has given [me?] a very valuable coin to have set as a locket; for they are very handsome and quite the fashion. Gaston proposes escorting us part way on our journey when we part on the 15th as we now propose doing.

I hope you have received the various illustrated letters.

May.

MS: Unlocated; copy by ABA at Houghton Library, Harvard University.

1. Poplin is a sturdy ribbed fabric, often made of cotton. A saque (also "sacque" or "sack") is a type of loose-fitting coat, the back hanging straight from the shoulders.

Louisa May Alcott to Anna Alcott Pratt

Dinan June 4th 1870.

All well.}

My Dear Nan,

Every one has gone to the grand pic nic but me, and I beguile my solitude by scribbling to my Betsey. I have just seen them off, in a great 'Bus, as gay as larks. Both the Dr.s Kane, the two daughters, Madame Forney, and her Gaston in full Breton rig, both our old ladies with May, Alice, Mrs Baxton, a *bonne*[1] in her quaint cap to wait at table. They started from the Porte St. Louis in great style, all the place turning out to see them go. May was a landscape in her blue cambric, and Alice in white piquè[2] perched on the top of the 'Bus with my Billy between them in his grey suit as gay as an old cock-robin. Behind him on the roof of the 'Bus in another perch was Pa Kane Amy the pretty daughter and Gaston who is "paying attention" as the country folks say. Inside are stored the "provisions" and the old ladies, all gabbling, smiling and wagging their funny bonnets, as tickled as children at the fun. They all kindly wailed and were "desolated" that I did'nt go, but it is twenty miles each way, and I get so tired with a little easy drive that I thought I would'nt take my poor bones so far, for I have to be very choice of 'em, or they drive me mad with pain. Away rumbles the party and I come back to the empty house with the four maids to fuss over me and "guard Mademoiselle" as Francoise says, shouldering her broom valiantly.

It is a perfect day and they will have a jolly time for which I am glad, as the girls are spoiling for a little fun and enjoy this sort of thing better than the queer French calls and parties in the house. The Kanes being English make it nice for May who is lost among Frenchfolks, and Alice who likes to plague Gaston who puts on killing airs and tries to get up a flirtation. Alice can be very fascinating if she likes, and when she wears white with little bows and gems bedropped here and there, the effect is quite captivating, though she is not pretty. May is absorbed in her sketching and lets the youth prance before her unheeded. She has done two pictures—one of the

FIGURE 34. "Mlle Kane," daughter of
Dr. John Kane, Dinan, France (1870), by
May Alcott. *Louisa May Alcott's Orchard
House/L. M. A. Memorial Association.*

FIGURE 35. Madame
Coste, Dinan, France
(ca. 1870). *Louisa
May Alcott's Orchard
House/L. M. A.
Memorial Association.*

old Duchess Anne's clock tower, and one of the *ruined Abbey Beaumaniors, which* are very fine.[3]

Dear old Costé gave me her photograph and was so pleased when I said I should send it to "ma mere" that I put it in. Please mount and keep it for me [see figure 35]. I will have one taken of your Sairy in her new rig that you may behold the gorgeous being in her grey silk and "ample hat."

It is after nine and at ten the Post comes round. I hope for a letter from you and shall weep copiously if I don't get one. 10.A.M. The Post has been but only left a letter from Italy for Alice. "Now she madded." Never mind, it will come round some time and I always have to wait for my things.

The only event of interest is the arrival of [the] English Edition of O. F. G. It is very handsome, scarlet and gold, with gilt edges and type that would delight father. Initial letters to the chapters and all very elegant. I suppose Niles will have one which you can see. Sampson and Low write me very polite notes and sent me a printed agreement to sign, giving them the "sole right to print during the legal term of copy right."[4]

If that means fourteen years as Loring says, I prefer not to do it, but should wait to hear from Niles about it before I sign. I think by their getting up such an elaborate edition, they might think well of it, and a cheaper edition of 2000 is to come.—The brother of Niles [see figure 36] also wrote to me, and they all seem much interested in the affair.[5] I have written to T. Niles, so you need not show him this. [I don't want my letters shown about or read to every one. Concord people are such gossips, I shall never put in any private plans, but trust to Ma's discretion not to tell C. and T. everything].[6]

I wish the boys had been with us the other day when we went driving, for we had a funny scene with a little black lamb. A flock were feeding by the road and all the rest ran away, when our dog Flo came trotting along, but one little bit of a black lamb didn't run, he put his head down and charged straight at Flo, who was twice as big, but not half so brave. Flo was scared at first and barked and went under the carriage, but Lammie pounced right after him and went butting among the wheels bent on giving Flo a good poke. They kept it up and were so funny that we stopped to see the fight. Such a plucky little chap as that brute was I never saw. He hopped at the horse, he chased Flo out of the road, he stood on his hind legs and pawed at us, he baaed and skipped, and tumbled down and didn't mind a bit, and all the flock stood and admired him till we drove off, and left him flying round after another carriage as bold as a little lion. I wish I could paint him for he was as black as ink, with yellow eyes and a little tail that flapped wildly against his legs, as he hopped and ran.

The present excitement is the wood, which Coste is having put in. Loads keep coming in queer heavy carts drawn by four horses each and two men to work the machine. Two men chop the gnarly oak stumps, and a woman puts it in down cellar by the armfull. The men get two francs a day, 40 cts. (Wouldn't our $3,00 a day workmen howl at that sort of wages!) When several carts arrive at once the place is a lively scene. Just now, there were three carts and twelve horses and eight were all up in a snarl, while half a dozen ladies stood at their doors and gave advice. One had a half-dressed baby in

London August 17th '71

FIGURE 36. William Niles, London
(May 1871), by May Alcott. *Houghton
Library, Harvard University.*

her arms, one a lettuce she was washing, another her distaff, and a fourth her little bowl of soup, which she ate at on the side walk in the intervals of gesticulating so frantically that her sabots rattled on the stones. The horses had a freefight and the man couldn't seem to manage one big grey one who romped about like a mad elephant, till the lady with [the] baby suddenly set the half naked cherub on the doorstep, charged in among the rampant beasts, and by some magic howl or jerk brought the bad horse to order, when she quietly returned to her baby, who had sat placidly eating dirt, and with a calm "Voila messieurs," she whipped little Jean into his shirt, and the men sat down to smoke.

Thursday, June 9. Private.

Nans letter dated May 23 has just come, the envelope so worn out that it was tied up with cord and sealed by Munroe and Co. I don't know where Nans others are; we have had only one from her. Why ours are so late, I *dont* see. We keep sending off great fat letters full of pictures and things and you never seem to get them. It's too bad.

I have no news to add, so will only reply to your letter. I'm disgusted that Barton did n't get his letter. I will write again and send it to you, so you can be sure that he gets it. It was very sweet in them to send the picture of old Lu, and I'm glad you like it. We have had a photograph taken to day of all three and will send next time when it is done.[7]

About "Hearth and Home". I don't wish any notice, but suppose I must, so Pa can give a few facts, when born and where, and just the most interesting bits of my life, Allens picture [see figure 37] or none.[8] Thank Marshall for keeping his word.[9] His pictures are vile.

I have blown Loring up and beg him not to say that "I think Moods" as it is "my best work," but as it was. He is a provoking man and ought in decency to have let me know his plan in time to change if I liked. I wish Niles would tell me what to do about Sampson and Low.

The Atlantic for June has a cool notice of O. F. G. Would like to see Curtis's?[10]

I'm so glad Mrs. C_____ is so nice and hope it will last: my respects to her.[11]

Tell Donny not to hurt the little turtles any more.[12] It was funny. I could

FIGURE 37. Louisa May
Alcott, by E. L. Allen,
Boston (ca. 1870).
*Louisa May Alcott's
Orchard House/L. M. A.
Memorial Association.*

see him swelling up red and blowzy splashing away. I send them my bird's
tail, it came out as I was catching the little toad to put him to bed. He dont
seem to mind but looks very droll without it. I am very sorry to hear about
John.[13] I wish he would try my iodine of potash. It has done me good and
he can take it without getting sick or changing habits, food, &c. I'll send
Dr. Kane's prescription, if he likes. It is simple and I have faith in it. Dear
old boy, give him the lovingest kiss that ever was, and tell him to meddle
in my affairs as much as he likes. Thank him. Dont have "Flower Fables"[14]
printed, for God's sake, or any other old thing—and if Loring writes lies
about "*Moods*," put a notice in the Transcript contradicting him.[15] I have
fears that Fuller will "bust" out, so keep an eye on him.[16] I forbid any book of
little tales, and have a *right* to do it Niles says. O dear, what a bother fame is,
aint it? Glad you had a nice time on the 23rd. I've told you many times how

I do, so will only repeat that, I'm better—voice very well though not clear, leg a plague at night, but improving! general health much better. Clothes all right. My photograph will show the new grey silk and "ample hat." My skirts were tucked in to get the figures into the same picture, which is not nice or flowing.

I think Concord must be awful with the Rs and other R's.[17] Glad I'm not there. What color is the new carpet? Is'nt it queer about A_____? Blow up Mrs. Singleton and get my letter.[18] Its mean[?]. Love to my Bartons. Glad you gave "Susta"[?] a picture.[19] Send me one.

Dinan is not near Rennes, Marmee, it is not far from Brest, southward.[20]

We go to Dr. K's to day to tea and croquet. They are very kind. Dr. William likes May very much; the girls are quite nice.

Now goodbye, my lovey. Keep a writing and in time we shall get them. Put on what steamer you send by.

Your Lu.

MS: Unlocated; manuscript copy by ABA in Houghton Library, Harvard University. Partially printed: Cheney 227–29.

1. The underlining and the previous comma were later inserted in pencil.

2. Cambric is a thin linen or cotton fabric; pique is a woven, ribbed fabric, made from natural fibers, such as silk or cotton.

3. May's sketch of Anne of Brittany's tower, often called the castle of Dinan, has not been located. May perhaps confused the castle, which does not contain a clock tower, for the nearby Carrefour d'Horloge, which has a tall granite clock tower. The ruined abbey, La Chapelle des Beaumanoirs, is in Lehon and, though roofless, it features a circular archway entrance. It was also the burial place of the Beaumanoirs family. See May's sketch (figure 19). LMA, inspired by her visit, later published the story "The Banner of Beaumanoir" in *St. Nicholas* 11.8 (June 1884); it was reprinted in *Spinning-Wheel Stories* (Boston: Roberts Brothers, 1884).

4. Sampson Low and Marston, located at 188 Fleet Street, London, would become LMA's official British publisher. Sampson Low (1797–1886), who had been involved in the book business since 1819, began his career as a publisher in 1848. Edward Marston (1825–1914) joined the firm in 1856. Low retired from the firm in 1875. The firm had written to LMA on 21 May 1870, forwarding two agreements for her to sign and promised to give her £20 since profits would not be immediately forthcoming. Thomas Niles wrote LMA on 8 June: "The sum and substance of Lows agreement is, that they agree to pay you one half the profits of every edition of O. F. G. which they print, *after they are sold,*

said profits being, the amount of sales calculated at ⅓ off from retail price, 13 or 12, less cost of printing &c. I should sign it by all means. As you say, you are at their mercy, but you can't lose any thing by signing it. On the contrary, if the book should prove to be a success in England, the house is an honorable & responsible one, and you would undoubtedly receive your share of the profits in exact accordance with the agreement" (ALS: Houghton Library, Harvard University).

5. William Niles, brother of Thomas Niles, served as Roberts Brothers's representative in England.

6. Brackets appear in the manuscript. C. is probably Ellery Channing, poet and Thoreau's first biographer, as the Alcott sisters refer to him several times in their European correspondence as being a town gossip. T. is probably Thomas Niles (LMA often refers to him as "Tom" or "Tommy"), as she suggests that he was often too free in sharing or publicizing the information she sent in her letters to him.

7. A photograph of the three women has not been located.

8. F. B. Sanborn's unsigned biographical sketch of LMA, titled "The Author of 'Little Women,'" would appear in the 16 July 1870 issue of *Hearth and Home*. The front-page article depicted an engraving of LMA, made from a photograph taken by E. L. Allen of Boston just before LMA traveled to Europe. Alcott liked Sanborn's piece but disliked the engraving and wrote across her copy: "Not a good likeness—Too dark, & nose all wrong" (See figure 50).

9. Augustus Marshall, in 1870, operated a photograph studio at 147 Tremont Street, Boston.

10. The unsigned review of *An Old-Fashioned Girl*, which appeared in the June 1870 *Atlantic Monthly*, began: "If we said that Miss Alcott, as a writer for young people just getting to be young ladies and gentlemen, deserved the great good luck that has attended her books, we should be using an unprofessional frankness and putting in print something we might be sorry for after the story of the 'Old-fashioned Girl' had grown colder in our minds." Later the reviewer asks: "we rather wonder where the power of the story lies." The review ends by calling the novel "charming and comfortable" (752–53). Probably George William Curtis (1824–92), novelist, essayist, lecturer (he also spent two years at the transcendentalist community Brook Farm), who became an editor of *Harper's Weekly* in 1863. No review by "Curtis" has been located. Curtis did, however, frequently write "The Editor's Easy Chair" and "The Editor's Literary Record" for *Harper's New Monthly Magazine*. In *Harper's* "Editor's Literary Record" for June 1870, an unsigned review of *An Old-Fashioned Girl* does appear, which states the book "belongs in a class by itself, being neither quite young enough for a children's story, nor quite old enough for a novel" (144).

11. Most likely Mrs. Conant. ABA, giving only the initial "C," draws a blank in the manuscript.

12. John Sewall Pratt, who turned five in 1870, was often called "Donny" as a child.

13. John Bridge Pratt, who complained of ill health throughout the summer, would die on 27 November 1870.

14. *Flower Fables*, LMA's collection of peaceful nature fairy tales inspired by Thoreau and first told as stories to Ellen Emerson, RWE's older daughter, was published by George W. Briggs of Boston in December 1854.

15. After the success of *Little Women*, Loring would publish several editions of *Moods* without LMA's permission, often giving the impression it was a "new" work.

16. Horace B. Fuller (1836–99) was the Boston publisher of *Merry's Museum*, a children's periodical that LMA edited and contributed to from January 1868 to December 1869. Fuller had also published LMA's *Morning-Glories, and Other Stories* in January 1868.

17. Probably Dr. Arthur Ricketson, who had recently moved to Concord, and his parents, Daniel and Louisa Ricketson. ABA later notes in his 12 September entry of his manuscript *Diary for 1870*: "Ricketson from New Bedford is here. A friend of Thoreau's and Channing's" (591).

18. A. is unidentified. Mrs. Singleton is probably a friend of the Alcott sisters when they lived at 43 Pinckney Street in Boston. See LMA to the Bartons, 17 June 1870.

19. "Susta" ("sister") may be a reference to May, suggesting that Anna sent May her photograph but not LMA.

20. Rennes, southeast of Dinan, lies further inland and was once the capital of Brittany; however, Murray's *Handbook* (1870) notes that it contains "few antiquities" and had "an entirely modern aspect" (130).

May Alcott to Abigail Alcott

Dinan June 5th 1870.

Dearest Mother,

Lu has told you about the starting off of the pic nic party yesterday. And I can only add that the whole excursion was a perfect success and I enjoyed it much, as it is great fun to drive through this lovely country on the top of a high diligence with pleasant people to talk to, and eat one's dinner in a lovely grove under shadows of great embattled towers, situated on a cliff, commanding the most superb view I ever beheld. After partaking of Gooseberry which I tasted for the first time, and found truly delicious, (which pleased the Kane's immensely) we sketched the towers, and then went to the little Chapel, famous for its painted windows and fine architecture.[1] I revelled in this as it suited my taste better than any church I have yet seen. Then having sang to the company, we mounted our 'bus, I being escorted by the gallant Dr. Kane, whom I like very much. We drove home, eating strawberries at intervals, singing college songs which were new to them and which they enjoyed exceedingly, and taking infinite satisfaction myself in the surrounding landscape glorifyed by the light of the setting sun. We did'nt get to bed till late, and this morning all the household seems rather used up and decidedly sleepy. Dr. Kane asked me to accept a Japanese umbrella, which is large when open, but shuts up in a very compact and convenient way, and is quite a swell concern. We also have bought a little tiny pair of sabots as ornaments, and the children will delight to see what queer things the young folk's here wear on their feet.

I have been painting a box for Alice in scarlet and black with black dragons round the keyhole and elaborate borders everywhere. She is delighted with it, and is very grateful for any little attention from us. She is very lively and entertaining and I am already much attached to her. She insisted on my riding her horse the other day while she and Lu went in the carriage, and I had a good tear over the hills often saying to myself can this be May Alcott mounted on a fine horse careening over La belle France. It seemed very strange, but was enchanting nevertheless. I am having very good times as Gaston is very devoted and goes sketching with me a good deal. I have sketched Gaston and Madame Fornier for you to see when I come [see figures 38 and 39]. I am very well, and if Lu could only be so, shouldn't have a wish ungratified. I have taken to filling a small sketch book with pen and ink likenesses of people about me and shall have a large collection for your benefit.

your May

MS: Unlocated; copy by ABA at Houghton Library, Harvard University.
1. The chapel is unidentified.

FIGURE 38. Gaston Forney, Dinan, France (1870), by May Alcott.
Houghton Library, Harvard University.

CH 97/8   *Madame Fornier*

FIGURE 39. Madame Forney, Dinan, France (1870), by May Alcott.
Louisa May Alcott's Orchard House/L. M. A. Memorial Association.

Louisa May Alcott to the Alcott Family

Hotel D'Universe

Tours June 17th 1870.

Dearest people,

Our wanderings have begun again, and here we are in this fine old city, in a cosy Hotel as independent and happy as three old girls can be.[1] We left Dinan Wednesday at 7 a.m. Gaston got up to see us off, a most unusual and unexpected honor. Also Mrs. Baxton and all the old ladies, whom we left dissolved in tears.

We had a lovely sail down the Rance to St. Malo where we breakfasted at Hotel Franklin, a quaint old house in a flowery corner.[2] At 12. we went by rail to Le Mans[3] a long trip, and arrived at 6. so tired that we went to bed in the moonlight while a band played in the square before the Hotel, and the side walks before the Cafe's were full of people taking ices and coffee round little tables. Next morning we went to see the famous Cathedral and had raptures, for it is like a dream in stone.[4] Pure Gothic of the 12th century with the tomb of Berengaria, wife of Coeur de Leon,[5] stained glass of the richest kind, dim old chapels with lamps burning, a gorgeous high altar, all crimson gold and ermine, and several organs. Anything more lovely and divine I never saw, for the arches so light and graceful seemed to soar up one above the other like the natural curves of trees, or the rise and [fall] of a great fountain. We spent a long time here, and I sat alone in the quaint old chapel with my eyes and heart full, and prayed a little prayer for my dear family. Old women and men knelt about in corners telling their beads and the priest was quietly saying his prayers at the altar. Outside it was a pile of grey stone with towers and airy pinnacles full of carved saints and busy rooks. I don't think we shall see any thing finer anywhere. It was very hot, for there had been no rain for four months, so we decided to start for town at 5. and get in about 8 as it is light then.

We had a pleasant trip in the cool of the day and found Tours a great city like Paris, on a small scale. Our Hotel is on the Boulevard, and the trees, fountains, and fine carriages make our windows very interesting. We popped into bed early and my bones are so much better that I slept without any opium or anything. A feat I have not performed for some time.

This morning we had coffee and rolls in bed; then as it was a fine cool day we dressed up clean and nice and went out for a walk. At the P.O. office we found your letters of May 31st,—one from Nan and Ma, and one from Loring, so we exalted, and went into the gardens and read them in bliss, with the Grand Cathedral right before us. Cathedral St Gatien, 12th century, with tombs of Charles VIII's children, the armor of St Louis, fine pictures of St. Martin dividing his cloak &c.[6] May will tell you about it and I shall put in a photograph if I can find one.

We are now—12 o'clock—in our pleasant room all round the table writing letters and resting for another trip by and by.

The Fëte Dieu is on Monday, very splendid, and we shall then see the Cathedral in its glory. To-day a few hundred children were having their first communion there, girls all in white, with scarlet boys, crosses, candles, music, priests, &c. Get a Murray and on the map of France follow us to Geneva, via St. Malo, Le Mans, Tours, Amboise, and Blois, Orleans, Nevers, Auxerre[?].[7] We may go to the Vosges instead of the Jura,[8] if Mrs Howe can go, as Alice wants to see her again. But we head for the Alps of some sort, and will report progress as we go.

My money holds out well so far, as we go 2nd class.

Private.

About letters—I think we have got all yours—the first April 12th Nan, Pa and Ma—2nd May 7th Nan 12 pages, Pa and Ma. 3d—May 23rd 8 pages from Nan and one from Ma and Pa dated May 10th and 15, and today, June 17th the last batch dated May 31st from Nan and Ma—5 budgets in full—Now as we are on the move just send all to Munroe's care and we shall keep him advised of our changes, and so miss nothing. He has told us how to send directly and safely to you, and we shall try his way henceforth. Brittany was a very out of the way place and English names puzzled the P.O. folks badly, so I think we have done pretty well on the whole. I am glad you have our letters now, and I will begin with this one and number it, so you will know if you miss any. We write once a week, sometimes oftener, but don't always hit the steamers I guess as we can't know when they go.

Now about dear old John. I can't have him get used up, and he must try my stuff, for I am really getting set up, and my leg is so little painful that I hardly think of it except at night. Tell the dear fellow to wear long woolen stockings and take the stuff after every meal, keep warm and dry and not walk too much, drink a little wine—something to warm the blood. If he can't feel to afford it please buy it with my money (and drink it with my blessing). He is too precious and good to let get run down if filthy lucre can set him up. So I beg and pray *you*, Nan, to see that he has good things and tries what may help him. I send my Dr.s prescription, any apothecary will put it up and it [is] not expensive. Do try it John and get your old poor legs well before you grow an invalid like me. Dr. K says it is probably with John as with me, the calomel he took in his fever out West is showing itself now that he is working hard and the climate is bad for it. Young folks can easily stop the rheumatic tendency only if they go at it in time. Take the iodine three months and perhaps longer: two months and less, have helped me immensely and I think the remedy is worth trying.

I got your letter about the Bartons &c. and shall write to them soon. Glad Mrs C_____ continues good. Dear Mum can sit in state. Cant Dr B. help the feet?[9]

Tom *is* rather—"ahem"—but at this distance I don't mind; it is rather fun to get his letters and notices, and Alice twits me about my rival publishers, for Loring writes long and elaborate letters to "my friend, Miss Alcott."

I am glad the parting don't weigh too heavily on my Sairys tender little heart. I don't feel far away, or in a strange land, and now that I am not in pain all the time, I enjoy my life *so* much, just the mere living and being—Thank the Lord, and sing Hallaluyer!

Dear Marme's letter in pencil was so faint we couldn't half read it, so please write with ink next time, Marmee, dear 'cause all the scribbles are precious now. My curlyheaded Donny! how I do want to see him; and my sober old Fred with big eyes and funny ways. Tell 'em Aunt Weedy saw some houses and barns made in the rocks and it looked very funny to see donkeys and cows and children popping out their heads from the funny doors and windows. Little boys here wear soldier coats and caps when they go to church and take walks, marching with a band playing all boys, and Fred and Jack would like to see the big drums and trumpets with small boys bamming and blowing on 'em.

Now, adieu, my family, keep a writing and we will also, and in time come home, two fat hearty old ladies to rejoice our generation with works of art and virtue.

Bless you, says Lu.

MS: Unlocated; copy by ABA at Houghton Library, Harvard University. Partially printed: Cheney 229–31.

1. Tours, once the capital of La Touraine, is situated in the fertile, flat Loire valley, between the left bank of the Loire River and the right bank of the Cher River. With a population in 1870 of 42,450 people, the city, according to Murray's *Handbook* (1870), "has long been a favourite residence for English, owing to the mildness of the climate and the unusual number of good houses to let" (201). The Hotel D'Universe, noted by Murray's *Handbook* (1870) as "very good and clean," was located on the Boulevard Heurteloup in Tours, France.

2. Hotel Franklin in St. Malo was located just outside of the town near the Casino.

3. Le Mans, an ancient town once occupied by the Romans, is located on the rising left bank of Sarthe River.

4. The Le Mans Cathedral, dedicated to St. Julian, the first bishop of Le Mans, was one of the leading churches of France. It consists of two distinct parts, the nave, dating from the eleventh to twelfth centuries, and the choir and transepts, which were rebuilt in the gothic style on a larger scale after 1217. The stained glass windows on the aisles are noted as among the oldest known. Murray's *Handbook* (1870) states that the choir is "*the crowning glory of the best period of Gothic art in France*" (116).

5. The tomb of Berengaria of Sicily (1163? 1165?–1230), wife of Richard the Lion-Hearted, was relocated to the Le Mans Cathedral from the neighboring abbey of Epan.

6. St. Gatien Cathedral in Tours, named for the saint who introduced Christianity into the Touraine region, sits on the site of two earlier churches in which St. Martin (ca. 316–397) and Gregory of Tours (d. 595) once officiated. Although the cathedral was begun in 1170, it was not completed until the middle of the sixteenth century. In the first chapel to the right of the choir is the tomb of two young sons of Charles VIII (1470–98) and Anne de Brittany (1477–1514). The marble tomb, decorated with the coat of arms of France, dolphins, bas-reliefs, and fleur-de-lis, depict the two princes being watched over by angels. Their early deaths led to the passing of the French throne to the line of Valois Orleans. Murray's *Handbook* (1870) notes: "In the beautiful old painted glass

surrounding the choir, and shedding a venerable gloom about the high altar, may be seen the arms of St. Louis, [and] of his mother, Blanche of Castile" (202). Blanche of Castile (1188–1252) ruled as regent of France from the death of her husband, Louis VIII, in 1226, until her son, Louis IX (1215–70), was old enough to assume the throne in 1234. Louis IX has been the only French monarch to be canonized. St. Martin, Tours's third appointed bishop, is a patron of France and of soldiers. He is often depicted in art as a soldier giving half his cloak to a poor man. Later, he told of a vision in which he saw Jesus wearing the torn cloak.

7. Amboise (population 4,188), located on the left bank of the Loire River, is described by Murray's *Handbook* (1870) as "an old and languid town" (197). Blois, an ancient and picturesque town, with a population of 20,008 inhabitants in 1870, is located on the steep right bank of the Loire River in northern France. Orleans, the ancient capital of Orléanais, is a small city in central France on the right bank of the Loire River. Nevers, a medium-sized town in rural central France, is situated at the confluence of the Loire and Nièvre rivers. Auxerre is located in the Bourgogne region of central France on the Yonne River.

8. The Vosages is a mountain range in central-western Europe. It is geographically located in France, rising along the west side of the Rhine and stretching from Basel, in northwest Switzerland, to Mainz, Germany. The Jura, part of the Alpine mountain system in central Europe, stretches approximately 225 miles along the boundary of eastern France and northwest Switzerland.

9. Dr. Josiah Bartlett (1796–1878) attended Harvard College and practiced medicine in Concord from 1820 until his death. He was the Alcotts' longtime physician.

Louisa May Alcott to the Bartons

Tours June 17th [1870]

My Dear Bartons,

I have only time for a tiny note, but as you never got my long one I must send something in its place & get John to give it safely into your hands.

Thank you very much for your gift to mother. It gratified her deeply & was a very sweet thing to do, though my old face would not be interesting to most people.

I hope it is a cheerful one, for I dont remember Allen's; I had so many they are all jumbled up in my mind. When you look at your copy be sure the original often thinks of you & thanks you very much for this & many other kindnesses.

You will like to know that I am mending fast, & the tiresome old "bones" begin to behave. May is fat, jolly & gay, & enjoys every thing with all her heart. Our friend is a treasure in every sense, & we travel in the most independent way imaginable. We shall have many funny adventures to tell when we get back & you come to Concord & we all sit in a jolly bunch & gossip. Where have you gone to? How do you do? & how does the Singleton flock prosper? Send us a little word some time; it is so pleasant to get letters from home.

May sends love & I am as always

affectionately yours
L. M. A.

Love to Miss Ames & my Francis, also Diane & the rest if you ever see them.

Love to Gracie & the fine doll.[1]

"I'll take" the law of "the old lady" if she loses my letters.[2]

ALS: Berg Collection of English and American Literature, New York Public Library, Astor, Lenox, and Tilden foundations.

1. Most likely these were friends of the Alcotts when they boarded at 43 Pinckney Street in Boston. See LMA to Anna Alcott Pratt, 4–9 June 1870. All are unidentified.

2. Probably Mrs. Singleton. See LMA's letter of 4–9 June 1870 to Anna, where she writes: "Blow up Mrs. Singleton and get my letter." She was probably given one of LMA's letters from Europe to read and had not returned it.

May Alcott to the Alcott Family

Tours June 17th 1870.

Dearest Family,

Lu will tell you about our journey from Dinan here, made during two very hot days, but quite jolly in spite of heat, dust, and dirty cars. At Le Mans we saw the most enchanting cathedral, in all France I thought then, but having just seen the one here, I can't say so now, for of all superb buildings I ever imagined this is the most so, and my second sensation since leaving America, I felt this morning when, turning a sharp corner suddenly we found ourselves in a large square and before us this grand church, with bronze[?] doors, and the whole front covered with the finest and most elaborate ornament, fine windows and bas relief. I was certainly breathless at the sight, and we subsided on a seat opposite the great lion and took sips of it and our letters (which we found awaiting us here,) alternately. After having a large dose of both, we entered the church through the grand door and found rows of little girls all in white receiving their first communion, and priests flourishing about, while the great organ boomed and the choir chanted in a very impressive way. I lost my wits over the fine stained windows which I never thought I should like, but the really fine coloring is beautiful, and here every thing is perfect in form and taste. I found also the best pictures I have yet seen, in the trancpts [i.e., transepts] of this cathedral; one very large of St. Martin dividing his cloak, I enjoyed immensely, and several smaller ones of saints and angels seemed very good coloring to me. But the immensity of both the Le Mans and this one strike me with awe, and it seems disrespectful to enter without falling on ones knees, like all the peasants, and saying a prayer to the good God who put it into the mind of man to make anything so wonderfully beautiful. I shall go there every day while we remain here, as one can't begin to see such a church in one visit; and I want to ascend the tower, as Murray says there is a superb view from it, and these certainly might be more than enough for the climb, as both the main towers of the front are very high.[1] I shall get a little photograph to send you; but no picture can give the very old, mossy, grey color of the stone, or show all sides which are very curious.

We have a lovely cool day for sightseeing, and after our writing are to sally again, and among other things purchase a large trunk, for things accumulate fearfully, and we have no room now, without crushing our clothes very much. This is a fine hotel and we have a lovely room with two canopied beds, large mirrors, bay windows, and a little room leading out of it, which Alice takes. Everywhere she is taken for the maid (as she wears her old dresses for travelling) Lu for the duenna, and I for the lady, which is very

FIGURE 40. Alice Bartlett (ca. 1870). *Louisa May Alcott's Orchard House/L. M. A. Memorial Association.*

amusing, as it really is so entirely the reverse. But the bills are all handed to me, and I am passed about like refreshments instead of being the pack mule of the party as I expected. I do wish I could perform the duties of courier, checking baggage, getting tickets, &c. but not knowing French enough, I can't be trusted to do things right, though if I was left alone, I am quite sure, I could get on perfectly well. Every one takes us for English ladies, and we are treated [with] perfect respect by this most civil nation. The entire order and quiet at the stations surprises me, so different from the rush and confusion at home. Yet every one is served and no one gets left. It would all please father very much, as it is certainly in accordance with his ideas of how things should be done.

FIGURE 41. Alice Bartlett and May Alcott (1870–71?). *Louisa May Alcott's Orchard House/L. M. A. Memorial Association.*

Don't be troubled about your letters, for I think we have received all you have sent, and think you have got almost all that we have written sooner or later. Have you had those containing little sketches of "La Garaye" and other places which I thought mother would enjoy; also little scribbles of our salon and our dressing room at Mdlle Coste's?

I am so sorry about John, and wish I could send him a few bottles of Europe for his rheumatism, as this fine air and Dr. Kane's medicine has certainly worked wonders for Lu, who looks and eats better than she has for several years, growing fat and rosy, and losing that drawn tired look which worried us all before she left home. Alice is also tip-top, and as for me, this luxurious lazy life is making me so fat and well, and you would hardly know me for the old tired thing you saw me in Boston. In short, Europe seems a cure for everything, and I only wish my whole family could be transported here in a feather bed, and put down in one of these healthy little French towns, for it would certainly rejuvenate you all.

We had a grand farewell at Dinan for every one turned out to say good bye, even the stable man and all the garcons "bon voyaged" to us, and Gaston got up at five in the morning to escort us to the boat. We had a most lovely sail in the early morning from Dinan to St. Malo, as you will see by your map, the directions we took to reach the Railroad. But I shall not enlarge[2] as Lu will give you so lively a picture of it that mine would be quite unnecessary.

We shall probably stay here over Sunday as that is a fête day, and there will be much to see.

Was'nt it too bad that two lovely Englishmen arrived at Coste's the night before we left? and we had to tear our selves away. They were very jolly and interested about America and could talk no more French than we, for there would have been great fun. I can't forgive them for not arriving earlier on the scene. However when we get to Switzerland and on the great route of travel I shall expect many adventures to befall us. Yesterday as we went through the street a party of boys stared very hard, and then broke out into a song, each line ending with "the pretty English girls" whereat every one smiled as they sang very pretty.

Give my love to the Rs'[3] and any Concord people who enquire for me.

Your May.

MS: Unlocated; copy by ABA at Houghton Library, Harvard University.

1. The Cathedral of St. Gratien, with its twin towers, each 205 feet high, dominates the city of Tours. Murray's *Handbook* (1870) states that "it will be worth while to ascend the towers for the view, which includes Amboise, Plessis les Tours, and the course of the Loire and the Cher. The woodwork of the roof, a masterpiece of carpentry . . . can be seen at the same time" (203). Begun around 1170, the cathedral was not completed until about 1547, thus accounting for its various architectural designs. The stained-glass windows are considered to be its centerpiece.

2. The word "digress" was deleted and "enlarge" inserted.

3. Probably Dr. and Mrs. Arthur Ricketson, whom May has mentioned several times.

Louisa May Alcott to the Alcott Family

Tours June 20th 1870

Dear People,

Before we go on to fresh "chateaux and churches new" I must tell you about the sights here in this pleasant, clean, handsome, old city. May has done the church for you, and I send a photograph to give some idea of it.[1] The inside is very beautiful, and we go at sunset to see the red light make the grey walls lovely outside and the shadows steal from chapel to chapel inside filling the great church with what is really "a dim religious gloom." We wandered about it the other evening till moonrise and it was very interesting to see the people scattered here and there at their prayers, some kneeling before St. Martin's shrine,[2] some in a flowery little nook dedicated to the infant Christ, and one, a dark corner with a single candle lighting up a fine picture of the Mater Dolorosa, where a widow all in her weeds sat alone crying and praying. In another, a sick old man sat while his old wife knelt by him praying with all her might to St. Gratien, (the patron saint of the church) for her dear old invalid. Nuns and priests glided about, and it was all very poetical and fine till I came to an imposing priest in a first class chapel who was taking snuff and gaping, instead of piously praying.

The Fête Dieu was yesterday, and I went out to see the procession. The streets were hung with old tapestry and sheets covered with flowers. Crosses, crowns, and bouquets were suspended from house to house, and as the procession approached, women ran out and scattered green boughs and rose leaves before the train. A fine band and a lot of red soldiers came first, then two different saints on banners, carried by girls and followed by long trains of girls bearing the different emblems. St. Agnes and her lamb[3] was followed by a flock of pretty young children all in white carrying tall white lillies that filled the air with their fragrance. "Mary Our Mother" was followed by orphans with black ribbons crossed over their breasts. St. Martin led the charity boys in their grey suits &c. The Host under a golden canopy was borne by priests, in gorgeous rig, and every one knelt as it passed with censers swinging, candles burning, boys chanting, and flowers dropping from the windows. A pretty young lady ran out and set her baby on a pile of green leaves in the middle of the street before the Host and it passed over the little thing who sat placidly staring at the show and admiring its blue shoes. I suppose it is a saved and sacred baby henceforth.

It was a fine pageant, and quite touching some of it, but as usual I saw something funny to spoil the solemnity. A very fat and fine priest who walked with his eyes upon his book and sung like a pious bumble bee, suddenly destroyed the effect by rapping a boy over the head with his gold prayer-book as the black sheep strayed a little from the flock. I thought the old saint swore also.

The procession went from the Cathedral to Charlemaignes' Tower, an old old relic, all that is left of the famous church which once covered a great square.[4] We went to see it and the stones looked as if they were able to tell wonderful tales of the scenes they had witnessed all these hundreds of years. I think "*The Reminiscences of a Rook*," would be a good story, for these old towers are full of them, and they are long-lived birds.[5]

Tuesday June 21st [1870]

Amboise, at the
Golden Lion.[6]

Here we go again! now in an utterly different scene from Tours. We left at 5 P.M. and in half an hour were here on the banks of the Loire in a queer little inn where we are considered Duchesses, at least, owing to our big trunks and Alice's good French. I am the Madame, May Mademoiselle and Alice the companion.

Last eve being lovely we went after dinner up to [the] Castle where Charles VIII was born in 1470.[7] The Arab chief Abd-el-Kadar and family were kept prisoners here, and in the old garden is a tomb with the crescent over it where some of them were buried.[8] May was told about the terrace where the Hugonuts hung thick and the Court enjoyed the sight till the Loire choked up with dead bodies forced them to leave.[9] We saw the little low door where Anne of Brittany's first husband Charles VIII "bumped his head" and killed himself as he was running through to play bowls with his wife.[10] It has been modernized and is now being restored as in old times, so the interior was all in a toss. But we went down the winding road inside the tower up which the knights and ladies used to ride. Father would have enjoyed the *pleached* walks, for they are cut so that looking down on them, it is like a green floor, and looking up it is a thick green wall.[11] There also Margaret of Anjou and her son were reconciled to Warwick.[12] Nan will like these bits of history, so I put them in. Read Murray, I beg and see all about it. We sat in the twilight on the terrace and saw what Fred would have liked, a little naked boy ride into the river on one horse after another and swim them round in the deep water till they were all clean and cool.

This morning at 7 we drove to Chenonceaux, the chateux given by Henri II to Diane De Poictiers.[13] It was a lovely day and we went rolling along through the most fruitful country I ever saw. Acre on acre of yellow grain, vineyards miles long, gardens and orchards, full of roses and cherries. The Cher is a fine river winding through the meadows, where haymakers were at work and fat cattle feeding.[14] It was a very happy hour, and the best thing I saw was May's rapturous face opposite me as she sat silently enjoying *every thing*, too happy to talk.

[This is a good lesson in history for her, and she will be ready to read up now, for she knows very little, and begins to find it out; as I do.][15]

The chataux built over the water was very interesting. Catherine de Medicis took it away from Diane when the king died, and her room is still seen as she left it.[16] Also a picture of Diane, a tall simpering woman in a tunic with hounds, stags, cupids and other rubbish round her. The gallery of pictures was fine, for here were old, old portraits and bas reliefs, Agnes Sorel, Montaigne, Rabelais, many kings and queens, and among them La Fayette, and dear old Ben Franklin.[17] There is a little theatre where Rousseau's plays were acted.[18] This place at the time of the Revolution belonged to the grandmother of Geo Sand, and she was so much respected that no harm was done to it.[19] So three cheers for Madame Dupin!! Among the pictures were Ninon D'Enclos and Madame Sevnegne holding a picture of her beloved daughter.[20] The Guidos, &c.[21] I don't care for much, as they were all grimy and convulsive; and I prefered pictures of people who really lived, to these impossible Venuse's and repulsive saints. (Bad taste, but I cant help it) The walls were hung with stamped leather and tapestry, carved chairs in which queens had sat, tables at which kings had eaten, books they had read, and glasses that had reflected their faces were all about, and I just revelled. The old kitchen had a fire place quaint enough to suit Pa, with immense turn-spits, cranes, andirons, &c. The chapel balcony, avenue, draw-bridge, and all the other pleasing bits were enjoyed, and I stole a sprig of jasmine from the terrace which I shall press for Marmee. [Pray take extra care of the photographs for if lost, we cannot replace them, and I want to make a fine Album of pictures with flowers and descriptions after I get home.][22]

We got back at 11 and had breakfast, then I napped till 3, when the girls went for a bath, and I sit here at the window looking up at the castle walls close before me as I write to you. I am steadily getting better, and my bones improve. I'm fat, and most of the time eat and sleep well. Now and then I get very tired and feel then that I'm not quite "firm fibre" yet. But all goes well and we enjoy much every day.

Love to all. I hope to see letters at Blois where we go tomorrow and shall stay awhile I think.

Lu.

MS: Unlocated; manuscript copy by ABA at Houghton Library, Harvard University. Partially printed: Cheney 231–35.

1. The nave of the Cathedral of St. Gratien has 23 chapels extending off of it. May's sketch of the cathedral has not been located.

2. St. Martin (ca. 316–97), Tours's third appointed bishop, is a patron of France and of soldiers.

3. St. Agnes (ca. 291–304) is the patron saint of chastity, girls, engaged couples, rape victims, and virgins. According to legend, St. Agnes, a Roman, was raised as a Christian. At the age of thirteen, she refused to marry the prefect Sempronius's son and was condemned to death. According to Roman law, however, virgins could not be executed, so she was ordered raped. But supposedly her virginity was preserved. The wood at the stake would not burn, so she was beheaded on January 21, which was later celebrated as her feast day. Often, she is portrayed in artwork with a lamb, as her name sounds like "agnus," the Latin word for "lamb."

4. Tour Charlemagne, so called because Luitgarde, Charlemagne's third wife, is supposedly buried beneath it, was built in the eleventh century and is, along with the Tour du Tresor, the only remains of the vast Cathedral of St. Martin of Tours, which was destroyed in 1790. The two towers are located on either side of the Rue St. Martin.

5. No story entitled "Reminiscences of a Rook" has been located.

6. Murray's *Handbook* (1870) notes the Golden Lion (Lion d'Or) as "cheap and homely" (197). In *Shawl-Straps*, LMA writes: "The Lion d'Or was a quaint place, so like

the inns described in French novels, that one kept expecting to see some of Dumas' heroes come dashing up, all boots, plumes, and pistols, with a love-letter for some court beauty in the castle on the hill beyond" (88).

7. The castle, constructed during the fifteenth and sixteenth centuries, had been, since 1434, the residence of the kings of France and until 1852 belonged to King Louis Philippe.

8. Algerian chief Abd-el-Kadar (1808 83), who had led the Muslim resistance against the French occupation of Algeria, was confined in the castle, which had long been used as a prison, from 1848 until his release by Napoleon III in 1852.

9. Led by Godefroy de Barry, lord of Renaudie, Huguenot conspirators planned to extricate the young King Francis II, from the influence of his Catholic uncles, François, duc de Guise, and Charles, cardinal of Lorraine, in March 1560. The conspiracy of Amboise, however, was foiled. Renaudie was captured and quartered and his body parts hung on the gibbet. Many of the prisoners were hung from the castle walls; others were drowned in the Loire. In all, approximately 1,200 or more Huguenots were killed, and the stench of the dead supposedly drove the royals from the castle.

10. Charles VIII was born in the castle in 1470; he died there in 1498, supposedly from the blow caused by striking his head on a low doorway at the end of the terrace.

11. Pleached walks are formed by intertwining boughs and twigs as in an arbor.

12. In 1470, the exiled Queen Margaret of Anjou (1430–82) and her son were reconciled to their former enemy, Richard Neville, Earl of Warwick. They were united in an attempt to oust King Edward IV and restore her husband, Henry VI, to the throne of England. Eventually, Warwick was killed in battle by Edward IV. Anjou's forces were defeated in May 1471 and her son killed. Her husband was then murdered in the Tower of London. She remained in captivity until the king of France ransomed her in 1474, at which time she returned to France in poverty.

13. Chenonceaux chateau, located about 7.5 miles from Amboise, was built on the Cher River. Constructed by Thomas Bohier, minister to Charles VIII, the chateau was given to the French crown after Bohier was accused of stealing from the royal treasury. In 1547, King Henri II presented it to his mistress Diane de Poitiers, some twenty years his junior. On the king's death in 1559, however, Diane was forced to relinquish the chateau to his widow, Catherine de Médicis, who became the regent of France. She enlarged it and used it for a retreat for almost twenty-five years. After her death, Louise de Lorraine, the wife of Henry III, de Médicis' third son, inherited the estate.

14. The Cher River begins in the Massif Central and flows for approximately two hundred miles northwest through central France to where it joins the Loire below Tours.

15. Brackets appear in the manuscript.

16. Catherine de Médicis' bedroom, decorated with sixteenth-century Flemish tapestries depicting the life of Samson, still retains its original sculpted furniture.

17. Catherine de Médicis (1519–87) was responsible for transforming the chateau into one of the most beautiful estates in France. She had a two-storied gallery, sixty meters long with eighteen windows, constructed over the bridge Diane had built to link the chateau to the bank of the Cher. The portrait of Diane as Diana, the Greek goddess of the hunt, by Le Primatice, from the Fontainebleau school, was painted at the chateau in 1556. Among the famous personages LMA mentions are the following: Agnès Sorel (ca. 1422–50), the acknowledged mistress of Charles VII of France from 1444 until her death; Michel (Eyquem) de Montaigne (1533–92), writer, lawyer, French courtier during the reign of Charles IX, most noted as the author of *Essays* (1572); François Rabelais (1483–ca. 1553), French writer and physician noted for his satirical works, such as *Gargantua* (1534); Marquis de Lafayette (1757–1834), French aristocrat who fought with American patriots during the Revolution and was appointed major general in 1777; Benjamin Franklin (1706–90), author, inventor, statesman, who, among his many accomplishments, served as minister to France during the American Revolution.

18. Jean-Jacques Rousseau (1712–78), French author and philosopher, tutored Madame Dupin's son at the chateau in 1747, a task that would later inspire his famous work about the education of children, *Emile* (1762). According to Murray's *Handbook* (1870), Rousseau's opera *Le Devin du Village* (1752) was performed for the first time at the chateau (200).

19. Madame Dupin (1706–99), grandmother (by marriage) of the French writer George Sand, bought the chateau in 1733. Her kind reputation spared the estate from destruction during the French Revolution.

20. Ninon de Lenclos, also called Anne de Lenclos (1620–1705), was a celebrated French courtesan. In 1632, she established a salon that attracted many prominent figures. Her scandalous attitude, however, caused King Louis XIV's mother, Anne of Austria, to have her confined to a convent in 1656. Sympathizers secured her release, and she defended her philosophy in *The Coquette Avenged* (1659). Madame de Sévigné, Marie de Rabutin-Chantal (1626–96), was of minor nobility but had access to the French royal court. She is most noted for her *Correspondence*, dating from 1648–96, during the reign of Louis XIV. Most of the correspondence covers a twenty-three-year period in which she wrote long letters twice a week from Paris to her daughter in Provence.

21. "Guidos" is probably LMA's derogatory term for Italian painters.

22. Brackets appear in the manuscript.

May Alcott to A. Bronson Alcott

Tours June 20th 1870.

Dear Father,

After having been to high mass, this morning, and seen the grand procession, I want to refresh myself by writing to you. I do wish you were here to sit with me in the supurb cathedral and enjoy the beautiful colored windows, such glass as I never imagined could be made by mortal hands, and I spent most of my time pervading the building, and enjoying the very coloring, which I think so ugly in King's Chapel at home,[1] but here the three primary colors are used only, and contrasted with such exquisite taste as would delight your critical eyes.

Alice and I are now going to vespers, as it is a great fête day, and all the services are particularly interesting.

We sent you day before yesterday a long letter from here, but could not get a photograph of the Cathedral in time to enclose it, but send it in this. It does not begin to give you any notion of the real beauty of this wonderful structure for in walking round it, we decidedly liked the rear hall as well as the front, there being just as elaborate carving about it, and the countless number of flying buttresses gave a light and wonderful effect to the whole. In short, this church can only be described by seeing it. In honor of the day, we found in our room two lovely great bouquts [i.e., bouquets] to give our already palatial apartment a little freshness. We are living in such perfect luxury that Lu often says to me, "May can this be the poor Alcott's travelling about and doing just as they like"! And it really does seem too good to be true. To-morrow we leave Tours for Amboise which you will show the boys on the map, and I shall imagine their little fingers following us along our route to Switzerland, but there are so many lovely places to see between this and the Alps that we shall take it very leisurely and perhaps stay some time at Blois, which, according to Murray, has much we shall want to see. Then from Amboise to Blois, then Orleans, then Bourges, then from Lyons to Geneva where we hope to find some cool peak to perch on for July and

FIGURE 42. Franklin B.
Sanborn. *Louisa May Alcott's
Orchard House/L. M. A.
Memorial Association.*

August.[2] Later our plan is to go to the Italian Lake's, and there, the longed
for Rome, Florence, Sorrento &c.[3] After seeing the best named places with
the addition of Naples and Milan, I shall be quite content to return without
seeing anymore lions for a great while. I have not been homesick yet.

We received your last letter here in which you say you may go to California next winter, which sounds very strange to us, but I suppose the Alcott
fame has even reached there, as it seems to be spreading in every direction
so rapidly.[4] I am very curious to see the notice of Lu in "*Hearth and Home*"
for such an interesting article might be made out of her. But I hardly think
Sanborn will put much imagination into it. [No, Bun is the last person who
should have done it. Lu.][5] Though I think he is as good a person for it as
anyone I know as he has always been such a good friend of yours, and is
interested in the family.

Amboise, June 21st.

We arrived here from town last night, and came to this funny little hotel where our room is on a kind of balcony and partly over a stable, but is picturesque being under the shadow of the great castle which we visited after dinner last night, and found so very interesting that I want to stay some time instead of only a day or two, as now proposed. I am a little tired of castles and wish I could only visit *one a month*, and then I could fully appreciate them. However the view from this one is truly supurb looking off on one side over the windings of the Loire, with the little town beneath its high walls; And on the other side we stood on the long balcony from which the Hugonots were hung, and we looked from the windows where Catherine De Medicis and Mary Queen of Scots witnessed their execution. Over the door of the little chapel is a fine bas relief of St. Hubert meeting the stag. I have got a picture of it, which if there is room, I will send in this envelope.[6] Please mount all the photographs on nice cards, so we can have an interesting Album when we come back.

At 7 oclock we started in a grand barouch[7] for Chenonceaux where we saw the rooms left just as they were used by the Kings and Queens so many years ago. I never enjoyed any thing more in my life, and arranged my hat in Mary Queen of Scots' mirror with great satisfaction.[8] Such tapestry and pictures as they did have and such taste as we don't see now; for fine paintings by Guido, Correggio, and Troyon,[9] beside plenty of other great people, hung everywhere among rich carvings, and supurb but fearfully old furniture all ornamented by the [May draws the royal symbol here] of Henry II and Diana of Poictiers. The whole castle is built on the river Cher, and dining room, kitchen, and servants rooms built in the arches over the water. I don't expect to see anything more interesting in all our travels, as the long gallery of fine portraits[10] in this curious place seemed so alive and the Queens and the surroundings even to smallest things, like pen and ink, hand mirrors used by the Queens &c. kept up [this] illusion so perfect that I began to feel a crown sprouting from my head, and ermine trailing behind me, and it was not till we were whirling along a very dusty road to the hotel, that I could bring my self to think or look at any thing short of royalty.

Friday there is a great fête here with all sorts of attractions, a regatta on the Loire, a balloon ascension, and peasants are to shin up grape poles. The latter performance, I think, will be very amusing, and I want to stay for it all very much.

Good bye, dear father, write again *to me this time* and all of you keep well till we come back, which may be sooner than we planned, if Lu goes on improving in health as fast as she does now.

I hope dear John is better. Tell him I look at my little ring and think of him often.

I never saw Mr. Ives though I heard about him last Summer.[11]

This is'nt the good letter I meant to write, but there is no time for doing better now.

Your loving May.

MS: Unlocated; copy by ABA at Houghton Library, Harvard University.

1. King's Chapel, located at the corner of Tremont and School streets, was organized in 1686 as the first Anglican church in Boston. In 1754, the current church, built of Quincy granite, replaced the original wooden building. Under the Rev. James Freeman, the church became Boston's first Unitarian church in the mid-1780s. Bronson and Abigail Alcott were married there in May 1830.

2. Bourges, the ancient capital of Berry, is located in the middle of flat country at the confluence of the Yevre and Auron rivers in central France. Lyons, located in the eastern part of central France at the confluence of the Rhone and Saône rivers, was founded in 43 BC as a Roman colony. By 1870, it was already a large economic center noted for its silk manufacturing.

3. Sorrento, an ancient town in Campania, Italy, is located on high cliffs rising approximately 160 feet above the Bay of Naples and is enclosed on its other sides by deep gorges. Set amid lemon and orange gardens, the small town was, by the early nineteenth century, a popular tourist location.

4. On 7 June, ABA wrote in his manuscript *Diary for 1870*: "Nothing will suffice, it seems, but for me to belt the continent with talk." He was thinking of arranging for October 1870 "a campaign throughout the great West. Every New Englander should see California" (332).

5. Brackets appear in the manuscript.

6. Located in the garden of the castle and constructed in the form of a cross for Anne of Brittany is a small chapel that Murray's *Handbook* (1870) describes as "one of the most exquisite morsels of profusely Gothic in France" (198). The chapel is dedicated to St. Hubert, whose meeting with the stag is carved above the door. St. Hubert (ca. 656–727), known as the Apostle of Ardennes, was the eldest son of Bertrand, duke of Aquitaine. A courtier, he loved to hunt and once saw a stag that turned to gaze at him. In its antlers,

Hubert perceived a crucifix. A voice warned him that unless he turned to the Lord and led a holy life he would go to hell. On asking what he should do, Hubert was told to find St. Lambert, bishop of Maastricht, who would instruct him. He did so and entered the priesthood. After the murder of Lambert, he became bishop of Maastricht and later was appointed bishop of Liege, where he converted the pagans in the Ardennes region of France. The photograph of the bas-relief of St. Hubert is located at Orchard House.

7. A barouche, a four-wheeled vehicle, had the undercarriage, lower quarter panels, and doors like a coach but had a folding top that covered the backseat. While the driver sat in the front seat, two seats inside the coach allowed four people to sit opposite each other. By the nineteenth century it was popular as a town vehicle in the United States.

8. Mary, Queen of Scots, also known as Mary I of Scotland (1542–87), was crowned queen of Scotland when only nine months old, although she did not assume power until after the death of her mother in 1560. At the age of five, she was sent to France under the protection of the French king, Henri II. On 24 April 1558, she married the dauphin François in Paris, and when the king died in 1559, Mary became queen consort of France and her husband became King François II. Mary was with her mother-in-law Catherine de Médicis during the Huguenot uprising in France on 6–17 March 1560. After François II's death in December 1560, Mary returned to Scotland, but, being a devout Catholic, she was not trusted by many of her subjects nor by her cousin, the Protestant Queen Elizabeth I of England. Mary was eventually put on trial for treason for supposedly trying to stage a Catholic overthrow and assume the crown of England. She was beheaded on 8 February 1587.

9. May possibly is referring to Guido Reni. Antonio da Correggio (1489–1534), the leading painter of the Parma school of the Italian Renaissance, is known for his paintings on both religious and mythological subjects. His art underwent a reevaluation during the age of Romanticism. His paintings "The Martyr" and "The Teaching of Love" (on wood) hang in Chenonceau. Constant Troyon (1810–65), a French painter of the Barbizon school, was well known for his animal paintings. May writes in *Studying Art Abroad* (1879) about visiting Chenonceau and states that "in the apartments of the present occupant (which are occasionally obligingly shown a visitor) are two magnificent Troyons, such as one seldom meets with even in small collections" (66).

10. The word "paintings" was deleted and "portraits" inserted.

11. Louis Thomas Ives (1833–94) was a Detroit artist, who had taken part in ABA's western Conversations. He wanted to arrange a lecture tour in the Midwest and serve as agent for ABA, RWE, and other New England speakers (See *Letters of ABA* 517, 519, 525).

Louisa May Alcott to Abigail Alcott

Dear Marmee,

On this Lizzie's and Donny's birth day,[1] Ill begin a letter to you. The last letter from home was from Pa, and we got it a week ago at Tours. I have a "feelin" that one from you and Nan is somewhere on the way and will soon appear. We found at the Post Restante here two "Moods" and a paper for me. One book from Loring and one from Niles. I think the pictures horrid and sent them floating down the Loire as soon as possible, and put one book at the bottom of my trunk and left the other where no one will find it. I could'nt read the story and try to forget that I ever wrote it. Much obliged to Niles for it. I don't get any letter from him about Sampson Low &c. Why dont he answer the letter I wrote ages ago, and tell me about figuring the agreement?[2] If he has written, the letter is lost and I must answer S. and L. soon or they will think I'm a Hottentot.[3] Ask Niles about it sometime when Pa is in town.

Blois is a noisy, dusty, soldierly city[4] with nothing to admire but the river (nearly dry now with this four months drought,) and the old castle where Francis I, Louis XII, Catherine de Médicis, and other great folks lived. It has been very splendidly restored by the Government, and the ceilings are made with beams blazoned with coats of arms, the walls hung with cameos painted with the same designs as the stamped leather in old times; and the floors inlaid with colored tiles. Brown and gold, scarlet blue and silver, quaint dragons and flowers, porcupines and salamanders, crowns and letters, glittered every where. We saw the guardroom and the very chimney where the Duc de Guise was leaning when the King, Henry III, sent for him; the little door where the king's gentlemen fell upon and stabbed him with forty wounds. The cabinet where the King and his mother plotted the deed, the Chapel where the monks prayed for its success and the great hall where the body lay covered with a cloak till the King came and looked at it and kicked his dead enemy, saying, "I did not think he was so large." We also saw the cell where the brother of the Duc was murdered the next day and the attic entire where their bodies were burnt, after which the ashes were thrown into the Loire by order of the King. The window out of which Marie de Médiciss lowered herself when her son Louis XIII. imprisoned her there. The recess where Catharine de Médiciss died, and many other interesting places.[5] What a set of rascals these old Kings and Queens were!

The Salle des Etats was very georgeous, and here in a week or so are to be tried the men who lately fired at the Emperor.[6] It will be a grand, a fine sight when the great arched hall is full. I got a picture of the castle, and one of a fire place for Pa. It is a mass of gold and color with the porcupine of Louis XII. and the ermine of his wife Anne of Brittany, their arms, in medallion over it.

At 5 P.M. we go onto Orleans for a day where I shall get some relics of Joan of Arc, for Nan.[7] We shall pass Sunday at Bourges where the great church is, and then either to Geneva or the Jura, for a few weeks of rest.

Private

Travelling gets more expensive as we come onto the great routes, for we have to stop at good hotels being women, and sometimes we must go first class when the trams are express. I hate to spend the money, but I'm getting better so fast and enjoying so much that I shall go on till my year is out, and then if the expense is very great, come home and go to work. I have May's washing and sundry little expenses for her which I did'nt expect, but her passage and dress took about all her money and she must be taken care of. I hope July will put a nice little plum "in crib" for us all. Let me know how it is, and what Lorings $12. was for.

Geneva June 29th 1870.

It seems almost like getting home again to be here where I never thought to come again when I went away five years ago with my Weld incumbrances. We are at the Metripole Hotel right on the Lake with a glimpse of Mount Blanc from our windows.[8] It is rather fine after the grimy little Inns of Brittany, and we enjoy a sip of luxury and put on our best gowns with feminine satisfaction after living in old travelling suits for a fortnight.

As we went into dinner yesterday, a voice called out as I passed, "Why Miss Alcott how do you do?" and a handsomely dressed lady at table put out her hand smiling and beaming. It was Mrs Bates whom I saw at Mrs Whipples' party last spring, the sister of the Mr. Howe who flirted and flattered on the same occasion.[9] It was pleasant to see a face I'd ever seen before, and as Alice knew her, and she is here with her brother, husband and three boys, it wont be bad to have them to go round with &c.

As it was rather a long haul from Lyons here we are to rest and write letters today, and tomorrow take the early boat to Villeneuve[10] where Alice's cousins, the Warrens[11] are, and then stay some weeks if we can find a good Pension.

I began my letter at Blois where we spent a day or two. At Orleans we only passed a night, but we had time to see the famous statue of the Maid put up in gratitude by the people of the city she saved. It is a fine statue of Joan in her armor on horseback with her sword drawn. Round the base of the statue are bronze bas-reliefs of her life from the girl with her sheep to the martyr at the stake. They were very fine but dont show much in the photograph which I got for Nan, remembering the time when she translated Schillers' play for me.[12]

At Bourges we saw the great Cathedral, but did'nt like it as well as that in Tours.[13] We only spent a night here, and Alice bought an antique ring of the time of Francis I.: an emerald set in diamonds. It cost $9.00, and is very quaint and handsome.

Moulins we reached Sunday noon, and at 3 oclock went to vespers in the old church[14] where we saw a good deal of mumbo jumbo by red, purple and yellow priests, and heard a boy with a lovely voice sing up [in] the hidden choir like a little angel among the clouds. Alice had a fancy to stay a week if we could find rooms out of the town in some farm house, for the handsome white cattle have captivated her, and we were rather tired. So the old lady at the Hotel said she had a little summer house out in the fields and we should go and see it with her in basket chay. After dinner we all piled in and went along a dusty road to a little dirty garden house with two rooms and a few cabbages and rose bushes round it. She said we could sleep and eat at the Hotel and come down here for the day. That did'nt suit at all, so we declined and on Monday morning we set out for Lyons. It was a very interesting trip under, over and through the mountains with two engines and much tunneling and up and down grading. May was greatly excited at the queer things we did and never knew that cars could [turn] such sharp corners. We wound about so that we could see the engines whisking out of sight round one corner while we were turning another, and the long tram looked like a snake winding through the hills. The tunnels were so long that lamps were lighted and so cold we put on our sacks while passing in the darkness. The scenery was very fine, and after we left Lyons, where we merely slept, the Alps began to appear, and May and I stared in blissful silence, for we had two fat old men opposite, and a little priest, so young that we called him the Rev. boy. He slept and said his prayers most of the time, stealing sly looks at May's hair, Alice's pretty hands, and my buckled shoes which were like his own and seemed to strike him as a liberty on my part.[15] The old boys were very jolly, especially the one with three chins, who smiled paternally upon us and tried to talk. But we were very English and mum and he thought we didn't understand French and confided to his friend that he didn't see "how the English could travel and know not the French tongue." They sung, gabbled, slept and slapped one another at intervals, and were very amusing till they left, and another very handsome Booth-like priest[16] took their places.

Hurrah! A knock just came to our door, and there was Sophy Bond! We howled and flew at her, and she told us Aunty and Mr. B. were below, so down we rushed and have had a good pow-wow.[17] All very "jolly and kind and so glad to see us." They are going to stay here some time in a Pension, so we shall see more of them. They saw our names in the book this A.M. and Sophy came up at once to find us. They arrived last eve after we did so we did'nt meet at dinner. Auntie is nicely, Sophy very handsome, and Mr B as jolly as ever. A Miss Wells[18] is travelling with them, and they were all in high feather and seemed to think it great larks to meet us here.

Evening.

We have had a busy pleasant day, for after a social chat, May and Sophy went out shopping, and Alice and I went with Mr Bond to the bankers. Then we took a drive. The Bonds are going to stay in a Pension here for a few weeks and we went to see if we could get rooms with them. We could, but not till Saturday, so as Alice's cousins were at the end of the Lake we thought we would only make one more. The Bonds went to their Pension in the P.M. and we called on them in eve and they showed us some lovely pictures. Mr.

B. and Sophy walked home with us, and we sat in the big parlor with some ladies whom they knew talking till 11, when we packed up and went to bed. Next morning at 8 we went to the boat, where Mr. Bond came to see us off, and after a fine sail of three or four hours came to Vevey and drove to Pension Du Rivage, near my old Pension Victoria.[19] A neat pleasant place where we pay 6 francs a day, live well, and have very nice rooms. Russian and English people with a Spanish Bishop are all who are here now. I was so tired that I have done nothing but rest since I came.

FIGURE 43. Alice Bartlett (1870–71?), by May Alcott. *Houghton Library, Harvard University.*

Vevey[20] July 2nd [1870]

Two days at a great Hotel, used me up as much as two weeks of travel. Alice and I both got cold by the way, and have laid round till today, when

A. has gone to see her cousins at Bex[21] and I begin to feel better. Things look very natural here, but more lovely than before, and the girls like it, so we may stay sometime. Aunt and Sophia may join us if Mr. B. goes to Austria. They wanted May to go to Chamonix[22] with them but as it costs about $20, she did'nt feel as if she ought. Mr B. might have invited her, but rich men always feel *so* poor, he did'nt. We telegraphed at once to Paris for our letters but none have come, and we are much disappointed, for there must be a pile somewhere.

I have kept this hoping to acknowledge yours in it, but shall send it off now and wait no longer, or you will think we are lost and gone.

[*Private*][23]

I have got a note from Niles and have signed the agreement. Aunty read me a letter from Lizzy Wells in which she says Mr Wells is very well and old Ben as usual, so they are not dying as you wrote us.[24]

This is a very dull letter, but I dont feel like writing now-a-days and have very little to tell.

5 P.M. May has just brought in some letters but none from you. One from Tilton asking me to write for "The Revolution,"[25] one from Low saying that £20 had been sent to Munroe,[26] and one from Munroe saying he had recieved the money for me, so that is all right. I am much disappointed but hope to get my home budget tomorrow.

Give my love to everyone who wants it, and don't read my letters to everybody for I hate to write if Tom, Dick and Harry are to see 'em.

By, By. It is "morning on the mountains" just now and it is very sweet for July 2nd.

Kiss my lovies.

Your Lu.

MS: Unlocated; manuscript copy by ABA at Houghton Library, Harvard University. Printed: *Selected Letters* 138–44; partially printed: Cheney 235–39.

1. John ("Donny") Sewall Pratt and Elizabeth Sewall Alcott, who died in 1858, shared the birth date of 24 June, she in 1835 and he in 1855.

2. Both Loring and Niles had sent LMA copies of *Moods*. On 8 June 1870, Niles wrote LMA: "I mailed you last week a copy of Loring's 'Moods'. He tells me [he] has printed

4000 & I imagine he may have sold 1000 in paper & 1500 in cloth. If I were you I would not worry about it; it is my opinion that the sales will not be large & all of it caused by the excitement consequent on the success of LW & O. F. G.. See if I am not right." Niles, however, wrote back on 8 November 1870 that the sales of *Moods* were larger than he had predicted: "Loring has not advertised it in newspapers, but *extensively* by hand bills in such a way that the inference was it was a new book. The great sale has been on Rail Roads. You see what *popularity* will do" (ALS: Houghton Library, Harvard University).

3. During LMA's time, "Hottentot" was used to describe a person of inferior intellect or culture.

4. Perhaps LMA refers to Blois as "soldiery" because of the castle, which dominates the town, and its military history. For example, Joan of Arc used the town as her base during the siege of Orleans. French soldiers were also stationed in the town in preparation for war with Germany.

5. Composed of several structures, the Château de Blois, located in the center of the town, was first constructed in the 13th century and completed in the seventeenth century. Near the end of the fourteenth century, the castle became the home of Prince Louis of Orleans, son of Charles V, king of France, for twenty-five years. In 1498 his grandson, King Louis XII, moved there, making Blois the royal capital. Louis XII fathered no sons, but Claude of France (1499–1524), his daughter by Anne of Brittany, married her cousin, Francis I (1494–1547), the heir presumptive of the throne, in 1514. At that time, women could not inherit the throne, so Francis I became king of France in 1515 and ruled until his death in 1547. He was succeeded by his son, Henry II (1519–59), who married Catherine de Médicis (1519–89) in 1533. Their fourth son, Henry III (1551–89), assumed the throne in 1575. Although he had persecuted the Protestants while he was still duke of Orleans and had aided his mother in the infamous 1572 St. Bartholomew's Day Massacre of thousands of Huguenots, he signed the Edict of Beaulieu in 1576, giving some concessions to Protestants, an event that caused Henry I, duke of Guise (1550–58), to form the Catholic League and pressure the king. As a result, Henry III rescinded many of his concessions. After the death of Henry III's brother, François, duke of Anjou, in 1584, Henri of Navarre (1553–1610), a descendant of Louis IX and a Protestant, was in line to be heir presumptive to the throne. The duke of Guise, however, forced Henry III to suppress Protestantism and block Henri of Navarre's line of ascension. The political power of the Catholic League grew, and by 1588, Henry III was forced to appoint Guise as lieutenant general of France. Henry III sought revenge. On 23 December 1588 Guise was summoned to Château de Blois to meet with the king; his brother, Louis II, the cardinal of Guise, accompanied him. Told that Henry III was waiting in the private room adjoining the royal bedchambers, the duke of Guise entered and was stabbed repeatedly by royal guards. As the attack was being perpetrated, monks in the nearby chapel were praying for its success. Supposedly the duke's body lay covered by a cloak

and a cross of straw for two hours until Henry III came to view it. Kicking the corpse in the face, he reportedly said, "Je ne le croyias pas aussi grand." The duke's brother was taken captive and murdered the following day. The bodies were ordered to be burned and the ashes tossed into the Loire. Several days later, on 5 January 1589, Henry III's mother, Catherine de Médicis died at the castle. The anti-Protestant duke of Guise had been a favorite with the French people and the government criminally charged the king, who then joined forces with Henri of Navarre. On 1 August 1589, Henry III was assassinated and died the following day. Henri of Navarre succeeded him as Henry IV, becoming the first of the Bourbon kings. The Catholic League, however, prevented him from assuming the throne, and military engagements soon took place. Although Henry IV succeeded in the fight, he was unable to conquer Paris. The popular support of the Catholic League began to crumble in the early 1590s as many people suspected them of being agents of the Spanish throne. Finally in 1593, Henry IV renounced Protestantism and became a Catholic. He was finally crowned king of France in 1594. Following the annulment of his marriage to his first wife, he married the Italian-born Marie de Médicis (1573–1642) in 1600. In 1610, Henry IV was assassinated and Marie de Médicis became regent of France. Her rule was marked by political unrest as she began to ally herself with Spain. In 1617 her son Louis XIII (1601–43) asserted his right to the throne and exiled his mother to the Château de Blois. She finally escaped in February 1619 by climbing out of the castle window during the night and fleeing. Although she was later briefly reconciled with her son, she was eventually exiled again and schemed against the rule of her son until her death in Cologne in 1642. In 1626, Louis XIII gave the Château de Blois to his brother Gaston d'Orléans on his marriage. After Gaston's death in 1660, the castle was essentially abandoned for almost 130 years. During the French Revolution, the castle was ransacked. King Louis Philippe declared the castle an historic site in 1841, and it was restored and opened as a museum.

6. Salle des Etats, located on the northeast part of the Château de Blois, is a hall dating to the early 13th century. Murray's *Handbook for Travellers* (1870) notes that "a row of pointed arches carried by circular piers with flowered capitals, supports its double, barn-like roof of wood" (194). The throne of the king of France was placed in the hall's center.

7. Joan of Arc (1412–31), a national heroine, was born in the rural village of Domrémy, France, where, as early as 1424, she claimed that she had visions commanding her to fight for France and end British domination during the Hundred Years War. She convinced Charles II, still uncrowned, to send her to Orléans, which was under siege. She inspired the troops and led them to end the siege in nine days. Other victories followed. She was wounded in an attack to retake Paris in September 1429 and was captured in a skirmish at Compiègne in May 1430. She was tried by the duke of Bedford, who had her burned at the stake in Rouen on 30 May 1541. She was canonized by Pope Benedict XV in 1920.

8. The Hotel Metropole, by the Jardin Anglais, is located on the left bank of Lake Geneva. Mount Blanc, with an elevation of 15,774 feet, is the highest mountain in Western Europe. Located between the Aosta Valley of Italy and the region of Haute-Savoie, France, the mountain has often been the subject of dispute since its summit lies almost on the border of each country and has been claimed by both.

9. Charlotte Hastings Whipple, wife of the critic Edwin Percy Whipple in New York City. Mrs. Bates and Mr. Howe are unidentified.

10. Villeneuve, Switzerland, a small town once occupied by the Romans, is located on the east bay of Lake Geneva, approximately a mile and a half from Chillon.

11. The children of Alice Bartlett's aunt and uncle Angelina Greenwood (1812–49) and Richard Warren (1805–75). He was the son of Henry and Mary Winslow Warren of Plymouth, Massachusetts, and a descendant of Richard Warren, who came to America aboard the *Mayflower*. Angelina Greenwood was the sister of Alice Bartlett's mother, Catherine Amelia Greenwood.

12. The bronze equestrian statue of Joan of Arc in Orléans was located in the Place du Martori. The 1857 bronze was by Royaltier with the bas-reliefs by Vital Dubray. Friedrich Schiller's (1759–1805) play *The Maid of Orleans* (1801) was first translated into English in 1835. Anna Alcott's handwritten translation, "The Maid Of Orleans, a tragedy," is dated 1 September 1852 and located at the Houghton Library, Harvard University (MS Am 1130.14[8]).

13. The Cathedral St. Étienne de Bourges was constructed from 1195 to 1270 and was the first cathedral of what is known as the high Gothic period. The design of the cathedral was fairly simple with double side aisles, a double ambulatory, and no transept. Flying buttresses, a rather new technique at the time, were used to support the pyramidal shape of the structure.

14. Moulins, located in central France, was the capital of the province of Bourbonnais and the seat of the dukes of Bourbon before the French Revolution. The Cathedral of Notre Dame in Moulins is a sixteenth- to seventeenth-century flamboyant Gothic structure with two towers and fifteenth- to sixteenth-century stained glass. It is most famous for its triptych painting (*Madonna Enthroned with Saints, Pierre de Bourbon and His Patron Saint*, and *Anne de France, Wife of Pierre de Bourbon*), dating from the end of the fifteenth century, by an unknown painter commonly referred to as the "Master of Moulins."

15. In *Shawl-Straps*, LMA writes: "The new-comer was a little priest; so rosy and young that they called him the 'Reverend Boy.' He seemed rather dismayed, at first; but, finding the ladies silent and demure, he took heart and read diligently in a dingy little prayer-book, stealing shy glances now and then from under his broad-brimmed hat at Amanda's [Alice's] white hands, or Matilda's [May's] yellow locks, as if these vanities of the flesh had not quite lost their charms for him" (80).

16. Probably a reference to the famous actor Edwin Thomas Booth (1833–93), son of

the actor Junius Brutus Booth. Edwin Booth made his acting debut in Boston in 1849 in Shakespeare's *Richard III*. His most famous role was that of Hamlet, a part he would play numerous times around the world. LMA first saw Edwin Booth on the Boston stage in May 1857: "Saw young Booth in Brutus and liked him better than his father" (*Journals* 84). In November 1858, she again saw him perform: "See Booth's Hamlet, and my ideal done at last" (*Journals* 91). On 1 April 1865, just two weeks before his younger brother John Wilkes Booth would assassinate Lincoln, LMA watched him perform and declared: "Saw Booth again in Hamlet & thought him finer than ever" (*Journals* 140). On 2 January 1876, she attended his performance in *Julius Caesar* at Booth's Theater in New York (*Selected Letters* 214).

17. Sophia Elizabeth Bond, born 1841, was the daughter of LMA and May's aunt and uncle Louisa Caroline Greenwood May Bond (adopted by Joseph May, Abigail's father) and George William Bond. Sophia's mother, Bond's first wife, Sophia A. May, died soon after the child's birth; her stepmother, Louisa, however, raised her after her marriage to Bond in 1843.

18. Miss Wells is unidentified.

19. LMA stayed at the Pension Victoria in Vevey with Anna Weld from October to December 1865. She described it in "Life in a Pension," published in the 7 November 1867 issue of the *Independent*: "Pension Victoria was pleasant, well kept, and as full as a beehive with a motley collection of lodgers from all over the world" (2).

20. Vevey, Switzerland, is located on the left bank of the Veveyse River, near its influx into Lake Geneva.

21. Bex is a small town on the Avancon River in the eastern part of the Lake Geneva region of Switzerland.

22. Chamonix, Switzerland, a small town popular with tourists, is located on both banks of the Arve River in the valley of Chamonix, bounded on the southeast by the Mont Blanc chain and on the northwest by the Aiguilles ranges.

23. Brackets appear in the manuscript.

24. LMA's first cousin Elizabeth Sewall Willis Wells (daughter of Abigail Alcott's sister Elizabeth Sewall May and Benjamin Willis) and her husband, Thomas Goodwin Wells. Lizzy Wells's letter must have been written after the onset of Benjamin Willis's illness because by August 2, ABA noted in his manuscript *Diary for 1870* that Benjamin Willis, Abigail's brother-in-law, had died the previous week (490).

25. Theodore Tilton, editor of the *Independent*, supported the *Revolution*, a feminist newspaper edited by Elizabeth Cady Stanton and Susan B. Anthony. The paper, serving as a mouthpiece for the National Woman Suffrage Association (NWSA), started publication in 1868. Many supporters of women's rights saw it as too strident, too uncompromising.

26. On 27 June 1870, Sampson Low wrote LMA to inform her that their banker was forwarding twenty pounds to Munroe (ALS: Houghton Library, Harvard University).

Louisa May Alcott to Sampson Low and Marston

Blois June 24th [1870]

Messrs Sampson Low & Marston

Gentlemen

I have delayed replying to your last letter till I heard from Mr Niles. His reply has just reached me & I at once sign & forward the agreement.[1]

When you send me whatever sum you may have will you be kind enough to put it in a bill of exchange on Baring Bros. as I can most easily use it in that form.[2]

Thanks for the copy of "Old Fashioned Girl". It [ms. torn] charming gotten up & very satisfactory, though here & there I find an omission or mistake. But as the former were probably made to render the book more agreeable to English readers, & the latter occur in the most carefully prepared books I have no complaint to make.

I hope it will be sufficiently successful to prevent the venture from being a loss to either party.

Please address me care of Munroe & Co. Paris & oblige

yours respectfully
L. M. Alcott.

ALS: Houghton Library, Harvard University (Autograph File).

1. Niles replied to LMA on 8 June 1870, urging her to sign the agreement.

2. Baring Brothers, the English banking firm, was located at 8 Bishopsgate Street, London.

May Alcott to the Alcott Family

Geneva[1] June 29th 1870.

Dearest Family,

Here we are on the loveliest lake in the world,[2] with mountains round us, and everything bright and summer like, though the air is very different from that we enjoyed at Dinan and along our route. Having exhausted all my adjectives on cathedrals and ruins, I have none left with which to describe the Alps, so shall leave it to Louisa to do for me, though I experienced a real thrill when I looked out of the car window and first saw those strange white peaks in the dim distance. I enjoyed our trip from Lyons here exceedingly as the landscape varied constantly, and kept me expecting new wonders at every turn; so imagine my utter disgust on exclaiming at the first sight of the Alps, to find I addressed a slumbering crowd, for the car was very full, and all were asleep but Lu. I retired to my corner and had a superb landscape all to myself.

About 5. oclock last night, we reached this grand Hotel,[3] and had just time to get refreshed before dinner. We were rather surprised on entering the long saloon to hear some one say, "Why how do you do Miss Alcott?" and there was a very dressy lady bowing and smiling, who proved to be a Mrs Bates that we met at our last party in America at Mrs Whipples. She and her brother Mr. Howe a very swell young gentleman, have been to see about rooms up the lake, and after resting here a day or two, we shall go to some more country place.

To our astonishment Sophy Bond has just appeared and we just rushed down to hug Mr. Bond and Aunty. I think we are now on the grand route of travel, we shall be continually meeting people we know. Aunty is much better, and they will probably stay here a week longer. After being in the wilds of Brittany it is quite pleasant to reach civilization again. Lu will give you a detailed account of all our doings, so I shall not digress, but only say, I am in Heaven and wish my family was here also. I hope John is better and C_____[4] continue a treasure.

Vevey July 1st. [1870]

We arrived here last night leaving Geneva in the boat and coming across this lovely lake in the early morning. The Bonds invited me to stay and go with them and others to Chamonix, but it was an expensive jaunt, so I fear I shall never see Mount Blanc any nearer than from the lake. This is the wildest scenery I ever imagined and I hope we shall stay some time here. There are a good many English and Spanish people here in the house, but all rather old, but the Howes and Bates are only a little way off, so I imagine we may see them. We are in a pleasant pension, the garden of which runs down to the lake with the mountains just across it, and Alice and I are going for a row this beautiful morning. There are many charming walks about, and it is very independent and countrylike, after the fashionable Geneva. I hope the Bonds will be persuaded to come here also, as this end of the lake is much the most beautiful. Aunty and Sophia were particularly sweet and affectionate, and wanted us [to] take rooms with them. I dreamt about my marmee last night and wish very much I could see her this morning.

Your loving May.

MS: Unlocated; copy by ABA at Houghton Library, Harvard University.

1. Geneva, capital of the canton of Geneva, lies at the south end of Lake Geneva, where the Rhone River emerges from it, dividing the town into two parts.

2. Lake Geneva (known as Lac Lehman in French), occupying approximately 224 square miles, is 45 miles long and 8.5 miles wide at its broadest point. On its north, the lake is bounded by sloping hills, vineyards, and small villages. To its east and south are the Swiss Alps of Valais and the French Alps of Savoy.

3. The Hotel Metropole.

4. Mrs. Conant, the Alcotts' housekeeper. ABA drew a blank after the initial.

Louisa May Alcott to the Alcott Family

Bex, Switzerland, July 8th 1870

Dear People,

I have not written since we left Geneva, for I got tired of writing letters and getting no answers. We hav n't had a letter from Ma and Nan since we left Dinan nearly a month ago. We had one from Pa at Tours and since then no news except through Niles who yesterday sent me a nice letter with his July account of $6,212. A neat little sum for the "Alcotts who can't make money."[1] S. E. Sewall will *invest* it safely, and so that you can draw the income. I shan't want any for some time.

We are now at Bex, a little place in the valley of the Rhone not far from Vevey. Alice's cousins, the Warrens,[2] are here, so she is happy, and May is in raptures with the grand mountains all round us. The Warrens are nieces of Judge Warren of Boston.[3] One has been an invalid for ten years and her sister travels with and takes care of her.[4] At Frankfort Emma was very ill and hearing of Count Sarpari a famous Hungarian doctor, they sent for him.[5] He had retired from work, but being persuaded to see Emma once was so charmed with, and so interested in the case that he devoted himself to her, and now travels with them and treats her for his own pleasure, being rich and old, and very fond of the "Pilgrim Sisters" as he calls them. He looks like old Henry May and is [a] very polite old sort.[6] He has a wife and fine establishment in Pesth where he goes now and then,[7] but always comes back to Emma, who is much better under his care. He only magnetizes her, but she is slowly improving and hopes to be well in time. She was ordered to Schwalbach[8] and it hurt her as it did A. Welds.[9] (By the way A. W. is engaged to a Mr. Perkins of the Navy)[10]

Lina the well sister is a bright jolly little lady, and she and May have gone to Mt. St. Bernard to day.[11] I am not strong enough to bear a mule-back ride of two hours or the snow air of the big mountains, though I much want to see the Hospice, the monks, and big dogs, that save people as Freddy knows. The trip will last two days but Lina knows the way, and has the best guide engaged, so they are gone to find adventures while Alice and I write letters and dawdle at home like two lazy mules.

It is a funny little place, Bex (pronounced Bay) right among the Alps, and we live in a rambling old Hotel all balconies and steps and trees and funny nooks. A fine garden full of big trees and rustic seats where we spend the days. A few English are here and a Polish Countess with her four servants, governess, two children, and her lover. The Count is in Paris and Madame flirts in a calm, cool way which rather amazes the Yankees. She is sitting close by me in the garden now knitting while her middle aged sweetheart reads the papers to her. She is neither young nor pretty, but they seem "fond and true."[12]

I will pay this letter and wish you would tell me how much you have to pay on it. We can pay only for part way and you only pay to England. Munroe pays ours and we shall have a nice little bill with him by and by.

I forgot the number of my last letter, but it was from Geneva, so let me know if you got it.

It is so hot, I'm most dead and have no ideas. Miss Warren thinks May a trump and they get on well together. I have just seen the sick one for the

first time, a pretty girl, very sweet and simple, but not particularly interesting. The little Count reminds me so of my Donny that I can hardly keep my hands off him.[13] Kiss my lovies for me.

Private

Bex July 8th [1870] 4. P M.

Ha!ha! The long desired letter has come! a nice fat one, dated June 23rd from Pa, Ma, Nan and Channing. The latter letter we could'nt read, but I've no doubt it was very fine. All the news of you is *so* good—thank the Lord.

[J. B. has begun early and Miss S. is an honor to her family.][14]

I am so sorry about John. Did you get my letter in which I sent Dr. Kane's prescription which has helped me. Do try it.

Niles sent me a notice in the gossipy old Republican telling about my "good old English Dr and my legs, and my grief for Dickens (dont care a pin) and all my plans and ails &c."[15] I suppose Channing or Bun wrote it, and I should like to knock their heads off for meddling with what dont concern them old tattle tails!—Another notice said I wrote diaries at 6, plays at 10, went out to service at 15, and was governess and dragged a baby round the Common. I recognized Pa's nice derangement of dates here, and fancy it was written by some of his admirers.[16] I suppose I ought to like it, but I dont. (Oh aint Lu cross?)

The photograph is very good only I'm sorry it was cut.[17]

Alice has just been telling me how careless S. E. S. is about his affairs, for he put down the rent she paid to another man's account and insisted that she had'nt paid it. I wish Pa would take a receipt for the $6000 on account, where and how it is invested, and the account of what S. E. S. already has. He said he would make out one for me, but did'nt, and if anything should happen to him I have no clear idea where my "fortin" is. Please have it fixed all shipshape and then if I fly out of my chrysalis some day, I may leave my affairs in order.

It does my heart good to hear of Ma's comfort and health. Long may she wave with Conant at the helm, and fussy old Lu safely over the sea.

My bones have achd [i.e., ached] badly lately and I cant ride, nor walk, nor sit, nor be in any peace. But the hot weather may ease them off and let me sleep without opium. Such a lazy life I lead lying round reading novels from morning till night, without an idea in my head or any desire for one. I'm afraid Niles will have to wait a long time for any new work from me. Did I tell that Tilton sent me a gushing letter asking me to write for "The Revolution." I shall not: for it is not our party unless the Boston and New York squabblers have joined forces. Have they? If I wrote for any woman's thing it would be for Livermore's paper.[18] I think I'd rather keep to my own work and lecture the public in a story, than hold forth a la Howe in the papers.[19] Old Tilton never answered my last letter, so he can wait for an answer to his signed "Yours, with all brotherly love".

The Countess in violet looking like Ma Lovering[20] is just passing my balcony with her son Severise[?], her daughter Rose Maria, and her brown lover Count Brindetske. Old Count Sarpari is smoking on his balcony, so you see I am in fine society. I fear I don't value it as I should, for I'd much prefer to be "hummin round" with my lovies, or sitting on the kitchen table eating Ma's messes in sisterhood.

I must leave room for May's raptures when she comes home tomorrow after her trip, for she will be bursting with news, if she is not burnt up or blown away on her journey.

Sunday P.M. May has told all her news, and as the lark ended safely, I have only to add love all round, and write soon to

Your Lu.

MS: Unlocated; copy by ABA at Houghton Library, Harvard University.

1. On 21 June 1870, Thomas Niles wrote LMA: "If you have not recovered your equanimity I hope the enclosed statement of our account will help you to do so. I do not now think of any author, male or female, in these U.S. who can congratulate him or her self on any like experience. The amount due you $6212.00, I pay over to Mr Sewall in July." On 7 July 1870, Niles again wrote to LMA and said that the balance due had been paid to Sewall (ALS: Houghton Library, Harvard University).

2. Lena Warren, Alice Bartlett's first cousin, was the daughter of Angelina Greenwood (sister of Bartlett's mother, Catherine Amelia Greenwood) and Richard Warren. Mr. Warren was a merchant and auctioneer in New York. Lena, who was approximately twenty-four years old in 1870, would later, in 1875, marry Siegmund George Nonne, secretary to the blind George V, ex-king of Hanover. The couple lived in Vienna and were

residing in Paris as late as 1895. Lena's brother, Henry Edward Warren, would marry Alice Bartlett in 1878.

3. Judge Winslow Warren, Jr. (1838–1930), an attorney in Boston, was the nephew of Richard Warren and the first cousin of the Warren children.

4. Emma Warren, Lena's sister, was born circa 1844. She later married Paul Guerra, a native of Colombia, South America, who was living in Paris. Emma gave birth to twins in 1877 and was residing in Paris as late as 1895.

5. Count Ferencz Szápáry de Muraszombath Szechysziget et Szapar (1804–75), born in Pesth, Hungary, was a noted healer and magnetopath who studied and practiced the effects of magnetism. In 1841, he directed "clinique magnetique" for eighty patients in Dresden, Germany. In 1858, he moved to Paris, where he stayed for twelve years. Often called "doctor of the incurables," he was, however, never licensed to practice medicine. He published nine books during his life, most written in French or German. His last work, *Testament Philosophique, Religieux et Social* (1870), best summarizes his ideas and philosophy. He was also the last keeper of the relics for the Order of Templars.

6. Old Henry May is unidentified.

7. Pesth, Hungary, was once the site of Celtic and later Roman settlements and was an independent city by the middle of the twelfth century. The Danube River separated it from the city of Buda. In 1849 a bridge was built connecting the two cities, and in 1873 the two became Budapest, capital of Hungary.

8. Schwalbach, Germany (called Langen-Schwalbach until 1927; now called Bad Schwalbach), is located in the Taunus Mountains, on the Aar River, approximately ten and a half miles northwest of Weisbaden. Noted for its mineral springs, the town became a health resort during the early part of the nineteenth century. Karl Baedeker writes in *The Rhine, Including the Black Forest and the Vosges: Handbook for Travellers* (Leipzig: Karl Baedeker, 1911): "The water, strongly impregnated with iron and carbonic acid, is used both internally and externally and is especially efficacious in anaemia, nervous affections, and female complaints generally" (264).

9. LMA had accompanied Anna Weld to Schwalbach in August to September of 1865. She writes: "The place is a narrow valley shut in between high hills . . . [Anna] began the water cure under Dr. [Adolph] Genth's care" (*Journals* 142).

10. On 15 September 1870, Anna Weld (age thirty-four) married U.S. Navy Lt. George H. Perkins (age thirty-five) from Concord, New Hampshire, the son of Hamilton E. and Clara Perkins. The Rev. James Freeman Clarke performed the ceremony.

11. The Pass of St. Bernard, utilized at least since the Bronze Age, is the oldest Alpine pass route. The Hospice of St. Bernard lies at its summit, over 8,100 feet in elevation.

12. In *Shawl-Straps* (1872), LMA writes that in Bex, a "Polish Countess, with her lover, daughter, and governess, conferred distinction upon the house" (130).

13. The little count is probably the Polish countess's son.

14. JB and Miss S. are unidentified. Brackets appear in the manuscript.

15. The *Springfield Republican* for 15 June 1870 published an unsigned column, "From Boston. Gossip, Literary and General," which noted: "One of the sincerest mourners for Charles Dickens will be Miss Louisa Alcott, who has heard of his death in her quiet retreat at Dinan in Brittany, which she will leave this week for Normandy . . . Your readers will be glad to hear that she has greatly improved in health . . . and, under the care of her good old physician, Dr. K., is beginning the recovery that he promises her if she will take sufficient doses of rest, air, simple food and delightful scenery. . . . Dr. K. reports that one cause of the lameness she now suffers is the calomel administered to her at the army hospital in Washington" (2). The author is probably Frank Sanborn, one of the paper's editors. ABA notes, on 12 June in his manuscript *Diary for 1870*: "Sanborn is here. He is curious about Louisa and May, and we read him passages from their letters" (350).

16. The article LMA refers to has not been located; however, a later article shows how ABA could distort the childhood events of his literary daughter. An unidentified newspaper clipping entitled "NEW ENGLAND AUTHORS / Conversations by A. Bronson Alcott / Sketches of American Literary Celebrities" is pasted into ABA's manuscript *Diary for 1870*. It details ABA's talk in Kanter's Hall in Detroit on 21 November 1870 and notes: "Miss Alcott first commenced word-sketching when seven or eight years old" (741–42).

17. The photograph LMA refers to is unidentified.

18. Mary Livermore (1820–1905) edited the *Woman's Journal* for two years. Lucy Stone and others, encouraged by support of the New England Woman Suffrage Association (NEWSA), formed a more moderate wing of the women's rights movement—the American Woman Suffrage Association (AWSA). *Woman's Journal*, which started publication in January 1870 and ceased in 1912, was their mouthpiece. Alcott did indeed contribute: she authored eighteen pieces, both fiction and nonfiction, for *Woman's Journal* between 1874 and 1887.

19. Julia Ward Howe (1819–1910), poet, abolitionist, social activist, and author of "The Battle Hymn of the Republic" (1862), was well known to the Alcott family. Living in Boston, she had been asked to join the Radical Club in 1867. She served as president of the New England Woman Suffrage Association from 1868 to 1877 and 1893 to 1910. With Lucy Stone and others, she helped form the American Woman Suffrage Association in 1869, and she edited and contributed to the *Woman's Journal*. In the 1880s, she participated in ABA's School of Philosophy in Concord.

20. LMA had tutored the children of Mr. and Mrs. Joseph S. Lovering of Boston in 1851.

May Alcott to the Alcott Family

Bex July 10th 1870.

Dearest Family,

I am almost afraid to begin a description of my trip to the pass of St. Bernard,[1] but as Lu didnt go, so cannot tell the tale, I must do my best to put before you our adventures "by flood and field and fire." For really a more exciting time I never had, as we were in danger many times, and even the guide thought us very courageous and *plucky*. Well, to begin, I must tell you that last Thursday Lena Warren and I determined on doing the great excursion by ourselves if nobody turned up to join us, and as that didn't happen, we decided to go immediately while we had fine weather and moonlight. So we telegraphed to Martigny[2] (an hours ride in the cars from here) to have a carriage and the guide, Maurice, ready for us at 4 oclock next morning and taking our bundles of water proof and thick saques, we bid our sisters an affectionate farewell as they evidently thought we never should return, and that it was the height of rashness to attempt a three days trip alone. However we felt fine, after studying Murray carefully, and finding out all particulars from a Polish gentleman here who just returned from the pass, that we could do it. So we turned our backs upon our friends and went at 9 oclock P.M. to Martygny, finding our room ready at the hotel, and tumbled directly into bed for a four hours sleep, as we were to be called so early. Then before sunrise we were up, had coffee and mounted our open barouch, with a nice man for driver and guide, and rode through the loveliest valley along the most turbulant little river, for eight hours, till we stopped at a little town, called Liddes,[3] for some refreshments, and to rest the mule. Then having been gradually ascending all the way, we now began to wind along the edge of a fearful precipice, but the road was so perfect that I was continually wondering how they ever built such on the straight side of the mountains. We kept meeting loads of tourists all in gay costume, with Alpine sticks, and the general bowing and *bon jouring* seemed so friendly and sociable that, though it had now began to rain and the covering of our carriage was buttoned down, yet our spirits rose higher and higher till we reached the Cantine, (as they call the place for leaving the vehicles and mounting mules.) We were ready for any thing, and lucky for us that we were, for things looked a little dubious. The rain poured in torrents, and it now being about 4. o clock P.M. we must either spend the night in this horrid little house already filled with people caught in the rain, and afraid to go on, or boldly plunge along in the storm climbing for two hours to reach the Hospice.[4] We persuaded the guide to take us along, and Lena mounted the mule, while I in my waterproof with thick boots and my sun umbrella over me, marched up and up, plowing through the mud and wading the river (which had burst all bounds and carried away the road in places) up to my knees in the ice-cold water. The lightening flashed and the tremendous claps of thunder seemed so near us, that the mules stopped and couldn't be persuaded to go on till a hard beating and *yanking* obliged him not only to start again, but to carry us through several places where the water came up to his belly and a false step would have sent us over a fall in one place and been certain death. All this, I really enjoyed intensely, and began to think I was a little courageous when the guide told me he had never been in such a storm on the mountains before as the thunder was always so near the peaks that people were often killed of lightening and it was considered dangerous, very dangerous to traverse these mountain passes at such times. My heart sunk within me, and my clothes clung to me so that it was like dragging a leaden weight after me every step I took. Ladies all ride up from the Cantine and Lena like the rest took her mule and though very wet, having no waterproof, was saved the immense execution of this very steep climb, in soaking garments. One can never calculate about the weather here, as it often rains on the mountains when perfectly clear below, and when we left Martigny, a more lovely morning I never saw, not a cloud in the sky, and we hardly expected a tempest a few hours later. But I wouldn't have missed seeing the mountains in the storms, for it was more fearfully beautiful then any thing I ever imagined. At last thoroughly wet to our skins we reached the Hospice, where a handsome kindly priest met us, and conducted us to a room with two pretty curtained beds in it and a grated window looking on the lake and toward Italy. A woman appeared and helped us off with our clothes which stuck tightly to us, being so wet, and brought us plain warm flannels, peasants' dresses, and under cloths. These we put on with rapture, being chilled with the cold air of this immense stone building. It was hard to find any skirt long enough for me, and we had great fun arranging one skirt over another as a kind of over dress, then my velvet jacket to cover up the waist, and putting on a pair of cloth slippers the size of mudscows, my toilet was finished. We descended to the salle a manger where our handsome priest awaited us, and complimented us immensely on our having accomplished such a fcat. Then putting us before an immense open fire, with an old English lady who spends her summers there we all sat round and talked and warmed ourselves till tea was served for our benefit, and a delicious dinner followed. Fine pictures hung about, presents from different visitors, and a piano from the Prince of Wales stood in a corner. The priests charge nothing for food and lodging but people leave what they choose behind there, and some tourists are very mean shrinking away without giving anything after receiving the lordly hospitality of this devoted brotherhood. From all the numbers at the Cantine none dared the storm but three English women and ourselves, all the gentlemen who started up, turned back in fear of the storm. The priest (for there is only one who sees and entertains the thousands of visitors who come every year) told us a great deal about how the Hospice was carried on and the adventures he had in the eleven years he had been there through summer and winter. Beside the average 13000 tourists that visit the establishment they rescue from the snow and storms not less than _____ peasants yearly.[5] They know what ladies need evidently up there, for on going to our rooms we found the beds had been warmed that we might not take cold, and every comfort was provided for us; and I never slept more delightfully than I did there after all our adventures and knowing also that we were only separated by a little grating from a host of priests.

At five, next morning, we were up to hear service in the chapel, and I enjoyed the music very much as I always do in these Catholic Churches. On going out for a clamber on the rocks we were startled by a tremendous howling and baying, and suddenly out from a kind of cellar, rushed six or seven great dogs who all bounded toward us licking our hands and smelling to see if we were hurt. They had the most human eyes I ever saw and could well imagine their wonderful feats in the winter, when they rescue so many travellers from the snow, for they are very powerfully built and look immensely strong, though so affectionate and gentle. I was glad I have seen the real St. Barnard dogs, and quite proud to have them slobber over and caress me. We walked into Italy which was an operation of ten minutes only, and I should have liked to have gone down on the Italian side to Aosta[6] and taken the cars from there, but the expense prevented. We went to the Morgue as they call a little dead house standing apart from the main building to receive the bodies of those found quite dead in the mountains, and the air is so rarified that they are left here just as they are found with no disagreeable consequences and the floor was strown thick with skulls and bones. We saw the lovely lake close to the Hospice and snow surrounded us every where, and we picked up some of the immense hailstones which fell the night before.

After a good hot breakfast we were shown photographs and various souvenirs which visitors like to carry away with them, and I bought several, one quite pretty device of a beautifully modelled little ivory hand holding a little magnifying glass through which is seen a photograph of the Hospice. I got photographs of the place and of the dogs [see figure 45]. We left a large piece of gold in the chapel *nave* and gave a good bit to each waiter then bid our dearest friends good bye, and trotted down the mountain at a good pace in the clear bracing air, and could hardly believe with our thick coats on that we should find it scorching hot in the towns below. Our guide followed with the mule and bundles and on our way I picked some Alpine flowers to press for mother. We could hardly realize that the way which seemed so cosy in the sunlight could have been so fearfully difficult the night before, for the roaring river had diminished to a brook and everything seemed peaceful and superbly grand. I much preferred the wild stormy scene and blessed my stars that everything had happened as it did. We reached the carriage and at five P.M. were in Martigny, and surprised at meeting the party from Geneva, that is—the elegant Mr. Charles Howe and his sister Mrs. Bates, who insisted on our coming into the hotel and having cake and wine, which we did, then took the cars and reached Bex at 8 oclock, rather tired and dusty, but two of the happiest mortals that ever embraced their friends. There was great rejoicing over our return and every one wonders at our performance.

I found your letter had come to console Lu, while I was away, and though

FIGURE 45. The dogs of St. Bernard Hospice (ca. 1870). *Louisa May Alcott's Orchard House/L. M. A. Memorial Association.*

it is intensely hot and I have nothing but a very bad pen to use, still I have done my best to tell you of the most exciting and most enjoyable trip that I ever took in my life.

Sophia Bond, Mrs. B. Augusta Curtiss and Miss Clara Wells[7] stopped here on their way home from Chamonix, while I was away, and I guess I had a better time as it was, than if I had gone with them. I may take the trip from here[?] if all goes well, for I am prepared for anything. Tomorrow I go to Geneva to select a fine engraving to send the priest who was so kind to us, for the money we left of course goes to the church, and we want to give him something.

I felt sure the Ricketsons would like Concord, and is the Dr. really in good practice so soon? Give them my love, and I wish Mrs R_____ would drop me a line about her fun and the Concord gossip.[8] Remember me to Mr Channing and tell him his letter was to Lu, and not me. Please say we are quite different people and I shall expect a very lucid one from him. It might be well *written* also, that I may read and appreciate it.

What a hard time John is having. Wont he try Lu's stuff? it would certainly do him good. Dear Marmee I look at your picture in my locket very often, though I'm not homesick yet.

Your loving May.

MS: Unlocated; manuscript copy by ABA at Houghton Library, Harvard University. Partially printed: *Boston Daily Evening Transcript*, 18 August 1870, 2; Ticknor 81–87. ABA also copies most of this letter, except for the last few paragraphs, in his manuscript *Diary for 1870* 463–72.

1. The Pass of St. Bernard was, for centuries, the only pass that linked northern and southern Europe for hundreds of miles on either side.

2. Martigny, located in southwest Switzerland in the canton of Valais, where the Rhone River makes a sudden sharp right turn, is a busy summer tourist town as it lies at the crossroads of Italy, France, and Switzerland.

3. Liddes is located in southwest Switzerland, west of Mt. Merignier.

4. In 962, Bernard de Menthon, who traveled to spread Christianity, founded the hospice. He was beatified soon after his death in the 1080s. Still in operation today, the hospice of St. Bernard, located at an elevation of 8,110 feet, is one of the highest winter habitations in Europe.

5. ABA leaves a blank in the manuscript.

6. The Italian border lies on the northwest side of the lake at the St. Bernard Pass. A short distance away is Aosta, a northern Italian town situated at the confluence of the Buthier and Dora Baltca and once an important Roman settlement. The Valle d'Aosta, one of the least populated areas of Italy, provides access to the Great and Little St. Bernard passes.

7. Clara Wells and B. Augusta Curtiss are unidentified.

8. Dr. Arthur Ricketson and his wife.

May Alcott to Abigail Alcott

Bex July 13th 1870.

Dear Mother,

I know how much pleasure you take in these little pictures of places where we stay for anytime, and as Miss Warren has just given me a good likeness of Bex as heading, I select one to send you. I have put a little cross on the house where we are, and you can see the lovely view that we look on of those superb white capped mountains and green hills a great deal of the time half hidden by a beautiful purple mist which I have always supposed to be exaggerated in pictures, but now I really see it, I think no picture can do justice to it.[1]

Yesterday morning Count Szapary invited me to drive with him to see some remarkable old trees, belonging to the estate of Lady Hope.[2] The Druids seem to have pervaded the continent pretty generally, for even these were thought to have been planted by them, and I am to sketch two of the most striking ones for the Count who is quite an antiquarian, and though I can't talk French enough to venture into much conversation with him, yet he is very attractive and gave me a lovely carved watch stand that shuts up in a very ingenious manner fitted for travelling. Also a photograph of himself when younger, and one of his cards with a grand flourish of titles and arms on it which is very imposing. He is a great dear, having the most polished manner, and is immensely rich.

John will laugh when I tell him I have really come to wearing blue eye glasses like his, as the glare on these white roads is fearfully trying, and even strong eyes suffer from it, and these glasses are universally worn both here and in Italy.[3]

Lena and I drove to Martigny, the other day, and hunted up our good guide to St. Bernard in order to be certain the large pictures for our handsome priest which we selected with great care at Vevey reached him safely. We could not find the head of St. Sebastian by Guido, that we wanted, but took the best we could get, being Mater Dolorosa and Guido's head of Christ, the pair making quite a handsome present for him.[4] Lena wrote a pretty note in French, and we hope soon to have an acknowledgment from him. Also Mr. Howe has promised us each a photograph of the priest himself, which of course we could n't get ourselves.

Last night we drove out by moonlight along the Rhone, and through St. Maurice,[5] where almost every one [one] meets has the horrible goitre,[6] or is a cretan and I hardly met an intelligent looking person all the way through this lovely valley where one would think to find nothing but beauty instead deformity poverty and filth. I dont like the Swiss as far as I have seen them, at all. They are insolent in their manners, very sordid and extremely dirty and diseased.

To day, the Polish Countess, her lover and suite left after bidding us a very cordial goodbye, for they have been reading Lu's books, and consequently take great interest in us, which is thought by the rest of the house to be very overwhelming.

We have had frightfully hot weather and Lu likes it as it suits her bones, but it is not very lively for me. Perhaps Sophia Bond will come to spend a few days with us, as she spoke of it when we left her the other day.

Last week Lena and I went to the "Grot des Fees,"[7] and had quite a fright, for we were alone, and after climbing the ascent to it, found a young and very unprepossesing guide ready to show us through it. Not knowing exactly what to expect we followed him into pitchy darkness, and were presented with two very dim lanterns by the uncertain light of which we found our way along, winding out of the narrow dark passage cut in the solid rock, with the man yelling in front to make the echoes and occasionally stopping to ask us if we didn't hear strange noises like the hard breathing of dying nuns, and other pleasing suggestions, which, as it was just the place for murder and robbery, they were anything but amusing. At last we reached a lake on which was a strange boat in which he begged us to embark, but we refused, though for fear of making him angry we chatted in the most cheerful and confiding manner with him, while he paddled round the inky pool with a great fall at the further end. Altogether when we got safely back to daylight, I thanked my stars for being allowed to live a little longer, as I hardly expected such good luck. It makes me shiver to think of the fearful cold and blackness of that place even now. Do you realize that I shall be 30 years old this month, for I don't and never felt younger in my life.[8]

Give my love to Emma Moore and ask her to drop a line in some of your letters. When is she to be married?[9]

Your loving May.

MS: Unlocated; manuscript copy by ABA at Houghton Library, Harvard University.

1. The photograph of Bex with May's cross mark on it has not been located.

2. Lady Hope, Louisa Anne Hatton (d. 1875), was the widow of Major General Charles Hope (1768–1828), the son of John Hope, the second earl of Hopetoun, whom she

married in 1807. Her estate, noted for its landscape gardens and fields, overlooked the village of Bex and the plain of the Rhone.

3. May had started to complain about her eyes around the age of twelve or thirteen, often commenting that her eyes troubled her or that she couldn't use her eyes. Intolerance to light seems to have been a major issue. Later in life, she would be unable to use her eyes for close work. The problem may have been trachoma, a bacterial disease.

4. Mater Dolorosa is a common title in art given to the Virgin Mary, stressing her role as the mournful mother of the crucified Jesus. May possibly is referring to the Bolognese Baroque painter Guido Reni (1575–1642), whose romanticized paintings of religious figures and scenes were popular in the nineteenth century. He had painted St. Sebastian seven or eight times, as early as 1616 and as late as 1640–42. He had also painted the head of Christ crowned with thorns during the 1630s. Interestingly, the British novelist George Eliot did not like Guido Reni and satirized him in chapter 60 of *Middlemarch* (1871–73) as "the celebrated Guydo, the greatest painter in the world." St. Sebastian (d. ca. 288), patron saint against plague and pestilence, was the son of wealthy Romans and served as an imperial bodyguard. When discovered to be a Christian, he was ordered executed by Diocletian and shot with arrows. He survived, however, and was then ordered clubbed to death. Renaissance paintings often depict him as a young man with Apollo-like beauty.

5. St. Maurice, Switzerland, an ancient Roman town, lies a short distance (three kilometers) south of Bex, where the Rhone narrows.

6. Goiter is caused by an enlargement of the thyroid gland and is usually visible as swelling on the front of the neck.

7. Grot des Fees (Fairies Grotto), first discovered in 1863, just north of St. Maurice, was carved into the stone by water. According to legend, all who dip their left hand into the Fairies Fountain found in the grotto will have their wish granted. The passageway in the grotto makes some sixty-three turns before opening onto a fifty-meter subterranean waterfall, whose crashing waters can be heard for great distances.

8. May was born 26 July 1840 in Concord.

9. Emma Frances Moore, aged twenty-two, married Charles Wilder Davis, aged thirty-six, a merchant from Chicago, on 22 September 1870. Emma, a neighbor to the Alcotts, was the daughter of John B. and Sarah Augusta (Hunt) Moore, who had sold ABA the Orchard House property in September 1857.

Louisa May Alcott to A. Bronson Alcott

Bex July 14th 1870.

Dear Pa,

As I have not written to you yet, so I will send you a picture-letter, and tell you about the very interesting old Count Szapary who is here. This morning he asked us to go to the hills and see some curious trees which he says were planted from acorns and nuts brought from Mexico by Attila.[1] We found some very ancient oaks and chesnuts and the enthusiastic old man told us a story about the druids who once had a church, amphitheatre and sacrificial alter up there. No one knows much about it and he imagines a good deal to suit his own pet theory. You would have liked to hear him hold forth about the races, and Zoroaster,[2] Plato, &c. He is a Hungarian of a very old family descended from Semiramade and Zenobia.[3] He believes that the body can be cured often by influencing the soul, and that doctors should be priests, and priests, doctors, as the two affect the body and soul which depend on one another. He is doing a great deal for poor Miss Warren who has tried many doctors and got no help. I never saw such a kindly, simple, enthusiastic old soul, for at 67 he is as full of hope and faith and good will as a young man. I told him I should like my Father to see a little book he has written, and he is going to give me one.

We like this quiet little place in among the mountains, and pass lazy days for it is very warm and we sit about on our balconies enjoying the soft air, the moonlight and the changing aspect of the hills.

May had a fine exciting time going up St. Bernard, and is now ready for another. Miss Lena Warren is a most congenial companion, as she is a frank, lively, energetic little woman full of enterprize and fond of adventures. A great lover of O. B. Frothingham[4] and very sensible not to say radical in her ideas. Alice is quite the conservative among us now, and we have fierce discussions about the great works of the day, as we sit in the garden or walk together.

The society of these well educated and rather superior girls will do May good, though as far as character goes, she is their superior, but in education and polish, we both feel much behind them.

I often wish you were with us to enjoy the new world we find over here. I dont think the Swiss are an attractive people; with all their freedom and independence they are rude, dull, and sickly. Every where we see horrible goitres, cretans, and dwarfs. They dont know how to live, for their houses are dirty damp and dark, they eat coarse food, and don't seem to be as fine a race as they ought to be, living in such a wonderfully beautiful country.

I am so glad that all goes well with you and Marmee, but very sorry that John has such trouble with his poor bones.

The Polish Countess and her daughter have been reading my books and are charmed with them. Madame says she is not obliged to turn down any pages so that the girl may not read them, as she does in many book's, "all is so true, so sweet, so pious, she may read every word."

I send by this mail the Count's little pamphlet. I don't know as it amounts to much, but I thought you might like to see it.

Love to every one, and write often to your

Affectionate daughter

L. M. A.

MS: Unlocated; copy by ABA at Houghton Library, Harvard University. Partially printed: Cheney 239–40.

1. Attila the Hun (ca. 405–53), the last king of the Huns, a confederation of Euroasian tribes, reigned from 434 until his death. His campaigns against the Roman Empire earned him a legendary reputation for cruelty. There is no evidence he was ever in Mexico.

2. Zoroaster, Iranian prophet (Zarathushtra) and founder of Zoroastrianism, which became the national religion of the Sassanian Empire of Persia. Recent scholars estimate he lived sometime between 1400 and 1000 BC. In classical antiquity he was considered to be the founder of the religion of the Magi. Most of his ideas were unknown to Western culture until the late eighteenth century when his name became associated with lost ancient wisdom. The Freemasons, as well as other groups, claimed they possessed the knowledge of Zoroaster's wisdom.

3. Semiramis (also known as Semiramide) was, according to legend, a powerful Assyrian queen. The daughter of the fish goddess Atargatis in Syria, Semiramis was kept alive by doves until Simmas, a royal shepherd, discovered her and raised her. She later married Onnes, general to the ruler Ninus. Awed by her bravery at the battle of Bactra,

Ninus married her—after Onnes killed himself. After Ninus died, she became queen of Assyria and, by conquest, ruled over much of Asia. She appears in Dante's *Divine Comedy* (ca. 1310–14), Voltaire's tragedy *Semiramis* (1748), and Rossini's opera *Semiramide* (1823). Zenobia was daughter of Zabaai ben Selim, an Arab chieftain. As regent for her son Vaballathus, she ruled as queen of Palmyra from 267 to 272. She claimed to be descended from Cleopatra and Mark Anthony and from Dido, queen of Carthage. She also claimed to be descended from the Assyrian queen Semiramis. In 272 the Roman Emperor Aurelian conquered her kingdom, and she and her son were brought to Rome, where Aurelian, in 274, paraded her bound in chains through the city. Supposedly impressed by Zenobia, however, Aurelian freed her and presented her with a villa in what is now known as Tivoli, Italy, where she remained for the rest of her life. In *Shawl-Straps*, LMA, commenting on their stay in Bex, writes: "An old Hungarian count, who labored under the delusion that he descended in a direct line from Zenobia, also adorned the scene" (130).

4. Octavius Brooks Frothingham (1822–95), LMA's distant cousin and leader of the Free Religious Association, was a prime mover in establishing the literary discussion group known as the Fraternity Club, which lasted from 1869 to 1874.

May Alcott to Abigail Alcott

Bex July 17th 1870

Dear Mother.

It is a rainy Sunday and every one is sitting about looking very solemn and stupid, and as I have nothing to read, I have taken to sewing and am hard at work making an overskirt to my blue daisy muslin. Every where I go I notice the fashions and pretty styles, and add a bow here or a ribbon their to suit the place I am in, and now by way of employment I shall modernize my long trailing skirt by having a little overskirt of the same trimmed with frills.

The great excitement of to day I may say the only one, is the present of a lovely inlaid box for gloves, such work as we only find in this part of the world, being a kind of yellow, pebbly wood with stripes of rosewood across it, and a flask of cologne, also a touching note in French from the Count,— all these attentions for me. He was so delighted with two sketches I made of his old trees, that Lena said he wanted to give me a coach and four, but they dissuaded him from anything extravigant in the way of jewelry &c. thinking

I should hardly like to accept such, so he at last got these for me, and the box is a perfect beauty, I assure you; handsome enough to offer a Princess. I really thought when I left America, after receiving thirty presents, that I could hardly expect any on this side the water, but everybody I meet seems to feel it their duty to offer me something which of course is very pleasant, but I sometimes wonder why it is so.

Bex July 21. [1870]

Mother's and Father's letters dated July 4th just received, also the Sanborn notice of Lu, copied from the "proof" we imagine. I think it excellently written and a good description of L. but I want to see the picture and hope the paper is on its way to us.[1] The photograph of me strikes me as exceedingly good, and if you can send some—one at a time—I should like them.[2] On the whole, you need not send them as we go to Venice where they take very superior pictures, and we shall all have some good one's taken, and then we will send you the new ones. The cost is much less here than at home and the Venetian ones are very famous.

To-day Lena and I are to take a trip to Geneva partly for the fun, and partly to see if we can find pleasant rooms for the coming month, as Bex is too hot, and this hotel too bad for comfort. We can't go to Italy yet and we don't retrace our steps very far in going to Geneva. It will be pleasant to be near the Bonds also, who are still there, though Mr. Bond has gone to England for a short time, and as every one is rushing from the war, Switzerland will be full and we may meet many friends quite unexpectedly.[3] Lu's fame follows her even here, in this out of the way little town: for yesterday a New York lady and her two stylish daughters were quite excited on looking over the hotel-book to see Miss Alcotts' name, and immediately enquired if it was the Miss Alcott who wrote "Little Women," and were much impressed when they found it was the lion. I don't think she realizes how great her success is and how [much] comfort she has given us all by this one effort. I am so happy that everything goes so smoothly at home, and I hope you will persuade Mrs Conant to go to Anna's for the winter, so you may not lose her for next summer. Such a treasure should'nt be allowed to slip through your fingers, as mother will always need just such a person about her, and they are hard to find.

Your kind messages gratify Alice very much, and I hope you will always remember to put in just a word to her. The other day, Lena and I went to the salt mines here.[4] It was a long walk through pitch dark subterranean passages with only an old woman carrying a flaming torch to light us through this strange place where the miners live, and must lead the most horrid lives. We had a fight with a drunken guide who insisted on going with us, and we had to pretend to give up going till he went off, and then we induced this old woman to show us what we had come to see. Then yesterday we went off in two grand carriages to "Villars" up on the mountain top among the clouds and snow having a most superb view all the way, and finding a jolly hotel full of English, and having a fine dinner at the Count's expense.[5] Then driving home by sunset and moonrise seeing the most superb landscape in the world by this beautiful light, we came very near an immense glazier, and though leaving Bex in the hottest weather now had to put on velvet jackets and water proofs over for warmth, the whole atmosphere changed so entirely[?]. They told us at the hotel they could hardly open the windows sometimes the clouds came in so damp and cold. It was a strange place and I enjoyed the whole spree immensely. In fact, I take great delight in my life just now, and wish every one was half as happy.

I am scribbling while waiting for the Bus' to take us to Geneva.

May.

MS: Unlocated; copy by ABA at Houghton Library, Harvard University.

1. F. B. Sanborn's "The Author of 'Little Women,'" which appeared in the 16 July 1870 issue of *Hearth and Home*, featured an engraving of LMA, made from a photograph taken by E. L. Allen of Boston.

2. Probably the Marshall vignette of May, which she mentioned earlier as her favorite. No copy of the Marshall photograph has been located.

3. Emperor Napoleon III of France declared war on Prussia on 15 July 1870, initiating the Franco-Prussian War.

4. The salt mine, Le Bouillet, the only working salt mine in Switzerland, is located three miles northeast of Bex.

5. Villars-sur-Ollon is a small town situated high above the Rhone Valley (elevation 4,120 feet); it commands wonderful views of the Diablerets, the Dent de Morcles, and part of the Mont Blanc chain.

Louisa May Alcott to the Alcott Family

Bex July 18th 1870.

All private.

Dear People,

The breaking out of this silly little war between France and Prussia will play the deuce with our letters. We have had none from you for a long time and Alexander, the English waiter here says that the mails will be left to come as they can, for the railroads are all devoted to conveying troops to the seat of war. The French have already crossed the Rhine, and rumors of a battle came last eve,[1] but the papers have not arrived, and no letters for any one, so all are fuming for news public and private and I am howling for my home letter which is more important than all the papers on the continent.

We have very little to tell except that all are well and doing nothing as usual. I have dropped my opium again and sleep well without it. My bones give me very little trouble while the heat lasts, and if I can only keep on as I have begun I shall have peace. Alice is enjoying her cousins, who are nice girls; and May is a general favorite as usual. The old Count admires her very much and thinks her sketches are wonderful. He put the finishing touch by having a rapture over her "handsome hands," often admiring them for some days and examining them through his glass. Alice, who rather prides herself on her white small hands and quiddles over her nails by the hour, was quite amazed that May's long skilful ones won the prize, for A. regards the Count as a gem of price and his good opinion worth "sums." May is much set up with his pretty glove-box and a flask of cologne and a fine French note from

"Votre tout recon nai sant /
Francois Compte de Szápany"[2]

He is a dear old soul so unworldly and absorbed that Lena Warren was to look after him and pay his bills &c. He was very rich, but the care of money disturbed his studies so he gave all but a little sum to his sons, and devotes himself to curing sick people, "for the love of God and humanity." As he speaks no English, May and I cannot [speak] with him, but we like each other and nod and smile when we meet quite beautiful to behold.

Dont be worried if you don't hear regularly, or think us in danger. Switzerland is out of the mess, and if she gets in, we can skip over into Italy, and be as cosy as possible. It will make some difference in money perhaps, as "*Munroe* in Paris" is our banker, and we shall be plagued about our letters, otherwise the war wont affect us a bit. I dare say you know as much about it as we do, and Marmee is predicting "a civil war" all over the world.

We hear accounts of the frightful heat with you, dont wilt away before we come.[3] I do hope it not so hot that Marmee cant get on her "dress boots" in a hurry. I imagine her flopping about upstairs with the "mainsail" in full bloat, I'm glad she tries my room, and like to think of her writing at my table, and hanging up her seven bobtailed jackets in my blessed[?] closet.

May and Alice and all the Warren party have gone on a trip up one of the lesser mountains today, so I am quite alone on my balcony. I sew and read and dawdle there, for the vines shade it and I can lie on my couch all day in the open air. The long drives tire me so, I dont try to go though I'd like to see the fine sights. But I came to get well, and [to] that end I devote myself with all my might, for it is too costly a cure to be wasted. Emma Warren [see figure 46] rides on a bed in the carriage for she cant walk a step.

Bex July 20.

A nice letter from Pa and Ma has just come, and I read them luxuriously in bed while May dressed and we both had shrieks over Bun's "large blue eye" portrait. It is very good, better than I expected and mostly true. Niles sent me a "Transcript" with two notices from London,—one by Conway I suspect.[4] I suppose you have seen them. Lady Amberley is a trump, and I am glad she says a word for her poor sex though she *is* a Peeress.[5] I'll drop a card on her if I go to London. I should like to have said of me what Hedge says of Dickens; and when I die I should prefer such a memory than a tomb in Westminster Abbey.[6]

As my "ten thousand income" has got into the papers, the tax men will know just how much to charge me. Does my being absent free me from taxes? or has Eaton called upon you for mine?[7] Do let me know all about it.

FIGURE 46. "Our Little Invalid," Emma
Warren, Bex, Switzerland (1870), by
May Alcott. *Louisa May Alcott's Orchard
House/L. M. A. Memorial Association.*

About S. E. S. and my money,[8] I have only to say that I want to know that $10,000 is invested, and the rest, if there is any over, so fixed that I can get it as I need it. For now that May's money is used up, I have many small expenses for her, as Alice only pays her travelling expenses. I have still $600. on my letter of credit which I have not touched; also $200 on my bills of exchange, for I have used only one. The war may affect money, but I guess we can do very well and I hope things easy for everyone. With $10,000 well invested, and more coming in all the time, I think we may venture to enjoy ourselves after the hard times we have all had. The cream of the joke is that we made our own money ourselves and no one gave us a blessed penny. That does sooth my rumbled soul so much that the glory is'nt worth thinking of. What arrangement did Pa make with Mrs. Stearns? do tell us. Also all the gossip of the town, for if you see Channing every week you get it all fresh and regular I suppose.

There are two little English boys here one of whom is so like Fred that I can hardly keep my hands off of him, long bright hair, big brown eyes, &c. and a fair face. Dear lovies! I dreamed that we went home, and to our horror found two tall men in tail coats instead of the dear little nannies! May and I got laughing in bed one day about Fred's one big white tooth and Donny's way of spluttering when excited. Alice heard us, and we convulsed her by telling about our "remarkable boys." Tell them this sad tale of a kitty. There is an old cat Ma puss with two dear little kits, and one day one kit went up so far in a tree that she didn't dare come down, and there she had to stay all night with it raining and thundering dreadfully. We couldn't get her down till next day, and then the old Ma puss did it in a very sly way. She purred and called the poor kit till she saw her, and then laid down at the foot of the tree and let the other kitty nurse. That was too much for the hungry little thing up in the tree, and down she scrambled and ran to her Mammar and bounced onto her so glad to get back that all we could see at first [were] three gray tails waving wildly. Wasn't it a nice Ma?

Send your letters by British steamers and mark them "Via England," and then they won't go off to Germany, for the German ships are all in a mess.

Alice thanks you for your messages. She is clever, but no saint, and we get on all the better for it. Just now we are thinking of a month in Geneva, for I cant go about and need amusement, and these little places are dull for Emma & me. I hope to have a good letter from Nan soon. May does the descriptions so well that I dont try it, being lazy.

Lu.

MS: Unlocated; manuscript copy by ABA at Houghton Library, Harvard University. Partially printed: Cheney 240–41.

1. Not until 15 July 1870, when Emperor Napoleon III declared war on Prussia, were French forces mobilized. While they had been preparing for war weeks earlier, they did not cross the Rhine. Instead, German troops crossed the border into France on 4 August 1870. Paris was surrounded on September 19, beginning a siege that lasted for over four months.

2. The note may be translated: "Your ever grateful François, Count of Szapany."

3. On 17 July ABA notes in his manuscript *Diary for 1870*: "Extreme heat for several days past" (445). The heat would continue, for on 25 and 30 July he would note that the temperature ranged from 90 to 100 degrees.

4. Sanborn's *Hearth and Home* article on LMA noted that LMA had blue eyes. Her eyes were actually grey. The 29 June 1870 *Boston Daily Evening Transcript* printed two brief notices, placed by Roberts Brothers, of *An Old-Fashioned Girl* under the title "John Bull Praises It": "'Who reads an American book?' used to be the query. Very shortly it will be, 'who does NOT read an American book?'" (3). The notice indicates LMA's most recent work has been reprinted in England and gives two brief excerpts, one from the 18 June *Athenaeum* and the other from the 11 June *Spectator*.

5. Lady Katherine Louisa Stanley (ca. 1844–74), daughter of Edward John Stanley, second baron Stanley of Alderly, married John Russell, Viscount Amberley, in 1864. The couple visited Concord in the fall of 1867, and ABA and RWE arranged for them to attend a meeting of the Radical Club. LMA noted: "Lord & Lady Amberly made a stir in B[oston]. Saw them at the Club" (*Journals* 159). For an account of this visit, see also *Letters of ABA* (414–15). She visited LMA in Boston in February 1868: "Note from Lady Amberly as I sat sewing on my nine-penny dress. She wanted to come see me, and I told her to do so, and I'd show her how I lived in my sky-parlor,—spinning yarns like a spider. Met her at the [Radical] Club, and liked her, so simple and natural" (*Journals* 165). A peeress is a female member of the nobility in Great Britain.

6. Charles Dickens died on 9 June 1870 in London and was buried in Westminster Abbey. Frederic Henry Hedge published an extract from a sermon on "The Moral Capital of Society" in the 18 June 1870 *Christian Register* where he says the following about Dickens: "This man, I say, has added to the moral capital of society. A power of healthful influence for this and future generations is funded by his works. . . . He should rank evermore with those who have added to the sum of human wealth" (2).

7. See ABA's manuscript *Diary for 1870*, where he pastes in an unidentified newspaper clipping that claims Roberts Brothers "has paid Miss Alcott for her books between $12,000 and $13,000 within two years, as author's percentage" (418); Lorenzo Eaton (1815–1901) was assistant internal revenue collector for Concord during the 1860s.

8. ABA's [August] 1870 letter to LMA provides details on the family's financial situation. Included with the letter is a financial statement detailing LMA's investments with Samuel E. Sewall. See *Letters of ABA* 520–21.

Louisa May Alcott to Anna Alcott Pratt

Sunday Bex July 24th 1870.

Private,

My dear Nan,

I feel to write you a letter all to your little fat self, though I have very little to say, for we lead such awfully lazy lives there is no news.

I am now writing in a salon, a large airy room with a painted ceiling, a polished floor, piano, and red sofas all round, with tables and books scattered about. All the six long windows are open on one side opening into the balcony or gallery that overhangs and leads into the court; on the other side a garden where a queer fountain drips into a trough where the women wash the salad and the clothes and men water their horses and fill great wooden things which [they] carry on their backs away.

May and Alice are reading at one table where I sit writing. At another table sit a Mr Louis Greenwood from England with his wife and two young ladies. At a third table is a stout imposing English lady in crimping[?] crape and a nose[?] fan,[1] she nods and bobs with sleep as she waits for her daughter Lizzy to come and escort her to church. They know Mrs. Eckley and her friend Miss Legget.[2] Lizzy is a very pleasant girl who has inspired me to begin a piece of worsted work. It is to be a cover for the little stool in the parlor, and to be green and black shaded like the carpet. A great work as you may imagine, a "Penelope".[3]

Mr. Tidey, the Pa of the pretty boys is a water-color artist and May likes his sketches very much, and has drawn a picture of little Alfred as he sat looking at papers [see figure 47] so like my Fred with his long goldy hair

FIGURE 47. Alfred Tidey, Bex, Switzerland (1870), by May Alcott. *Louisa May Alcott's Orchard House/L. M. A. Memorial Association.*

FIGURE 48. One of the Tidey boys, Bex, Switzerland (1870), by May Alcott. *Louisa May Alcott's Orchard House/L. M. A. Memorial Association.*

and great brown eyes.[4] They have sweet soft manners and voices so like the lovies that it does my heart good to hear them. They come from Sussex and are plain quiet folks, very fond of each other and particularly to the mother who is very sad for the loss of her eldest son lately dead.

The Warrens dont particularly interest us. Lena is a stubby little girl of 24, very blunt, smart, common-sensical and rough. Her one soft spot is her dog, a scrabbly Skye, whom she frets and fusses over more than she does her sister [see figure 49]. She is full of fight as a game chicken, but kind and funny. Emma, 30 years old, is pretty and mild, but affected, and not at all interesting. She sits or lies in a wheel-chair all the time. Alice thinks she is lovely and is very fond of her, which is a good thing as it gives A. something to do.

Just now we are full of plans, for it is rather hot here and we have seen all there is to see, having stayed three weeks. So we have a dozen plans a day, the last being a villa at or near Geneva where we all live together, which would make it cheap for every one. I don't care where we go, if it is only warm and I dont have to fuss about any thing. The weather is superb and day after day we wake to find the sun shining and a cool air blowing from the hills. Even the hottest days when I am in a drip, I feel well, so I'm content to sit and fan fearing to fare worse if I go farther. May is fat and jolly enjoys every thing and gets gifts and praise from every one. Alice is funny and kind and we move on peacefully in spite of every thing.

The war along the Rhine is sending troops of travellers to Switzerland for refuge, and all the large towns are brimful of people flying from Germany. It won't trouble us, for we have done France and don't mean to do Germany. So when August is over, we shall trot forward to Italy and find a warm place for our winter quarters. At any time twenty-four hours carries us over the Simplon,[5] so we sit at ease and dont care a straw for old France and Prussia. Russia, it is reported, has joined in the fight,[6] but Italy and England are not going to meddle, so we can fly to either in case of fire.

I have been hoping to get a nice gossipy letter from my Nan all the week and hope still, and often sit and fancy you trotting round the house, making blanc-mange for tea,[7] or pants for the boys, or putting on a "little dear dress" and blue bow for Pa Pratt at night, or writing to your old lass with a

FIGURE 49. Lena Warren with her dog,
Bex, Switzerland (1870), by May Alcott.
Houghton Library, Harvard University.

loving tear in your dear eyes as you long to see "the girls;" who long, one at any rate, to see you all so much, she puts a iss here X X X X. Mother would have fits over the *goitre* which nearly every one has in some stage or other. At St. Maurice they are so big that they have to be tied up with ribbons and people ornament them with lockets. Idiots and *goitres* are the rule here and I don't wonder living as they do in dark dirty houses and inter-marrying generation after generation.

July 27th [1870]

Bless you my Sairy! Your nice long letter has just come and we have been revelling in it all the forenoon. Such a fat beamy one, and only one little bad news—my missis being poorly. She well is now she hoped. With yours came one from Tommy with the picture and notice in "Heart [i.e., Hearth] and Home." The picture is as good as such things ever are, better than many [see figure 50]. I think the Black picture the best and wished it had been used,[8] only as there was no negative there would have been a good deal of trouble. The notice is excellent, kindly and simple and flattering. I shall write to tell Sanborn, I'm much obliged to him for finding out that I am related to Longfellow.[9]

I opened it at breakfast table, and the girls, A. and M. and Lena, howled over the paper, and the Yankee party Ma Bates and her two girls were dying to know what it was all about.

I read them about the Jones and Bartletts parties and they thought it great fun.[10] You need'nt send me the letters that come, and don't answer them or send my picture, Marmee. People will see I'm away and won't expect it.

If my princely Freddy gets countryfied and rejects his Ma, I shall be grieved. He must be a "trotty drau" like his Pa. The little english boys went yesterday, and came to say goodbye, putting up their rosy faces to kiss us, so like my lovies' that I gave them a good hug. May won their hearts by singing to them, and the last eve they were here every one swarmed into the parlor while she was singing and applauded and gave her flowers, and she made quite a sensation.

We thought some of going to St. Luke with them, but it is high up and far away from every one,[11] and Alice don't like it, so we shall probably stay here longer.

FIGURE 50. Louisa May Alcott, engraving,
Hearth and Home (1870), with LMA's
comments about it. *Louisa May Alcott's Orchard
House/L. M. A. Memorial Association.*

FIGURE 51. Frontispiece to *Little Women, Part One* (1868), by May Alcott.

You ask if I am not in bliss? No. I find that I've lost the power of enjoying as I used to, and though I like to see the fine scenes, I get tired of it very soon, and want to rest and be still. If I could have had a party like this four years ago I should have enjoyed it with a real relish. Now I feel so old and stupid and wimbly, I don't deserve to be in the way of such things and you should be here in my place. I'm getting better steadily, and yesterday went up to Leppz,[12] a long drive over the most wonderful road I ever saw, so steep that it wound & zig zagged till at one place I looked down on six turns. We were gone all day, yet I was not very tired and had no pain but slept well all night without opium and feel well to day. This is a decided gain, for I have not been able to drive because the jar hurt me. The heat and soft air at Bex seem to suit me, and as it only costs $7,00 a week, it is a good place to stop in and economize, for Italy is very expensive A. says. The Warrens wont move and A. wants to be with them, and we dont find any better place, so we shall stay.

You need not send me notices for Tommy sends all of any consequence, and I had rather have letters from you. I pay 10 cents here and you ought not to pay anything on our letters. Do you have to? I think I know a little fat lady who will go to Selwyne now and then, if Fetcher is there. Wish I could see him again.[13]

I did n't hear about the birth day tea party. Give my Donny isses from Aunt Weedy.[14] X X X X. Does Ma leave C[onant]. to be "boss-mammas" while she is gone? Hope Marmee will come to you and shut up the house before Pa goes, so that no cold weather can nip her up. This is a double letter and I shall pay franc 20 cts. for it, and it will be enough if the old troops and war fuss don't interfere and delay it. Two Frenchmen and one Prussian have been killed and that is all the news as yet.

We heard of Dickens' death some weeks ago, and have been reading notices &c. in all the papers since. One by G. Greenwood in the Tribune was very nice.[15] I shall miss my old Charley, but he was not the idol he once was. I hope Tommy will send me "Every Saturday" with the picture in it.[16]

Did you know that Higginson and a little girl-friend had written out the Operatic Tragedy in "Little Women" and set the songs to music, and it was all to be put in "Our Young Folks?"[17] What are we coming to in our old age? Also I hope to see the new designs Tommy has got for Little Women. I know nothing about them. I hope the "Jo Worshippers" were not regaled with my papers. *Has* the old box ever been nailed up? I squirm to think of my very old scribble being trotted out. I am so glad you were there to do the honors and fill the posy-pots[?]. Dear little parlor! I often think of it and imagine you in it, Ma mending hose at her window or reading Johnson,[18] Pa among his newspapers, and you with the work basket that seldom is empty. I wonder if I shall ever see it again!

I'm glad Alice sends good accounts of us. She seems very fond of me to my surprise, for May was the first love. Thank you for telling me.

Let me know how S. E. S. has invested my chink, and if Pa keeps any account of things, for if S. E. S. should die, I don't know where my *fortune* is.

Riches bring care and my $20,000 will be "wearing" if we don't keep our eye out on our investments, &c.

Ha! Ha! It is droll, but I cant make the fortunate Miss A. seem me, and only remember the weary years, the work, the waiting and disappointment—all that is forth in my mind; the other don't belong to me, and is a mistake somehow. Perhaps it will come real when I get used to rest and comfort, and not feeling as if "the hounds were after me." God bless and keep us all to enjoy the late honest wealth which Marmee and Pa sowed in the chaotic *pastur*

called Lu.

P. S.

That Miss *writes* often to her Miss and Nannies[?].

May is funny, but very clever and improves daily being with folks who have some of the polish which she likes. I think I don't care for it as much as I once did; for the folks who have it don't have what I value more—character and simplicity.

May says "our moral remarks will convulse the folks at home," but we are rather out of our element without any reformers or sages or bow wows, and so we "digress."

MS: Unlocated; manuscript copy by ABA at Houghton Library, Harvard University. Partially printed: Cheney 241–42, where it is printed as two separate letters.

1. Crimping crape has a succession of small folds or frills.

2. Perhaps Mrs. Eliza Seaman Leggett of Detroit, Michigan. ABA, on his Western tour, had held a Conversation at her home in late January 1870. Mrs. Eckley is unidentified.

3. In Homer's *Odyssey*, Penelope, wife of Odysseus, waits twenty years for her husband to return from the Trojan War. Many suitors press her to marry, insisting Odysseus is dead. She finally declares she will wed when she completes weaving the burial shroud of Laertes, her father-in-law. For three years, she weaves the shroud but unravels a portion of it every night to delay selecting a husband.

4. Mr. Tidey may be related to the artist Alfred Tidey (1808–92), who was also from Sussex, England. See May's sketch of little Alfred looking at papers (figure 47). In *Shawl-Straps*, LMA writes: "An artist with two pretty boys, named Alfred Constable Landseer Reynolds and Allston West Cuyp Vandyke, afforded Matilda [May] much satisfaction" (130).

5. The Simplon Pass, in the southern Swiss Alps, connects Italy to Switzerland. The Simplon Road was built by Napoleon in the period 1800–1806.

6. Russia never joined the fight; however, they did use the early French defeats to denounce clauses in the Treaty of Paris of 1856, which declared the Black Sea neutral waters and limited the number of Russian naval forces on the sea.

7. Blancmange, a sweetmeat made of dissolved gelatin boiled with milk.

8. J. W. Black had taken an earlier photograph of LMA circa 1868–70. In 1870, his "Photograph Rooms" were located at 163 and 173 Washington Street, Boston.

9. In his *Hearth and Home* article, Sanborn had written that "Miss Alcott and the poet Longfellow are descended from a common Massachusetts ancestor, Henry Sewall, of Newbury, whose daughter Anne married William Longfellow, the first of the name in New-England" (1).

10. The Joneses and Bartletts are unidentified.

11. St. Luc, located in the Valais canton of southern Switzerland, is on a steep slope high above the Val d'Anniviers, with beautiful views of the valley below and the Alps beyond.

12. Les Plans, located approximately five and one half miles from Bex, was noted for its health resorts and spring water. The road from Bex borders the left bank of the Avancon River and offers superb views of Dent du Midi.

13. The Selwyn Theatre, managed by John H. Selwyn, was located on Washington Street near the corner with Essex Street in Boston and operated from 1867 to 1870. In 1870, it was renamed the Globe but burned in 1873.

14. John Sewall Pratt was born 24 June 1865.

15. Grace Greenwood was the pseudonym of Sara Jane Lippincott (1823–1904), poet, essayist and journalist. Her first-person account of a June 1852 meeting with Dickens in London formed the basis for her tribute "Recollections of the Great Novelist" published in the 5 July 1870 *New York Daily Tribune* (6) under the initials "G. G."

16. On 7 July 1870, Niles wrote LMA: "Next week 'Every Saturday' will have a full page cartoon from 'Little Women' of 'Joe & the Professor' under the umbrella. It is superb" (ALS: Houghton Library, Harvard University). *Every Saturday: An Illustrated Journal of Choice Reading* (23 July 1870) carried a full-page illustration of "Jo and the Professor" from *Little Women* on page 536.

17. Thomas Wentworth Higginson (1823–1911), author, reformer, soldier, and friend of the Alcott family, notes in his diary that he saw *Little Women* performed at the home of young Annie Bigelow on 18 June 1870. By June 21, he says that he had begun writing "Acting Little Women" and had completed it by 6 July. See the manuscript diary of T. W. Higginson, Houghton Library, Harvard University (bMS Am 1162 [8] 1870). On 7 July 1870, Niles had written LMA that Higginson had composed a long introduction to Bigelow's play and that someone had drawn illustrations. On 30 August, however, Niles

wrote her that Fields had rejected the manuscript for *Our Young Folks* and that Higginson had "brought it to me. A hasty reading did not impress me very favorably and though on a more careful review I might have formed a different opinion, as he was anxious to do something else with it, I returned it to him" (ALS: Houghton Library, Harvard University). No record has been located of the adaptation being published.

18. Dr. Samuel Johnson (1709–84), British poet, lexicographer, and essayist, was Abigail Alcott's favorite author.

May Alcott to Anna Alcott Pratt

Bex July 25 1870

(Private)

Dear Nan,

Here we are still at Bex (pronounced Bay) and there is so much difficulty in finding just the right place to go that I begin to think we may stay here a month longer. Lena and I went to Geneva looking for a good pension the other day, but the prices have risin so owing to the war, and the place is so full of strangers that we were almost discouraged. Besides the difficulty of finding six rooms that would suit the members of the party. Alice of course wishes to be with her cousins as long as possible, and as they prefer Geneva we all decided to go, if it was found possible to get rooms. So off Lena and I started going to Montreux[1] by cars and then across this lovely lake for a four hours' sail, and reaching Geneva rather late for two young women alone. However, I am quite hardened now, and think nothing of poking round strange cities alone, for I never find any trouble in getting back to the hotel. We went directly to Madame Bovet where Aunty and Sophia still are, but found no possibility of even a room for the night but succeeded in getting in at a Pension next door, where we slept in a little room looking directly out on a yard and street and as I felt a little suspicious about the kind of house we had got into, I kept my eye on the long low window just by my bed, and hardly slept a wink all night though I felt quite ready to cope with any burglar that should try to frighten us as we were each armed with our long sharp daggers, (for Lu, really purchased one merely that we might have something in case of emergences) and I felt quite ready for a scene, but nothing happened, and very likely the house was the most peaceful one imaginable.

Next morning we started in search for rooms, and after much trouble found some not far from the great hotel and not very high in price, so we satisfied our consciences with having dragged all over the city, Murray in hand, so there we began to enjoy our plans by taking an ice-cream, peach pie and delicious cake of all kinds for lunch, and going shopping afterwards till it was time to take our train home.

The first thing I saw was a ready made grey waterproof dress, with a border and fringe like a shawl, the very last style from Paris, and as it was very cheap and becoming, after trying it on in the store behind a funny little screen, I decided to buy it and wear it home to surprise Lu and Alice. I hav'nt any autumn or winter travelling dress and the moment I saw this decided to have it, and walked out of the store with it on. The clerks all took a deep interest in my purchase and all smiled approval, when I *bon joured* all round and sailed out in my new robe, leaving my old one to be put to the station. I have been wearing my old grey one with black underskirt ever since we came here, having it washed at intervals, and so felt I could now indulge in a new one.

The Geneva stores are the most distracting I ever beheld, and I should spend a fortune if I had it, for every thing is so cheap, lovely watches with hunter[?] cases, one $15 only, (and I hope Lu will get one it is such a chance,) most heavenly jewelry of all kinds, fine carved things, ready made robes of white muslin; and in short, every thing that one can imagine that is tempting. I was so sure that I saw Herbert Pratt in the street that I went to the hotel from which he came and looked over the book of names but found no H. J. P. However Alice dropped a line to him as soon as I told her I thought I saw him, and he may appear, but I think it is doubtful as we saw his name at a great dinner in Paris.

I hope you will all think of me on the 26th. and take satisfaction in the thought that I am very happy and not at all troubled by my advanced age.[2] I enjoy the two little English boys immensely because they remind me so much of Freddy and Johny though larger and taller than the lovies; the father is an artist and we have nice talks together.

We have just got your letters and the pictures of Lu in the paper, which is as good as any of those horrid wood cuts ever are. I think it a very cool proceeding in Fields' part to put two illustrations of "Little Women" in the "Young Folks," and should'nt think Niles would allow such liberties with his particular authoress. Of course it will make a great sale for the paper and I am sorry they should have the profits.[3]

Give my love to dear John and ask him why he never writes to us: particularly to his beloved May who wears his little ring on her little finger[4] and yanks it with great effect for the Count's benefit, but thinks of her dear old beau at home enjoying rheumatics.

Lu does seem more than ever on the crest of the wave, and it wont do her any harm to have such success after her hard times. Alice is very much attached to her, and the Warrens think her splendid. Every where we go we meet people who recognize her as a lion and treat her accordingly, which she does'nt object to in her sweet heart I think. Poor Nanny, I wish you could be with us & have some of our everlasting leisure, for I have no ambition to work this hot weather; sleep overpowers me at all hours, and I give up to it as it seems to do me good, and I realize how run down I was when I left America. I should'nt have held out much longer working as I did.

I send 100 kisses for my birthday present to you all

Your loving May.

MS: Unlocated; copy by ABA at Houghton Library, Harvard University.

1. Montreux, Switzerland, actually made up of several small villages, sits on the north shore of Lake Geneva at the fork of the old Roman road that goes to Italy over the Simplon Pass.

2. May Alcott was born on 26 July 1840 in Concord, Massachusetts.

3. In a search of *Our Young Folks* for 1870–71, I did not locate any illustrations from *Little Women*. It is possible that the illustrations May refers to here were printed on the inside wrappers of an issue. I have been unable to locate, however, a complete run of the magazine in wrappers for 1870.

4. John Pratt had given May his seal ring, which had a symbol or emblem that was used to press into wax when sealing a letter (see May to Abigail Alcott and Anna A. Pratt, 9–12 April 1870).

May Alcott to Abigail and A. Bronson Alcott

Bex July 26 1870

Dear Mother and Father,

  I send you a little picture of Bex which will give you an idea of the lovely valley we are in, and a glimpse of the Dent de M'orcle which we look up to every day from our windows and where we mean to go as an excursion sometime next week.[1] Lu took a long drive yesterday and slept all the better for it last night; she has used no opium for some time and improves daily I think. There is really nothing of interest to tell you but I thought it hardly kind to let this the 26th go by without writing to the dearest parents that a young woman of 30 was ever blessed with. I feel quite sure that within the last year or two my views and opinions about things in general, and a womans life in particular have been getting right and that my real life was beginning, and think when I come home, father will find I have grown a little near him and we shall have some good talks together. There is nothing like travel for bringing out one's character and improving one's mind; and I now knowingly regret not having had the eyes to have read more books of general information that I might see and enjoy things more understandingly in this delightful tour we are now making. I am digging at Italian, for we shall so soon be in that enchanting land of pictures and I can be so useful to the party with only a smattering of the language.

  I have had five pretty presents to day, which is more than I expected. I miss mother's little cake with a posy in it for the birth-day, but think of you all the more and see the value of all our little celebrations more than I ever did before.

  Do tell me about "Tablets" being translated into German. What an honor for dear old Pa![2]

Kisses to both of you
from your loving
May.

FIGURE 52. Bronson Alcott in his study, Orchard House (1869–70?), by May Alcott. *Louisa May Alcott's Orchard House/L. M. A. Memorial Association.*

MS: Unlocated; copy by ABA at Houghton Library, Harvard University.

1. Dent de Morcles (elevation 9,775 feet) is located in Bernese Alps of Switzerland, commanding fine views of Lake Geneva and Mount Blanc.

2. ABA's *Tablets* had been published by Roberts Brothers in September 1868. In his manuscript *Diary for 1870*, ABA notes: "Miss Jane Hosmer is here from Syracuse N. Y. where she is teaching. She informs me that she has heard my 'Tablets' are translated into German. I am not surprised to learn that my book interests speculative thinkers and finds a readier reading in Germany than with us" (431). No copy of a German translation has been located.

May Alcott to A. Bronson Alcott

Bex July 30th 1870.

Dearest Father,

I fear this war is going to be more of an inconvenience than we at first imagined, for if Italy joins in it, or does not remain entirely neutral as she now declares herself to be, we cannot go there in September according to our plans. Of course, I can bear such a great disappointment, but it will be rather hard for both Louisa and myself to forego seeing Rome. However we will hope that the most may be only a delay of some months, not the giving it up altogether. Here in Switzerland we are safe enough, but in case of a prolonged struggle it may be very hard to get our money through Munroe; whereas if we were in England we could charge to Baring, and receive our funds without trouble. What do the papers say in America?—for it is impossible to get any news here, and you hear everything sooner than we do.

Louisa is so well, sleeping naturally without narcotics, having no pain, and growing so strong and well, that it would be too bad if she was obliged to winter in England, or by any possibility return to America, as the change of climate must do its work thoroughly to prevent the horrors of last winter from being repeated. We shall probably be here sometime longer, and as for me I am quite content to remain in this lovely valley, with my windows directly under the snow peaked "Dent du Midi" on one side, and the enchanting "Diableret" on the other, with Lake Geneva only a little way off.[1] I should feel fully repaid for crossing the ocean by what I have already seen, and very thankful that I came, even if we posted home tomorrow. But we shall hope that there will be [a] little convenient corner found for us over here to hide in till the worst is over.

We received a long nice letter from Anna, and one from Mr and Mrs Barton, which told us all home items and news about our last winter friends at No 43. A Mr. Harden whom we knew there and was extremely polite and kind to us, has asked through the Bartons for one of the Marshall vignette photographs of me,[2] and I very much wish he should have one of them, if you have one of the best ones to spare; the one you sent me, I think perfect, the smiling profile without any dress to be seen. The small common size if you have such without ordering a dozen or half a dozen taken. I should like it put into an envelope and directed to Mr. Harden with the complements of Miss May Alcott and put with the enclosed letter to the Bartons. Now papa, dear, you will do this all nicely for me *without going to any expense*, and I shall be pleased to have it all done.

I am glad your hearing is so much better and hope you will have a successful winter trip at the West, where you can celebrate your girls as much as you like, for it seems to pay excellently.[3] Louisa wrote Sanborn a charming letter, thanking him for his notice in "Hearth and Home," and expressing her satisfaction with the whole thing. I know [it] will please him. Do remember me to him whenever you see him, as I dont think he knows what a sincere admirer he has in me.

You have never told us how the matter was settled with Mrs. S_____ for of course you have had an interview with her about the money and I am curious to hear what she has to say.[4] Louisa's prosperity of course will bring any old auditors about you, if any such there be, clamoring for funds, and our friends will henceforth consider us rolling in money, and never by any possibility be in need of help. I am amazed at Fields putting the picture of Jo into "Every Saturday;" but it only shows how ready he is to bite the dust now, after telling her, "*She had better keep to schoolkeeping.*"[5] She has a great chance now for making more fame and money, and I am therefore all the more anxious that she should stay abroad long enough to get her poor head quite strong again and ready for work;—for her next book will be her best, I think. The income from her money already in S. E. S.'s hands would support you and mother I should suppose and that seems a great deal for her to have done. The continued sale of her books will be steady income which will allow her to rest when she feels like it, and remove the tremendous pressure that she has felt so long.

The Misses Warren are reading "Little Women," and enjoying the whole very much. They are parishioners of O. B. Frothingham in New York and great admirers of his. They like Lu, and enjoy having a good look at the lion, though at first they had heard so much about her fame that they were afraid. They each gave me a present on my birthday—a pretty breast-pin made of the crystal found at the "Gorge de Trient."[6] I read aloud to them a great deal and they are very fond of me. I regret so much not bringing a copy of "*Tablets*" with me, as we have met several people who would enjoy seeing it, and I delight to show my Papa's books, I think them so lovely myself.

Why do you have a brown and green carpet when everything is red in your study? I hope the old red table clothe is kept at the window in my studio behind your bust.

Give my love to Ellen Emerson when you see her, and tell her we enjoyed Edward's *champagne* very much.[7]

Your affectionate

May.

MS: Unlocated; manuscript copy by ABA at Houghton Library, Harvard University.

1. From Lake Geneva, Dents du Midi (Teeth of the Moon), elevation 10,685 feet, are the mountains prominently seen from the south of the lake. Seven major "dents" can be seen. Mt. Diableret, noted for its glacier, rises to an elevation of 10,650 feet.

2. Augustus Marshall, photographer, was located at 147 Tremont Street, Boston. The photograph May refers to may be the one pasted into ABA's *Autobiographical Collection* for 1870 (165), located in the Houghton Library, Harvard University (Ms Am 1130.11[8]).

3. On 2 May 1870 ABA noted in his manuscript *Diary for 1870* that he had visited Dr. Smedley in Boston about his ear; Smedley "pronounces the deafness which has been troubling me for the last year, especially in conversing with persons sitting at some distance, curable." Claiming the loss of hearing was caused by catarrh, the doctor says that for one hundred dollars he can restore hearing if ABA visits him twice a week for three months (251). He begins treatments and by 26 September reports that he left Smedley's office "with my sense of hearing, as far as I could discern, perfectly restored" (611). Bronson wrote LMA in August 1870: "My prospects are fair as to my Western tour. I ought not to return home without my $2000 at least, since I go advertised and arrangements

are made for me in the cities and towns from Syracuse to Debuque and St. Louis, and I may get as far as San Francisco" (*Letters of ABA* 520–21).

4. Probably Mrs. Stearns. ABA drew a blank line after the initial "S."

5. Early in her writing career, the publisher James T. Fields (1817–81) had advised LMA: "'Stick to your teaching; you can't write'" (*Journals* 109).

6. Gorges du Trient is located at Vernayaz, a small village, near Martigny, Switzerland. Almost forty thousand years earlier, a U-shaped profile had been shaped in the valley by glaciers. Formed from the snow and glacier melting, the river had cut a notch there in a V-shape. During the eighteenth century, a glassworking factory had been opened.

7. Ellen Emerson (1839–1909) was one year older than May Alcott and a close friend of the Alcott sisters throughout their lives. Edward Emerson, at the request of his sister Ellen, had presented the Alcott sisters with a case of champagne for their European voyage in April 1870. See Ellen Emerson's 25 March 1870 letter to Edward Emerson in *The Letters of Ellen Tucker Emerson*, vol. 1., ed. Edith E. W. Gregg (Kent, Ohio: Kent State University Press, 1982), 542–43.

Louisa May Alcott to Abigail Alcott

3 P.M. Bex July 31ˢᵗ 1870.

Dear Marmee,

As May wants to send some notes, I must have a finger in the pie and put something in the envelope.

We are all in a stir here, for the bankers begin to act as if money was to be scarce, and travellers begin to feel as if they must tread toward home. Mrs Bates, the American here had to take Swiss paper money instead of gold yesterday, and as it is not good out of Switzerland, she must use it here and trust to luck by and by. I shall draw my £20 from Munroe as that is all he has in hand, so if he scrimps or gets into a muddle I don't lose any thing. *Don't send any money to him for me till I write*, for I may have to cut away to England and there Baring is the best banker. I have only spent about $200 in these four months for self and May which is cheap living. In Italy it will cost more, but as Italy sides with France and war is likely to break out there, we may have no choice except between Switzerland and England. We all prefer England for we could go early in the fall and see what we could before November. Then go to Torquay or Penzance on the coast of Cornwall for the winter.[1] An English lady here, an invalid, tells us that Penzance is a lovely place for delicate people in winter, consumption and rheumatism both, as it is warm and dry.

I am so much better that I think any mild place will do by that time and the good food in England suits me well. Alice has friends and so have I in England, and we can have good times if we *are* driven there. I regret Italy on May's account but the war may be over by spring, and being this side the sea we can start off again in spring and still see Rome.

Papers are suppressed by the Government, so we know nothing about the war except the rumors that float about. But people seem to think that Europe is in for a general fight, and there is no guessing when it will end.

The trouble about getting into Italy is that civil war always breaks out there, and things are so mixed up, that strangers get into scrapes among the different squabblers. When the Perkin's were abroad during the last Italian fuss, they got shut up in some little city and would have been killed by Austrians, who were rampaging round the place drunk and mad, if a woman had not hidden them in a water closet for a day and night and smuggled them out at last when they ran for their lives.[2] I don't mean to get into any mess, and between Switzerland and England we can manage for a winter. London is so near home and so homelike that we shall be quite handy and can run up to Boston at any time. Perhaps Pa will step across to us.

All these plans may be knocked in the head tomorrow, and my next letter may be dated from the Pope's best parlor or Windsor Castle, but I like to spin about our ups and downs, so you can have something to talk about at Apple Slump. Uncertainty gives a relish to things, so we chase about and have a dozen plans a day. It is an Alcott failing you know.

Private

It will please you to know that I am steadily getting on, and see a plump, rosy, old face in my glass. To-day I put on my boots for the first time for weeks and they are cosy. The bunches are nearly gone, and I have no pain even at night and enjoy my sleep as only *I* can. I am so tickled to wake every morning after a long sound sleep that I can't believe it is *me*, and bless old Kane every day of my life. I can walk and ride and begin to feel as if a chain of heavy aches had fallen off and left me free. If this goes on without any break down for a month or so I shall feel as if my trip was a brilliant success, and be satisfied even if I never see Rome. I think the dry hot weather here the last month came just when I needed it, and did a great deal to perk me up. The climate is so very mild and soft, it relaxes my strung up nerves, and is better than a more bracing place just now, so I am resigned to stay longer and be ready in September to go wherever fate and the war leads us.

August 2nd [1870]

To Marmee,

The envelope is so full and postage has risen, so I can only add a word. Please put Mrs Cheney's note in an envelope and send it, and let me have her reply soon, so I can get her shawl in Paris if we go in a month or so.

We got a letter from Pa yesterday with a second edition of my pictures. Tommy sends all those things, so don't fill your letters with them. I'd rather have news, so keep the papers &c. and send me letters.

I am looking out for Nan and Ma's now. Thanks to Papa for his; he is very good to write us so often. Does he *really* mean to go to California?[3] Isn't he perky in his old age? Hurra for the plucky old philosopher!

Love to all and bless you

Ever Yours
Lu.

MS: Unlocated; copy by ABA at Houghton Library, Harvard University. Partially printed: Cheney 242–43.

1. Torquay is a town on the south coast of England in the county of Devon. Because of its healthy climate, it became a fashionable seaside resort during the nineteenth century. Penzance is a port town in the Penwith district of Cornwall, England, and it faces southeast into the English Channel. Its location in the shelter of Mount's Bay provides the town with a subtropical climate that is warmer than the rest of England.

2. The Perkinses are unidentified.

3. ABA was contemplating undertaking Conversations in the West, including California, in October 1870. He left for his Western tour on 26 October 1870 and returned home four months later on 3 March 1870. Iowa, however, was as far west as he would travel.

OH 97/12   The Golden Goose.

Louisa May Alcott to Thomas Niles

Bex August 7 1870.

Dear Mr. Niles,

I keep receiving requests from editors to write for their papers or magazines. I am duly grateful, but having come abroad for rest, I am not inclined to try the treadmill till my year's vacation is over. So, to appease these worthy gentlemen and excuse my seeming idleness I send you a trifle in rhyme[1] which you can (if you think it worth the trouble) set going as a general answer to everybody, for I cant pay postage in replies to each separately, "its werry costly."

Mr Ford said he would pay me $10, 15, 20, for any little things I would send him, so perhaps you will let him have it first.

The war makes the bankers take double toll on our money, so we feel very poor and as if we ought to be earning not spending, only we are so lazy we can't bear to think of it in earnest. Street and Smith of the "N.Y. Weekly" were the last applicants, asking for a serial, and in a brief business way, and ending with, "Name your own price".[2] But I did not like the list of contributors Ned Buntline, Lu Billings, Spaulding, Philander Doesticks, and other great lights, so I could not think of it, and prefer the "heavy moral."[3]

We shall probably go to London next month, if the war forbids Italy for the winter, and if we cant get one dollar without paying five for it, we shall come home disgusted.

If a chance ever comes to get hold of "Morning Glories" please do it for me.[4] Perhaps if I can do nothing else this year, I could have a book of short stories old and new for Christmas. Ford and Fuller have some good ones, and I have the right to use them. We could call them, "Jo March's Necessity Stories." Would, would it go with new ones added and good illustrations?

I am rising from my ashes in a most phoenix-like manner.

L. M. A.

FIGURE 53. "The Golden Goose," Louisa May Alcott, Bex, Switzerland (1870), by May Alcott. *Louisa May Alcott's Orchard House/L. M. A. Memorial Association.*

The Lay of a Golden Goose

Long ago in a poultry yard
   One dull November morn,
Beneath a motherly soft wing
   A little goose was born.

Who straightway peeped out of the shell
   To view the world beyond,
Longing at once to sally forth
   And paddle in the pond.

"Oh! be not rash" her father said,
   A mild Socratic bird;
Her mother begged her not to stray
   With many a warning word.

But little goosey was perverse,
   And eagerly did cry—
"I've got a lovely pair of wings.
   Of course I ought to fly."

In vain parental cacklings,
   In vain the cold sky's frown,
Ambitious goosey tried to soar,
   But always tumbled down.

The farm yard jeered at her attempts;
   The peacocks screamed, "Oh fie!
You're only a domestic goose,
   So don't pretend to fly."

Great cock-adoodle from his perch
   Crowed daily loud and clear,

"Stay in the puddle, foolish bird,
     That is your proper sphere."

The ducks and hens said, one and all,
     In gossip by the pool,
"Our children never play such pranks;
     My dear, that fowl's a fool."

The owls came out and flew about,
     Hooting above the rest,
"No useful egg was ever hatched
     From transcendental nest."

Good little goslings at their play,
     And well-conducted chicks,
Were taught to think poor goosey's flights
     Were naughty, ill-bred tricks.

They were content to swim and scratch,
     And not at all inclined,
For any wild-goose chase in search
     Of something undefined.

Hard times she had as one may guess,
     That young aspiring bird,
Who still from every fall arose
     Saddened but undeterred.

She knew she was no nightingale,
     Yet spite of much abuse,
She longed to help and cheer the world,
     Although a plain gray goose.

She could not sing, she could not fly,
     Nor even walk with grace,

And all the farm-yard had declared
    A puddle was her place.

But something stronger than herself
    Would cry, "Go on, go on!
Remember, though a humble fowl,
    You're cousin to a swan."

So up and down poor goosey went,
    A busy, hopeful bird.
Searched many wide unfruitful fields,
    And many waters stirred.

At length she came unto a stream
    Most fertile of all *Niles*,
Where tuneful birds might soar and sing
    Among the leafy isles.

Here did she build a little nest
    Beside the waters still,
Where the parental goose could rest
    Unvexed by any *bill*.

And here she paused to smooth her plumes,
    Ruffled by many plagues;
When suddenly arose the cry—
    "This goose lays golden eggs."

At once the farm-yard was agog;
    The ducks began to quack;
Prim Guinea fowls relenting called,
    "Come back, come back, come back."

Great Chanticleer was pleased to give
    A patronizing crow,

And the contemptuous biddies clucked,
   "I wish my chicks did so."

The peacocks spread their shining tails
   And cried in accents soft—
"We want to know you, gifted one,
   Come up and sit aloof."

Wise owls awoke and gravely said,
   With proudly swelling breasts,
"Rare birds have always been evoked
   From transcendental nests!"

News-hunting turkeys from afar
   Now ran with all thin legs
To gobble facts and fictions of
   The goose with golden eggs.

But best of all the little fowls
   Still playing on the shore,
Soft downy chicks and goslings gay,
   Chirped out, "Dear Goose, lay more."

But goosey all these weary years
   Had toiled like any ant,
And wearied out she now replied,
   "My little dears, I can't.

When I was starving, half this corn
   Had been of vital use,
Now I am surfeited with food
   Like any Strasbourg goose."

So to escape too many friends,
   Without uncivil strife,

She ran to the Atlantic pond
And paddled for her life.

Soon up among the grand old Alps
She found two blessed things,
The health she had so nearly lost
And rest for weary wings.

But still across the briny deep
Couched in most friendly words,
Came prayers for letters, tales or verse,
From literary birds.

Whereat the renovated fowl
With grateful thanks profuse,
Took from her wing a quill and wrote
This lay of a golden goose.

Bex, Switzerland, Aug. 1870.

MS: Unlocated; manuscript copy by ABA at Houghton Library, Harvard University. Printed: *Selected Letters* (without the poem) 144–45; partially printed: Cheney 243–44. ABA's copy of "The Lay of a Golden Goose" is located at the end of his bound volume of Louisa's and May's European letters. The original manuscript has not been located. A handwritten six-page manuscript of the poem, signed by LMA, is located at the Houghton Library, Harvard University (MS Am 1817[12]). It bears the following notation: "Written by Louisa May Alcott & copied into this book by her—L. W." The manuscript appears to be three pages removed from a notebook or autograph book and therefore suggests LMA merely copied her poem for "L. W." It has no textual significance. L. W. possibly was Louisa Wells, LMA's cousin.

1. The poem LMA includes, "The Lay of a Golden Goose," was not given to Daniel Ford's *Youth's Companion* as LMA suggested but was first printed in the 8 May 1886 *Woman's Journal* and later reprinted in Cheney 204–7. This sixteen-year delay in publication was most likely due to Niles, who wrote to LMA on 30 August 1870 after receiving the poem: "I enjoyed 'the Lay' hugely & blush while I think of & thank you for the compliment *laid* to me. But pray dont print it. I would rather give you ten times its pecuniary value than have it published. Its effect would be very prejudicial I am sure.

It is best to forget the neglect and 'outrageous fortune' of past years and you can well afford to do so; pocket the insults & the dollars & do nothing which will 'damn up the waters of the Nile'—let the torrent rush on with gradually accumalating waters. . . . This is Tom's sermon and you can take a nap while reading it if you choose, and order him to print the 'lay' & he will do so without getting mad" (ALS: Houghton Library, Harvard University).

2. Francis Scott Street (1831–83) and Francis Shubael Smith (1819–87) were publishers of the *New York Weekly*, a pulp paper that ran gripping serials. Niles also told LMA in his letter of 30 August: "Do not be tempted with offers to write stories, which you can turn out *ad libitum*—result, money without fame—but devote yourself *entirely* to works which will insure you both a permanency in the niche of fame and a handsome income" (ALS: Houghton Library, Harvard University).

3. The dime novelist Ned Buntline, pseudonym of Edward Z. C. Judson (1823–86); the humorists Josh Billings, pseudonym of Henry Wheeler Shaw (1818–85) and Philander Doesticks, pseudonym of Mortimer Thompson (1831–75); the journalist James Reed Spaulding (1821–72).

4. *Morning-Glories, and Other Stories* was published by Horace B. Fuller of Boston in January 1868. An abridged version of the book had been published by Carleton in New York in December 1867. Roberts Brothers eventually acquired the rights to *Morning-Glories*, and LMA reprinted most of the stories in *Aunt Jo's Scrap-Bag. Volume 6. An Old-Fashioned Thanksgiving* (Boston: Roberts Brothers, 1882).

Louisa May Alcott to Thomas Niles

Forwarded by Politeness of
   Pa Plato.

                                             Vevey Aug. 10th 1870

Dear Mr Niles,

   Will you please send all letters to me that come to your care to my family at Concord, and not to me? Most of them are enthusiastic little bursts from boys and girls who want auto- or photographs which I can't send them; so they may as well go to Concord and be kept for future settlement. Munroe asks sums for forwarding our letters, therefore we want only of the important ones and the dears must wait till I come back, or take it out in looking at the damp and earwigly, "Home of the great American authoress."[1]

FIGURE 54. Thomas Niles, LMA's editor at Roberts Brothers.

We are enjoying the lake now at Vevey in a cosy Pension called "*Paradise*,"[2] where we have French counts and Spanish grandees to play croquet with us, boats to go paddling in, and three or four ex kings and queens to stare at when we take our walks abroad.[3]

The war seems to be coming to a "*focum*," as they[?] would say,[4] and when the last Prussian has calmly slaughtered the last fiery little Turco we shall be able to get a trifle of money from the agitated bankers and go to Italy, if they dont get up a general revolution. I want to have a warm winter and come home via England next spring, "bearing my sheaves." Of what my gleanings will consist, I dont know but as my bones cease "worseting" my brains begin to simmer, and by another month the engine will insist on working, and when the steam *is* up, it must have a "went," or there will be an explosion. I sent you a superb *pome* the other day, hope you got it.[5]

Best of wishes from

Yours truly,

L. M. A.

MS: Unlocated; copy by ABA at Houghton Library, Harvard University.

1. LMA's reference to the "Home of the Great American Authoress" is unidentified. It was probably a promotional photograph or illustration of Orchard House issued by Roberts Brothers.

2. LMA, in *Shawl-Straps*, calls Pension Paradis in Vevey "the best *pension* that ever received the weary traveller. Standing in its own pretty grounds, and looking out upon the lake, Pension Paradis deserves its name. Clean and cosy within, a good table, a kindly hostess, and the jolliest old host ever seen" (133–34).

3. In *Shawl-Straps*, LMA wrote: "Vevey was swarming with refugees. Don Carlos, or the Duke of Madrid, as he was called, was there with his Duchess and court, plotting heaven knows what up at his villa, with the grave, shabby men who haunted the town. Queen Isabella reigned at one hotel, and Spanish grandees pervaded the place. There were several at the Pension Paradis, and no one guessed what great creatures they were till a *fête* day arrived, and the grim, gray men blossomed out into counts, marquises, and generals covered with orders, stars, and crosses splendid to behold" (134).

4. I have been unable to locate the origin of the phrase "come to a 'focum.'" In a letter of 5 April [1860] to Alf Whitman, an old Concord friend, however, LMA ends her letter by saying: "My paper is at a 'focum'"(*Selected Letters* 53). Both uses of the phrase by LMA imply "coming to an end or drawing to a close."

5. The poem was "The Lay of a Golden Goose."

May Alcott to Abigail Alcott

Pension Paradis.

Vevey August 10th 1870

Dearest Mother,

Here we are again back at Vevey, in a large airy room looking on the lake which is to me is a great source of enjoyment, for I have never seen any water that approached it in beauty of coloring. We left Bex on Monday last and shall stay here till events decide us to turn either toward Italy, (which is hardly to be hoped) or England, though Montreux close by us here, is called the Italy of Switzerland, as the climate is exquisite and the hotels swarm with invalids through the winter, it may prove just the place for Lu, if Alices dislike of the Swiss could be overcome. Just now everything looks rather black for the French. McMahon having just lost this last battle and it being thought necessary to fortify Paris, it seems as if the Emperor

FIGURE 55. "Pension Paradis," Vevey, Switzerland (1870), by May Alcott. *Louisa May Alcott's Orchard House/L. M. A. Memorial Association*

had underrated the strength of the Prussians.[1] It seems such a silly war that it makes it all the more provoking to have our plans so upset just be cause one man wants a little more territory. All travellers are more or less embarrassed about their money, and a party of Russians have just left here for home as their coin would not pass anywhere but there in the present state of things. The Bonds are uncertain about their movements also, as I suppose you know that the business which called Mr Bond to England so suddenly, was to intercept Mr Wilson one of their partners in Boston, who had decamped with a large sum of money belonging to the firm, and had sailed for England, where Mr. B. met him as he landed and succeeded in getting a part of the funds back, and a promise from him to meet him in London and return more, if not the whole of the amount.[2] There was some reason why he could not arrest him on the spot, but I dont know exactly what it was. Aunty and Sophy wrote to us at Bex from Geneva where they are still at Madame Bovets,[3] waiting command from Mr. B. whether to meet him in Paris, or remain till he could come to them as they sail for America in October from England. If we knew exactly when they go from Geneva, we may be able to send a little parcel by them.

You must see the "Lay of the Golden Goose," that Lu has written and sent to Niles, for it is exceedingly clever and bright. She hopes she will get $15 or 20 for it which can be handed to you as such trifles are always welcome at Apple Slump *if I remember right.* With her relief from pain, comes good spirits and the desire to write, though it makes her head ache she says. Yet I think she is preparing for a *vortex,* and if we remain quiet here for anytime, she will accomplish something in that line in spite of the temptation of an excellent circulating library. She will tell you how lovely everything is in Paradis, even to the tumbling into bed at nine and sleeping (without any pill) *till nine the next morning.* Also there are beaux provided for all single ladies, free of extra charge. A superb old Russian for Lu, his son a handsome young fellow for Alice, and a Frenchman who plays croquet with me all day, is especially my delight. Alice has written to her friends the Misses Bigelows and their brother Jo. Bigelow[4] to come here from Berne[5] and take rooms in this house, which would be very jolly, I think, as this moving continually does not give one a chance to see much society. The Warrens and dear old Count Szapany follow us in a week, going to the next Pension, which will be quite sociable. The day we left Bex, I put a flower in the counts' buttonhole which so pleased him he not only kissed my hand devoutly but went on a long string of praises about me to the Warren's and gave me many touching snotties[?] from his bon bons at dinner.[6]

I am very robust, growing fatter every day, but my eyes have troubled me a good deal lately, so much so that I dont draw or read at all as I think a few months rest, might cure them entirely, and I shall never have a better chance to give it to them than now, much as I want to study, and draw the lovely things about me. They have never recovered from the pen and ink strain, and though I feel no pain, they are very sensitive to the light, and the glare on the white roads here is very trying.

Do please after this put 5 3 cents stamps on your letters to us, or *one fifteen cent one,* as there be huge postage bills at Munroes for us if you dont, and all your letters now are marked "short postage," which makes it expensive.

I wish I could send you some of the delicious white grapes we have every day, for they are so cheap and so wholesome we live on them, besides having large plums and pears and apricots. For ten cents we get enough to surfeit us. Does not this sound like living in Paradise? We have most delicious curried chickens. I only wish I could send Mr. Channing some.

I had a fine swim in the lake the other morning with Alice.

As I lie in my bed till late these fine mornings, I imagine I hear mother saying at the foot of the stairs, "Come girls, morning glories all out, and a beautiful day. breakfast nearly ready, come do get up for these are the most [word missing?] hours of the day." So I call to Lu, in remembrance of home, but we dont get up.

Your loving

May.

MS: Unlocated; copy by ABA at Houghton Library, Harvard University.

1. Patrice Maurice de MacMahon (1808–93), of Irish descent, had served as governor general of Algeria from 1864 until the beginning of the Franco-Prussian War, when he returned to command the First and Fifth French Corps on the southern border of the Rhine. On 4 August 1870, the Prussian army attacked and defeated MacMahon, capturing the city of Wissembourg and then Woerth two days later. As the French Rhine army retreated from the advancing Prussians, MacMahon left his corps and joined with Napoleon III. The French troops, however, could not withstand the advance and lost a three-day battle in August along the Meuse River and again at the city of Sedan. Supposedly, MacMahon's failure to act with decisiveness allowed the Prussians to completely surround Sedan. During the battle on 1 September, MacMahon was wounded and the command passed to General De Wimpffen, who surrendered the French army. MacMahon later served as chief of state for France from 1873 to 1875 and then as the first president of the Third Republic from 1875 to 1879.

2. G. W. Bond and Company, wool brokers, was located at 167 Congress Street, Boston, in 1870. Mr. Wilson is unidentified. The words "of Milton" appeared after "Mr. Wilson" in the sentence but were deleted.

3. Madame Bovets probably operated the pension where the Bonds were staying.

4. Adie A. (b. ca. 1843), Anna Smith (b. 1852), and Joseph Smith (1849–1930) were three of the six children of Horatio and Annie L. Smith Bigelow of Boston. Joseph was a civil engineer and in 1877 married Mary C. Bryant of Boston. He went into business and in 1897 became president of the Atlas National Bank of Boston. When it merged as Webster and Atlas National Bank in 1904, he served as vice president until 1914.

5. Bern ("Berne" in French), situated just west of central Switzerland, is the capital of the canton of Bern and, since 1848, the seat of Swiss government. The town (founded

1191), which has more medieval features than any other large town in Switzerland, is constructed on a peninsula of sandstone rock formed by the Aare River that flows some one hundred feet below.

6. "Snotties" may be a form of "snotter," which was used figuratively to indicate something of little importance.

Louisa May Alcott to Abigail Alcott

Vevay Pension Paradis
August 11th 1870.

Dear Marmee,

It is a dull rainy day and I have devoted the A.M. to reading novels and eating grapes; half a pound at a time of great green sweet juicey bunches in which I revel, for they only cost 10 cents a pound. May is wandering about our two rooms, for she cant read or draw, and she has just done a job of work for Alice who is very funny about her clothes. She has just cut up a black silk mantle to make a pocket for her water proof—which has desolated May. Alice is writing at our round table and I am at the little work table in the west window scribbling to you. (May has now laid down for a nap though it is only 12½ P.M.)

This used house is very cosy and the food excellant. I thought it would be when I heard that gentlemen liked it; they always want good fodder. There are only three now. An old Spaniard and his son, and a young Frenchman. We see them at meals and the girls play croquet with them. Alice's friends Annie and Addie Bigelow and their brother Joe, are coming here soon, and then the girls will have good times.

The Warrens will be in a pension near us and that will suit me better than to be in the same with them. Emma dont interest me and Lina is not very good tempers. So we shall see enough of them as it is.

Our rooms are very pleasant; ours looks on the lake and has two west windows sunny and gay. A's room opens into ours, and we roam to and fro, have parties in dressing sacks, smoke cigarettes, eat fruit, drink our private wine, and carouse in a truly festive manner. There is a pretty salon below opening onto the lake and lawn, and the old lady Madame Nicond is very gossipy and pleasant.[1] The weather has been rainy all this month and dull, but my bones dont ache, so I keep warm and take runs between the showers.

This is the gay season here and in spite of the war Vevey is full. The Ex Queen of Spain[2] and her family are here at the Grand Hotel, also Don Carlos, the rightful heir to the Spanish throne.[3] Our landlady says that her house used to be full of Spaniards who every day went in crowds to call on the two Kings, Alphonse[4] and Carlos. We see brown men and women with saucy black eyes driving round in fine coaches with servants in livery, who I suppose are the court people.

The papers tell us that the French have lost two big battles, the Prussians are in Strasbourg, and Paris in a state of seige.[5] The papers are also full of theatrical messages from the French to the people asking them to come up and be slaughtered for "La Patrie," and sober cool reports from the Prussians. I side with the Prussians, for they sympathized with us in our war and old Nap. did'nt.[6] I guess he is going to get a good thrashing, and he deserves it. Hooray for old Pruss!

Sunday [August] 13th [1870]

No letter for a long time, and I dare say ours have not reached you owing to the war. Don't be troubled at our silence; every thing is in a mess and often no mails from Paris come for a day or two. France is having a bad time. Princess Clotilde[7] passed through Geneva the other day with loads of baggage flying to Italy, and last week a closed car with the imperial arms on it went by here in the night, supposed to be Matilde,[8] and other royal folks flying away from Paris. The Prince Imperial[9] has been sent home from the seat of war, and poor Eugenie[10] is doing her best to keep things quiet in Paris. The French here say that a Republic is already talked of, and the Emperor is on his last legs in every way.[11] He is sick and his doctor wont let him ride, and so nervous he cant command the army as he wanted to. Poor old man! He is a polygog, but one cant help pitying him when all his plans fail.

We still dawdle along getting fat and hearty. The food is excellent and we eat like pigs. A breakfast of coffee tiptop bread, and fresh butter with eggs or fried potatoes at 8. A real French dinner at 1½ of soup, fish, meat, game, salad, sweet messes, and fruit with wine and at 7 cold meat, salad, sauce,

FIGURE 56.
"Americans
Leaving Paris"
(17 December 1870),
Harper's Weekly.

tea and bread and butter. It is grape time now, and for a few cents we get pounds on which we feast all day at intervals. I walk and sleep as well as anyone and feel so well I ought to do something.

May's eyes worry her, and we mean to see a famous oculist who comes from Berne, just to ask him if they need any thing but rest.[12] I shan't advise any experiment, but she will feel better to know that she is not neglecting them. You know if we had taken Marmee's [indecipherable word] she might have kept both. So we are going to "take time by the fetlock."[13]

Fred and Jack would like to look out of my window now and see the little boys splashing in the lake. They are there all day long like little frogs, and lie around on the warm stones to dry, spanking one another for exercise. One boy having washed himself is now washing his clothes, and all lying out to dry together. May and Alice had a swim at the bath house right at our back gate yesterday and it was very nice. I dont dare to try it yet.

This is a dull letter but I have nothing to tell. I sent Niles a poem the other day, but dare say he wont get it. If he does dont send me a copy, he will do that if it is printed. Do pay your letters right, *15 cents*, for Munroe marks all "short paid," and we shall have to pay entire for each, so your 12 cts are of no use.

Goodby, drop a line Sairy.

Ever your
Lu.

MS: Unlocated; copy by ABA at Houghton Library, Harvard University. Partially printed: Cheney 244–45.

1. Madame Nicond operated the Pension Paradis in Vevey.

2. Isabella II (1830–1904) was the oldest daughter of Ferdinand VII, king of Spain, and his fourth wife, Maria Christina, a Neapolitan Bourbon. On the king's death in 1833, Isabelle, at age three, was proclaimed queen of Spain and Maria became queen regent. Isabella's right to ascend to the throne was disputed by Ferdinand's brother Carlos V (1788–1855), known as the first pretender, and this became the basis for the Carlist Wars, which continued in Spain throughout much of the nineteenth century. At age thirteen, Isabella was officially declared queen of Spain and assumed rule. In 1843 Isabella was forced to marry her cousin Prince Fernando I, Francisco de Asis de Bourbon-Cadige, a match that pleased the French. Political intrigue and disputes over the throne finally

forced Isabella to go into exile in September 1868. She abdicated on 25 June 1870 and her son Alfonso XII assumed the throne. Isabella lived in France the remainder of her life.

3. Carlos VII, Carlos Maria de los Dolores (1848–1909), son of the second pretender, Carlos VI (1818–61), was known as the duke of Madrid. He was the fourth pretender and claimant to the Spanish throne from 1868 to his death. He and his wife Princess Marguerite had a son, Jaime I, born in Vevey, Switzerland, on 27 June 1870; Jaime, duke of Anjou and Madrid, would be claimant from 1909 until his death in 1931 (he was also the legitimist claimant to the French throne, where he was known as Jaime III).

4. Alfonso XII (1857–85) was the son of Isabella II, queen of Spain. In 1868, his mother abdicated in favor of her son, not quite eleven years old. He went back to England, where he was pursuing military studies at the Royal Military Academy Sandhurst. While at the academy, Alfonso XII proclaimed, on 1 December 1874, that he was the rightful and only Spanish monarch. He returned to Spain and in 1876 took part in the war against the Carlists, defeating Don Carlos VII, who gave up the struggle for the throne.

5. The French army was defeated by the Prussians on 4 August at Weissenburg and on 6 August at Wörth. On 7 August, Paris was declared in a state of siege. Strasbourg was surrounded by the Prussians and ordered to surrender on 10 August 1870.

6. Germany supported the Union during the Civil War while France, who thought a weaker United States would be in their political favor, were sympathetic with the Confederacy.

7. Princess Clotilde Maria Teresa of Saxony (1843–1911), daughter of Victor Emmanuel II of Sardinia, married Napoleon Joseph Charles Paul (1822–91) in 1859. Known as Prince Napoleon or "Plon-Plon," he was a close advisor to his cousin, Napoleon III. In August 1861, Prince Napoleon and Princess Clotilde, who was eighteen, had visited America and met President Lincoln in Washington.

8. Princess Mathilde Bonaparte (1820–1904) was the daughter of Napoleon I's brother Jerome Bonaparte and his second wife, Catharina of Württemberg. She grew up in Rome and Florence and married the wealthy Russian Anatole Demidoff in 1840 in Italy. She separated from her husband in 1847 but was always supported by the imperial court in St. Petersburg because her mother was Emperor Nicholas I's first cousin. She moved to Paris, where she was part of the aristocracy of Napoleon III's Second French Empire (her brother was Prince Napoleon, "Plon Plon"), and where she established a literary and artistic salon. After Demidoff's death in 1870, she married the French artist and poet Claudius Popelin.

9. Napoleon Eugène Louis Jean Joseph, Napoleon IV, Prince Imperial (1856–79), was the only child of Emperor Napoleon III and Empress Consort Eugénie de Montijo. In 1870, at age fourteen, he joined his father at the front in the Franco-Prussian War. He fled with his family to England after the defeat of the French and settled in Chislehurst, Kent. Serving as an officer in the British army, he was killed during the Zulu War in Africa.

10. Empress Eugénie de Montijo (1826–1920) was born to Spanish nobility but educated in Paris. She married Napoleon III in 1853 and served as his regent during his absences in 1859, 1865, and 1870. After the defeat of the Second French Empire, she and her husband settled in England, at Chislehurst, Kent. Twelve years after the death of her husband in 1873, she retired to her villa, Cyrnos, in Farnborough, Hampshire.

11. Charles Louis Napoleon Bonaparte, Napoleon III, Emperor of France (1808–73), was the son of Hortense de Beauharnais (who was the daughter of Napoleon I's wife Josephine de Beauharnais by her first marriage) and Louis Bonaparte, Napoleon I's brother. With his family forced into exile after the defeat of Napoleon I and the restoration of the Bourbon monarchy in 1815, Louis Napoleon was raised in Germany, Italy, and Switzerland. Twice, in 1836 and in 1840, he helped lead failed coups to restore a Bonaparte to the French throne. His second attempt led to his imprisonment from 1840 to 1846. He managed to escape and lived in England until the revolution in France in 1848, which deposed the monarch and established the French Second Republic. He immediately returned to France and was elected president by an overwhelming majority of voters. He seized total control of the government near the end of his third year in office, however, and a year later, December 1852, he became Emperor Napoleon III, leader of the Second French Empire. After being turned down by two royal princesses, he married the Countess of Teba, Eugénie de Montijo. During the Franco-Prussian War, he left his wife as regent in Paris and took command of French forces at the front. He was captured on 2 September 1870 in the battle of Sedan and deposed two days later. He spent the remaining years of his life in exile in Kent, England.

12. Dr. Henri Dor (1835–1912) was a noted Swiss ophthalmologist. Born in Vevey, he earned his medical degree in Zurich and then studied with specialists across Europe. He returned to Switzerland and established his practice in Vevey in 1860, but he moved to Berne in 1867, accepting a chair in ophthalmology at the university. In 1876, he moved to Lyons, France, where he established an eye clinic and practiced medicine until his death. He was one of the founders of the French Ophthalmologic Society and among his many honors was becoming a chevalier of the Légion d'Honneur.

13. To "take time by the fetlock" means to grab time by its shackles and take control of it. LMA also uses this phrase in chapter 10 of *Little Women* ("The P. C. and the P. O."); Nathaniel Winkle (Amy) writes to Mr. Pickwick in "The Pickwick Portfolio" that he must submit a French fable instead of original work because he has too much schoolwork to do but promises to "take time by the fetlock" in the future and accomplish his task.

Louisa May Alcott to the Alcott Family

Vevey Aug 18th 1870.

Dear Folks,

My letter has dragged along expecting to get one from you to answer. But none has come and I want S. E. S. to see about my money, so I send along this dull budget. Will you send my little note to S. E. S. at *once*, for it takes so long to hear it must [be] under way soon. If he is away, and you cant get at Ham,[1] T. Niles will do it for me as he is a business man, and kindly offered to lend me a hand anytime. Pa is rather *vague* at such times, and it must be done *right* or it is not good, and John is too busy, besides neither of the dear old fellows know anything about such matters. S. E. S. or Niles must sign a paper promising to be responsible for the sum I ask for or something of that sort, so it must be a known and responsible party.

I dare say my Munroe letter will do, but it may be so costly to get gold that I cant afford it, and might fall back on England. This confounded war is *such* a plague I wish they would all blow up together and get done with it. The French here tear their hair and wail at their defeats. I think the Prussians behave well, but I dont love any of them, because I cant go to Italy. I begin to think I am *never* going to hear from you anymore, so I dont feel the interest in life that I otherwise should. Hope you will get this in the course of ages, and all go well.

Bless you all! May is hard at croquet with the little Spaniard and Frenchman.

Adoo! and Alice sends you all a fancy line about us both. She is well but not so fat as we are, and so she is mad at us.

Ever yours
Lu.

MS: Unlocated; copy by ABA at Houghton Library, Harvard University.

1. Hamilton Willis (d. 1878), LMA and May's first cousin, was the son of Abigail Alcott's sister Elizabeth May Willis and Benjamin Willis. His wife, Louisa Willis (d. 1862), was the daughter of Charles W. Winship (whose first wife was Abigail's sister Catherine)

and his second wife, Martha Ruggles Winship. LMA was good friends with both "Ham" and "Lu" as she called them. In the summer of 1855, she had stayed at their Walpole, New Hampshire, home. Both had encouraged her writing for the theater. Hamilton Willis was, in the mid-1850s, editor of a financial gazetteer for the *Boston Saturday Evening Gazette* and *Boston Journal*.

Louisa May Alcott to Samuel E. Sewall

Vevey August 18th 1870

Dear Mr. Sewall,

Miss Bartlett has just sent to Mr. Thomas[1] asking him to get her a letter of credit on Baring Bros. London, so that if French money gives out she will have something to use. We find that since the war the French bankers ask so much for gold that we cant afford it, and their paper is of no use out of France. So I think I had better follow her example and have an English letter of credit also. I have never used mine on Munroe except for the £20 which Low of London paid me for "Old Fashioned Girl."

I have still between two and three hundred dollars by me, but it takes so long to hear from home, and the war may render my Munroe Letter of Credit too expensive to use, so I think I had better have $500 or 1000 arranged so that I can get it as I want through Barings. I believe the mere letter dont cost anything, and is no loss if I dont use it. We may not be able to go to Italy, and be forced to spend the winter somewhere in England;—at any rate French money is in a very uncertain state, and many people are going home on account of it. I dont want to do that yet unless I must.

Will you kindly arrange it for me, and I will send Baring my address in a few weeks, so that he will be able to let me have money if I want it. By that time, I fancy he will have heard from his agent in America and it will all be right.

Love to all and many thanks from your troublesome cousin,

L. M. A.

P. S./ We are all well and enjoying much. I am mending very fast.

L. M. A.

MS: Unlocated; copy by ABA at Houghton Library, Harvard University.

  1. Mr. Thomas probably managed Alice Bartlett's financial matters.

May Alcott to Anna Alcott Pratt

Pension Paradis

Vevey August 20th 1870.

Dear Anna,

    In the midst of entertaining the Bonds, who spent yesterday with us, came your and mothers letters dated July 26th, when I imagine you were all thinking of your old baby, who wrote to you all on that day from Bex where we spent a very peaceful month. I am glad you liked my letter about the Hospice of St. Bernard though my description could not begin to give you the least idea of the real romance and excitement of the whole adventure for I felt like the heroine of some novel, and it only needed a gallant knight in place of our excellent guide, to bear us in his arms across the raging torrent, to make the illusion quite perfect. Though the knight did appear in the shape of the handsome priest, who not only entertained us beautifully, but went so far toward forgetting his vows as to really flirt with us, and made our evening before the great open fire, with the safest dogs lying round, and the English lady to do propriety, one of the most enchanting I ever spent. We felt so grateful for all their kindness to us that Lena and I purchased two exquisite pictures, of the Mater Dolorosa and Guido's Head of Christ, and sent to our devoted priest and have just received a pretty french note from him in return, showing that he was greatly pleased with the attention, and that he would not soon forget the visit of the two young Americans.

    Here we have adventures of another kind for Alice and I row a good deal on the lake, and the other day it being a superb morning, we stepped out of our back gate in our boating dresses to find one handsome boatman waiting for us with a little light boat and four oars and the American flag flying at the stern. After dismissing him, we did our prettiest to make the boat fly, and I assure you our speed was nothing to be ashamed of, for these months of leisure have made me stronger than I thought, and everyone is kind enough to say that if I could practice for a time, I ought with my broad shoulders make quite a crack oarsman.

We went to Montreux about four and a half miles to the bankers for money and then came back in time to take a turn round the steamer which was just coming up the new pier, and the firing of guns and waving of flags of all nations. We also have croquet from morning till night, as the gentlemen here have nothing to do apparently (though the Spaniards are really hard at work plotting with Don Carlos) and as I cannot use my eyes much I am glad to play at all hours. They call me Mlle Mitrailleuse after the famous french gun that is doing so much execution in the present war,[1] and we have great fun being Prussian and French.

Yesterday Sophia Bond played with us till time for them to take the boat when Lu and I escorted them to the pier and said good bye to them for the last time this side the water for their passages are taken the 10 of October from England. We gave them a little box for you, with Lu's silver watch for Papa in a little carved case from me which he will find useful in travelling, a painted porcelain for mother, and gloves for Nan.[2] I should like to have something to you all, but not having any money of my own, can hardly make presents, besides Sophia could hardly take any thing larger than the little parcel we have sent. I find I have only sent half my note in the box, as I took two sheets by mistake and fear you can hardly find a beginning or end to the scrap that will reach you.

This is very sad business for Mr. Bond to face just as he was leaving the business to the younger men. It seems that Wilson decamped with 10,000 dollars, took his mistress and came abroad for a long lark, and that Mr. Bond could not arrest him in England for being a partner in the concern, but succeeded in getting back $30000, which is a very small proportion. Aunty said the Lynn house belonging to them which Aunt Cary[?] has, will have to be sold, and Rocky Nook also if they get a good offer for it, as it is too expensive an establishment to keep up merely for three people.[3] She said she must forego the anticipated pleasure of giving me a dozen Balbrighan stockings,[4] which would last me all my life, as she had intended to do, and the same for Anna, for now they must economize till the firm was afloat again. The merchants had all come forward very handsomely, and offered help and sympathy, but it [was] hard for all to suffer by this one scoundrel. They were sweet and kind and we read them extracts from your letters just received about the death of Ben. Willis and other items which they had not heard. It is possible if Mr. Bond goes to Munich that Aunty and Sophia may be persuaded to come here for a solstice with us, and as the Bigelows come Monday or Tuesday we may have very gay times. I don't object to it in the least. This is the season for Vevey, and the young Spaniard is an exile with a string of titles even longer than his fathers; but they are both living *incog* just now. I am not afraid of their titles, and the young one and I sing "Zuper die" together as if he were a student of old Harvard, instead of a Spanish Grandee. I am teaching him college songs.

You speak as if the Tyrol was in the front yard here, but I beg to believe it is some distance off.[5] Bex is just this side of Martigny which you say you can find on your map. I have got a photograph of the St Bernard dogs for mother. How sad about the Mansfields. I hope Lu will be persuaded to write May a nice note.[6] I would if I could do it well.

Your envelopes are so thin that they get all worn out before reaching us and several have come from Monroes lately tied up with strings. So if you can use thinner paper and thicker envelopes it will be safer.

Give my love to Ellen Emerson and tell her I wish she would slip in a note to your envelope sometime, telling me of all the Concord doings, news of which never reaches Apple Slump you know till all is very stale.

Remember us to the Miss Andrews[7] and Emma Moore.

your loving May.

MS: Unlocated; copy by ABA at Houghton Library, Harvard University.

1. A mitreilleuse was an early form of the machine gun developed by the French and first used during the Franco-Prussian War. Mounted on a horse-drawn carriage, the gun had thirty-five barrels that could fire all at the same time.

2. Abigail Alcott recorded in her manuscript diary for 29 October 1870 that she had received her daughters' box from the Bonds and noted: "They must know how great a void their absence makes in our home" (Houghton Library, Harvard University).

3. Lynn, Massachusetts, situated on the Atlantic Ocean in Essex County, is a small town just north of Boston; Rocky Nook, Massachusetts, is located on the coast just north of Plymouth, approximately thirty-one miles from Boston. The Bond family were still residing at their home, Rocky Nook, in 1880, when "Auntie Bond" wrote to LMA

regarding May's death (ALS: Houghton Library, Harvard University, bMS Am800.23.13). The Bonds' Aunt Cary[?] is unidentified.

4. Balbriggan stockings, originally manufactured in Balbriggan, Ireland, were made from a knit fabric of unbleached Egyptian cotton.

5. The Tyrol, located in the eastern Alps, is a region in western central Europe that included the Austrian state of Tyrol (including Salzburg) and the Italian regions of South Tyrol and Trentino.

6. Frances (Fanny) Hildreath Mansfield Estabrook (1841?–70), wife of John D. Estabrook, died in Gloucester, Massachusetts, on 27 July 1870 from tuberculosis. She was the daughter of Major James Mansfield (1801–82) and his wife Frances Gilman Hildreth Mansfield (b. 1816). In 1859 LMA had written Alf Whitman that F. B. Sanborn's school had a "fresh crop" of boys and "several pretty girls—Fanny Mansfield, 'Major' as we call her is the best, she is Abbys [May's] firm ally, rows rides shoots & dances like a trump" (*Selected Letters* 48–49). In 1864, LMA noted that in September she had gone "to Gloucester for a fortnight with May at the Mansfield's. Found a family of six pretty daughters . . . Had a jolly time boating, driving, charading dancing & picnicing. . . . While at the M's Fanny was engaged, & there being a house full of girls, it made a great stir" (*Journals* 131). Abby Davis Mansfield Brooks (1842–70), Fanny's first cousin, also from Gloucester, was the daughter of Alfred Mansfield (1806–70) and Abigail Somes Davis Mansfield (1811–1900). Abby died 22 July 1870 in Saginaw, Michigan, where she was living with her husband, George B. Brooks. May was Fanny Mansfield's younger sister, two years her junior.

7. Miss Andrews is unidentified.

Louisa May Alcott to Abigail Alcott

Vevey Aug 21st 1870

Dear Marmee,

Your letters of July 26th came just after our last was sent. The Bonds were here, and by them I sent my watch for Pa, a little Madonna Dolorosa for you, and a pair of gloves for Nan. I wanted to send the plaid purple silk, as I dont wear it, and it is a pity Nan should not have it, but Sophy had but little room, so the box is all.

I had such a droll dream last night, I must tell you. I thought I was returning to Concord after my trip, and was alone. As I walked from the Station, I missed Mr. Moore's house,[1] and turning the corner, found the scene so changed that I did'nt know where I was. Our house was gone, and in its

FIGURE 57. Orchard House, Concord, Massachusetts (with Bronson Alcott and his grandson on porch). *Louisa May Alcott's Orchard House/L. M. A. Memorial Association.*

place stood a great grey stone castle with towers and arches and lawns and bridges very fine and antique. Somehow I got into it without meeting any one of you, and wandered about trying to find my family. At last I came across Mr. Moore papering a room, and asked him where his house was? He did n't know me and said, "Oh! I sold it to Mr Alcott for his school, and we live in Acton² now." "Where did Mr. Alcott get the means to build this great concern", I asked. "Well, he *gave* his own land and took the great fortune his daughter left him, the one that died some ten years ago." "So I am dead, am I?" says I to myself, feeling so queerly. "Government helped build this place, and Mr. A. has a fine College here," said Mr Moore papering away again. I went on wondering at the news and looked into a glass to see how I looked dead. I found myself a fat old lady with grey hair and specs, very like E[lizabeth]. P[almer]. P[eabody].³ I laughed, and coming to a Gothic window, looked out and saw hundreds of young men and boys in a queer flowing dress roaming about the parks and lawns, and among them was Pa, looking as he looked thirty years ago, with brown hair and a big white neckcloth as in the old times. He looked so plump and placid and young and happy, I was charmed to see him, and nodded, but he did n't know me, and I was so grieved and troubled at being a Rip Van Winkle,⁴ I cried, and said I had better go away and not disturb anyone, and in the midst of my woe, I woke up. It was all so clear and funny. I can't help thinking that it may be a foreshadowing of something real. I used to dream of being famous, and it has partly become true. So why not Pa's College blossom, and he yet young and happy with his disciples? I only hope he won't quite forget me when I come back, fat and grey and old. Perhaps his dream is to come in another world where every thing is fresh and calm, and the reason why he did'nt recognize me was because I was still in this work-a-day world, and so felt old and strange in his lovely castle in the air. Well, he is welcome to my fortune, but the daughter who did die ten years ago, is more likely to be the one who helped him build his School of Concord up aloft.

I can see how the dream came, for I had been looking at Silling's boys in their fine garden, and wishing I could go in, and know the dear little lads larking about there.⁵ Then in the forenoon, I had got a top knot at the barbers and talked about my grey hairs, and looking in the glass thought how fat and old I was getting, and had shown the Bond's, Pa's picture, which they thought saintly, &c. I believe in dreams, though I am free to confess that "cowcumbers" for tea may have been the basis of this "*ally-gorry-cal vision.*"

May has two devoted croquet followers, the young Frenchman and the little twenty years old Spaniard with the dark blue eyes and black lashes. His name is Silvio Mirandola and his Pa is a Count.⁶ Both were in the army and are refugees not daring to go home yet. Vevey is full of Spaniards who are gathered round the Ex-Queen Isabella and Don Carlos, all plotting and planning some mad revolution. Mysterious little brown men come and take the Count out from his meals to jabber darkly in corners, and then vanish as mysteriously as they came. Don Carlos, a plain brown man of twenty four, goes driving round with his little wife and baby. At the christening of said baby all the dingy Spaniards in Vevey burst forth in grand rigs with orders and stars, and our old ladys nineteen generals were gorgeous to behold, she says. One funny weak little man who sits opposite me at table, and spills his soup, puts his knife in his mouth and talks fearful French, turns out to be a great Spanish General, and on gala days is stuck as full of orders as [a] cushion of pins: blue ribbon round his neck with stars, red ribbons on the left breast, yellow ditto on the right, and a green one with a great gold key hanging down his back. His clothes are very shabby, and his hands very dirty, but the orders cover the shabbyness, several rings adorn the unwashed hands, and the little hero is as perky and mild as a baa-lamb when he is not plotting privy conspiracy and rebellion, like a bald-headed demon.

There are a good many strangers in town now. The Weld party have been at the Grand Hotel, and we saw many American names in the list of strangers. The Bigelows, sister and brother, come to morrow to visit Alice and will stay a little while. So a week more will slip by pleasantly, and then we can decide what to do. Mr Bond thought we could go to Italy with perfect safety if the money question is fixed. We have had to get new passports from Berne and they are viséd for Italy, so we can be at Milan in a day or so, if we like. I dont want to be cheated out of my Italian winter, and the war can't last long if Prussia goes on beating the French in every battle, and the French continue to mow down the Prussians like grass before they retreat. It will be like the Kilkenny cats,[7] and old Nap will retire to private life a last piece of unnecessary wickedness. I don't envy him. His people hate and distrust him and things look badly for the Naps.

As we know the Consul at Spezia,[8] that is, we have letters to him as well as to many folks in Rome, &c, I guess we shall go, for the danger of Europe getting into the fight is over now, and we can sail to England or home any time from Italy.

Don't send me any more letters from *so cracked* girls. I can't answer them, and have to pay Munroe for every one he forwards. Just put them away and dont reply to them; it is too expensive, and the rampant infants must wait.

I put in a bit of a note to Tommy on the same subject, for I dont want any "*hifalutin*" notes to come disappointing me when I look for letters from family.

I am tip top now and keep so in spite of rain or shine, and a warm winter will finish me off I trust, and let me come home in the spring to work "*in moderation*", for doing nothing is *awful* when I have nt "my bones" to tend.

Use thicker envelopes for yours are worn out, and have to be tied up before we got them.

Love to every one. I'll write to the poor Mansfields.

Kiss *my lovies* for me.

Ever your

Lu.

MS: Unlocated; manuscript copy by ABA at Houghton Library, Harvard University. Printed *Selected Letters* 146–49; partially printed: Cheney 245–47, where it is listed as being written to Anna Alcott Pratt.

1. John Brooks Moore (1817–87) had sold Orchard House to the Alcotts in September 1857.

2. Acton, Massachusetts, is a small town approximately six and one-half miles from Concord and twenty-five miles northwest of Boston. In 1870, Moore lived several hundred yards up from the Alcotts at No. 343–55 Lexington Road.

3. Elizabeth Palmer Peabody (1804–94) was an educator, author, reformer, and member of the transcendentalist circle. In 1834 she assisted ABA in his Temple School in Boston and published her account of the venture in *Record of a School* (1835); however, she left the school in 1836 because she disagreed with his methods of teaching. She later published the *Dial*, the transcendentalist magazine, from 1841 to 1843. In 1860 she opened the first English kindergarten in the United States in Boston and was assisted for a time by LMA. Peabody's sister, Sophia, married Nathaniel Hawthorne in 1842, and her other sister, Mary, married Horace Mann in 1843.

4. Rip Van Winkle, the character in Washington Irving's story "Rip Van Winkle" (1820), who falls asleep for twenty years in the Catskill Mountains and returns home to find all is changed.

5. Edovard Sillig ran Bellerive School in Vevey. It was comparable to Frank Sanborn's academy in Concord.

6. In *Shawl-Straps* LMA describes Silvio Mirandola: "One particularly silent, shabby little man with a shaven head and fine black eyes, who was never seen to smile, became an object of interest on that occasion by appearing in a gorgeous uniform with a great gilt grasshopper hanging down his back from a broad green ribbon. Who was he? . . . No one ever knew, and all the artful questions put to the young Spaniard, who played croquet with the girls, were unavailing. Nothing was discovered except that little Mirandola

had a title, and might be sent back to Spain any day to lose his life or liberty in some rash plot" (135).

7. Kilkenny cats were two cats that supposedly fought each other until only their tails remained. The term perhaps derived from Kilkenny, a city and county in Ireland, which once stationed a large garrison of British soldiers, who occupied their free time by tying the tails of two cats together and wagering on the outcome of the fight. The term then came to signify two foes who fought until each was annihilated.

8. Spezia, a popular winter residence for the English on the Mediterranean coast in northern Italy.

Louisa May Alcott to Thomas Niles

August 23rd 1870

Dear Mr Niles,

Your note of August 2nd has just come with a fine budget of Mag's, and a paper, for all of which many thanks,—for I seldom hear from our papers except Miss Bartletts "Nation" and that "sarces me."

Dont give my address to any one. I don't want the young ladies notes. They can send them to Concord, and I shall get them next year.

The Lippincott notice was very good. Who is C.L.P.[1] I thought at first it was my friend Mr Davis, husband of "Margaret Howth" Davis.[2]

I hope in correcting the plates of "O. F. G." that the word "Six" on page 223, English edition, was changed to "Five." I corrected it in the proof once or twice, but it was not changed in the English edition.

The pictures in the end of Lippincott of Laurie &c. are to go into some new edition, May says. I forgot if it is so, and should like to know. They are all right except my *Laurie* who is too *cravatly* and stiff.[3]

The boys at Sillings school here are a perpetual source of delight to me, and I stand at the gate, like the "Peri" longing to go in and play with the lords.[4] The young ladies who want to find live Lauries can be supplied here for Silling has a large assortment always on hand.

Miss Bartlett says, "she is constantly trying to incite me to literary effort, but I hang fire." So I do, but only that I may go off with a bang by and by, "a la mitrailleuse."

I pleasant cruise to the Nile boat. Bartlett is always raving about that part of the world.

Respects to Messr[5]

L. M. A.

MS: Unlocated; copy by ABA at Houghton Library, Harvard University.

1. *An Old-Fashioned Girl* was reviewed by "C. L. P." in *Lippincott's Magazine of Literature, Science and Education* 6 (August 1870): 230 32. C. L. P. is unidentified.

2. L. Clarke Davis (1834–1904), abolitionist, journalist, and author, married Rebecca Harding (1831–1910) in 1863. Harding's most famous work, *Life in the Iron Mills*, had already appeared in the 1861 *Atlantic Monthly*. Her novel *Margaret Howth* was published the same year. LMA had met Harding when she came to Boston in 1862: "A handsome, fresh, quiet woman, who says she never had any troubles, though she writes about her woes. I told her I had lots of troubles; so I write jolly tales" (*Journals* 109).

3. In a search of *Lippincott's Magazine of Literature, Science and Education* for 1870–71, I did not locate any illustrations from *Little Women*. It is possible that the illustrations LMA refers to here were printed on the inside wrappers of an issue. I have been unable, however, to locate a complete run of the magazine in wrappers for 1870.

4. A Peri is a benevolent spirit (or person) or fairy.

5. "Roberts" was originally written after "Messr" but was erased. The closing "your Lu" was also erased.

May Alcott to A. Bronson Alcott

Vevey August 23rd 1870.

Dear Father,

The Bonds' mean to return in October, and I wish them to have one of the *Marshall* profile vignetts of me, one of the good Smith vignetts from Mrs Hildreths crayon of you,[1] and one of the best vignetts of Lu, as we have'nt any with us to give them, and they want them very much, and have given us some excellent ones of themselves taken in Venice. If we go there, I mean [for] Lu at least [to] make another trial for a good likeness, and as she has improved so immensely in appearance there is more hope of succeeding now than ever before.

Anna and mother wrote me on my birth day, but no letter from Papa to his baby, though there may be one on the way. I cannot give you any longer

FIGURE 58. Bronson Alcott, from Caroline Hildreth's crayon portrait (1857). *Louisa May Alcott's Orchard House/L. M. A. Memorial Association.*

description of my Bernard trip as I don't in the least remember what I have already told you, and it seems so long ago that it all happened and I wrote about my adventures.

I hope the watch will reach you in time for your Western trip; it is a per-fect time keeper and will remind you not to keep your audiences *too long*, as a good lecture loses its power if *ten* minutes to long. At least so thinks your practical daughter whose only use in the world has been to keep the Alcott balloon within sight of common folks you know. I should like to take you and mother out for a row on this lovely Lake about sunset some evening for the boats are cushioned to such an extent and look so festive with the pretty flags and awnings that even mother would enjoy a trip in them. After our rows we take a bath, a good deal as you have described the Connecticut boy's doing,[2] for all are swimmers in this part of the world, and a long procession of girls run down the long platforms with a springboard at the end and dive off into good deep water swimming and playing round, like so many young lobsters, for scarlet is the prevailing color of the bathing suits, and it has quite a picturesque effect, especially when shrouded in long sheets, we sit about in the hot sun and dry off, for that is the fashion here, and is thought to be most healthy to take this sun bath after the ducking. Then we eat a good hearty dinner and repose till it is cool enough to play croquet. This sounds like a good wholesome way of spending one's days does'nt it?

I am determined to see the oculist here before leaving as he is very famous.

The Bigelows have come. They are the two daughters and son of Horatio Bigelow,[3] who with his wife have been called home, and have left the young people here.

Alice delights to hear all your letters read, and is always pleased with any message to her. She is very kind and we both are very much attached to her.

Remember and put fifteen cents on your next letters as that will not only take them to New York but also there will be nothing extra to pay here, which is quite a consideration.

We begin to think after all our doubts on the subject that we may see Italy in the fall.

Your affectionate

May.

MS: Unlocated; copy by ABA at Houghton Library, Harvard University.

1. Caroline Negus Hildreth (1814–67), wife of the historian and philosopher Richard Hildreth (1807–65), had drawn a crayon portrait of ABA in 1857. Abigail Alcott, who admired the portrait, wrote her: "You have converted my long, sharp, angular spouse into a peerless prophet and seer" (26 February 1857; copy by ABA, manuscript *Diary for 1857*, Houghton Library, Harvard University).

2. ABA was born and grew up in rural Connecticut.

3. Horatio Bigelow (1814–88), a Boston attorney, attended Harvard Law School in 1833–34. In 1870 he and his wife, Annie Lenthal Smith, lived at 17 Beacon Street in Boston. Bigelow and his son Albert S. Bigelow were also owners of a number of mines, and Albert became known as a copper magnate.

Louisa May Alcott to the Alcott Family

Vevay August 29th 1870.

Dear People,

We sent you an extra fat letter last week, so we shall send a thinnish one this time for postage has "riz" again, because there are two ways to send letters,—one cheap and unsafe by way of Berne, and one secure and double pay by Geneva. We choose the safe way and pay 1 franc 20 centimes, or 25 cents, so we wont waste any papers in long yarns.

The Bigelow girls are here and we like them much, pretty, gay, kind and accomplished. With the Warren sisters we are seven jolly girls and have little frolics among ourselves.

M. Nicond, the owner of this house, a funny old man with a face so like a parrot that we call him M. Parrot, asked us to come and visit him at his châlet up among the hills. He is building a barn there and stays to see that all goes well, so we only see him on Sundays when he convulses us by his funny ways. Last week seven of us went up in a big landau,[1] and the old dear entertained us like a Prince. We left the carriage at the foot of a little steep path and climbed up to the dearest old châlet we ever saw. Here Pa Nicond met us, took us up the outside steps into his queer little salon and regaled us with his forty year old wine, and nice little cakes. We then set forth in spite of clouds and wind to view the farm and wood. It showered at intervals, but no one seemed to care, so we strolled about under umbrellas, getting mushrooms, flowers and colds, viewing the Tarpean rock,[2] and sitting on rustic seats to enjoy the "belle vue," which consisted of fog. It was such a droll lark that we laughed and ran and enjoyed the damp pic-nic very much. Then we had a tip-top Swiss dinner, followed by coffee, three sorts of wine, and cigars. Every one smoked, and as it poured guns, the old Parrot had a blazing fire made, round which we sat talking many languages, singing and revelling. We had hardly got through dinner and seen another foggy view when tea was announced and we stuffed again, having pitchers of cream, fruit and a queer but very nice dish of slices of light bread dipped in egg and fried, and eaten with sugar. The buxom Swiss maid flew and grinned and kept serving up some new mess from her tiny dark kitchen. It cleared off, and we walked home in spite of our immense exploits in the eating line. Old Parrot escorted us part way down, and we gave three cheers for him as we parted. Then we showed Madame and the French governess and Don Juan (the Spanish boy) some tall walking though the roads were very steep and rough and muddy. We tramped some five miles, and our party (May, Alice, the Governess and I) got home long before Madame and Don Juan, who took a short cut, and wouldn't believe that we did'nt get a lift some how. I felt quite proud of my old pins, for they were not tired, and none the worse for the long walk. I think they are really all right now, for the late cold weather has not troubled them in the least, and I sleep, oh ye gods! how I do sleep! ten or twelve hours sound, and get up drunk with dizziness, it is lovely to see. A,int I grateful? Oh, yes, oh, yes.

We began French lessons today; and May and I of the French governess, a kind old girl who only asks two francs a lesson. We *must* speak the language for it is so disgraceful to be so stupid, so we have set to work and mean to be able to *parley-vous* or die.

The war is still a nuisance and we may be here sometime, and really need some work, for we are so lazy we shall be spoilt if we don't fall to. Alice is tired of fussing with us, and we are tired of being perfect noodles.

Saturday a Mrs Willard called on us. She saw Pa in Chicago and her husband knew him I think.[3] I did not see her but May did, and so we had to return the call yesterday. I found them kind and ordinary people, the Ma clever and the girl pretty. Dont think we shall care much for them, but will be civil if they were good to Pa.

I gave Count Szapany Pa's message and he was pleased. He reads no English, and is going to Hungary soon, so Pa had better not send the book. He is a little cracked on some points I find, but a kindly old man and has helped Emma.

It was kind of Emma Moore to send such a pleasant letter. Give her our congratulations and best wishes through her family, as the wedding will be over before this reaches you.

We have sent lots of letters since the St. Bernard ones which you speak of in your last. Hope you will get them. In my last sent one, I asked S. E. S. to fix $1000 so I could get it if I wanted through Baring, when in Italy, for

FIGURE 59. Bois de Boulogne in Paris Cut Down (22 February 1871), *Harper's Weekly*.

Munroe is not good, he charges so much, and it is so difficult to get French money anywhere. I repeat this because that letter may have got lost, and it takes time to do these things. Baring is always safe and a letter of credit dont cost anything, so if I dont use it there is no loss. Alice and her friends have sent for English letters, and I do the same as Paris is in a flurry getting ready for a siege. Strangers are ordered to leave, the Bois de Boulogne is cut down for fortifications[4] [see figure 59] and peasants for miles around are bid[5] to bring in all the provisions &c. they can get, so the enemy may find no plunder when he comes. Things look badly and people fly round for papers and gabble excitedly in the streets though Switzerland is not in the quarrel. Speaking of war, the old dog Vino was shot here to-day because of his age and feebleness.

I'm glad May's St. Bernard sketch is to be put in some paper, for it is lively and well written.[6] I hope you corrected and fixed it over, for she writes carelessly.

Never put any thing of mine anywhere till you have my leave. Now mind and dont let Tom or Bun extract or do anything stupid.

Lu.

MS: Unlocated; copy by ABA at Houghton Library, Harvard University. Partially printed: Cheney 248–50.

1. A landau, first manufactured in Germany, is a four-wheeled carriage whose top, made in two parts, may be open or closed.

2. The original Tarpeian Rock is located on the Capitoline Hill in Rome. People convicted of treason were thrown over the rock. LMA is probably referring to a local rock face named after Rome's infamous rock.

3. ABA had first held talks in Chicago in December 1858, and he had returned there to speak in mid-February 1870 as part of his winter speaking engagements. Mrs. Willard and her husband are unidentified.

4. Bois de Boulogne, located on the western edge of Paris, was formed from the "Boulogne Woods," ancient oaks from the forest of Rouvray, and was established as a park in 1852 by Napoleon III. Comprising approximately 2,090 acres, it was later informally landscaped with beech, linden, cedar, chestnut, and elm trees.

5. The word "hired" was deleted and "bid" inserted.

6. May's letter of 10 July 1870 to the Alcott family, which describes her ascent to the St. Bernard Hospice, was partially published in the *Boston Daily Evening Transcript*, 18 August 1870, 2.

May Alcott to Abigail and A. Bronson Alcott

Vevey August 30th 1870

Dear Mother and Father,

You can hardly believe in the midst of the intense heat at home,[1] how we have really suffered from cold the last week, and I am now wearing an under flannel and my thick velvet sacque over my shoulders to be even comfortable. Much snow is lying on the mountains, and though the days begin bright and sunny, we are sure to have rain or heavy clouds before sunset. Happily the snowy air does not affect Lu, and through all the changes her rheumatism has not returned, and she is quite unconscious of such things as *bones*.

She will give you a funny description of our visit to the country house of Monsieur Nicond who is a most entertaining old man, and came here the other day on purpose to have a game of croquet with me, as they had told him I could'nt be beaten. He worked very hard, and as they have only had the game here a little while and play in the old fashioned way with two hands, I came off triumphant.

Yesterday the Misses Bigelow, Alice and ourselves drove to a mountain town called Châlet St. Denis, from which we had a most supurb view, though it was so cold we got out and walked at intervals in order to get up a glow.[2] The Bigelows are charming. Mr Joe and myself having nice talks together, for he was in Will Simmons class[3] and knows all of our set, is very jolly and sensible, likes croquet (at which I beat him, which is a great feather in my cap) and we had a nice walk to the grand promonade above the town the afternoon of his arrival. Yesterday he went to Chamonix and will not return for several days, which is quite sad, as I enjoy having someone who talks my native tongue, about.

We have had a letter from Prescott Baker and wife in Berlin. They seem very happy, and so far the war has not troubled them, except by the increase of prices every where. The Prussians have taken Chalons and are marching towards Paris which is in a state of siege.[4] People seem to think Munroe is not being safe, and I am glad Lu has no money there now, though Alice has and may lose it. After the next battle we may decide to go to Italy, but every thing is still doubtful though Lu and I want if possible to put our eyes on Rome if no more.

Father's letter and Emma Moore's came yesterday, and if I thought an answer would reach her before she left for her trip, I should write to Emma, though there is very little that is interesting to tell just now. I wish her all joy on the great occasion and hope to see her when I come home though it will seem a little strange to call her *Mrs Davis*.

Did you ever receive a note directed to Fanny Lombard,[5] as I sent one a long while ago in one [of] the home envelopes?

How is dear John, and why does'nt he write to his devoted May who wears his picture in her locket opposite the one of her Marmee.

A Mrs Willard from Chicago who is educating her two children here called on us and seemed to know father, or had heard him lecture, and was a great admirer both of his and of Lu's. We are going to see her this P.M. and to the tower which gives the name to La Tour.[6]

Monday P.M. Lu and I have just returned from seeing Dr. Dorr who to my great joy said the optic nerve was in a fine healthy condition, and my late discomfort was owing entirely to inflamation of the lids both in the up per and underside. It is nothing in the least dangerous, only it will be a long time before they are perfectly well, as it has been growing worse and worse for some years, and he comes tomorrow to make an application which he says will be very painful for the first few times, but as it is very necessary I can bear it, and am only too thankful that I persisted in seeing him now, rather than waiting till I really suffered with them. He is very famous, having just returned from Scotland where he went to perform an operation. Also it is a great advantage that the prices are so much less here than at home, for an examination is only $2.00 instead of $10 as with us. He is highly accomplished and agreeable, and speaks English which delights me, as I could'nt talk freely in French and there might be great misunderstanding. His wife is an English lady and they have a most lovely house with charming pictures and every thing attractive. He knows Dr Derby.[7]

Yesterday we got your letters of August 14th, but to day we hear that all communication between France and England [is] being cut off. I don't exactly see how we shall see your next letters.

I think it very funny if Niles put my St. Bernard adventure in the paper, as I could have made it much better if I had really tried to make a good description. I hope you looked it over before it went to press.

The Bigelow's have just gone and some Monroes from Syracuse have come who will probably know Uncle Sam.[8] Remember me to Miss Hoar[9] and Mr Sanborn as I love them both.

Good bye all round and write soon to your

loving May.

MS: Unlocated; copy by ABA at Houghton Library, Harvard University.

1. On 31 July 1870, ABA noted in his manuscript *Diary for 1870* that the temperature in Concord ranged from 90 to 100 degrees during the last few days (479).

2. Châtel St. Denis (elevation 2,670 feet), a small town in western Switzerland, is situated on the Veveyse River in the Fribourg canton.

3. William Hammatt Simmons (1848–1920) was originally from Springfield, Massachusetts. He graduated from Harvard in 1869, studied medicine in Vienna, Austria, and received his MD from the University of Würzburg, Bavaria, in 1872. By 1878 he was a physician in Bangor, Maine.

4. The remains of MacMahon's French forces reached Châlons, France, on 16 August 1870, where he was joined by Emperor Napoleon III's troops. On 20 August the French abandoned Châlons and marched north; the Prussians occupied the town by 27 August.

5. Fanny Lombard was from Cambridge, Massachusetts, and a friend also to the family of novelist Henry James. While painting in Europe, May later met up with Lombard again. In a letter of 1877 to LMA, May writes from Paris of visiting the Salon exhibition: "The next day I took Fanny Lombard, dressed in her fine new suit, and we had a jolly time together" (Ticknor 200–201).

6. La Tour-de-Peilz, Switzerland, a small town in the district of Vevey, is located on Lake Geneva between Montreux and Vevey. The castle, constructed in the thirteenth century by Pierre of Savoy, once oversaw traffic and customs on the lake. Although the structure was almost destroyed by the wars of Burgundy in 1476, it was rebuilt in 1747.

7. Dr. Haskett Derby (1835–1914), a celebrated ophthalmologist, was born in Boston. He received his medical degree from Harvard in 1858 and later studied at the University of Vienna and the Graefian Clinic. He began his practice in ophthalmology in Boston in approximately 1861. He later founded the Eye Clinic in the Carney Hospital in Boston in 1887.

8. The Monroes are unidentified. Abigail's brother Samuel Joseph May lived in Syracuse, New York.

9. Elizabeth Hoar (1814–78) had been engaged to RWE's brother Charles when he died in 1836 and had remained a close friend of the Emerson family.

Louisa May Alcott to the Alcott Family

Vevay September 2nd 1870.

Your letters dated August 7th and 10th came yesterday with pictures &c. I am much obliged, but you need not send any papers, for Niles always does it, and as we have to pay Munroe for every letter forwarded, besides most of the postage from America, because it is *never* right, it is very expensive and one paper from Niles is enough. Pa's last letter had only two 2 cent stamps

FIGURE 60. "Tom and Polly" (20 August 1870), *Every Saturday.*

on it, and should have had 16 cent put on it in stamps, or I pay 25 or 30 cents here. Do be smart and have things straight. I don't wish to fuss, but the war makes such a difference in my money that I have to be as careful as I can, and after this shall send short letters and save the spins till we come. May's Dr. bill will be large I think so I must be careful, but it is necessary, and I gladly pay it.

We have no news for the days go quietly and pleasantly walking, reading, sewing, and playing games in the eve, for the house is now full of old and young.

A young German, Eugene Knorring very elegant and pleasant, but shy is here, also two Russian ladies, one dying of consumption.[1] A Polish General, the young Spaniard, and the Bigelow and Alcott party.

I dont think "Tom and Polly" good at all [see figure 60]. The "Brittany" one is excellent.[2] Your bits of news were all nice. I gave the Count Pa's message and he sends thanks and complements. Lina was pleased at being remembered.

I am so sorry you have had such a bad summer. We are in splendid health now. I walked to Chillon and back this week 12 good miles, and in one morn.[3] We met Howe a gay Yankee bird, and he gave us a fine lunch, and escorted us part way back.

May's eyes are better for the Drs. little salve. The underside of the lid is out of order, and he is to put it right by the salve &c. A sweet man and very celebrated.

This is a bad letter but studying French makes me cross and I hate it. Good bye and bless you all. I often wish spring was here and I going home.

Your Lu.

MS: Unlocated; copy by ABA at Houghton Library, Harvard University.

1. LMA describes Eugene Knorring in *Shawl-Straps*: "A bashful Russian, who wore remarkably fine broadcloth and had perfect manners, was likewise received into the good graces of the ladies, who taught him English, called him 'the Baron' in private, and covered him with confusion in public by making him talk at table" (135–36). The two Russian ladies are unidentified.

2. *Every Saturday: An Illustrated Journal of Choice Reading* NS 1.34 (20 August 1870) printed a full-page illustration entitled "Tom and Polly" from *An Old-Fashioned Girl* (536). The paper notes: "The picture represents them in Tom's 'den,' Polly in grandmother's chair and in the absence of grandmother, at Tom's request, giving him sage counsel; while Tom, seated on a stool at her feet, is tearing in pieces the note his fair-weather sweetheart Trix has written releasing him from his engagement" (531). Niles wrote LMA on 30 August 1870: "'Tom & Polly' wh. has been sent you, will not perhaps please you as much perhaps; Polly is too dignified & Tom too much of a man, but still it is excellent. All of them have certainly given a new 'Vein' to the sale of the book. . . You ask why Fields allows pictures of your heroes to appear in Every Saturday. Because he wishes to sail *it* into popularity, not *you*" (ALS: Houghton Library, Harvard University). The same issue of *Every Saturday* also published a full-page illustration titled "Washerwomen in Brittany" (540), which depicts the women in traditional Brittany clothing with the famous "fly-away" caps.

3. Located on Lake Geneva near Montreux, the Castle of Chillon appears to rise out of the water and is connected to the mainland by a wooden bridge. The location had been the site of a fortress dating back to the Bronze Age, but the present castle was constructed in the thirteenth century under Count Pierre II of Savoy. François Bonivard, who championed the Reformation, was chained in its dungeon from 1530 to 1536 and became the subject of Lord Byron's famous poem "The Prisoner of Chillon" (1816).

May Alcott to Abigail Alcott

Pension Paradis
Sept 5th 1870.

Dear Mother,

I have seated myself just outside our garden, on the edge of the Lake, meaning to write you a good long letter, but looking down this pretty lane to the Pension Victoria, where Lu stayed when here before (and where she met the Polks)[1] I am tempted to use the little time I have before sunset in putting this bit on paper as a heading, rather than try to fill this page with our doings, which of late have not been very exciting. The war news of course is the great subject of conversation and Napoleon's surrender caused quite a panic to the French, here in the house.[2] I dont see how there can be much more fighting, and you need not be surprised if our next letters are dated Stresa which you know is on Lake Maggiore,[3] and where Nelly Low is staying with her maid only. Alice is fond of her, and thinks we should have good times sketching together, as she is talented and an extremely pleasant companion. It sounds very attractive as the drive from Brieg to Stresa is most exquisite,[4] and as we shall probably do it starting in the early morning I imagine it will be something that we shall remember all our lives—Alice has an Italian teacher and a French one comes three times a week which keeps us all hard at work, and now the Bigelows have gone to Zermatt,[5] we have quit [i.e., quiet] days and pleasant evenings, for I have taught the young German Professor from St. Petersburg, and the Spaniard, *Muggins*, which game they now delight in, and it is a never ceasing source of enjoyment; sometimes for variety, we have *slap*[?] *everlasting*,[6] and now and then the German and I play chess, for he is an old hand at it, and we have hard fights. Lu, Lena, and I walked to Villeneuve the other day and back, making about 11 miles in the whole, which was pretty well for a rheumatic invalid who was as chipper on her return as when she started, and finished up with eating an immense dinner, such as would have delighted mothers' eyes to behold. She seems so well and bright, I can think it only little less than a miracle that air and potash should have accomplished so much in five months, and we had a good laugh over the Allen photograph which looks like a death's head compared to her round brown face as it is now. Dr. Dorr has made my eyes as good as new and by killing the intense inflamation on the underside of both lids. He gave me my choice of a short and very painful cure, or a long and comparatively painless one. I, of course, chose the former: and really thought the first application of the blue stone had put my eyes out as I suffered intensely for two hours, but each treatment since has hurt less, so now that it is nearly over, I am truly grateful I decided on the short course, and Father will delight in his daughters good clear eyes bought for a few francs in Switzerland.

Nan's letter dated August 20th has just come and a nice gossipy one it is too, just the sort we like to get. You seem to be having many visitors, and Concord appears to have waked up to the benefit of the Ricketsons, who I was quite sure would like the old town if they once got into it.

Lu has told you how H. J. Pratt surprised us the other night and it really is very entertaining to hear about his adventures, for he tells them well, and as he went to Tunis and Constantinople where every thing was exceedingly foreign, it sounds quite like a romance.[7] We have good times sketching and walking together, and it seems like old Concord days to have nothing to do but ramble about and enjoy oneself. He is handsomer and more manly than formerly, and after all it is great comfort to have an American gentleman to speak to, though they dont have titles.

This uncertainty about Italy is dreadful, but I can only wait with patience.

Lena Warren wants four "Transcripts" with my *Mount St Bernard Sketch* sent to her address, "Pension Du Rivage, La Tour, Vevey, Swizn," as she means to send them about to her friends instead of writing the account herself. You need not send us one as Niles is devoted, and forwards every thing to us.

I feel greatly complemented that Emma Moore should want my picture.

Give a great deal of love to John and tell him how sorry I am that neurolgia has got hold of him, but his walk to Mount Desert will do him ever so much good.[8]

FIGURE 61. Herbert J.
Pratt, Vevey,
Switzerland (1870), by
May Alcott. *Houghton
Library, Harvard
University.*

Remember me to the Emersons and Ricketsons, and write soon dear
Marmee to

Your May.

MS: Unlocated; copy by ABA at Houghton Library, Harvard University. ABA writes
Lena Warren's address on page 7 of his copy: "Miss Lena Warren / Pension Du Rivage /
La Tour, Vevey, / Swizn."

1. LMA stayed at the Pension Victoria in Vevey with Anna Weld from October to December 1865. Colonel Polk and his family, whom LMA described as "rebels, & very bitter
& rude to us," were from South Carolina (*Journals* 144). She goes on to describe Polk
and her other fellow boarders in "Life in a Pension" in the *Independent* 19 (7 November
1867). It was also here that LMA met Ladislas Wisniewski, a Polish youth who became
the partial inspiration for the character "Laurie" in *Little Women.*

2. Emperor Napoleon III of France surrendered to the Prussians on 2 September 1870. On 5 September in Paris, the empire was declared over and the new republic of France began.

3. Stresa is situated on the west bank of Lake Maggiore in northern Italy.

4. Brieg (German for Brigue), located in northern Switzerland, is the beginning point for the Simplon Road.

5. Zermatt, located in northern Switzerland, is situated in a green valley surrounded by mountains. On the southwestern side of the town rises the majestic Matterhorn. Because of its beautiful scenery and its mountaineering opportunities, the town had long been a popular tourist attraction.

6. Muggins was a popular card game where the players would try to dispose of their cards by laying them down in a certain order. "Muggins" was the name given to the last player holding cards. Muggins was also a popular domino game also called All Fives. Slap-everlasting is unidentified. In *Shawl-Straps* LMA writes of the young Spaniard, Silvio Mirandola, playing muggins with them: "It is also to be recorded that the doomed little Don was never seen to laugh but once, and that was when the girls taught him the classical game of Muggins. The name struck him; he went about saying it to himself, and on the first occasion of his being 'mugginsed,' he was so tickled that he indulged in a hearty boy's laugh; but immediately recovered himself, and never smiled again, as if in penance for so forgetting his dignity" (135).

7. Herbert James Pratt (1841–1915) was born in Medford, Massachusetts, the son of James and Caroline Bartlett Pratt (the sister of Alice's father, Dr. George Bartlett). He was educated at the Boston Latin School and graduated from Harvard College in 1863. He entered Harvard Medical School but soon enlisted in the U.S. Army, where he served as acting assistant surgeon until he was discharged in May 1864. He resumed his studies and graduated from Harvard Medical School in July 1868. He traveled abroad extensively (Europe, Asia, Africa) for most of the rest of his life and was both an accomplished musician and a linguist skilled in seven languages. He died in Plymouth, Massachusetts, survived by his unmarried sister, May Pratt. In *Shawl-Straps* LMA described Herbert J. Pratt: "A cheerful comrade was the 'Peri,' and a great addition to the party, who now spent most of their time . . . listening to the pranks of this sprightly M.D., who seemed to be studying his profession by wandering over Europe with a guitar à la troubadour. Sounding the lungs of a veiled princess in Morocco was the least of his adventures, and the treasures he had collected supplied Lavinia with materials for unlimited romances" (139–40).

8. Mt. Desert, Maine, located in Hancock County, is an island in the Gulf of Maine; it was already a resort area by the mid-nineteenth century.

Louisa May Alcott to the Alcott Family

Vevey September 10th 1870.

Dear People,

As all Europe seems to be going to destruction, I hasten to drop a line before the grand smash arrives. We mean to skip over the Alps next week if weather and war permit, for we are bound to see Milan and the lakes, even if we have to turn and come back without a glimpse of Rome. The Pope is beginning to perk up, and Italy and England and Russia seem ready to join in the war now that France is down. Think of Paris being bombarded and smashed up like Strasbourg. We never shall see the grand old Cathedral at Strasbourg now, it is so spoilt.[1]

Vevey is crammed with refugees from Paris and Strasbourg. Ten families applied here yesterday. It is awful to think of the misery that wretch Nap has made, and I don't wonder his people curse him after he got them into such a war, and then slipt out like a coward. Hope his ills will increase, and every inch of him will suffer for such a shameful act. I wish you could hear the French talk about him; they stamp and rave and scold, like theatrical children as they are. I like them less and less, the more I see of them. They are so unstable and absurd. Now they howl, "Vive la Republique," and within months they ask one of the Bourbons to come back and reign over them. A bad lot.

Our house is brim full and we have funny times. The sick Russian lady and her old ma make a great fuss if a breath of air comes in at meal times, and expect twenty people to sit shut tight in a smallish room for an hour on a hot day. We protested, and Madame put them in the parlor where they glower as we pass and lock the door when they can. The German professor is learning English and is a quiet pleasant man. The Polish General, a little crooked, is very droll and bursts out in the middle of the general chat with stories about transparent apples and golden horses. Mrs Munroe and Julia, her daughter, (with a Russian lover whom Julia is to marry next month) are from Syracuse N.Y. and know Uncle Sam.[2] They are rather ordinary, and we dont say much to them. They asked the first thing for my works,

FIGURE 62.
Strasbourg Cathedral
(19 November 1870),
Harper's Weekly.

"for the Russian bear to read." Benda, the crack book and picture man here asked May, "if she was the Miss Alcott who wrote the popular books," for he said he had many calls for them, and wished to know where they could be found.[3] We told him at London and felt puffed up.

The other eve, as we sat in our wrappers, the maid came up with H. J. Pratts card. We asked him up and he appeared as brown and jolly and handsome as ever. He had been to Bex for us and hunted all day along the Lake to find us. At Montraux he met Charley Howe who told him the Alcotts' were here and on he came. He has been here some days and will remain till we go to Italy, when he will go on to Paris, if Paris is'nt blown up. We have had lively times since he came, for he has traveled far and wide, and can tell his adventures well. He went to Tunis and Carthage[4] and dug up marbles among the ruins for classic sleeve buttons, &c. He dances wild dances for us, sings songs in many languages. We had a moonlight ball in the road the other night coming from the Warrens—fine affair. He is much improved and quite appals us by talking Arabic, French, German, Italian, and Armenian in one grand burst.

May and I delve away at French, but it makes my head ache and I don't learn enough to pay for the trouble. I never could study, you know, and suffer such agony when I try, that it is piteous to behold. The little brains I have left, I want to keep for future works, and not exhaust them on grammar— vile invention of Satan! May gets on slowly and dont have fits over it, so she had better go on, the lessons only cost two francs.

I don't know as you will ever get this letter or the others lately sent, for Paris is in such a mess no letters go in or come out, and all ours *from* you go Munroe's care, so when we see them, no one knows. Alice has written to have her letters sent to the care of "Baring Brothers, London." I think we had better do the same. So direct your next letters *there*, and I will send Baring our address in Italy, if we go.

MS: Unlocated; manuscript copy by ABA at Houghton Library, Harvard University. Printed: *Selected Letters* 149–50; partially printed: Cheney 250–51.

1. The Strasbourg Cathedral was built on the foundation of a much older cathedral when construction began in 1176 under the direction of Bishop Heinrich von Hasenburg. One of the finest examples of high gothic architecture, the cathedral was finally

FIGURE 63. "Flight of French Peasants," (5 November 1870), *Harper's Weekly.*

completed in 1439 when its north tower was finished; a south tower was planned but never executed. The tower, which could be seen from the Vosage Mountains and the Black Forest across the Rhine, made the structure the tallest building in the world from 1625 until 1847. While Strasbourg suffered greatly from the Prussian bombardment during the war, the town surrendered on 27 September with the cathedral basically unharmed. *Harper's Weekly* for 19 November 1870 reports: "The gunners were instructed to spare, if possible, this magnificent monument of medieval art, and probably there was not one among them who would not rather have lost his right hand than direct a single shot against the wonderful structure" (748).

2. In *Shawl-Straps* LMA describes Mrs. Munroe and Julia: "One other party there was who much amused the rest of the household. An American lady with a sickly daughter, who would have been pretty but for her affectation and sentimentality. The girl was engaged to a fierce, dissapated little Russian, who presented her with a big bouquet every morning, followed her about like a dog and glared wrathfully at any man who cast an eye upon the languishing damsel. . . . It was evident that the Russian . . . was going to marry Mademoiselle for her money, and the weak old Mama was full of satisfaction at the prospect. To others it seemed a doubtful bargain, and much pity was felt for the feeble girl doomed to go to Russia with a husband who had 'tyrant' written in every line of his bad, *blasé* little face and figure" (138–39).

3. B. Benda was a publisher and bookseller in Vevey. In 1870, his shop was located in the Hotel Monnet.

4. Tunis, an ancient city located on a large Mediterranean gulf (now the Gulf of Tunis) in North Africa. Carthage, an ancient city near Tunis, was founded in 814 BC by Phoenicians from the city of Tyre. In 146 BC the Romans, during the Third Punic War, destroyed both Tunis and Carthage, but Augustus rebuilt the cities and they became important Roman centers.

Louisa May Alcott to Anna Alcott Pratt

Private *Sunday 11th* [September] 1870

Dear Nan,

Your letter of August 24th has just come! I am lying on my bed with a *head ache*. Herby and Alice sit on the sofa talking Italian, and May is finishing off a sketch of "H having a funeral" [see figure 64]. We are all "obese" with dinner, as May says, and very jolly, so I read bits of news in the midst of "questo," "hasto," &c. and May touches up Herbys nose. Yes, deary, Nan, we

do cot on your reamy letters, and all bits of news have a relish, even Reuben Rice with his "*yaller* canopy."[1]

When we read that the parlor chairs must go, we wailed and May hoped you would take off her precious green rep, so we could cover other old chairs.[2] When we got to the A_____ tribe and the big dinner, I flew up and declared I *would'nt* keep hotel and when we read of the strangers swarming round, I *fairly panted for my garden hose and a good chance to blaz away at 'em*. Is'nt it dreadful? and am I not glad I am safe? I delight to have my family live in luxury but I do hate to spend my substance on old strangers. I am glad you got Mum a nice shawl. Over haul every clothes she has this fall and buy a whole piece of flannel for her, so she can revel in it, and never say again, holding up an old gray rag of a petticoat, "I really have'nt the necessaries of life." I never forgot that time and beg you don't take her word for having clothes, as I did and then find that she was half naked.

Do tell me about Mrs Stearns. Did Pa have any money? and how did old S_____ take it? A'int she mean? Oh Lu!

I hope Donny will find time to love Aunt Weedy a little. Dont let him spindle up too high. I must find my little rosy, round "Coopid" when I come back. Read Miss Marletts "Countess Giscela", and see if the pastors' wife and children are not lovely.[3] They made me long for my nannies so much I quite squirmed 'cause I couldn't grab at once. Always tell me all you can about the dears. I am glad John is off for a lark and hope it will set him up. Can't he run over here next spring and meet us in England, and come home with us after a little trip. I should think one of his rich uncles could afford to help him. If they can't, I will go halves as far as I can for health is better than money, and he must not get invalided at thirty. No, by Jove!

I shall surely come in the spring, for travelling is not very interesting to me now, and if I am well, I had rather be at home. So take care of Mum this winter and I'll be at the fore in six months God willing. Alice and May can stay if they like.

What a funny mess of company you have had. Lizzy Wells sent me a note by Auntie last week and I answered it.[4] Poor Eliza, I dont think she bettered herself much.

This Miss beed[?] very glad that her dear Miss beed[?] weller[?], and she wished she settled with her in the dinin room kissed her, and sawed[?] the

FIGURE 65. Anna Alcott
Pratt (ca. early 1860s).
*Louisa May Alcott's
Orchard House/L. M. A.
Memorial Association.*

new sucker-to-seer dress and the blue bow, and goed to the Globe theatre with her Lain at[?] Fechter, Oh, say, she did'nt find nothing so filling as her family after all, though she did blow their heads off frequent and parse[?] them daily[?]. They scused her and she [indecipherable word] of them. I have *never* heard of L. W. Is it a poem?[5]

We are thrown aback to day by the news that Italy is getting under arms just where we want to go.[6] Russia and England must hurry and make peace or Europe will be in a general toss, and we shall have to go to England. Speaking of Italy, Alice has a very handsome Italian teacher who rolls his eyes and complements her to her hearts content. She said one day that the war kept her here, and he responded with a Roman languish "Thank God for the war then." Tender but not patriotic. I have to sit in the room and play propriety, for Italians don't understand American fare and casinofs[?] and get presuming, Alice says.

The writing of this letter is not full, but I write so little I really dont know how. Nan, I want you to send me the number of inches in one of your skirts—down the front of the skirt. I mean to get you a little "ress" here where silk's are cheap and must half make the skirt on account of duties. Don't forget. Shall it be black or gray? long or short?

Good bye love to every one. Dont read this stuff loud. I dont write for the public now,—let May do that.

Be sure and send us one of Mays Mount St. Bernard letters, if Niles dont, and do, do, pay your postage 16 cts, not 4.

Ever Your Lu.

MS: Unlocated; copy by ABA at Houghton Library, Harvard University.

1. Reuben Rice (1814–85) settled in Concord with his parents in 1829 but eventually moved to Detroit to work for the Michigan Central Railroad. He returned to Concord in 1867. A member of the Concord Social Circle, Rice was active in community affairs. The yellow canopy perhaps refers to his carriage, for on 25 August, ABA noted in his manuscript *Diary for 1870* that "Mr Rice offers his carriage and I take Mr. Mellon [of Detroit] to Sleepy Hollow Cemetery . . . and return to dinner" (526).

2. Rep is a fabric, usually wool, silk, or cotton, that is ribbed or corded.

3. *Countess Giscela* (Leipzig, 1869) by E. Marlitt, pseudonym of the German best-selling author Eugenie John (1825–87), was translated from German by A. L. Wister and published in America by Lippincott in 1869.

4. Eliza May Wells, the eldest child of LMA's cousin Elizabeth Sewall Willis Wells, had married Samuel Greele on 5 September 1866, a marriage that LMA had called "a foolish match" (*Journals* 153). Samuel Sewall Greele was the son of LMA's uncle Samuel Greele, who had married Louisa May, Abigail's sister, in 1823.

5. LMA, at times, engaged in this type of childish language in her letters to Anna.

6. During the Franco-Prussian War, Napoleon III withdrew his garrison from Rome, unable to protect the Papal State while fighting Prussia. Although many people in Italy demanded the Italian government seize Rome, no action was undertaken until the French army was defeated at Sedan. King Victor Emmanuel II then proposed a peaceful settlement with Pope Pius IX. The Pope refused, and on 11 September 1870, the Italian army began its nine-day advance toward Rome. The Alcotts and Bartlett waited in Switzerland until Rome was taken by the Italian army on 20 September before finally setting forth in early October for Italy.

Louisa May Alcott to the Alcott Family

Vevay September 19 1870.

Dear People,

    We are having pleasant times now with "*Herby dear*" M. de Knorring, the German Professor, and Mr Sturater, a Vermonter, whom we call the "Fat Boy," as he is stout, pompous, and very ordinary. Michael De Knorring from Courland[1] is a blond, shy, dignified Russian German, a real gentleman, and we like him very much. Alice is trying to draw him out, and he seems glad to come as he dont care to mix with some disagreeable Russians and French in the house. So we have nice walks together, our party of six Alice and Konorring, May and H. J. P. myself and Lena, or the Fat Boy (who has left now to our satisfaction, for he was not a speciman of our blessed countrymen of whom we could be proud.)

    To-morrow we go with old Mr. Nicond to the theatre here, for two good plays are to be done by a company from Geneva. Last week Alice and I went to Geneva with the Bigelows, who are to stay there some time. The Lake was rough, and I was ill, but the rest had a good pleasant sail. Sickard[?] was herself again as soon as her foot was on her naked hearth, and after a lunch at a Cafe, we flew about the city in a gale of wind, to hunt watches. Alice and I made a bargain, she gave me her lovely Francis Ist ring—antique emerald and diamond, in a quaint setting,[2] also a pretty gold chain for watch or locket, and I was to give her a crystal watch, now the rage. It was a fine bargain for me, for the chain was worth $25 or 30 in America and the ring would bring sums among a certain antiquity-loving set. The watch is a round crystal ball by a chain from a hook at the belt. I don't admire them but A. does, and was going to sell the ring and chain to get one. So I exchanged and as her watch only cost $28, it was a good speculation. I got a plain new unminted[?] watch for $30, and with my chain am all fixed. We had great fun over the bargain, and the Bigelows offered sums for my ring, but as a piece of "portable property" I prefer to keep it, and speculate on it in America, where I can do better. My watch is by a good maker and he gave me a sort of pledge to keep it in order through his agents in Rome, London, Paris, Madrid, or New York, whenever I applied to them to regulate it.

May wanted me to get a "crystal goblet" as we call A's, but it is only a fancy thing and not suitable for me, so I resisted the temptation, and got a plain one. So far I like it very well, and think it was a good job.

Our pension is brimming full, and some of the gentlemen have rooms over the stable, for the fame of the table seems to attract people. We have a French family now, a funny fat old lady with a white beard and a vast purple bonnet in which she lives day and night apparently, and her married daughter, a handsome shrill blonde, who dresses in as delicate violet and white, and picks her teeth at table with a *hairpin*! I thought Alice and H. J. P. would have fainted at the full spectacle; but we are fast getting used to the little peculiarities of foreigners and I trust they will forgive us many sins in return. Miss Munroe and her Russian lover, go roaming about while the Marmee pegs away at French, so she can confer with the Russian Ma who smokes strong tobacco and is a very high and haughty female, to judge from her appearance. Alice has dismissed her comely Italian teacher, and is to take riding lessons now so that she can learn to leap and be ready to hunt on the Campagnia when at Rome.[3]

May devotes herself to sketching and "funeral," with frequent "arbors," and in the eve, we go "*in mass*" to Pension du Rivage and call on Emma Warren. H. J. P. is in full feather and frolicks as of old. I poke about as usual, sew, read, eat, sleep, walk, sit in corners and take notes, and wonder what the world was made for.

The weather is as cool and autumnal as at home, and I dont think the climate would suit us much longer. We are only delaying our Roman trip on account of May's eyes, for Dr. Dorr says they are doing well and need only a little more treatment to be quite right. So, as it was also well to see what the Pope and King intend to do, we decided to stay a week or two longer and finish May up, and then set forth on our Italian journey. Advice differs so that we mean to abide by our own observations and experience and see the Lakes any how, unless a general explosion in Northern Italy makes it rash to cross the Alps.

Tell Fred, that when Herbert Pratt was a little boy and his teeth were loose he used to tie a thread round the loose one when he went to bed, a[nd] leave the thread hanging out of his mouth. Then his grandmother used to come up when he was asleep and tweak out the tooth, and little Herby would wake up and cry for a minute and then be glad to go to sleep again. Fred had better try it.

Lu.

MS: Unlocated; copy by ABA at Houghton Library, Harvard University.

1. Courland, an historical Baltic province, was, from the early thirteenth century, primarily owned by nobles who were descendants of German invaders. From 1795 until 1918, Courland was a province of imperial Russia. Today it is part of Latvia.

2. Francis I (1494–1547) ruled France from 1515 until his death, becoming France's first Renaissance monarch. He was a patron of the arts and his reign saw great cultural advances in the country.

3. Campagna di Roma, the low-lying land that surrounds Rome, is approximately eight hundred square miles. Although it was populated during Roman times, it was later abandoned for centuries due to malaria. It was reclaimed as a farm and pasture region during the nineteenth century.

Louisa May Alcott to the Alcott Family

Private

Vevey September 20th 1870.

Dear People,

Pa's letter containing Marmee's picture and Mr Sewall's Accounts has just come.[1] The picture is very soft and pleasant though not quite clear and strong enough, but it will be a great comfort to us, for the old one is so faded you can hardly see it. Alice and Lena who were with us at the P. Office admired it very much, and Lena said at once, "What a dear, lovely, motherly face, I must know her when we go home." She lost her own mother when a child and does not like her step-mother, so I told her she should come and love my Marmee.[2]

The Account looks all right, but I don't seem to know much about it, and am willing to take it on trust. I am only sorry that Mrs S———— had any of

FIGURE 66. Orchard House, Concord, Massachusetts (1870s). *Louisa May Alcott's Orchard House/L. M. A. Memorial Association.*

my money, for I never wanted to accept the favor, and don't think she had any right to be paid. However we are out of the mess now, and I hope can keep so.

I have only to say, as before, about the *money*, I should like the sums that Roberts pays me safely invested somewhere and we live on the interest so far as we can. When I get home and at work again I can supply all the extra needs by short tales &c, so till then I suppose we must draw and spend, and trust to luck to make the sums hold out. I see that my trip is to cost a good deal more than I expected, for being in a party, I have to pay my share in some things that I dont care for, though Alice is perfectly fair and generous, and kind. May has no money for her private wants, and these I shall of course supply—Drs. bills, French Lessons, and amusements included. So that I shall spend a thousand or two before I get back. If I get well and May has a good time it will be worth the money and I shan't complain.

I dont see why S. E. S. dont invest some of the money in *Government Bonds*, they cant fail like railroads, and every one says they are an excellent investment. If I have a good sum in January from Niles, I wish S. E. S. would buy me some bonds. John will draw the dividends for Ma while Papa is gone. I wish her to have all she wants, to pay Nan a good board—$6 or 8 a week, and have without stint every comfort or luxury she expresses the least wish for. Now our John must see to it that she is well cared for in every way, and let her feel that the income of my money is all her own to use and enjoy to her heart's content. Another thousand by and by will be all May and I shall want, for I have'nt spent my first money yet, and *that* can be put aside in a lump when the January return comes in—the second $1000 I mean. Niles sent me a long letter about Low &c. I suppose he has told you the story, so I won't repeat. I hope Low will "play fair," and Tom keep his temper, and not spend too much in puffing the books, which seem to be doing well enough to be let alone now. I don't think the printing of the "Lay of the Golden Goose" would do us any harm, but I don't care any thing about it either way, so you can let it pass. I am glad the books continue to go well since I am doing nothing now. I am afraid I shall not write till I get home, for all I do is to scribble odds and ends as notes, and dawdle round without an idea in my head. Alice says no one does anything in Italy, so after another six months of idleness, I may get back and go to work. In the spring one of us will come home to run the machine. I fancy it may be May, if I can make up my mind to stay, for Alice cant remain without duenna, and I can be one and also *pay my own way*. A year of pleasure at A's expense is all May should expect or accept *I* think, and she is ready to fall to again, being grateful for sips of fun. I dont want to stay, but if I'm not tip top by spring, I should feel as if I ought, for fifteen years' mischief cant be mended in twelve months, at least not thoroughly, I am afraid. However, I shall leave that point for time to settle.

I think Plato had better not try San Francisco. He would be as much out of place as a saint in a bar-room, besides, he is too old to [be] slamming across the continent in a week. Dont!

Please give the note to Niles and tell him to send our next letters to Baring Brothers, London.

I hope that Nan and Ma are getting off a fat letter to us.

Good bye to all

May sends love, but is rather "absorbed" just now.

Your Lu.

MS: Unlocated; manuscript copy by ABA at Houghton Library, Harvard University. Printed: *Selected Letters* 151–52.

1. S. E. S. had detailed LMA's account on 24 August 1870; ABA included a copy of it in his August 1870 letter to LMA. The account showed that LMA's income from 3 May 1869 to 27 July 1870 was $10,485, and it listed the more than $9,000 in stocks that LMA owned (see *The Letters of ABA* 520–21).

2. Lena's mother, Angelina Greenwood, had married Richard Warren on 12 October 1836. She died on 21 March 1849, a few days past her thirty-seventh birthday. Lena (Angelina Langdon Warren) was her mother's namesake and last child. Richard Warren married his second wife, Susan B. Gore, daughter of Jeremiah Gore of Portland, Maine, on 3 January 1855.

May Alcott to Abigail Alcott

Lake Como, Cadenabbin.

Oct. 8, 1870.

Dearest Mother,

I want to write you a circumstantial account of our triumphal entrance into Italy over the Simplon Pass for since my St. Bernard adventure
nothing has equalled the excitement of the last few days. We left Pension
Paradis Vevey in the early morning having bid the weeping household
Adieu the night before. I really believe it was not merely a French display
of sentiment but they were honestly sorry to see the last of us particularly
Mlle. Nicond who was up betimes cutting flowers and fixing a delicious
luncheon for us but she quite broke down as we stepped into the carriage
and said her only comfort was the hope we should sometime return to her
house and that there would always be a corner for us. As we steamed along
I ruminated on the importance of being amiable and sociable on all occasions for I find even the sternest officials melt beneath a smile and a polite
word, and I am quite sure our party might be traced all over Europe by the
pleasant impressions we have left behind us, though this is not for me to
say yet as a hint to future travellers I dash[?] it down and think it should be
first and foremost in all guide books. From Vevey past the dear old Castle
of Chillon standing out in the water grey and solemn in the early light, by
our old friend the white capped "Dent de Midi" and up the lovely valley of
the Rhone is something to remember but after taking [a] diligence at Sierre[1]
and arriving at Brieg that evening rather tired after our first day of travel
our adventures really began. All the party were up at four the next morning
and lighted by lanterns for it was pitch dark, we were conducted to a square,
where surrounded by our luggage we waited patiently till it was announced
that there were no places in either of the immense diligences which stood
before us ready to start immediately. This was enough to dampen the arder
of a less gay crowd than ours, but we fell upon the official and smiled to
such an extent that he suddenly ordered out a calêche with two horses and
a superb driver dressed in a red coat, cocked hat with gold lace and yellow small clothes who whirled us out of the square and then though it was
still star-light we began the steady ascent. The air grew colder and colder,

Crossing the Simplon Oct 3rd / 70

till at last after having applied the bottle many times in vain I got out and walked to warm myself. The other two remained in the carriage wrapped up to such an extent that only eyes were visible and the sketch I took looks like a portrait of Egyptian women. They hardly dared uncover their hands enough to eat a bit of chicken with comfort for fear of a nipped finger and it was funny to see the horses covered with a little hoar frost.[2] But in spite of cold I tingled with delight when Monte Rosa opened before us with its dazzling white snow against a perfectly clear blue sky and behind us the Bernese Alps and the glaciers.[3] This was something to have lived for and as we climbed still higher while white peak after white peak showed itself in the direction of Brieg and over the valley we had left so far below us.

We had a miserable dinner at Simplon[4] and then I nearly stood on my head with delight at the intense beauty of the valley of Gondo for any thing wilder and more picturesque cannot be imagined. Then this wonderful road which we had traversed so far in safety led along the edge of precipices, through tunnels and over cataracts to such an exciting extent, that nothing

OH 345/1

short of the little farce which was now to be enacted could have taken my
attention off the magnificent scenery about us. At Iselle[5] our baggage was
to be examined and passports demanded, but I not having one of the latter
was to play the part of ladies maid, so out came my ear rings—up went my
curls and tying a veil over my rather dressy hat and throwing a waterproof
over my swell new travelling dress I dismounted to help the ladies out and
arranging the cloaks and bundles stood quietly [to] one side hoping the
sharp eyed officials would overlook me.

They didn't however, and after examining every parcel in the carriage,
looking at me from head to foot as if taking an inventory of all my clothing and thoroughly hauling over all the trunks, we were allowed after great
deliberation to continue our descent through this enchanting valley everything growing more and more Italian in appearance till we entered Domo
D'Ossola[6] by sunset and from there drove to Stresa by moonlight.

FIGURE 68.
Monte Rosa,
Switzerland
(5 October 1870), by
May Alcott. *Louisa
May Alcott's Orchard
House/L. M. A.
Memorial Association.*

This I consider making a Pass successfully for its not every traveller who sees sunrise in the Alps, an Italian sunset and first sight of Lago Maggiore by moonlight all in one day.

The next morning we rowed to Isola Bella the loveliest of the Borromean Islands[7] and though the situation on the great rock is charming yet the chateau and gardens are not at all to my taste being too fantastic and not in harmony with the surrounding scenery. At 2 o'clock we took the steamboat to Luini[8] and here among the jeers and shouts of an Italian crowd, Alice and I mounted to the very top of a high diligence and sat with perfect complacency amid the baggage while Louisa from the coupé begged us to come down and the inside passengers craned their necks to see of what nation the insane travellers could be who preferred to view the landscape from that great elevation. But I wouldn't have missed the enjoyment of the next few hours for all the ridicule in the world and the beauty of that drive from Luini to Lugano can hardly be overrated. We had a last glimpse of Lago Maggiore and Monte Rosa by sunset and following the shores of the lake drove into Lugano by moonlight with our superb cocker playing a festive tune on a Robin Hood's horn which hung by gilt bands at his side, putting on two brakes, driving four horses and making himself agreeable to us all at the same time. I consider this man, a person of mind for he spoke three languages easily, and did everything with such a superior air that I felt intensely honored to have him lift me down in his great arms when we reached the Hotel Washington and stopped in a crowded square.[9] As a very proper ending to this delightful day Lu and myself can only say that we went to the opera in our robes-de-suit for from the window of our palatial apartment we looked directly onto the stage and behind the scenes of the theatre on the opposite side of a very narrow alley and heard the last two acts of Traviata finely sung.[10] It reminded me so much of the old days when Annie dressed in the velvet puffs and everlasting yellow top boots sang baritone to Lu's soprano and brought down the house in every act.[11]

The next morning we went to the church of San Angelo[12] and saw some striking frescoes by Luino who was the master of Leonardo da Vinci[13] and it is easy to see that the latter has copied this very fresco in the arrangements of the principal group in his Last Supper. Then we steamed up this Lugano, which to me is the most beautiful of all the lakes to Porlezza and drove by carriage to Menaggio,[14] where taking a funny sail boat we arrived here in Cadanabbia Thurs. Oct 6th after a varied journey and found Miss Nellie Low (more charming than ever) to welcome us. She proves a kindred spirit in the way of art and as we follow her to Milan Monday, I hope to have many good times with her. Como is charming but I must repeat nothing equals the beauty of Lugano to me, and our taking first a little boating and then a little driving has so broken up our trip that there has been no fatigue and nothing to mar the perfect enjoyment of this series of beautiful pictures and now more than ever I am convinced we travel under a lucky star.

Oct. 11th. Milan—Off to see the Cathedral,[15] to the galleries to see fine frescoes and pictures and to La Scala, to hear Travatore[16] which I consider a pleasant programme for a day with the sun shining and the softest air I ever felt to warm us after the chilly peaks of Switzerland. Good bye dear family and we can only hope that a balloon will bring us some letters from Paris before long as we pine for one—

Your loving May.

L. F. M.[17]

ALS: Houghton Library, Harvard University. This letter is bound into ABA's volume of his copies of LMA's and May's letters from Europe. Partially printed: Ticknor 90–94.

1. Sierre, in northern Italy, is a small town often frequented as a health resort.

2. May's rudimentary sketch of LMA eating chicken is located at Houghton Library, Harvard University. See her sketch "Crossing the Simplon" (figure 12).

3. Monte Rosa (elevation 15,203 feet) in the Alps dividing Switzerland and Italy is part of both countries. It is a gigantic glacier-covered mountain with ten summits, four of which are the highest peaks in the Alps. Glaciers cover the northern section of the mountain toward the fields of the Zermatt Valley. The southern side of the mountain is filled with rugged precipices that drop to verdant valleys below.

4. Simplon, Switzerland, is a pastoral village set at the northeast base of the Fletschhorn.

5. Iselle di Trasquera, Italy (elevation 2,155 feet), is located in the Val Diverdo near the Diveria River.

6. Domodossola, Italy, is a small town at the junction of the Bogna and the Toce rivers at the foot of the Italian Alps and is the point of Italian and Swiss customs examinations.

7. The Borromean Islands, situated in the western bay of Lake Maggiore. Baedeker's says its "scenary . . . rivals that of the Lake of Como in grandeur and perhaps surpasses it in the softness of its character" (*Switzerland* 372).

8. May appears to have confused the town of Luino with the painter Bernardino Luini, who was believed to have been born there (see note 13 below), thus accounting for the misspellings.

9. The Hotel Washington was located on the Via Genzanna.

10. *La Traviata* (1853) composed by Giuseppe Verdi (1813–1901) was derived from Alexander Dumas's *La Dame aux Camelias* (1852).

11. Anna and LMA acted in amateur dramatic companies in both Concord, Massachusetts, and in Walpole, New Hampshire, during the 1850s and early 1860s. For more information, see Madeleine B. Stern, "Louisa Alcott, Trouper: Experiences in Theatricals, 1848–1880," *New England Quarterly* 6 (June 1943), 175–97.

12. The convent of Santa Maria degli Angioli houses frescos by Bernardino Luini (ca. 1470–1532), including Luini's largest fresco (1529), depicting the Passion of Christ and containing several hundred figures. A smaller fresco on the church's wall depicts the Last Supper.

13. Leonardo da Vinci (1452–1519), Renaissance painter, architect, inventor, perhaps best known for his paintings *Mona Lisa* and *The Last Supper*. No direct evidence exists that supports the assertion that Luini was a student of da Vinci's; however, he was certainly influenced by him. Luini's coloring and design more closely resembles da Vinci's art than any other painter's of the period. While Luini painted both mythological and religious scenes, he, according to art critics, sentimentalized da Vinci's style, which garnered him a large following during the second half of the nineteenth century.

14. Porlezza, a small town situated on the northeast arm of Lake Lugano, Italy.

15. Milan, once an important Roman city, was in the 1870s a wealthy manufacturing and financial center, as well as the most populous city in Italy. The Milan Cathedral, founded by Gian Visconti in 1386, is one of the largest of the great cathedrals, holding over forty thousand people and extending over fourteen thousand square yards. Constructed over the basilica of Santa Maria Maggiore, the cathedral, built over several centuries, is adorned with over two thousand statues.

16. The opera *Il Trovatore* (1853) was composed by Giuseppe Verdi. Teatro alla Scala, located on the northwest Plaza della Scala, was constructed in the period of 1776–78; at the time it was one of the largest theaters in Europe, holding approximately 3,600 people.

17. The letters possibly stand for "Letter from May" or "Love from May."

Louisa May Alcott to Abigail Alcott

Lago Di Como,[1] Oct. 8, 1870.

Dearest Marmee,   A happy birthday, and many of 'em! Here we actually are in the long-desired Italy, and find it as lovely as we hoped. Our journey was a perfect success,—sunlight, moonlight, magnificent scenery, pleasant company, no mishaps, and one long series of beautiful pictures all the way.

Crossing the Simplon is an experience worth having; for without any real danger, fatigue, or hardship, one sees some of the finest as well as most awful parts of these wonderful Alps.

The road,—a miracle in itself! for all Nature seems to protest against it, and the elements never tire of trying to destroy it. Only a Napoleon would have dreamed of making a path through such a place; and he only cared for it as a way to get his men and cannon into an enemy's country by this truly royal road.

May has told you about our trip; so I will only add a few bits that she forgot.

Our start in the dawn from Brieg, with two diligences, a carriage, and a cart, was something between a funeral and a caravan: first an immense diligence with seven horses, then a smaller one with four, then our *calèche*[2] with two, and finally the carrier's cart with one. It was very exciting,—the general gathering of sleepy travellers in the dark square, the tramping of horses, the packing in, the grand stir of getting off; then the slow winding up, up, up out of the valley toward the sun, which came slowly over the great hills, rising as we never saw it rise before. The still, damp pine-forests kept us in shadow a long time after the white mountain-tops began to shine. Little by little we wound through a great gorge, and then the sun came dazzling between these grand hills, showing us a new world. Peak after peak of the Bernese Oberland[3] rose behind us, and great white glaciers lay before us; while the road crept like a narrow line, in and out, over chasms that made us dizzy to look at, under tunnels, and through stone galleries with windows over which dashed waterfalls from glaciers above. Here and there were refuges, a hospice, and a few *châlets*, where shepherds live their wild, lonely lives. In the P.M. we drove rapidly down toward Italy through the great Valley of Gondo,—a deep rift in rock thousands of feet deep, and just wide enough for the road and a wild stream that was our guide; a never-to-be-forgotten place, and a fit gateway to Italy, which soon lay smiling below us.[4] The change is very striking; and when we came to Lago Maggiore lying in the moonlight we could only sigh for happiness, and love and look and look. After a good night's rest at Stresa, we went in a charming gondola-sort of boat to see Isola Bella,—the island you see in the chrome over the fireplace at home,—a lovely island, with famous castle, garden, and town on it.[5] The day was as balmy as summer, and we felt like butterflies after a frost, and fluttered about, enjoying the sunshine all day.

A sail by steamer brought us to Luino,[6] where we went on the diligence to Lugano.[7] Moonlight all the way, and a gay driver, who wound his horn as we clattered into market-places and over bridges in the most gallant style. The girls were on top, and in a state of rapture all the way. After supper in a vaulted, frescoed hall, with marble floors, pillars, and galleries, we went to a room which had green doors, red carpet, blue walls, and yellow bed-covers,—all so gay! It was like sleeping in [a] rainbow.

As if a heavenly lake under our windows with moonlight *ad libitum* was n't enough, we had music next door; and on leaning out of a little back window, we made the splendid discovery that we could look on to the stage of the opera-house across a little alley. My Nan can imagine with what rapture I stared at the scenes going on below me, and how I longed for her as I stood there wrapped in my yellow bed-quilt, and saw gallant knights in armor warble sweetly to plump ladies in masks, or pretty peasants fly wildly from ardent lovers in red tights; also a dishevelled maid who tore her hair in a forest, while a man aloft made thunder and lightening,—and *I saw him do it*!

It was the climax to a splendid day; for few travellers can go to the opera luxuriously in their night-gowns, and take naps between the acts as I did.

A lovely sail next morning down the lake; then a carriage to Menaggio[8]; then a droll boat, like a big covered market-wagon with a table and red-cushioned seats, took us and our trunks to Cadenabbia, for there is only a donkey road to the little town.[9] At the hotel on the edge of the lake we found Nelly L[ow]., a sweet girl as lovely as Minnie, and so glad to see us; for since

Lugano Oct 6th/7...

her mother died in Venice last year she has lived alone with her maid. She had waited for us, and next day went to Milan, where we join her on Monday. She paints; and May and she made plans at once to study together, and enjoy some of the free art-schools at Milan and Naples or Florence, if we can all be together. It is a great chance for May, and I mean she shall have a good time, and not wait for tools and teachers; for all is in the way of her profession, and of use to her.

Cadenabbia is only two hotels and a few villas opposite Bellagio, which is a town, and fashionable.[10] We were rowed over to see it by our boatman, who spends his time at the front of the stone steps before the hotel, and whenever we go out he tells us, "The lake is tranquil; the hour is come for a walk on the water," and is as coaxing as only an Italian can be. He is amiably tipsy most of the time.

To-day it rains so we cannot go out, and I rest and write to my Marmee in a funny room with a stone floor inlaid till it looks like castile soap,[11] a ceiling

FIGURE 69. Lake Lugano, Italy, by May Alcott. *Louisa May Alcott's Orchard House/L. M. A. Memorial Association.*

in fat cupids and trumpeting fairies, a window on the lake, with balcony, etc. Hand-organs with jolly singing boys jingle all day, and two big bears go by led by a man with a drum. The boys would laugh to see them dance on their hind legs, and shoulder sticks like soldiers.

All looks well, and if the winter goes on rapidly and pleasantly as the summer we shall soon be thinking of home, unless one of us decides to stay. I shall post this at Milan to-morrow, and hope to find letters there from you. By-by till then.

MS: Unknown. Printed: Cheney 251–54. There is no copy of this letter in ABA's bound collection of LMA's and May's letters from Europe.

1. Lake Como, located in northern Italy, is thought to be one of the most beautiful lakes in the region, with many villages and villas lining its border and mountains rising above it to an elevation of 8,560 feet. Baedeker's says: "In the forests above, the brilliant green of the chestnut and walnut contrasts strongly with the greyish tints of the olive" (*Switzerland* 380).

2. A caleche is a type of light carriage with low wheels and a folding top.

3. The Bernese Alps are a group of mountain ranges in Switzerland's western Alps. Among its peaks are the Jungfrau, the Eiger, Dent de Morcles, and the Wetterhorn. Although the name derives from the Bernese Oberlan region of the Swiss canton of Bern, the ranges actually are located in six other cantons as well.

4. The Ravine of Gonda is described by Baedeker's as "one of the wildest and grandest [ravines] in the Alps, becoming narrower and more profound at every step, till its smooth and precipitous walls of mica-slate completely overhang the road" (*Switzerland* 258).

5. Isola Bella, one of the four islands, was a barren rock with only a church and several cottages until Count Vitaleo Borromeo (d. 1690) built a chateau and gardens there as his summer home. Baedeker's writes that the garden rises "on 10 terraces 100′ above the lake" and holds "the most luxuriant products of the south: lemon-trees, cedars, magnolias, cypresses, orange-trees, laurels, magnificent oleanders, etc. Grottos of shells, fountains (dry), mosaics, statues etc. meet the eye in profusion" (*Switzerland* 371).

6. Luino, a small industrial town, lies on the Italian shore of Lake Maggiore, near the junction of the Margorabbia and Tresa rivers.

7. Lugano, the largest town in the Swiss canton of Ticino, lies on the banks of Lake Lugano and is noted as a summer retreat because of its mild climate. The town itself is more Italian in character than Swiss. Lake Lugano is some 20 square miles with a depth of 945 feet. Baedeker's notes that the lake "presents a succession of the most beautiful landscapes, and is a worthy rival of its more celebrated and imposing neighbours the

Lakes of Como and Maggiore. In the vicinity of Lugano the banks are picturesquely studded with villas and chapels, and planted with the vine, fig, olive and walnut" (*Switzerland* 379).

8. Menaggio is a small town located on the west bank of Lake Como in northern Italy.

9. The village of Cadenabbia is situated on the west bank of Lake Como, approximately one-half mile northeast of Tremezzo and two miles south of Menaggio.

10. The Lake of Como divides into two arms (the Lake of Como to the east and the Lake of Lecco to the west) at the Punta di Bellagio. The small town of Bellagio, considered by many to be one of the most beautiful on the three lakes, is located in the Bay of Como on the west bank of the Punti di Bellagio.

11. Castile soap is an un-perfumed white soap made from lye and olive oil.

May Alcott to A. Bronson Alcott

Florence Oct. 30th 1870.

Dearest Father, your letters through Baring have just reached us, and now all of them will come safely I think. Last night we went to a party made for us at the house of the sculptor Ball[1]; who with his wife called on us immediately on our arrival, saying they had been expecting us, and looking forward with great pleasure to doing the honors of Florence to us. We returned their call and saw Mr. B. in his fine studio, among his marbles—all lovely but none so strong and full of power as his "Washington" in the Boston Public Garden.[2] He had never seen it since it was finished in bronze; and was pleasantly surprised by the unanimous approbation it has met with from *critical* Boston.

Last night Mr. Powers and Hart besides several other sculptors and artists were introduced to us and invited us to their studios.[3] It seems "Little Women" is as well known here as in Boston and has made many friends for Louisa. She was showered with compliments from the distinguished people here, Mr. Marsh (who is a literary man himself); also Miss Foley the cameo cutter and several ladies from Rome who would return there in a few weeks, and were full of kind offers about apartments &c.[4] Mr Gould was not there and we hear that he and his wife go into society very little, however we mean to see him at his studio, if possible.[5] Mr Hart who is a gray haired

Florence Oct. 30th 1870.

Dearest Father, Your letters through
Baring have just reached us, and now
all of them will come safely I think.
Last night we went to a party made
for us at the house of the sculptor Ball;
who with his wife called on us immediately
on our arrival, saying they had been expecting us, and looking forward with
great pleasure to doing the honors of
Florence to us. We returned their call and
saw Mr. B. in his fine studio, among his
marbles — all lovely but none so strong
and full of power as his "Washington" in the
Boston Public Garden. He has never
seen it since it was finished in bronze,
and was pleasantly surprised by the unanimous approbation it has met with from
critical Boston.

Last night Mr. Powers and Hart
beside several other sculptors and artists were

bear, but quite devoted to me, begs me to take a corner of his studio, and model a bust or little head of Lu, as he thinks I could clear a few hundreds by the sale of it, as her reputation seems spreading so rapidly. I also want to copy one of the enchanting Fra Angelio[6] angels, blowing her trumpet, a rose colored figure, on a gold background but as every thing seems uncertain about the climate suiting the invalid, I donot dare begin anything and devote myself to sight seeing, studying the fine pictures at the Uffizi and Pitti—digging at Italian.[7] I am greatly disappointed in finding there is no free school of painting here as my plan was to enter some such, and make the most of my time while here.

I can hardly begin to tell you how much some of the great pictures interest me and how disappointed I am in others. Every visit I make to the Uffizi, though I go intending to get some idea of the whole collection, I never get any farther than the Tribune, a small room containing the gems of the collection.[8] In this room a large Madonna of Andrea del Sarto is a constant delight to me[9]; also one by Correggio, no not *one* but *all* that I have seen of his seem most beautiful, particularly his frescoes at Parma, the cherubs of the chase, on the sixteen compartments of the Abbess' room in the old convent are too enchanting; and the watercolors and engravings are very perfect copies.[10] I can now more perfectly appreciate the fine set of his, belonging to Mrs. Stearns. But dreadful to relate the few Raphael Madonnas I have seen disappoint me and I am even so depraved as to prefer the fine steel engravings of them to the original paintings; they are charming in a way, but do not impress and interest me as much, as I expected.[11] His Fornarina is really distasteful to me.[12] Titians Venus[13] though a wonderful piece of flesh is not beautiful, (to me). But I like the Sibyl of Guercino,[14] and everything of Fra Angelio's they are so simple and sweet though often stiff and outdrawing[?], yet the beauty of the mans own character, seems to have crept into his work; and the frescoes in his convent of St Marks are perfectly touching.[15] His illuminations are very numerous and beautiful and it adds greatly to the charm of seeing where he lived and worked, to be shown all of this by a custodian who is so proud and fond of each, spoke of the great mans brushs, as any father could be. He was so gratified by our real interest in, and great admiration for everything we saw that he presented us with tickets to private and very exclusive exhibitions as a mark of his satisfaction.

FIGURE 70. May Alcott to Bronson Alcott, 30 October 1870. *Houghton Library, Harvard University.*

Then the pictures by Cimabue and Giotto are interesting and curious as the beginning of art, and a very old Madonna by the former, on a gold background, I like very much and am glad to have seen it in the church of Santa Maria Novella and created a great excitement when first uncovered for the Florentines.[16] I cant be reconciled to this city so full of history, and so connected with remarkable people looking so modern and new that it might be New York or any flourishing American city. The Arno is also [a] disappointing river, of an ugly color, and being just now particularly low, showing broad flats on both sides, and the bridges are the only redeeming feature.[17] I imagine we shall soon be on our march to Rome though we have letters to Dr. Appleton and Mr. Jarvis.[18] I hardly think we shall present them; as Lu does not care to go into company, though I should like it much to see how easily we could spend a gay month here. Dear papa do write from the West and we shall put an answer in home envelope to be forwarded to you. I dont wish any likeness of me put any where but wish Osgood would make a little money for me this Christmas out of the sketches.[19] x x I hope you will *make* a heap. May.[20] You must tell me about the new arrangement of Concord sketches. Is it one you have for yourself or one to be published. I want to know the exact arrangement.

ALS: Houghton Library, Harvard University. This letter is bound into ABA's volume of his copies of LMA's and May's letters from Europe. Partially printed: Ticknor 96–97.

1. Thomas Ball (1819–1911), born in Charlestown, Massachusetts, was a painter and sculptor. In 1844, he went to Florence, Italy, to study. He returned to work in Boston in 1857 but then went back to Florence in 1865, where he remained for over thirty years. In 1897 he moved to Montclair, New Jersey, and opened a studio in New York.

2. Ball's most famous work is his 1869 statue of George Washington, the first equestrian statue of the former general and president. It is located on the west side of the Boston Public Gardens, facing the Arlington Street gate.

3. Hiram Powers (1805–73) was born in Woodstock, Vermont, but moved to Ohio with his father in 1819. He was inspired to become a sculptor when he visited the studio of Frederick Eckstein and began to study art seriously. In 1834, he moved to Washington DC, where his work began to attract attention. In 1837, he went to Florence, Italy, where he spent the remainder of his life. His most famous work was the 1843 statue *The Greek Slave*, which was shown at the Crystal Palace Exhibition and immortalized in a sonnet by Elizabeth Barrett Browning. Joel Tanner Hart (1810–77), born in Winchester, Kentucky, began his career as a stonecutter and from there became a sculptor. In the 1840s,

he moved to Florence, Italy, where he lived until his death. His most famous works were the busts of Andrew Jackson (1838) and Henry Clay (1847). Hart also executed the bas-relief for the tombstone of Theodore Parker in the English Cemetery in Florence.

4. George Perkins Marsh (1801–82), son of a U.S. senator, was born in Woodstock, Vermont. He graduated from Dartmouth College in 1820 and a few years later began to practice law in Burlington, Vermont. From 1843 to 1849, he served the state as U.S. representative. In 1861 President Lincoln appointed Marsh as the first U.S. minister to the new kingdom of Italy, a post he held until his death at Vallombrosa, Italy. Marsh was also a noted philologist and scholar, writing numerous articles, reviews, and books. Among his works are *The Origin and History of the English Language* (1862) and *Man and Nature* (1864), a book that is considered an early important work of ecology. Margaret F. Foley (1827–77) grew up in rural New England, working for a time in the textile mills of Lowell, Massachusetts. Self-taught, she began her career carving small wooden figures and busts from chalk. She moved to Boston in 1848, where she earned recognition as a cameo cutter. In 1860 she moved to Florence, Italy, becoming friends with the American sculptor Harriet Hosmer. During the last part of her career, she began to focus on larger medallion portraits.

5. Thomas R. Gould (1818–81) was born in Boston, Massachusetts, and operated a successful dry-goods business with his brother prior to the Civil War. In the early 1850s, he studied with the Boston sculptor Seth Cheney (husband of Ednah Dow Cheney). In 1863, two of his sculptures, the heads of *Christ* and *Satan*, were exhibited at the Boston Athenaeum. In 1868, he and his family moved to Italy, settling in Florence until his death.

6. Fra Angelico (ca. 1395–1455), born Guido di Pietro, became a Dominican monk in Florence in 1418. Working first as an illuminator, he later began to execute frescoes at the various convents where he lived. In 1436 he moved to the new monastery of San Marco in Florence, where he completed one of his famous works, the altarpiece of San Marco. He was called to Rome by the pope in 1445 to paint frescoes at St. Peter's Cathedral. One of the most important artists of the early Italian Renaissance, Fra Angelico was beatified by Pope John Paul II in 1982. May probably is referring to Fra Angelico's *Linaioli Tabernacle* (ca. 1433). When its doors are closed, it depicts St. Mark and St. Peter. When the doors are open, the Virgin Mary and Child sit on a throne while, on the inside of the doors, St. John the Baptist and St. Mark flank the Madonna. Around the Madonna are small panels with angels holding instruments. Sophia Peabody Hawthorne was also impressed with the painting when she viewed it. See comments in her *Notes in England and Italy* (New York: G. P. Putnam and Son, 1869), 356.

7. The Uffizi Gallery, one of the most famous art museums in the world, was constructed in Florence during the period 1560–81 as offices ("uffizi" in Italian) for local magistrates. Portions of the palace were then used to display the artwork owned by the Medici family, paintings and sculptures that later became the core of the Uffizi's

collection and helped create one of the early modern art museums. In 1765, the gallery was opened to the public. The Palazzo Pitti, located on the south side of the Arno River, was originally constructed for the Florentine banker Luca Pitti in 1458, but it remained unfinished at his death in 1472. The palace continued to undergo various additions into the eighteenth century. Purchased by the Medici family in 1539, it remained a Medici residence until 1737. Napoleon later occupied the Pitti during his reign over Italy. The Palatine Gallery, composed primarily of the art collection owned by the Medicis and the palace's subsequent residents, was opened to the public in the late 1700s by the Grand Duke Pietro Leopoldo. When Florence became briefly the capital of the newly created kingdom of Italy, the palace became the royal residence of Victor Emmanuel II until 1871. It was finally presented to the people of Italy in 1919 and opened as one of the city's largest art galleries.

8. The Tribuna, or Tribune, an octagonal room in the Uffizi, was designed by Bernado Buontalenti and built by Francesco de' Medici in the period 1585–89 to showcase the museum's finest works of art.

9. Andrea del Sarto (1486/87?–1531) was born in Gualfonda near Florence, Italy, to a tailor ("sarto" in Italian) and became one of the most admired painters of the Italian High Renaissance. He was first apprenticed to a goldsmith, then to a wood-carver, before finally turning to painting. While his early work were frescoes, his best-known painting was the one admired by May Alcott. *Madonna of the Harpies* (1517) was originally commissioned as the altarpiece for the nuns of San Francesco dei Macci. The work depicts the Virgin Mary and child standing on a pedestal decorated with monstrous creatures (thus the name Harpies) and flanked by St. John the Evangelist and St. Bonaventure. Almost two hundred years later, Prince Ferdinando de' Medici so admired the painting that he bought it from the nuns, presenting them a copy of the work by Francesco Petrucci and engaging Foggini to remodel and restore the decorations of their church. It was placed in the Tribuna in 1785.

10. Antonio da Correggio (1489–1534), the leading painter of the Parma school of the Italian Renaissance, is known for his paintings on both religious and mythological subjects. His *Adoration of the Child* (1524–26) was placed in the Tribuna in 1617, and his *Madonna and Child in Glory* (ca. 1520) had hung in the Uffizi since 1753. By 1516, Correggio was in Parma, Italy, where he stayed until 1530. His first major works there, executed between 1519 and 1520, were frescoes for the ceiling of the private dining room of Giovanna da Piacenza, the abbess or mother superior of the convent of St. Paul (Camera di San Paolo). Consisting of sixteen separate segments, the frescoes depict the goddess Diana on the hunt with numerous cherubs. Other notable frescoes in Parma include *The Vision of St. John on Patmos* (1520–21), painted on the dome of the church of San Giovanni Evangelista, and the complex *Assumption of the Virgin* (1526–30), on the dome of the Cathedral of Parma.

11. Raphael (1483–1520), Italian painter and architect from the Florentine school of the Italian High Renaissance, was born in Urbino, Italy. By 1501 he was starting his career as a painter and made his way to Florence in 1504. By 1508, he was commissioned by Pope Julius II to paint rooms at the Vatican palace. He remained in Rome, painting and also serving as an architect for St. Peter's Cathedral; he died unexpectedly in the city in 1520 and was buried in the Pantheon. May probably saw his *Madonna of the Grand Duke* (ca. 1505) and *Madonna della Seggiola* (*Madonna with Child and Young St. John*) (1513–14) at the Pitti and his *Madonna of the Goldfinch* (1505–6) at the Uffizi. LMA apparently shared her sister's dislike of his art. She wrote in *Shawl-Straps*: "Raphael won't suit yet. Sad for me, but I cannot admire Madonnas with faces like fashion-plates, or dropsical babies with no baby sweetness about them" (157). Raphael collaborated on engravings with Marcantonio Raimondi (ca. 1480–ca. 1534), an important Italian Renaissance printmaker; some were specially designed by Raphael, who made the initial drawings, and others were copies of his paintings. These engravings were, until the twentieth century, the way that most people around the world were exposed to Raphael's work.

12. Raphael's painting *The Portrait of a Young Woman*, also called *La Fornarina* (1518–19), was supposedly a portrait of one of his lovers, Margherita, the daughter of Francesco Luti, a baker ("fornaro" in Italian). Legend has it that Raphael died after a wild night of sex with her. The woman is depicted with bare breasts, which may have led to May's dislike of it.

13. Tiziano Vecelli, more commonly called Titian (ca. 1488/90–1576), was the foremost painter of the sixteenth-century Venetian school of the Italian Renaissance and was known for his portraits, landscapes, and paintings of religious and mythological subjects. Titian's *Venus and Cupid* (ca. 1550) and his *Venus of Urbino* (1538) were displayed in the Uffizi. Both portrayed Venus as a reclining nude. Ten years after the Alcotts viewed Titian's paintings, Mark Twain, in his travel narrative, wrote, tongue in cheek, that *Venus of Urbino* was "the foulest, the vilest, the obscenest picture the world possesses" (*A Tramp Abroad*, Hartford, Conn.: American Publishing Co., 1880, 578).

14. *The Samian Sibyl* by the Italian Baroque painter Guercino (1591–1666) is displayed in the Tribuna at the Uffizi. Born Giovanni Francesco Barbieri in Cento, Italy, Guercino moved to Bologna by 1615 and began to earn a reputation as an excellent painter. By 1621 he was in Rome working on commissions for Pope Gregory XV.

15. The convent of San Marco, in Florence, is located where a Vallombrosan monastery once sat. In 1435, Dominican monks replaced the Benedictines there, and two years later, with financial help from the Medici family, they began rebuilding, under the direction of the Italian architect Michelozza, a Renaissance structure. The Dominicans lost control of the convent during the Napoleonic Wars in 1808, and by 1866 the convent became the property of the Italian government. It is now open as a museum. Fra Angelico, who lived at the new monastery from 1436 to 1445, executed a number of small

frescoes in the cells of the monks' cloister and larger ones in other portions of the convent. Among the more famous ones are the following: *The Annunciation* (1450), *Transfiguration* (1440–41), *Adoration of the Kings* (1438–46), *Crucifixion and Saints* (1441–42), *Saint Dominic Adoring the Crucifixion* (1440s).

16. Cenni di Pepo Cimabue (ca. 1240–ca. 1302) was born in Florence and is now considered one of the great painters (he also worked in mosaics) in the Byzantine tradition; he was also considered to be the master of Giotto, though this has never been proven. Little is known of his life and few of his works are known to exist today. His *Crucifix* (1287–88) at the Basilica di Santa Croce in Florence and his *Madonna of San Trinita* at the Uffizi are among his few surviving works. The Madonna that May refers to is *Madonna with Child Enthroned and Six Angels*, also known as the *Rucellai Madonna* (ca. 1285). It is not the work of Cimabue; rather it was painted by Duccio di Buoninsegna (ca. 1255–60), an artist from Siena, Italy, who is now considered an important influence on the international Gothic style of painting and the master of the Sienese school. Little is known about his life. One of his major works was *Maestà* (*Madonna with Angels and Saints*), painted for the cathedral of Siena in the period 1308–11. On 9 June 1311 the multi-paneled painting was carried in a procession through the streets of Siena and placed in the cathedral. In *The Lives of the Most Excellent Painters, Sculptors, and Architects* (1550; rev. 1568), an early and influential art history book (and one May would surely have read), the artist and author Giorgio Vasari, in an attempt to glorify his native Florence, ascribed the *Rucellai Madonna* to Cimabue and elevated him as one of the earliest masters of Italian art. Taking an event from the career of Duccio, he even declared that the people of Florence had watched as Cimabue's Madonna was carried through the streets in triumph when it was placed in the church. May saw the *Rucellai Madonna* at the Basilica di Santa Maria Novella, where it was originally placed (the painting is now in the Uffizi). The church (ca. 1246–ca. 1360), constructed in Florence by the Dominicans, contains numerous important works of Italian art. Giotto di Bondone (1267–1337) was born near Florence, the son of a farmer. His most famous work is the Arena Chapel cycle at Padua, a series of frescoes completed around 1305 that go around the interior of the church and illustrate the life of the Virgin Mary and the Passion of Christ. After spending ten years in Rome working for Pope Benedictus XII, he returned to Florence and painted two fresco cycles for the church of Santa Croce. Giotto is now seen as the first significant artist of the Italian Renaissance.

17. The Arno River, which flows through Florence, runs approximately 149 miles from Mount Falterona in the Apennines to the Tyrrhenian Sea at Marina di Pasa.

18. Probably Dr. B. B. Appleton. Frank Preston Stearns, a friend of the Alcott family, writes: "Dr. B. B. Appleton, an American resident of Florence, is here on a flying visit. We have heard from many sources of the kindeness of this man to American travellers, especially to young students. In fact, he took P_____ into his house while at

Florence, and entertained him in the most generous manner. He has done the same for Mrs. Julia Ward Howe and many others" (*Cambridge Sketches*, Philadelphia and London: J. B. Lippincott, 1905, 336–37). James Jackson Jarves (1818–88), born in Boston, established the first newspaper published in Honolulu, a work that became the official organ of the Hawaiian islands. He moved to Florence, Italy, in 1852 and was appointed U.S. vice consul in Florence from 1880 to 1882. While in Italy, he collected and wrote about art. His Italian art collections are now at the Yale School of Fine Arts and the Cleveland Museum of Art.

19. James R. Osgood (1836–92) had published May's *Concord Sketches Consisting of Twelve Photographs from Original Drawings* (Boston: Fields, Osgood and Co., 1869). Another edition was never published. May perhaps confused her book with a new project that ABA had begun contemplating, *Concord Days*, which was to be in diary form and contain sketches of famous Concord citizens as well as ABA's thoughts about his favorite authors. *Concord Days* was eventually published on 21 September 1872 by Roberts Brothers.

20. The xx's, which appear in the manuscript, serve as insertion symbols. The sentence following them, along with May's closing signature, is interlined above the sentence beginning, "You must tell me . . ."

Louisa May Alcott to Anna Alcott Pratt

[December? 1870?]

Dear Nannie: You need not be told what he was to me, or how I mourn for him, for no born brother was ever dearer, & each year I loved & respected & admired him more & more.[1] His quiet integrity, his patient spirit, so cheerful & so persistent, his manly love of independence & his brave effort to earn it for those he loved. How beautiful simple & upright his life looks now. Good son, brother, & husband, father friend. I think that record is a noble one for any man & his 37 quiet years are very precious to those who knew him. He did more to make us trust & respect men than any one I know & with him I lose the one young man whom I sincerely honored in my heart. Good bye my dear, honest, tender, noble John! your place never will be filled your love never lost, your life never forgotten. The world is better for your simple virtues, & those who loved your riches for the faithful heart you showed them.

FIGURE 71. John Bridge Pratt with son
(mid-1860s?), by May Alcott. *Houghton
Library, Harvard University.*

MS: Unknown; manuscript copy (partial) at the Berg Collection of English and American Literature, New York Public Library, Astor, Lenox, and Tilden foundations. Printed: *Selected Letters* 153.

1. John Bridge Pratt died on 27 November 1870, in Maplewood, Massachusetts.

Louisa May Alcott to Daniel Noyes Haskell[?]

RECENT EXCITING SCENES IN ROME

Rome, December 29, 1870.

My Dear Mr.[1] —— : As we are having very exciting times just now I will send you a little account of the two last "sensations" though I dare say the news will be rather old by the time you receive it.

Yesterday morning at breakfast our maid, Lavinia, came flying in from market with the news that the Tiber had overflowed its banks[2] and inundated the lower part of the city, that people just outside the walls were drowned, others in the Ghetto[3] were washed out of their houses, the Corso[4] was under water, and the world generally coming to an end. We instantly went out to see how things stood, or rather floated, and found that Lavinia's story was true. The heavy rains and warm winds had swelled the river and melted the snow on the mountains, till the Tiber rose higher than at any time since 1805, and had done much damage in a few hours.

When we reached the Piazza di Spagna[5] it seemed as if we were in Venice, for all the long streets leading up to it from the lower part of the city were under water, and rafts and boats were already floating about. The Piazza del Popolo[6] was a lake, with the four stone lions just above the surface, still faithfully spouting water, though it was a drug in the market. Garrett's great stables[7] were flooded, and his horses and carriages were standing disconsolately on the banks about the Piazza. In at the open gates rolled a muddy stream bearing haystacks and brushwood from the country along the Corso. People stood on their balconies, wondering what they should do, many breakfastless, for meals are sent in, and how were the trattoria boys[8] to reach them with the coffee-pots across such canals of water? Carriages splashed about in the shallower parts with agitated loads of people hurrying

to safer quarters, many were coming down ladders into boats, and flocks stood waiting their turn with little bundles of valuables in their hands.

THE SOLDIERS AND PRIESTS

The soldiers were out in full force, working gallantly to save life and property, making rafts, carrying people on their backs, and later, going through the inundated streets with boatloads of food for the hungry, shut up in their ill-provided houses. It has since been said that usually at such times the priests have done this work, but now, they stand looking on and smile maliciously, saying it is a judgment on the people for their treatment of the Pope.[9] The people are troubled because the priests refuse to pray

FIGURE 73. Army
Guards, Rome, Italy
(winter 1871), by
May Alcott. *Louisa
May Alcott's Orchard
House/L. M. A.
Memorial Association.*

for them, but otherwise they snap their fingers at the sullen old gentleman in the Vatican, and the brisk, brave troops work for the city quite as
well (we heretics think better) than the snuffy priests. Some of the saintly
young Jesuits amused themselves by throwing stones at the soldiers while
they were working during the flood, for which cowardly trick the afore-
said heretics feel a strong desire to box the long-coated boys' ears and cast
their shovel-hats in the mud. By the way, I heard that one whole college of
lads left in a body and went to the free school the King has opened,[10] de-
manding to be taken in and taught something, being disgusted with their
Jesuitical masters, a sure sign that young Italy is waking up. Three cheers
for the boys!

THE FLOOD

To return to the flood. In the Ghetto, the disaster was really terrible, for the flood came so suddenly that the whole quarter was under water in an hour. At five no one dreamed of such a danger, at seven all the lower part of the city was covered, up to the first story in many places. A friend who promptly went to the rescue of the Jews, told us that the scene was pitiful, for the poor souls live in cellars, packed like sardines in a box, and being washed out all of a sudden were utterly destitute. In one street he saw a man and woman pushing a mattress before them as they waded nearly to their waists in water, and on the mattress were their little children — all they could save. Later in the day, as the boats of provisions came along, women and children swarmed at the windows, crying "Bread! bread!" and their wants could not be supplied, in spite of the generosity and care of the city authorities. One old woman who had lost everything but her life besought the rescuers to bring her a little snuff for the love of heaven, which was very characteristic of the Italian race. One poor man, in trying to save his wife and children in a cart, upset them, and the little ones were drowned at their own door. Tragedy and comedy, side by side.

Outside the city houses were carried away, and people saved with difficulty, so sudden and rapid was the overflow. A bridge near the Ghetto was destroyed, and a boatful of soldiers upset in the current and several men drowned. In the Corso several shops were spoilt, and many people were ruined by the mishap. Friends of ours from Boston were cut off from supplies for two days, and lived on bread and water till help came. A pleasant little experience for the Christmas holidays.

We fared better, for our piazza is on the hill and our Lavinia, forseeing a famine, laid in stores, among them live fowls, who roost in the kitchen with the cats and L.'s relatives, who infest that region in swarms. If the heavy rains continue we may come to want, for the woodyards are under water, the railroads down in all directions, and the peasants from outside cannot get in to bring supplies, unless the donkeys swim. So far we enjoy the excitement, for the sleepy old city is all astir, and we drive about seeing unexpected sights in every direction. Being a Goth and a Vandal,[11] I enjoy it more than chilly galleries or mouldy pictures. It thrills me more to see one live man work like a Trojan to save suffering women and babies, than to sit hours before a Dying Gladiator who has been gasping for centuries in immortal marble.[12] It's sad, but I can't help it.

DARKNESS

Last night the gas went out in many parts of the city, and people were ordered to put lamps at their windows—for thieves abound. We prepared our arms, consisting of one pistol, two daggers, and a heavy umbrella, and slept peacefully, although it was possible that we might wake to find ourselves floating gently out at the Porta Pia.[13] My last idea was a naughty hope that the Pope might get his pontifical petticoats very wet, be a little drowned, and terribly scared by the flood; for he deserves it.

NOVEL SCENES

Today the water is abating, and we are becoming accustomed to the sight of boats in the market-place, gentlemen paying visits on the backs of stout soldiers, and family dinners being hoisted in at two-story windows. All the world is up on the Pincio[14] looking at the flood, and a sad sight it is. Outside the Popolo Gate[15] a wide sea stretches down the valley, with roofs and trees sticking up dismally from the muddy water. A raging river foams between us and the Vatican, and the Corso is a grand canal where unhappy shopkeepers float lamenting. The Pantheon[16] is under water over the railing, the Post Office has ceased to work, the people have become amphibious, and Rome is what Grandmother Rigglesty[17] would call "a wash."

THE POOR

The city officers are working splendidly, having fed and housed the poor, but there will be much misery, and beggars already begin to come to us with long tales of their woes. Lavinia's five grandmothers, six aunts and two dozen small nephews and nieces will settle for the winter in our tiny kitchen probably, although none of them have suffered by the flood, and we shall not have the heart to object, they look so comfortable and be so easy about it. Lavinia herself is as good as a whole opera troupe, she is so dramatic and demonstrative. Ristori[18] is feeble beside L. when she shakes her fist at the Pope and cheers for the King, with a ladle in one hand, and her Italian eyes flashing as she prances with excitement, regardless of our *polenta* burning in the frying-pan.

———————————————

January 1, 1871.

THE CLIMATE AND THE KING

A happy new year to you and a pleasanter day than we have here in balmy Italy, which, by the way, is the greatest humbug in the way of climate that I ever saw. Rain, wind, hail, snow and general disorder among the elements. Boston is a paradise compared to Rome just now. Never mind, we had a new sensation yesterday, for the King came in the first tram from Florence to see what he could do for his poor Romans. He arrived at 4 A.M., and though unexpected, except by a few officials, the news flew through the City, and a crowd turned out with torches to escort him to the Quirinal.[19] Lavinia burst in like a tornado to tell us the joyful news, for the people have begun to think that he never would come, and they are especially touched by this prompt visit in the midst of their trouble. He is to come on the 10th of January and make a grand entry, but the kind soul could not wait, so came as soon as the road was passable, and brought 300,000 francs for the sufferers with his own royal hands.

VICTOR EMMANUEL

Of course we rushed up to the Quirinal at once, though it rained hard. Before the palace stood a crowd waiting eagerly for the first sight of the King, and cheering heartily every one who went in or out.

There was a great flurry among the officials, and splendid creatures in new uniforms flew about in all directions. Grand carriages arrived, bringing the high and mighty to welcome the King. General Marmora, looking like a seedy French rowdy, went in and out, full of business.[20] Dorias and Collonas[21] gladdened our plebeian eyes, and we cheered everything, from the Commander-in-Chief to somebody's breakfast, borne, through the crowd by a stately "Jeames" in a splendid livery.[22] We stood one mortal hour in a pelting rain, and then retired, feeling that the sacrifice of our best bonnet was all that could reasonably be expected of a free-born

FIGURE 74. Alice Bartlett, Rome, Italy (March 1871), by May Alcott. *Houghton Library, Harvard University.*

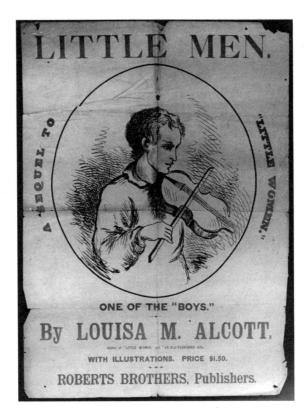

FIGURE 75.
Advertising poster
for *Little Men*
(1871). *Louisa May
Alcott's Orchard
House/L. M. A.
Memorial Association.*

American. We consoled ourselves by putting out Lavinia's fine Italian banner, supported by our two little ones proudly bearing the stars and stripes, and much perplexing the boys and donkeys who disport themselves in the Piazza Barberini.[23]

Feeling that neuralgia would claim me for its own if I went out, I sat over the fire and read Roba di Roma;[24] while M. and A. took a carriage and chased the King all over the city, till they caught him at the Capitol.[25] They had a fine view of him as he came down the steps of the Capitol, through a mass of people cheering frantically and whitening the streets with waving handkerchiefs.

ENTHUSIASTIC RECEPTION

My enthusiastic damsels mounted up with the driver and cheered with all their hearts, as well they might for it certainly was a sight to see. They

FIGURE 76. Frontispiece
for *Little Men* (1871).
*Rare Book Collection,
University of North
Carolina at Charlotte
Library.*

had another view of the King on the balcony of the Quirinal; for the people
clamored so for another sight of "Il Re" that the Pope's best velvet hangings
were hastily spread on the balcony and Victor Emmanuel came out and
bowed to his people, "who stood on their heads with rapture," as one young
lady expressed it. He was in citizen's dress, and looked like a stout, brown,
soldiery man, M. said. He hates ceremony and splendor, and would not
have the fine appartments offered him, but chose a plain room and said:
"Keep the finery for my sons, if you like; I prefer this." He asked the city
fathers to give the money they intended to spend on welcoming him, to the
poor. But they insist on giving him a Roman welcome when he comes on
the 10th. He only passed one day here, and went back to Florence last night
at five. All Rome was at the station to see him off. Ladies with carriages full
of flowers were tearing by at dusk, and there was a great demonstration, for
this kingly sympathy has won all hearts.

We are preparing to decorate our balcony for the 10th, and have our six windows full of cheering Yankees, for our rooms are directly on the street he will pass by, and our balcony on the Piazza, where two great arches are now being set up. The prudent A. suggests that we let these windows and make our fortunes but we decline and intend to hurrah our best for the "honest man," as they call Victor Emmanuel—and that is high praise for a king ×××

LITERARY WORK

I hope the New Year opens well and prosperously with you. I was just getting well into my work on "L. M.," when sad news of dear "John Brooke's" death came to darken our Christmas and unsettle my mind.[26] But I now have a motive for work stronger than before, and if the book can be written, it shall be, for the good of the two dear little men now left to my care, for long ago I promised to try and fill John's place if they were left fatherless.

We all send best wishes and I am as ever

Yours truly, L. M. A.

MS: Unlocated. Printed: "Recent Exciting Scenes in Rome," *Boston Daily Evening Transcript*, 3 February 1871, 1; *Selected Letters* 153–59. In the same issue of the *Transcript* is the following: "The Letter from Rome on our first page will be read with pleasure not only for its lively and graphic descriptions of recent events in that city but also for the assurance it gives of the improved health of an author whom tens of thousands have learned to value as a friend. Without the help of the initials appended to it, readers will at once see from whose pen it comes and rejoice at the intimation in the last paragraph that the 'Little Women' are to be matched ere long with the 'Little Men' even whilst they sympathize with the sorrow implied in the added motive for the care to be taken of the fatherless boys" (2).

1. This letter may have been written to Daniel Noyes Haskell, editor of the *Transcript*. Earlier, reports had been circulating in the Boston papers about LMA's supposed ill health and even death. Niles tracked the rumors back to a letter from Mrs. Howe to her brother in which she said LMA had died of diphtheria. Beginning his letter of 20 January 1871 to LMA with "Are you dead?" Niles went on: "I have had a continual stream of excited individuals men, women, boys, & girls rushing in, with tears in their eyes, to ascertain the facts" (ALS: Houghton Library, Harvard University). This public letter may have been LMA's way to stop such rumors.

2. The Tiber River, in central Italy, flows 252 miles from Mount Fumaiolo to the Tyrrhenian Sea, making it the third longest river in the country. It intersects the city in three large bends that are approximately 65 yards wide. Rising on the Tiber's left bank are the "Seven Hills" of Rome, where the city was founded.

3. Rome's approximately four thousand Jews were forced by Pope Paul IV to relocate into seven acres of land known as the Ghetto in 1555. This walled part of the city was across the Tiber from Trastevere, their original home in ancient time. Wearing yellow scarves and hats, Jews could go outside the walls by day but had to return by curfew at night. Some freedom was extended to Jews during Napoleon's reign over the city (1805–14), and the wall itself was destroyed in 1848. The Jews were granted rights and citizenship only after the end of papal rule in 1870.

4. Corso Umberto Primo was one of the central streets in Rome and the main artery of traffic prior to the modern growth of the city. It runs southward for almost one mile from the Piazza del Popolo to the Piazza Venezia.

5. Piazza di Spagna is the public square at the foot of the Scalla di Spagna, the Spanish Steps. The construction of the 135 steps was ordered by Pope Benedict XIII in the period 1721–25, and they were designed by Francesco de Sanctis. At the foot of the steps is the war-vessel-shaped fountain "La Barcaccia" ("The Bark") by Bernini. In the southern end of the plaza is the Palazza de Spagna, the location of the Spanish embassy since the seventeenth century.

6. Piazza del Popolo (Plaza of the People) lies inside the northern gate of the Aurelian Walls. It is bounded on the east and west by arcades with groups of statues. On the north stands the church of Santa Maria del Popolo and on the south are the twin churches, Santa Maria in Monte Santa (1679) and Santa Maria dei Miracoli (1681), one on each side of the Corso. An obelisk rises 78 feet (117 feet with pedestal and cross) in the center of the plaza. Brought by Emperor Augustus from Egypt, the obelisk of Ramses II originally was placed in the Circus Maximus but moved and erected in the square in 1589. In 1818 fountains in the form of four Egyptian lions were added around the obelisk's base.

7. Garrett's stables are unidentified.

8. A trattoria is a restaurant in Italy.

9. Italy's King Victor Emmanuel had upset Pope Pius IX by taking possession of church revenues, allowing the opening of the first Protestant church in Rome, and upholding secular law over ecclesiastical. In return, the Pope refused to receive the king's official congratulations on his Papal Jubilee on 16 June 1871.

10. The free school opened by the king is unidentified.

11. The Goths were a Germanic tribe who supposedly originated in Scandinavia. During the third century, they divided into two groups: the Visigoths and the Ostrogoths. In 263, the Visigoths invaded Rome, one of the first "barbarian" attacks on the empire, and later, in 267, they destroyed Byzantium. By 271, they were defeated and driven across

the Danube River and settled in the old Roman province of Dacia. They would again attack Rome and sack it in 410. By 475, the Goths dominated the majority of the Iberian peninsula. The Visigoth kingdom eventually ended in 711 after the Umayyad invasion of Andalusia. The Vandals were an East Germanic tribe who sacked Rome in 455, plundering many valuable treasures, including the riches from the Temple of Jerusalem, which had been brought to Rome by Titus. The term "vandalism" comes from the tribe's actions. The Vandal kingdom ended when it was eventually defeated by the Byzantines in 534. By the seventeenth century, both the Goths and Vandals were considered barbarian tribes who had helped destroy the glories of the much-admired Roman Empire. John Dryden would write in "To Sir Godfrey Kneller" (1694): "Till Goths, and Vandals, a rude Northern race, / Did all the matchless Monuments deface" (ll. 47–48).

12. *The Dying Gladiator* (also called *The Dying Gaul* or *The Dying Galatian*) is located in the Capitoline Museum in Rome. It is a replica of one of the ex-voto group dedicated to Pergamon by Attalius I to celebrate the victories over the Galatians in the third and second centuries BC. The famous sculpture, by an unknown artist, depicts the dying man, sitting on his shield with blood pouring from his wounded breast.

13. Porta Pia was a relatively new gate in the Aurelian Walls around Rome. Ordered by Pope Pius IV and designed by Michelangelo, the gate was built between 1561 and 1565. The outer walls of the Porta Pia were rebuilt by Pope Pius IX in 1868. In 1870 the gate was made famous as the entryway for the Italian troops into Rome as they took control of the city.

14. The Pincio (165 feet high) is the northernmost hill in modern Rome. In ancient times, it was covered only with gardens. Its modern grounds were designed and laid out in the period 1809–14, during Napoleon's time.

15. The Porta Popolo, just to the north of the Piazza del Popolo, was the northern gate of Rome. Built in 1562 by Vignola, it was reconstructed on its interior by Bernini in 1655 on the orders of Pope Alexander VII.

16. The Pantheon was originally built as a temple in the period 27–25 BC by Marcus Agrippa but destroyed by fire in 80 AD. The current Pantheon, the best preserved of all Roman buildings, was constructed in the period 118–26 by the Emperor Hadrian as a temple to all gods. In 609, Pope Boniface IV consecrated the temple as a Christian church, Santa Maria ad Martyres, commonly referred to as La Rotunda. The circular edifice has walls that are twenty-one feet thick and a concrete dome. The porch is supported by sixteen Corinthian columns that are forty-one feet in height.

17. Grandmother Rigglesty is a character from John Townsend Trowbridge's (1827–1916) abolitionist novel *Neighbor Jackwood* (1857). The book was adapted into a play soon after it was published and ran for several years in Boston, where it was popular.

18. LMA had first heard the famous Italian performer Adelaide Ristori (1822–1906), often called the "Marquise," sing at the opera in Nice in April 1866.

19. The Quirinal (170 feet high), one of the original "seven hills" of Rome, adjoins the Pincio on the southeast.

20. Alfonso Ferrero La Marmora (1804–78), born in Turin, was an Italian general and statesman. In charge of the Piedmontese army during the Crimean War (1855), he also led the Italian army during the Third War of Independence (1866) but was defeated at Custoza and retired. He was also prime minister of Italy from 1864 to 1866. After the Italian army occupied Rome in 1870, he was appointed lieutenant-royal of the new capital.

21. Doria-Pamphilj-Landi was a princely Roman family of Genoese extraction. The Colonna family was a powerful noble family in medieval and Renaissance Rome, producing one pope and over twenty cardinals. The family has been prince assistants to the papal throne since 1710. After unification in 1870, two members of the family were guarantors of the new government and appointed senators.

22. Jeames, a humorous name for a liveried footman, comes from William Makepiece Thackeray's (1811–63) character in *The Diary of C. Jeames de la Pluche, Esq.* (1859).

23. The Piazza Barberini lies at the point where the Via Sistina, Via Quattro Fontane, and Via del Tritone converge. It is perhaps most famous for its centerpiece, the Fontana del Tritone (1643) by Lorenzo Bernini, a fountain with Triton blowing a conch shell.

24. William Wetmore Story's *Roba di Roma* (1862).

25. The Capitol, or Capitoline Hill, is the smallest of the seven hills of Rome, and had long been the center of municipal government. A flight of stairs leads up the hill to the Piazza del Campidoglio, which was designed by Michelangelo.

26. John Bridge Pratt's romance with Anna Alcott had inspired the character of John Brooke in *Little Women*. Brooke dies in *Little Men*.

Louisa May Alcott to Elizabeth Wells

Rome Jan. 9th [1871]

Dear Lizzie

Annie in her letters speaks of your being with her during that sad week & of your helping to make dear John ready for his last sleep. Also that Marmee is to make you a little visit. All these kind & tender things come right home to my heart though so far away, & I *must* thank you in this poor way.

Annie bears her loss so beautifully that it makes it possible to stay away now in order that I may be more useful by & by. But *you* know how hard it is for me to be even in Rome when my heart is at home & every day a burden till I can come.

FIGURE 77. John Bridge
Pratt in theatrical
costume (1860s). *Louisa
May Alcott's Orchard
House/L. M. A. Memorial
Association.*

John leaves so sweet & precious a memory of his simple upright life
& lovely character that Annie has much to sustain & comfort her. Real
goodness is so rare & beatiful [i.e., beautiful], & he possessed it so truly
that the dear boys inherit a better fortune in their father's virtues & honest
name than millions of money or much fame. The ten perfectly happy &
united years Annie has spent with John are a treasure which nothing can
take away, for such a love must be immortal & will not be divided even by
death.

Dear Lizzie, I hope I need not say to you what your own loving heart
will prompt you to do, *fill my place a little till I come*, for of all our many

relatives you are the nearest & dearest to us. Your daughterly care & love for Mother in her dark hour is never forgotten by me, or your regard for John who loved you much. Both mother & Annie find great comfort in your thoughtful kindness, & *I* hold it as one of the debts which I shall hope to pay in the years to come if your daughters are sick or absent when you need them. My heart is very anxious about mother & I ache to go to her, but winter, distance, health, & my duty to Alice hold me till April. I think God will keep my Marmee for me because I couldn't bear to miss my Good bye & the keeping of my promise to close her dear eyes. Annie says she is not well & so I dread another loss before I have learned to bear the last. God bless you dear L.

Ever yrs
L. M. A.

ALS: Houghton Library, Harvard University. Printed: *Selected Letters* 159–60.

Louisa May Alcott to Mrs. Edward Barton

Rome Jan. 9th [1871]

My Dear Little Woman,

Annie sends me your kind message & pleasant news of your motherly hopes. I am truly glad to hear of your happiness, & it does me good even in this sad time. You & your husband knew & valued my dear brother & he was grateful to you for your kindness to us, so I am sure of your sympathy in my sorrow as you may be of mine in your joy.

I cannot wish you both any better wish than many years of such love & happiness as the ten which have blessed Annie & John. The memory of them is her best comfort in the present & the certainty of knowing a still happier & more united life here after is her sustaining hope in the future. She bears her loss so beautifully that I know the burden will not be too heavy or life lose all its satisfactions.

We are well & living cosily in a nice little appartement here in Rome. May paints, visits galleries, & goes to some pleasant gatherings of artists & Romans. The Howitts, Sheridan, the King & other great creatures come

Orchard House.

FIGURE 78. Orchard House, with removable
winter doorway (1870s). *Louisa May Alcott's
Orchard House/L. M. A. Memorial Association.*

& go, & now & then we have a flood, an earthquake or an eclipse by way of variety.[1]

I am getting so fat & rosy that I dont know myself, & Miss Vincent,[2] who is here said "Why, Miss Alcott, I never saw such a change from a ghost to hearty looking woman."

I shall come home as early as it is safe, & one of the first visits I make will be to my Bartons. I hope I shall find a cradle in the house & a rosy little Edward Henry in it, ready to welcome his Aunt Weedy.

I'd like to hear from you so pray you write. With best wishes & the hearty sentiment God bless baby Barton! I am as ever

your loving friend
L. M. A.

May sends best love to *all*.

ALS: Berg Collection of English and American Literature, New York Public Library, Astor, Lenox, and Tilden foundations.

1. The British writers, William (1792–1879) and Mary (1799–1888) Howitt, who by 1870 were spending winters in Rome. Former Civil War General Philip Sheridan (1831–88), who at the request of President Ulysses S. Grant was an observer during the Franco-Prussian War and was a guest of the king of Prussia at the surrender of Napoleon III. After the war, he toured Europe.

2. Mrs. Vincent is unidentified.

Louisa May Alcott to Mrs. Ellen Conway

May 1st [1871]

Dear Mrs Conway[1]

We are engaged tomorrow, but on the 11th will certainly come— D.V.

Our escort gave out & I was afraid to lead my virgin perch forth in search of unknown regions in the eve without a body guard. Not strong-minded but prudent, & on the whole I rather incline to the old fashioned ways fast being forgotten.

On Wed. week we hope to settle at Mrs Grovers',[2] as she has a room for May & I want to see the baby of the family in safe quarters before I leave. Miss Bartlett sails a week from tomorrow. I am sorry she has been so occupied with friends, & at times not well enough to see & visit the friends I wanted her to know. But she is very delicate & I let her do as she likes.

With thanks & regards from all I am

affectionately yours
L. M. Alcott.

Excuse this paper—I'm all out & can['t get any] at this [moment]

ALS: Fruitlands Museum, Harvard, Massachusetts.
  1. Ellen Conway, wife of Moncure Daniel Conway.
  2. Mrs. Grover is unidentified.

Index

Abd-el-Kadar, 103, 106n8

Acton, Mass., 196, 200n2

Adams, Henry, xvii

Albano, Italy, lx, lxi

Alcott, Abigail May, xvi, xviii, xxvii, xxviii, 3, 4n4; diaries of, xx, 95n2; employment of housekeeper for, 68n1; illness and death of, lxvii; inheritance of, xix; intelligence office opened by, xx; letter to, xl; letters to, from LMA, 3–4, 16–17, 113–22, 169–71, 185–90, 196–201, 239–43; letters to, from May, 41–43, 77–78, 88–89, 143–45, 181–85, 233–38; letters to, from May, with Amos Bronson Alcott, 65–68, 165–66, 208–11; letters to, from May, with Anna Alcott Pratt, 4–10, 23–27, 36–39, 51–54; LMA's and May's departure to Europe, xxxiv; marriage of, 63n5, 111n1; on May's return home, lxv; sister of, 122n24; summer return of, to Orchard House, 63n4

Alcott, Amos Bronson (ABA), xviii, xxvii, 3; Conversations of, 4n4; distorts facts of LMA's early writings, 128, 131n16; employment of housekeeper for, 68n1; final visit by LMA and death of, lxx; greets LMA on her 1871 return home, lxiii; hearing problems of, 76, 77n6; letter to, from LMA, 141–43; on letter writing, xv; letters to, from May,

108–12, 166–69, 202–4, 243–51; on LMA's and May's departure to Europe, xxxiii; marriage of, 63n5, 111n1; on May's death, lxviii, lxix; meets Ednah Dow Cheney, 27n3; nicknames LMA, 32n5; and repair of Orchard House, xxi; seventy-second birthday of, lxv; summer return of, to Orchard House, 63n4; Temple School teaching of, xviii; western Conversations of, 111n4, 167, 168n3, 171, 171n3, 203

—diaries of, xx, xliv; and Abigail May Alcott's comment on Caroline Hildreth crayon, 204n1; on Abigail May Alcott's reaction to receiving Alcott sisters' letters, 68n2; on birth of May, xviii, xix; on Conversations in California, 111n4; on death of Benjamin Willis, 122n24; on German translation of *Tablets*, 166n2; on Healy's portrait of LMA, lxiv; on hearing problems, 168n3; on heat wave in Concord, 150n2, 210n1; on hiring Mrs. Conant as housekeeper, 68n1, 73n7; on LMA's income, 151n7; on publication of "Lay of a Golden Goose," xlix; on repaying Mary P. Stearns, 68n3; on returning to Concord for summer (1870), 63n4; on Rice, Reuben, 226n1; on Ricketson, Daniel, 88n17; on Sanborn inquiring

Alcott, Amos Bronson, diaries of (*cont.*)
about LMA in Dinan, 131n15; on
western Conversations, 168–69n3
—works of: *Concord Days,* xv, 251n19;
Tablets, 165, 166n2, 168
Alcott, Elizabeth Sewall: birth of, xviii;
birthday of, 113, 118n1; death of, xxi;
funeral of, 9n7
Alcott, Louisa May (LMA), xvii, lxx;
on ABA going to California, 232;
agreement of, to visit Europe in 1870,
xxxi; birth of, xviii; childhood of,
in Concord, xx; Civil war nursing
experience of, xxv, 64, 65n11; crosses
Alps into Italy, 239, 240; death of, lxx;
departure of, to America in 1871, lxiii;
early reading of, xviii; early stories of,
xx, xxiv; edits *Merry's Museum,* xxvii;
European trip of, in 1865, xxvi–xxvii;
on ex-royalty in Vevey, 186; friendship
of, with Alice Bartlett, 66, 67; health of,
86, 128, 129, 147, 170, 171, 200; health of,
treated by Dr. Kane, 46, 48, 50, 58, 64,
65, 66; on *Hearth and Home* engraving,
87n8; income of, 147, 148; inquiry of,
about London publishers, 56; lack of
enjoyment of, on trip, 157; letter of,
to ABA, 141–43; letter writing of, xvi;
on letters from fans, 179; letters of, to
Abigail May Alcott, 3–4, 16–17, 113–22,
169–71, 185–90, 196–201, 239–43; letters
of, to Alcott family, 19–22, 27–29,
32–36, 43–48, 49–51, 54–55, 64–65,
73–77, 92–96, 102–7, 125–31, 146–51,
191–92, 205–8, 211–22, 227–32; letters
of, to Anna Alcott Pratt, 57–63, 79–88,
151–61, 222–26, 251–53; letters of, to
May about Abigail May Alcott's death,
lxviii; and Loring's new edition of
Moods, 33, 73, 84, 85, 88n15; on May's
art lessons, xxii; on May's changes in
Europe, 159; on Napoleon III, 199, 218;
partial payment by, of Anna's purchase
of Thoreau house, lxvii; privacy of
letters of, xv; and publication of
Moods, xxvi; publishing agreement of,
with Sampson Low, 84; recovery of,
from typhoid fever, xxv; and Roberts
Brothers' total royalties, lxx; royalties
of, 125, 128; sale of photographs of, 76;
and Sanborn's article for *Hearth and
Home,* 109, 155, 167; success of, 159;
and support of family in 1880s, lxx;
on Swiss people, 142, 155; and Temple
School, xviii; thirty-ninth birthday
celebration of, lxv; thousand-dollar
gift of, to May, lxvi; travel expenses of,
62, 114, 231; twenty-sixth birthday of,
xxii; voyage of, to Europe, xxxiv, xxxv;
on Warrens, 153; writing of, for the
woman's rights movement, 129, 131n18;
writing while abroad, 231
—*Journals* of, xv, xx, xxvii; on Abigail
May Alcott's death, lxvii, lxviii; on
Amberly, Lady, 150n5; on ambition,
xx; on Booth, Edwin, 122n16; on
celebrity seekers, lxvi; on Civil War
nursing experience, xxv; on death of
Elizabeth S. Alcott, xxi; on decision
to travel abroad in 1870, xxx; on
Emerson, Ralph Waldo, xxi; on fall
of 1871 illness, lxv; on fame, xxix; on
Fields, James T., 169n5; on illness,
xxx; on Mansfields in 1864, 196n6; on
marriage of Anna Alcott, xxi–xxii; on
May's art lessons, xxiii; on May's art
study in Paris, lxvii; on May's death,
lxix; on May's good fortunes, xxiv,
xxvi; on May's Paris Salon exhibit
of 1877, lxvii; on May's return home

in 1871, lxv; on meeting Rebecca Harding, 202n2; on *Moods,* xxvi; on Polks in 1865, 216n1; on return home from Europe in 1866, xxvii; on return to Orchard House in 1871, lxiv; on success of *Hospital Sketches,* xxv; on Weld, Anna, xxvi; on Wisniewski, Ladislas, xxvi; on writing *Little Women,* xxviii; on writing *Shawl-Straps,* lxvi

—works of: *Aunt Jo's Scrap-Bag,* lxvi; *Aunt Jo's Scrap-Bag, volume 6: An Old-Fashioned Thanksgiving,* 179n4; "The Banner of Beaumanoir," 86n3; "La Belle Bayadère," 51n4; "Betrayed by a Buckle," 51n4; "The Cost of an Idea," 35, 36n12; *Eight Cousins,* lxvi; *Flower Fables,* xxi, xli, 85, 88n14; "Grandma's Team," 36n10; *Hospital Sketches,* xv, xxv, 9n7; *Hospital Sketches and Camp and Fireside Stories,* xxx; *The Inheritance,* xx; "Jo March's Necessity Stories," 173; *Jo's Boys,* lxvi; "The Lay of a Golden Goose," xlviii, xlix, 173, 174–78, 178n1, 180, 181n5, 183, 231; "Life in a Pension," 216n1; *Little Men,* lvi, lix, lxi, lxiii, lxxi; *Little Women* (see *Little Women*); "Love and Self-Love," xxiv; *Lulu's Library,* lxix; *A Modern Mephistopheles,* lxvi; *Moods* (see *Moods*); *Morning Glories and Other Stories,* 88n16, 173, 179n4; "Mother's Trial," 36n10; "An Old-Fashioned Boy," 36n12; *An Old-Fashioned Girl* (see *Old-Fashioned Girl, An*); "Pauline's Passion and Punishment," xxiv; "Pelagie's Wedding," 45n2; *Proverb Stories,* lxvi; "Recollections of My Youth," xx; "The Reminiscences of a Rook," 103, 105n5; "The Rival Painters," xx; *Rose in Bloom,* lxvi; *Shawl-Straps* (see *Shawl-Straps*); *Spinning Wheel Stories,* lxvi; *Under the Lilacs,* lxvi; *Work,* lxvi

Alcott, May, xv, xvi; birth of, xviii; crosses Alps into Italy, 233–35; death of, lxviii; early childhood of, xix; early education of, xx; and European art, xviii; eye problems of, 138, 140n3, 183; eyes of, treated by Dr. Henri Dor, 188, 190n12, 204, 210, 213, 215, 228; fascination of, with Dinan architecture, 41; first reactions of, to France, 69; friendship of, with Alice Bartlett, 66, 67; independence of, in Europe, lxxi; letter writing of, xvii; letters of, to ABA, 108–12, 166–69, 202–4, 243–51; letters of, to ABA and Abigail May Alcott, 65–68, 165–66, 208–11; letters of, to Abigail May Alcott, 41–43, 77–78, 88–89, 143–45, 181–85, 233–38; letters of, to Abigail May Alcott and Anna Alcott Pratt, 4–10, 23–27, 36–39, 51–54; letters of, to Alcott family, 48–49, 97–101, 123–25, 132–40; letters of, to Anna Alcott Pratt, 69–73, 161–63, 193–96; on LMA's health, 72, 77, 165, 166, 167 214; on LMA's prosperity, 167; on LMA's success and people's opinion of her in Europe, 163; marriage of, lxviii; painting and sketching of, 69; and Paris Salon exhibit of 1877, lxvii; reading of, 65; return of, to America in 1871, lxv; return of, to Europe in 1876, lxvii; on Sanborn's *Hearth and Home* article, 109; second European trip of, in 1873, lxvi; sketches in Dinan, 23; studies art, xxi; studies art in London, lxiv; teaches art, xxiv, xxviii; thirtieth birthday of, 165; as travel companion of Alice Bartlett, xxxi; travel

Alcott, May (*cont.*)
    enlightens, 165; trip of, to Mount
    St. Bernard, 132–37; voyage of, to
    Europe, xxxiv, xxxv, weight of, 42
—art lessons of, xxii–xxiv; with
    Crowninshield, Frederic, liv; with
    Hunt, William Morris, xxix; with
    Johnston, David Claypoole, xxiv;
    with Rimmer, William, xxv; with
    Tuckerman, Stephen Salisbury, xxii
—works of: *Concord Sketches,* xxx, 54n2,
    246, 251n19; *Little Women* illustrations,
    xxviii; *Negresse* (in Paris Salon exhibit
    of 1879), lxviii; *Studying Art Abroad,*
    lxviii, 112n9
Alcott family: letters to, from LMA,
    19–22, 27–29, 32–36, 43–48, 49–51,
    54–55, 64–65, 73–77, 92–96, 102–7,
    125–31, 146–51, 191–92, 205–8, 211–22,
    227–32; letters to, from May, 48–49,
    97–101, 123–25, 132–40; move of, to
    Boston, xx; move of, to Concord, xxi;
    move of, to Fruitlands, xix; move of,
    to Hillside, xx
Alfonso XII, 186, 189n2, 189n4
Allen, E. L., xlii, 48n5, 96; photograph of,
    used for *Hearth and Home* engraving,
    84, 87n8, 145n1, 214; and sale of LMA's
    photograph, 9n16, 47
Amberly, Lady (Lady Katherine Louisa
    Stanley), 147, 150n5
Ambois, xlvi, 93, 96n7, 103, 106n13, 108;
    Alcotts' arrival in, 110; letters from,
    103–7
American Woman Suffrage Movement,
    131nn18–19
Andrews, Miss, 195, 196n7
Angelico, Fra, liii, 245, 247n6, 249n15
Anjou, duke of (François), 119n5

Anjou and Madrid, duke of (Jaime),
    189n3, 198, 199
Anne of Austria, 107n20
Anne of Brittany, 17n13, 38, 111; daughter
    of, 119n5; husband of, 103; royal arms
    of, 114; tomb of children of, 95n6;
    tower of, 15, 17n13, 30, 43, 81, 86n3
Anthony, Susan B., 122n25
Antwerp, Belgium, lxi
Aosta, Italy, 135, 137n6
Apple Slump, xxi, 71, 72n6, 170, 183, 195
Appleton, Dr. B. B., 246, 250n18
Arno River, 246, 250n17
Athenaeum, 150n4
Atlantic Monthly, xxiv, 68n4, 84, 87n10
Attila, 141, 142n1
Aubrey House, xxvii, lxi
Aunt Jo's Scrap-Bag (LMA), lxvi
*Aunt Jo's Scrap-Bag, volume 6: An Old-
    Fashioned Thanksgiving* (LMA), 179n4
Austria, 118
Auxerre, France, 93

Baedeker's: on Borromean Islands, 238n7;
    on Isola Bella chateau and gardens,
    242n5; on Lake Como, 242n1; 242n7;
    on valley of Gonda, 242n4
Baker, A. Prescott, 8, 9n16, 45, 209; in
    Germany, 76; marriage of, 46, 48n4, 65
Baker, Amos and Matilda, 9n16
Ball, Thomas, liii, 243, 246n1; statue of
    Washington by, 243, 246n2
"Banner of Beaumanoir, The" (LMA),
    86n3
Baring Brothers (bankers), 123, 123n2, 169;
    Bartlett, Alice, gets credit from, 192;
    letters sent care of, 221, 232, 243; LMA
    requests $1000 credit from, 206, 207
Barry, Lord Godefroy de , 106n9

Bartlett, Alice, xv; birth of, xxx; death of, lxii; departure for America, lxii; family of, xxx–xxxi; friendship of, with LMA, lxii, lxiii; marriage of, lxi; and May's death, lxix
—works of: "The Downward Road," 59, 63n6; "The French Provinces," lxii; "Our Apartment," lviii, lix; "Some Pros and Cons of Travel Abroad," lxii

Bartlett, Catherine Amelia Greenwood, xxx, xxxi, 121n11, 129n2

Bartlett, Dr. George, xxx, xxxi, 217n7

Bartlett, Hannah Jackson, xxx

Bartlett, Dr. Josiah, 94, 96n9

Bartlett, Truman, xxix

Bartlett, William Pitt Greenwood, xxxi

Bartlett, Capt. Zaccheus, xxx

Barton, Edward Henry, 34, 36n8, 84, 86, 94, 96, 167, 269; letter to, from LMA, 96–97

Barton, Mrs. Edward Henry Barton, 34, 36n8, 86, 94, 96, 167, 267, 269; letters to, from LMA, 96–97, 267–69

Bates, Mrs., 115, 121n9, 124, 135, 155

Baxton, Mrs., 92

Beaumanoirs, La Chapelle des, 32n4, 81, 86n3

Beaumanoirs family, 32n4

Bellagio, Italy, 241, 243n10

"Belle Bayadère, La" (LMA), 51n4

Benda, B., xliii, 221

Berengaria, tomb of, 92, 95n5

Berne, Switzerland, 183, 184n5, 190n12, 205

Bernese Alps, li, 234, 242n3

Bernese Oberland, li, 239, 242n3

"Betrayed by a Buckle" (LMA), 51n4

Bex, Switzerland, xlii, xlvii, 182, 193, 195; Alcotts leave, 181; Bartlett, Alice, visits Warrens in, 118; letters from,

125–79; location of, 122n21; Pratt, H. J., searches for Alcotts in, 221

Bigelow, Adie, 183, 184n4, 185, 205, 209

Bigelow, Albert S., 204n3

Bigelow, Anna Smith (Annie), 160n17, 184n4, 185, 205, 209

Bigelow, Annie Lenthal Smith, 183, 184n4, 204n3

Bigelow, Horatio, 184n4, 204, 204n3

Bigelow, Joseph Smith, 183, 184n4, 185, 209

Bigelow family, 195, 199, 204, 210, 212, 214, 227

Billings, Josh (Henry Wheeler Shaw), 173, 179n3

Black, J. W., 155, 160n8

Blanc, Mount, xlvii, 114, 121n8, 124, 145n5, 166n1

Blanche of Castile, 96

Blois, Chateau de, 113, 119–20n5, 120n6

Blois, France, xlvi, 93, 96n7, 108, 113, 115, 119n4; letters from, 113, 114, 123

Bohier, Thomas, 106n13

Bois de Boulogne, 207, 208n4

Bologna, Italy, liii

Bonaparte, Mathilde (princess), 186, 189n8

Bond, George William Bond, xlvii, 122n17, 124, 199, 195; Alcotts meet, in Geneva, 116, 117, 118; business partner of, steals money, 182, 184n2, 194; departs for England, 144

Bond, Louisa Caroline Greenwood May, xlvii, 122n17, 124, 125, 182, 195; Alcotts meet, in Geneva, 116, 118; letter of, to LMA on May's death, 195n3

Bond, Sophia A. May, 122n17

Bond, Sophia Elizabeth, xlvii, 122n17, 124, 125, 136, 139; Alcotts meet, in Geneva, 116, 117, 118; departs Geneva, 194;

Bond, Sophia Elizabeth (*cont.*)
    possible stay of, with Alcotts in Vevey,
    195; writes from Bex, 182
Bond family, 124, 125, 144, 193, 195n3;
    Abigail May Alcott receives box from,
    195n2; plans to return to America, 202;
    visits Alcotts in Vevey, 196, 198
Bonivard, François, 213n3
Booth, Edwin, 116, 121–22n16
Borromean Islands, lii, 236, 238n7
Borromeo, Count Vitaleo, 242n5
Boston, 170; Alcotts' 1847 move to, xx;
    LMA and May board on Pinckney
    Street in, xxx; LMA rents room in,
    xxviii; LMA's 1871 return to, lxiii; May
    studies art in, xxii, xxiii, xxiv; May
    teaches art in, xxviii
Boston Commonwealth, xxv, xxvi, 9n7, 56
Boston Daily Evening Transcript, xli, lvii,
    lix, 35n5, 85; LMA's departure from
    New York recounted in, 50, 51n5;
    LMA's letter from Rome in, 262, 262n1;
    May's account of St. Bernard trip in,
    137, 208n6; *Moods* ad in, 33, 35n4;
    Niles, Thomas, sends, to LMA, 67; *An
    Old-Fashioned Girl* notices in, from
    London papers, 147, 150n4
Boston Journal, 192n1
Boston Museum of Fine Arts, xxvi, liv
Boston Olive Branch, xx
Boston Public Garden, 243, 246n2
Boston Saturday Evening Gazette, 192n1
Boston School of Design, xxii–xxiii, xxv
Bourges, France, xlvi, 108, 111n2, 114
Bovets, Madame, 182, 184n3
Braxton, Mrs., 74
Brest, France, xxxv, xl, 3, 3n2, 4, 10,
    55, 69
Brieg, Switzerland, li, 214, 217n4, 233, 234,
    239

Britaiyne, 21
Brooks, Abby Davis Mansfield, 196n6
Brooks, George B., 196n6
Brown, T. Quincey, 6, 9n8
Browning, Elizabeth Barrett, 246n3
Bryant, Mary C., 184n4
Buntline, Ned (Edward Z. C. Judson), 173,
    179n3
Byron, Lord, 213n3

C. L. P., 201, 202n1
Cadenabbia, Italy (Cadenabbin), liii, 233,
    237, 240, 243n9; letters from, 233–43
Cadorna, General, lviii
Caen, France, 62, 63n10
California, 109, 171, 171n3
Campagna, Italy (Campagnia), liv, lxii,
    228, 229n3
Capitol, the, 260, 265n25
Capitoline Hill, 208n2, 265n25
Carleton (publisher), 179n4
Carlos V (first pretender), 188n2
Carlos VI (second pretender), 189n3
Carlos VII, 186, 189n3, 189n4, 194, 198
Carthage, 221, 222n3
Cary, Aunt, 194, 195n3
Cassatt, Mary, lxvii
Châlons, France, 209, 211n4
Chamonix, Switzerland, 118, 122n22, 124,
    209
Channing, Ellery, xxx, 65, 68n2, 136, 184;
    as gossiper, 82, 87n6, 149; letter from,
    128
Channing, William Ellery, 68n2
Charlemagne, tower of, 102, 105n4
Charles, cardinal of Lorraine, 106n9
Charles II (king), 120n7
Charles V (king), 22n1, 119n5
Charles VII (king), 107n17
Charles VIII (king), 17n13, 103, 106n10,

106n13; castle of, 103, 106n7, 106n10, 110; death of, 103, 106n10; tomb of children of, 93, 95n6

Charles IX (king), 107n17

Chase, Mr., 67, 76

Chateau De Lahon, 30. *See also* Beaumanoirs, La Chapelle des

Châtel St. Denis, Switzerland, 209, 211n2

Cheney, Ednah Dow, 24, 27n3, 171, 247n5

Cheney, Seth, 27n3, 247n5

Chenonceaux chateau, lxvi, 104, 106n13, 110

Chicago, Ill., 206, 208n3

Chillon, castle of, 213n3, 233

Chillon, Switzerland, 213, 213n3

Chislehurst, Kent, England, 189n9, 190n10

Christian Register, 150n6

Christian Union, lxv

Christina, Maria (queen regent), 188n2

Christmas Stories (Dickens), 9n14

Cimabue, Cenni di Pepo, 246, 250n16

Clarke, Rev. James Freeman, 130n10

Claude of France, 119n5

Clomadoc, Jules, xxxvii, lxvi, 28, 30, 34; wedding of, 44, 45n2

Clotilde, Maria Teresa, of Saxony (princess), 186, 189n7

Cologne, Germany, lxi

Colonna family, 258, 265n21

Como, Lake, liii, 233, 239, 243n8, 243n9; beauty of, 237, 238n7, 242n1, 243n7; two arms of, 243n10

Conant, Mary, 65, 68n1, 73n7, 87n11, 94, 124, 125n4, 144, 158

Concord, Mass., 86, 196; ABA and Abigail May Alcott's return to, for summer of 1870, 35, 49, 63n4, 65; Alcotts' 1845 return to, xx; Alcotts move to, xviii;

funeral of John Bridge Pratt in, lv; gossiping in, 82; LMA buried in, lxx; LMA recollects childhood in, xx; May born in, xviii; May's 1874 return to, lxvi; Orchard House purchased in, xxi; Thoreau house purchased in, lxvii

Concord Art Center, lxvi, lxvii

Concord Days (ABA), xv, 251n19

Concord Sketches (May Alcott), xxx, 54n2, 246, 251n19

Constantinople, 215

Conway, Dana, 57n5

Conway, Ellen, xxvi, xxviii, lxi, 270n1; letter to, from LMA, 269–70

Conway, Emerson, 57n5

Conway, Eustace, 57n5

Conway, Mildred, 57n5

Conway, Moncure Daniel, xxvi, xxviii, lxi, 55, 56n1, 57n5, 62, 270n1; letter to, from LMA, 55–57; and notice of *An Old-Fashioned Girl,* 147

Cooper Union School of Design, xxvi

Cornwall, England, 169, 171n1

Correggio, Antonio da, liii, 110, 112n9, 245, 248n10

Corso, the, 253, 256, 257, 263n4, 263n6

"Cost of an Idea, The" (LMA), 35, 36n12

Coste, Madame, xxxvi, xxxvii, 13, 15, 16, 17nn10–11, 46, 47, 62, 67; on Alcotts' departure, 76; concern of, for LMA's health, 34, 37, 44; on lack of crime in Dinan, 70; pension of, 101; photograph of, 81; stores wood, 82

Courland, 227, 229n1

Couture, Thomas, xxix, lx

Crowninshield, Frederic, liv

Cruikshank, George, xxiv

Curtis, George William, 84, 87n10

Curtiss, Mrs. B. Augusta, 136, 137n7

da Vinci, Leonardo, 236, 238n13

Daisy Miller (James), lxii

David Copperfield (Dickens), 48n3

Davis, Charles Wilder, 140n9

Davis, L. Clarke, 201, 202n2

Davis, Rebecca Harding, 201, 202n2

de la Garaye, Claude Toussaint Comte, 29n5

del Sarto, Andrea, liii, 245, 248n9

D'Enclos, Ninon (Ninon de Lenclos), 104, 107n20

Dent de Midi, 166, 233

Dent de Morcles, 145n5, 165, 166n1, 242n3

Derby, Dr. Haskett, 210, 211n7

Diableret, Mount, 166

Diablerets, 145n5

Dial, 200n3

Diana (goddess), 107n16

Dickens, Charles, xliii; death of, 128, 131n15, 147, 150n6, 158; Grace Greenwood's tribute to, 160n15

—works of: *Christmas Stories,* 9n14; *David Copperfield,* 48n3; "Holly Tree Inn," 7, 9n14; *Martin Chuzzlewit,* 9n15, 63n1; *The Pickwick Papers,* 76n4

Dinan, France, xxxv, xlvi, 12, 101, 124, 125; Alcotts' departure from, 92; letters from, 12–89

Dinard, France, 32n3, 44, 45n5

Doesticks, Philander (Mortimer Thompson), 173, 179n3

Doll (photographer) 8, 9n16, 76

Doll and Hendersons (photographers), 67

Doll and Richards (photographers), 10n17

Domodossola, Italy (Domo D'Ossola), lii, 235, 237n6

Don Carlos, l

Dor, Dr. Henri, 188, 190n12, 210, 215

Doria-Pamphilj-Landi (Dorias), 258, 265n21

d'Orléans, Gaston, 120n5

Dorr, Dr. *See* Dor, Dr. Henri

"Downward Road, The" (Alice Bartlett), 59, 63n6

du Guesclin, Bertrand, 19, 22n1, 30, 39n2

Dupin, Madame, 104, 107n18, 107n19

Dying Gladiator, The, 257, 264n12

Eaton, Lorenzo, 147, 151n7

Eckley, Mrs., 151, 159n2

Edward IV (king), 106n12

Eight Cousins (LMA), lxvi

Eliot, George, 140n4

Elizabeth I (queen), 112n8

Emerson, Charles, 211n9

Emerson, Edith, xliv

Emerson, Edward, xxxiii, 6, 9n6, 168, 169n7; medical practice of, in Concord, 27n2

Emerson, Ellen, xxi, xliv, lxii; *Flowers Fables* told to, 88n14; May sends love to, 168, 169n7, 195

Emerson, Ralph Waldo, xviii, xx, xxi, xxx, xxxii, 8n6; as brother of Charles, 211n9; as father of Ellen, 88n14; home of, 52, 54n2; on foreign travel, xvii; on May's death, lxviii, lxix; meets Alice Bartlett in Italy in 1873, lxii; as member of Saturday Club, 73n8

Emerson family, 216

Emmanuel, Victor. *See* Victor Emmanuel II

Estabrook, Frances Hildreath, 196n6

Estabrook, John D., 196n6

Eugénie de Montijo (empress), 186, 190n10, 190n11

Every Saturday, 158, 160n16; illustration of Jo March in, 167; illustration of *An Old-Fashioned Girl* in, 213n2

Fanny, Miss, 44

Farnborough, Hampshire, England, 190n10

Ferdinand VII (king), 188n2

Fetcher, Charles A., 35, 36n11, 158, 225

Fields, James T., 163, 167, 169n5

Fields, Osgood and Company, xxx

Fireside Companion, The, 35, 36n9

Florence, Italy, liii, lviii, 109, 241; letter from, 243–51; Victor Emmanuel II arrives from, 258; Victor Emmanuel II departs for, 261

Flower Fables (LMA), xxi, xli, 85, 88n14

Foley, Margaret F., 243, 247n4

Ford, Daniel, 35, 36n10, 173, 178n1

Fornarina, La (Raphael), 245, 249n12

Forney, Alice, lxvi, 14, 17n11, 30; wedding of, 43, 45n2

Forney, Gaston, lxvi, 14, 15, 16, 17n11, 20, 23, 28, 38; on Alcotts' departure from Dinan, 101; in Breton costume, 59, 62; farewell of, to Alcotts, 92; gifts from, 73, 78; May's sketch of, 89; picnic with, 79; wedding of sister of, 44

Forney, Madame, xxxviii, 14, 15, 17n11, 34; May's sketch of, 89; picnic with, 79; wedding of daughter of, 43

Forney family (Fourniss), 23

Fornier, Alice. *See* Forney, Alice

Fornier, Gaston. *See* Forney, Gaston

Fournier, Madame. *See* Forney, Madame

Fourniss, Gaston. *See* Forney, Gaston

Fourniss family (Forney), 23

Francis I (king), 115, 229n2, 227; castle of, 113; marriage of, 119n5

Francis II (duke), 17n13

Francis II (king), 106n9

François (duc de Guise), 106n9

François (duke of Anjou), 119n5

François II (king), 112n8

Francoise, 70

Franco-Prussian War, xlix, 144, 145n3, 148, 150n1; as cause of travelers' money problems, 169, 191, 192; end of, appears near, 180, 199; French losses in, 181, 182, 184n1, 186; Italy's position in, 166, 170; LMA's account of Europe after surrender of France in, 218; Paris under siege during, 186; Prussians take Châlons during, 209, 211n4; refugees from, arrive in Switzerland, 153; Russia rumored to join, 153, 160n6; Switzerland as neutral in, 147

Frank Leslie's Illustrated Newspaper, xxiv

Frank Leslie's Lady's Magazine, 51n5

Franklin, Benjamin, 104, 107n17

Fraternity Club, 143n4

Free Religious Association, 143n4

Freeman, James, 111n1

French, Daniel Chester, xviii, xxix, 68n6

French, Henry and Pamela, 68, 68n6

French, Sarah (Sally), 68, 68n6

French Ophthalmologic Society, 190n12

"French Provinces, The" (Alice Bartlett), lxii

Frothingham, Octavius Brooks, xxx, 141, 143n4, 168

Fruitlands, xix

Fuller, Horace B., xxvii, xli, 85, 88n16, 173, 179n4

Garrett, stables of, 253, 263n7

Geneva, xlvi, xlvii, 125, 125n1, 126, 135, 136; Alcotts' arrival in, 114, 123; Alcotts contemplate staying in, 149, 153; on Alcotts' itinerary, 93, 108; Bigelows stay in, 227; Bonds stay in, 182, 183; Clotilde passes through, 186; letters from, 114–17, 123–24; letters safe via, 205; stores in, 162

Geneva, Lake, xlvii, 123, 166, 166n1, 168n1; description of, 125n2; Hotel Metropole located on, 121n8; La Tour-de-Peilz located on, 211n6; Montreux located on, 163n1

Giotto di Bondone, liii, 246, 250n16

Globe Theater, 225

Gloucester, Mass., 196n6

Godkin, E. L., 68n4

Goethe, Wolfgang von, lxvi

Gonda, valley of (Gondo), li, 234, 240, 242n4

Gore, Jeremiah, 232n2

Gore, Susan B., 232n2

Gorges du Trient, 168, 169n6

Goth, 256, 263n11

Gould, Thomas R., 243, 247n5

"Grandma's Team" (LMA), 36n10

Grant, Ulysses S., lx, 269n1

Gratien, St., xlvi

Greele, Samuel, 226n4

Greenwood, Grace, 158, 160n15

Greenwood, Louis, 151

Greenwood, Mary Langdon, xxxi

Greenwood, Dr. William Pitt, xxxi

Gregory of Tours, 95n6

Gros, Baron, lx

Grot des Fees, 139, 140n7

Grovers, Mrs., 270, 270n2

Guercino, 245, 249n14

Guerra, Paul, 130n4

Guidos, 104, 107n21

Guildo, Le, 46, 48n2

Guise, duc de (François), 106n9

Guise, duke of (Henry I), 113, 119n5

Hale, Edward Everett, lix

Hamilton, Alexander, xxv

Harden, Mr., 167

Harmon, Adolph, 50

Harper's Hand Book for Travellers in Europe and the East, xliv

Harper's New Monthly Magazine, 87n10

Harper's Weekly, 87n10

Hart, Joel Tanner, liii, 243, 246n3

Haskell, Daniel Noyes, 262n1; letter to, from LMA, 253–65

Hatton, Louisa Anne (Lady Hope), 138, 139n2

Hawthorne, Nathaniel, xx, xxi, xxix, lx; marriage of, 200n3; seat of, 52, 54n2

Hawthorne, Sophia, 247n6

Healy, G. P. A., lx, lxiv

Healy, Mary, lx

Hearth and Home, xliii, 84, 87n8, 109, 145n1, 160n9; LMA thanks Sanborn for article in, 167; received from Thomas Niles, 155

Hedge, Frederic Henry, 150n6

Hendrickson, Doll, and Richards (photographers), 10n17

Henri II (king), 106n13; 112n8

Henri of Navarre (Henry IV), 119n5

Henry I (duke of Guise), 113, 119n5

Henry II (king), 110; marriage of, 119n5

Henry III (king), 106n13, 113, 119n5

Henry IV (Henri of Navarre), 119n5

Henry VI (king), 106n12

Higginson, Thomas Wentworth, 158, 160–61n17

Hildreth, Caroline Negus, 202

Hildreth, Richard, 204n1

Hoar, Elizabeth, 210, 211n9

"Holly Tree Inn" (Dickens), 7, 9n14

Holmes, Oliver Wendell, 73n8

"Home of the Great American Authoress," 179, 181n1

Hope, Lady (Louisa Anne Hatton), 138, 139n2

Hope, Maj. Gen. Charles, 139n2

Hoppin, Martha J., xxix

Hosmer, Harriet, 247n4

Hospital Sketches (LMA), xv, xxv, 9n7

Hospital Sketches and Camp and Fireside Stories (LMA), xxx

Howe, Mr., 115, 121n9, 124, 213

Howe, Mrs., 262n1

Howe, Charles, 135, 138, 221

Howe, Dr. Estes, 7, 9n10, 63n10, 64, 67

Howe, Mrs. Estes, 7, 9n10, 62, 63n10, 64, 67, 93

Howe, Julia Ward, 129, 131n19, 251n18

Howitt, William and Mary, 267, 269n1

Hugo, Victor, xxxvi, 13, 16n6

Huguenots, hanging of, 106n9, 110

Hunt, William Morris, xxix

Independent, 45n2, 122n19, 122n25, 216n1

Inheritance, The (LMA), xx

Irving, Washington, 200n4

Isabella II (queen), 186, 188n2, 189n4, 198

Iselle di Trasquera, Italy, 235, 237n5

Isola Bella, lii, 236, 240, 242n5

Italy, unification of, 225, 226n6

Ives, Louis Thomas, 111, 112n11

Jaime (duke of Anjou and Madrid), 189n3, 198, 199

James, Henry, lxii, 211n5; *Daisy Miller,* lxii

Jarves, James Jackson (Mr. Jarvis), 246, 251n18

"Jo March's Necessity Stories" (LMA), 173

Joan of Arc, 114, 119n4, 120n7; statue of, 115, 121n12

Johnson, Samuel, 158, 161n18

Johnston, David Claypoole, xxiv

Jo's Boys (LMA), lxvi

Judson, Edward Z. C. (Ned Buntline), 173, 179n3

Jura, the, 93, 96n8

Kane, Amy, 79

Kane, Dr. John, 47n1; daughters of, 79; picnic with, 79; on treatment of LMA, 75

Kane, Dr. William, xlv, 47, 49; admiration of, for Hawthorne, 52; on LMA's health, 64; no longer treats LMA, 75; picnic with, 79, 89; prescription of, 85, 93, 100, 128; treats LMA's health problems, 46, 47n1, 48, 50, 58, 65

Kane family, 88

Kilkenny, 199, 201n7

King's Chapel, 108, 111n1

Knorring, Eugene, 212, 213n1, 214, 218, 227

Krug, Edouard, lxvii

La Garaye, Chateau de, 28, 29n5, 41, 42; May's sketch of, 100

La Scala, 237, 238n16

La Tour-de-Peilz, Switzerland, 210, 211n6

Lafayette (steamer), 3, 3n1, 4; letters from, 3–9

Lafayette, Marquis de, 104, 107n17

Lahon, France. *See* Lehon, France

Lambelle, France (Lamballe), 12, 16n3, 44

Lane, Charles, xix

Latimer, Elizabeth Wormeley, xvii

Lavinia, 253, 256, 257, 258, 259

Lawrence, Dr. Rhoda, lxx, lxxi

"Lay of a Golden Goose, The" (LMA), xlviii, xlix, 173, 174–78, 178n1, 180, 181n5, 183, 231

Le Bouillet salt mine, 145, 145n4

Le Mans, cathedral of, 92, 95n4, 95n5, 97

Le Mans, France, xlvi, 92, 93, 95n3, 97

Lecco, Lake of, 243n10

Lee, Robert E., xxxi

Lee, William Fitzhugh, xxxi

Legget, Eliza Seaman, 151, 159n2

Lehon, France, xxxviii, xl, 19, 22n3, 29n5, 32n4; May's reaction to, 70

Lenclos, Ninon de, 104, 107n20

Les Plans, Switzerland (Leppz), 157, 160n12

Leslie, Frank, xxviii, 50, 51n4

Liddes, Switzerland, 132, 137n3

"Life in a Pension" (LMA), 216n1

Lincoln, Abraham, lx, 189n7, 247n4

Lippincott, Sara Jane (Grace Greenwood), 158, 160n15

Lippincott's Magazine, 201, 202n1, 202n3

Little Men (LMA), lvi, lix, lxi, lxiii, lxxi

Little Women, xvii, xxvi, xliii, lxx, 225; admirers of, in Europe, 144; Amy's dream of being artist in, xviii; author of, xxxii, xlii, lxvi; comparison of, with *An Old Fashioned Girl,* 43; Demi and Daisy in, 22n11; illustration from, in *Our Young Folks,* 163, 163n3; illustration of Jo from, in *Every Saturday,* 160n16; inspiration for "Laurie" in, 216n1; Loring capitalizes on popularity of, xli; new designs for, by Thomas Niles, 158; new illustration for, 202n3; "Operatic Tragedy" of, set to music, 158, 160n17; part 2 of, published, xxix; phrase "take time by the fetlock" used in, 190n13; Warren sisters read, 168; well-known in Italy, liii, 243; writing of, xxviii

Livermore, Mary, 129, 131n18

Lock of Le Châtelier, 28, 29n4

Lodge, Henry Cabot, 17n9

Lodge, James, 17n9

Lodge, Mary Langdon Greenwood, 13, 15, 17n9

Lombard, Fanny, 209, 211n5

London, England, liv, lxi, 170, 173, 221; letter from, 269–70

Longfellow, Henry Wadsworth, lx, 73n8, 155

Loring, A. K., xli, lix; letters from, received, 93, 94; LMA's anger with, 84; and publishers' rights, 82; reprints *Moods,* 33, 35n4; sends LMA new *Moods,* 113, 118–19n2

Louis of Orleans (prince), 119n5

Louis VIII (king), 96n6

Louis IX (king), 96n6, 119n5

Louis XII (king), 17n13; castle of, 113; children of, 119n5; royal arms of, 114

Louis XIII (king), 114, 119n5, 120n5

Louis XIV (king), 107n20

Louisa Wells (Lu), 67, 68n5

Louise de Lorraine, 106n13

Louis-Philippe (king), 120n5

"Love and Self-Love" (LMA), xxiv

Lovering, Joseph, 131n20

Lovering, Mrs. Joseph, 129, 131n20

Low, Nellie (Nelly), 214, 231, 237, 240

Low, Sampson, lxi, 56, 57n3; publishing agreement of, with LMA, 82, 84, 86n4, 113; and royalty on *An Old-Fashioned Girl,* 118, 122n26

Low, Sampson, and Marston, 63n3, 123; letter to, from LMA, 123

Lowell, James Russell, 73n8

Lugano, lii, 236, 240, 242n7

Lugano, Lake, liii, 236, 237, 238n14, 242n7

Luini, Bernardino, 236, 238nn12–13

Luino, 236, 238n8, 240, 242n6

Lulu (Louisa May Nieriker), lxviii, lxix

Lulu's Library (LMA), lxix

Lynn, Mass., 194, 195n3

Lyons, France (Lyon), xlvi, 108, 124, 190n12

MacMahon, Patrice Maurice de, xlix, 181, 184n1, 211n4

Maggiore, Lake, l, lii, 214, 217n3, 236, 238n7, 240, 242n6, 243n7

Malleson, Elizabeth Whitehead, 56, 57n7

Malleson, Frank Rodbard, 57n7

Malleson, J. P., 57n7

Malo, St., 44, 45n5

Mann, Horace, 200n3

Mansfield, Abby (Brooks), 195, 196n6

Mansfield, Abigail Somes Davis, 196n6

Mansfield, Alfred, 196n6

Mansfield, Fanny (Frances Hildreath Estabrook), 195, 196n6

Mansfield, Frances Gilman Hildreth, 196n6

Mansfield, Maj. James, 196n6

Mansfield, May, 195, 196n6

Mansfield family, 195, 196n6

Margaret of Anjou (queen), 104

Margaret of Foix, 17n13

Marguerite (princess), 189n3, 198

Marie (stewardess), 3, 4n3

Marlitt, E. (Eugenie John), 224, 226n3

Marmora, Alfonso Ferrero La, 258, 265n20

Marsh, George Perkins, 243, 247n4

Marshall, Augustus, xliii, 84, 87n9; photograph of May by, 145n2, 167, 168n2, 202

Marston, Edward, 86n4. *See also* Low, Sampson, and Marston

Martigny, Switzerland, 132, 135, 137n2, 138, 195, 169n6

Martin Chuzzlewit (Dickens), 9n15, 63n1

Marvaile, Miss (Madlle Mervaille), 20, 22n4, 28

Marvales family, 44

Mary, Queen of Scots, 110, 112n8

Mathematical Monthly, xxxi

Mathilde, Princess (Bonaparte), 186, 189n8

Maximilian I (emperor), 17n13

May, Henry, 126, 130n6

May, Col. Joseph, 75, 77n5

May, Samuel Joseph, 210, 211n8, 218

McMahon, Patrice Maurice de. *See* MacMahon, Patrice Maurice de

Médicis, Catherine de, 104, 106n13, 106n16, 107n17, 110; castle of, 113; death of, 114, 120n5; marriage of, 119n5

Médicis, Marie de, 114, 120n5

Menaggio, liii, 237, 240, 243n8

Merry's Museum, xxviii, xxx, 88n16

Mervaille, Madlle (Miss Marvaile), 20, 22n4, 28

Metropole, Hotel, 114, 121n8, 124, 125n3

Milan, liii, 238n15, 241, 242; Alcotts plan to visit, 109, 218, 237

Milan, Cathedral of, 237, 238n15

Millet, Jean-Francois, xxix

Mirandola, Silvio, 198, 200n6, 214, 217n6

Modern Mephistopheles, A (LMA), lxvi

Monroe, George (Munro), 36n9; letter from, 195

Monroe family, 210, 211n8

Montaigne, Michel de, 104, 107n17

Monte Rosa, lii, 233, 237n3

Montreux, Switzerland (Montraux), 161, 163n1, 181, 194, 211n6, 213, 221

Moods (LMA), xxvi, lx, xli, 84, 85, 88n15; 1882 revision of, 76n1; LMA's reaction to Loring's new edition of, 73, 76n1; Loring's new edition of, 33, 113, 118–19n2

Moore, Emma, 195, 206, 209, 215; marriage of, 139, 140n9

Moore, John B., 140n9, 196, 197, 200n1

Moore, Sarah Augusta Hunt, 140n9

Morlaix, France, xxxv, 4, 16n1, 23, 76; Alcotts' arrival in, 10; Alcotts' departure from, 12; letters from, 10, 12; location of, 8n3; May's initial reaction to, 69

Morning Glories and Other Stories (LMA), 88n16, 173, 179n4

"Mother's Trial" (LMA), 36n10

Moulins, France, xlvi, 115, 121n14

Mount Desert, Mass., 215, 217n8

Mount St. Bernard, 126, 141

Munich, Germany, lxi, 195

Munro, George, 36n9; letter from, 195

Munroe (banker), 10n18, 84; Alcotts' plan to advise him of their moves, 93; charges of, for forwarded letters, 179, 199, 211; charges of, for postage due, 126, 183, 188; difficulty of getting funds from, during war, 147, 166, 169, 191, 207; direct letters to, 8, 26, 45, 52, 56, 62, 64, 68, 123; LMA deposits Low's royalty with, 118, 122n26, 192; LMA has no money with, 209

Munroe, Mrs., 218, 228

Munroe, Julia, 218, 228

Murdock, Mrs., xxi

Murray, John, xxxvi, xxxix, 4, 8n4, 16, 16n5, 93, 98, 104; on Amboise, 96n7; on Blois, 108; on Brittany, 27n1; on Chapel of St. Hubert, 111n6; on Chenonceaux, 107n18; on Dinan, 16n4; on Hotel de Europe, 72n1; on Le Mans Cathedral, 95n4; on Lehon, 22n3; on Lion d'Or inn, 105n6; on Morlaix, 72n4, 72n5; on Rennes, 88n20; on Rue de Jerzual, 39n3; on Salle des Etats, Blois, 120n6; on St. Gatien Cathedral, 95–96n6, 101n1; on Tours, 95n

Nantes, France, 50, 51n3

Naples, Italy, 108, 241

Napoleon, Joseph Charles Paul (Plon-Plon), 189n7

Napoleon I, 239, 248n7, 263n2

Napoleon III, xlix, lviii, 1, 17n6, 106n8, 114, 181; as cousin to Prince Napoleon, 189n7; declares war on Prussia, 145n3; establishes Bois de Boulogne park, 208n4; family and history of, 190n11; as father to Napoleon IV, 189n9; joins forces with MacMahon, 184n1, 211n4; LMA's opinion of, 186; marriage of, 190n10; surrender of, 214, 217n2, 269n1; withdraws garrison from Rome, 226n6

Napoleon IV (prince imperial), 186, 189n9

Nation, The, 67, 68n4, 201

National Woman Suffrage Association, 122n25

Negresse (May Alcott), lxviii

Nevers, France, 93

Neville, Richard (Earl of Warwick), 104, 106n12

New England Quarterly, 238n11

New England Woman Suffrage Movement, 131n18

New York Daily Tribune, 158, 160n15

New York Tribune, 48n6

New York Weekly, 173, 179n2

Nicond, Madame, 185, 188n1, 233

Nicond, Monsieur, 205, 209

Nieriker, Ernst, lxviii

Nieriker, Louisa May, lxviii, lxix

Niles, Thomas, xvii, xxviii, 27, 29n1, 35, 45n1; and author's rights, 85; business duties for LMA performed by, 191; Conway's notices sent by, 147; and *Every Saturday* publication, 158, 160n16, 213n2; gossip of, 82, 87n6; greets LMA on return home, lxiii; *Hearth and Home* article sent by, 155; on Higginson's "Acting Little Women," 160n17; *Hospital Sketches* copyright obtained by, xxx; informality of, 94;

"Jo's Letters from Abroad" requested by, lxv; and "The Lay of a Golden Goose," 173, 178–79n1; letters from, 45, 171; letters from fans forwarded by, xlii, 199; letters to, from LMA, 173–81, 201–2; and *Little Women* designs, 158; LMA requests note forwarded to, 232; LMA's permission needed by, to reprint material, 208; and Loring's edition of *Moods,* 33, 35n1, 43, 113, 118–19n2; and Low publishing agreement, 84, 86n4, 118, 123, 123n1, 231; May's St. Bernard letter placed in *Transcript* by, 210; notices forwarded by, 47, 50, 54, 58, 128, 158, 171, 215; and *An Old-Fashioned Girl,* xli, 20, 21, 22n9, 26, 42; on *Our Young Folks* illustration, 163, 163n3; papers sent by, 211; and royalty statements, 42, 54, 125, 129n1, 231; on rumors of LMA's death, 262n1; *Transcript*s sent by, 67; waits for new work by LMA, 129
Niles, William J., lxi, lxiv, 82, 87n5
Nonne, Siegmund George, 129n2
Normandy, France, 64, 65n2
Norton, Caroline Sheridan, 29n5
Notre Dame, cathedral of (Moulins), 115, 121n14
Notre Dame, church of (Lambelle), 16n3

Old and New, lix, lxii
Old-Fashioned Girl, An, xxxiv, lxxi, 87; *Atlantic* review of, 84; British edition of, 57n5, 63n3, 81, 123; British reviews of, 58, 150n4; correction in British edition of, 201; illustration from, in *Every Saturday,* 213n2; LMA's comments on, 47; Loring capitalizes on popularity of, xli; mention of, in *Transcript,* 51n5; passengers read, on

the *Lafayette,* xxxv, 6; publication of, 9n9; published in *Merry's Museum,* xxx; reviews of, 48n6; royalties from, 32, 35n1, 192
Orchard House, 140n9, 200n1; Alcotts' purchase of, xxi; LMA's 1871 return to, lxiv
Orleans, France, xlvi, 93, 108, 119; Alcotts in, 115; siege of, 120n7
Osgood, James R., 246, 251n19
"Our Apartment" (Alice Bartlett), lviii, lix
Our Young Folks, 158, 161n17

Padua, Italy, 250n16
Pantheon, 249n11, 257, 264n16
Paradis, Pension, 180, 181, 181n2, 183, 185, 214, 233
Paris, France, xlix, 171, 183, 221; under bombardment, 218; May studies in, lxvii; under siege, 186, 189n5, 207, 209, 221
Parker, Harvey D., 73n8
Parker House, 73n8
Parma, Italy, liii, 245, 248n10
"Pauline's Passion and Punishment" (LMA), xxiv
Peabody, Elizabeth Palmer, 198, 200n3
Peabody, Mary, 200n3
Peabody, Sophia, 200n3
"Pelagie's Wedding" (LMA), 45n2
Penelope, 151, 159n3
Penzance, England, 169, 170, 171n1
Perkins, Lt. George H., 126, 130n10
Perkins family, 170
Pesth, Hungary, 126, 130n5, 130n7
Piazza del Popolo, 253, 263n4, 263n6, 264n15
Piazza di Spagna, 253, 263n5
Pickwick Papers, The (Dickens), 76n4
Pierce, Benjamin P., xxxi

Pierre II of Savoy, Count, 213n3

Pincio, the, 257, 264n14

Pisa, Italy, liii

Pitti, the, liii, 245, 248n7, 249n11

Pius IX (pope), lvii; anger of, at king of Italy, 254, 257, 263n9; refuses peaceful settlement with king of Italy, 226n6

Plato, 141, 232

Plymouth, Mass., 217n7

Poitiers, Diane de, 104, 106n13, 107n17, 110

Polk family, 214, 216n1

Popolo Gate (Porta Popolo), 257, 264n15

Porlezza, Italy, liii, 236, 238n14

Porta Pia, 257, 264n13

Porta Popolo, 257, 264n15

Powers, Hiram, liii, 243, 246n3

Pratt, Anna Alcott, xvi, xvii, xxii, 3, 4n4, 8n1, 22n11; engagement of, xxi–xxii; hearing of, 76, 77n6; letter to, xxxix, xl; letters to, from LMA, 57–63, 79–88, 151–61, 222–26, 251–53; letters to, from May, 69–73, 161–63, 193–96; letters to, from May, with Abigail May Alcott, 4–10, 23–27, 36–39, 51–54; marriage of, 63n5; purchase of Thoreau house by, lxvii; residence of, in Maplewood, Mass., 63n2; teaches school, xx; tenth wedding anniversary of, 58; translation of *Maid of Orleans* by, 115, 121n12; visit of, to Temple School, xviii

Pratt, Caroline Bartlett, 217n7

Pratt, Donny. *See* Pratt, John Sewall

Pratt, Frederick Alcott, lvi, 3, 4n4, 22, 22n11, 31, 32n5, 35, 77n8, 94, 126, 149; desires to see boys swimming, 188; manners of, 155; on pulling teeth, 229; resembles Alfred Tidey, 151; Tidey boys remind May of, 162

Pratt, Herbert J., xlvii, xlviii, 42, 43n2, 162, 227, 228; arrival of, 221; arrival of, in Vevey, 215; life of, 217n7; May sketches, 223; May thinks she sees, in Geneva, 162; on pulling teeth, 228, 229

Pratt, James, 217n7

Pratt, John Bridge, xxii, xxvii, lvi, 3, 4n4, 22n11, 39, 57, 124; Abigail May Alcott's grief over, 266; Alcott sisters' desire for, to visit in London, 224; care of Abigail May Alcott by, while ABA is out West, 231; death of, lv, lvi, lxiii, 251, 253n1, 262, 267; engagement of, xxi; escorts LMA and May to New York, xxxiv, 8; eye troubles of, 138; on handling LMA's business, 191; health of, 137, 142; illness of, 85, 88n13, 93, 100, 111, 128, 215; LMA's grief over, 265, 266; marriage of, 63n5; May wears ring of, 163, 163n4; May's inquiry regarding health of, 209; and photograph of LMA, 96; residence of, in Maplewood, Mass., 63n2; on sale of LMA's photographs, 46, 67

Pratt, John Sewall (Donny), lvi, 3, 4n4, 22, 22n11, 31, 32n5, 35, 77n8, 85, 87n12, 94, 128, 149; birthday of, 113, 118n1, 158, 160n14; desires to see boys swimming, 188; growing up of, 224; Tidey boys remind May of, 162

Pratt, May, 217n7

Pratt, Minot, xxi, lxv

Proverb Stories (LMA), lxvi

Prussia, xlix, 146, 153, 226n6; France declares war on, 145n3, 150n1; king of, 269n2; LMA favors, l, 186

Putnam's Magazine, xvii

Quirinal, the, 258, 261

Rabelais, François, 104, 107n17

Radical Club, 131n19, 150n5

Rance valley, xxxvi, 30, 32n3

Raphael, liii, 245, 249n11

"Recollections of My Youth" (LMA), xx

Record of a School, 200n3

Redpath, James, xxv

"Reminiscences of a Rook, The" (LMA), 103, 105n5

Reni, Guido, 110, 112n9, 138, 140n4, 193

Rennes, France, 12n3, 86, 88n20

Revolution, 118, 122n25, 129

Rice, Reuben, 224, 226n1

Richard the Lion-Hearted, 92, 95n5

Richards (photographer), 17n10

Richardson, Caroline, 39n6

Richardson family, 39

Ricketson, Dr. Arthur, 24, 27n2, 86, 88n17, 101, 101n3, 137n8, 216; settles in Concord, 65, 136, 215

Ricketson, Daniel, xxx, 27n2, 88n17

Ricketson, Louisa, 27n2, 88n17

Ricketson, Louise Dolben Bliss, 27n2, 86, 101, 101n3, 137n8, 216; settles in Concord, 65, 136, 215

Ricketson family, 86

Rimmer, William, xxv, xxvi, xxix

"Rip Van Winkle," 198, 200n4

Ristori, Adelaide, 257, 264n18

Rivage, Pension Du, 117, 215, 228

"Rival Painters, The" (LMA), xx

Roberts Brothers, xxvii, xxx, xlii, lx, lxvi, lxviii; obtains rights for *Morning Glories,* 179n4; publication of revised 1882 *Moods* by, 76n1

Rocky Nook, Mass., 194, 195n3

Rodin, lxvii

Rome, xxxix, liii, lvi–lvii, lx, lxvi, 1, 109, 166, 170, 199, 208n2, 218, 246; Alcotts desire to see, 209; letters written from, 251–69

Rose in Bloom (LMA), lxvi

Rousseau, Jean-Jacques, 104, 107n18

Rowbotham, Thomas Charles Leeson, liv, lxi

Rowbotham, Thomas Leeson, lxi

Ruskin, John, lxvi

Russell, John, Viscount Amberly, 150n5

Russell, Thomas, lxiii

Saginaw, Mich., 196n6

Salle des Etats, 113, 120n6

Salzburg, Austria, 196n5

Sampson Low and Marston, 63n3, 123; letter to, from LMA, 123

San Angelo, Church of (Santa Maria degli Angioli convent), 236, 238n12

San Francisco, Calif., 232

San Marco, convent of, 245, 247n6, 249n15

Sanborn, xxv, 6, 9n7; academy of xxiv, 196n6, 200n5; claims LMA related to Longfellow, 155, 160n9; *Hearth and Home* article of, xlii, 109, 87n8, 144, 145n1, 147, 150n4; LMA thanks, for *Hearth and Home* article, 167; and LMA's letters, 208; LMA's opinion of *Hearth and Home* article by, 155; May sends her regards to, 210; review of *An Old-Fashioned Girl* by, 20, 22n10; and *Springfield Republican* notice, 128, 131n15

Sand, George, 104, 107n19

Sandhurst, Royal Military Academy, 189n4

Santa Maria degli Angioli, convent of, 236, 238n12

Santa Maria Novella, church of, 246, 250n16

Sarpany, Count. *See* Szárápy, Count Ferencz Sarpari

Saturday Club, 73n8

Saturday Evening Gazette, lix

Schalbach, Germany, 126, 130nn8–9

Schiller, Friedrich, 115, 121n12

School of Philosophy, Concord, 131n19

Scraps, xxiv

Sedan, France, 184n1, 190n11, 226n6

Selwyn Theater, 158, 160n13

Semiramide, 141, 142n3

Sévigné, Madame de (Sevnegue), 104, 107n20

Sewall, Joseph S., 32n6

Sewall, M. R., 47, 48n7

Sewall, Mary, 32n6

Sewall, Mary Joe, 32, 32n6

Sewall, Mary K. (Polly), 27, 29n2, 32n6; letter to, from LMA, 29–32

Sewall, Samuel E., 29n2, 54, 62, 191; investment of July 1870 royalties by, 125; investments of, 149, 151n8; letter to, from LMA, 192–93; LMA reviews account of, 229, 232n1; and LMA's desire for account in writing, 128; and LMA's desire to invest in bonds, 231; and LMA's desire to know about investments, 158; and LMA's $1000 credit through Baring, 206; and support of ABA and Abigail May Alcott, 167

Sewall, Thomas, xxii, 29n2

Sewall family, 73n7

Shaw, Henry Wheeler (Josh Billings), 173, 179n3

Shawl-Straps, xv, xxxii, xxxvii, lix, lxiii, lxv, lxxi, lxxii, 9n11; Bartlett's poem "The Downward Road" in, 63n6; on Forney, Gaston, 17n11; Knorring, Eugene, description in, 213n1; on the Lion d'Or inn, 105n6; on Mirandolo, Silvio, 200n6, 217n6; Mrs. Munroe and Julia's description in, 222n2; on

"Pelagie's Wedding," 45n2; on Pension Paradis, 181n2; on Polish Countess in Bex, 130n12; on Pratt, Herbert J., 217n7; on Raphael, 249n11; on refugees and ex-royalty in Vevey, 181n3; on "Reverend Boy," 121n15; on Szárápy, Count, 143n3; on Tidey children, 159n4

Sheridan, Gen. Philip, 267, 269n1

Sicily, Italy, xxxii

Sierre, Italy, 233, 237n1

Sillig, Edovard (Silling), 198, 200n5, 201

Simmons, William Hammatt, 209, 211n3

Simplon, Switzerland, 234, 237n4

Simplon Pass, li, lxvi, 153, 160n5; Alcott's crossing of, 233, 239

Simplon Road, 217n4

Singelton, Mrs., 86, 88n18, 97n2

Singleton family, 97

Smedley, Dr. Alvin, 76, 77n6, 168n3

Smith (photographer), 202

Smith, Ellen T., 48n4

Smith, Francis Shubael, 173, 179n2

Smith, Harold F., lxvi

"Some Pros and Cons of Travel Abroad" (Alice Bartlett), lxii

Sorrel, Agnés, 104, 107n17

Sorrento, Italy, xxxii, 109, 111n3

Spaulding, James Reed, 173, 179n3

Spectator, 150n4

Spezia, Italy, 37, 39n1, 199, 201n8

Spinning Wheel Stories (LMA), lxvi

Springfield Daily Union, 48n6

Springfield Republican, xliii, 20, 22n10, 35; notice regarding LMA's English doctors in Dinan, 128, 131n15

St. Agnes, 102, 105n2

St. Bartholomew's Day Massacre, 119n5

St. Bernard, 137n4

St. Bernard, Hospice of, 130n11, 133, 134, 135, 137n4, 138, 193, 208n6

St. Bernard, May's letter of, 207, 208n6, 210, 215

St. Bernard, Mount, 203, 206

St. Bernard, Pass of, 130n11, 132, 137n1, 137n6

St. Étienne de Bourges, cathedral of, 115, 121n13

St. Gatien Cathedral, 93, 95n6, 98, 101n1, 105n1

St. Gratien, 102, 103

St. Hubert, 110, 111n6

St. Louis, armor of, 93, 96n6

St. Luc, Switzerland, 155, 160n11

St. Luke, Switzerland (St. Luc), 155, 160n11

St. Malo, church of, 39, 39n5, 60

St. Malo, France, 32n3, 92, 95n2, 93, 101

St. Marks, church of. *See* San Marco, convent of

St. Martin, xlvi, 95–96n6, 102, 105n2; painting of, 93, 98

St. Maurice, Switzerland, 138, 140n5, 155

St. Melanie, tower of, 12, 16n1

St. Peter, cathedral of, 249n11

St. Sauveur, church of, 38, 39n2, 49, 49n3

St. Sebastian, 138, 140n4

St. Servan, France, 45n5

St. Serves, church of. *See* St. Sauveur, church of

Stanton, Elizabeth Cady, 122n25

Stearns, Frank Preston, 250n18

Stearns, George Luther, xxvi, 68n3

Stearns, Mary Preston, xxvi, 224; Correggio engravings of, 245; debt of, repaid, 65, 68n3, 149, 167, 168n4; LMA angry regarding payment to, 231

Stern, Madeleine B., 238n11

Stone, Lucy, 131nn18–19

Stowe, William W., xvii

Strasbourg, xlix, 186, 189n5, 218, 221n1

Strasbourg, cathedral of, 218, 221n1

Street, Francis Scott, 173, 179n2

Stresa, Italy, lii, 214, 217n3, 235, 240

Studying Art Abroad (May Alcott), lxviii, 112n9

Sturater, Mr., 227

Sumner, Alice Mason, lxii

Sumner, Charles, lxii

Syracuse, N.Y., 218

Szárápy, Count Ferencz Sarpari, 126, 129, 130n5, 138, 141; admiration of, for May, 146, 147; flirts with May, 183; leaves for Hungary, 206; May flirts with, 163; May sketches trees for, 138, 143

Tablets (ABA), 165, 166n2, 168

Tarpeian Rock, 205, 208n2

Taylor, Clementia, lxi, 56, 57nn6–7, 62

Taylor, Peter Alfred, xxvii, lxi, 57nn6–7

Temple School, xviii, xxii, lvi, 200n3

Thomas, Mr., 192, 193n1

Thomas of Cantorbury, Sir, 22n1

Thompson, Mortimer (Philander Doesticks), 173, 179n3

Thoreau, Henry David, xx, xxx, 27n2, 88n14; as friend of Channing, Ellery, 68n2, 87n6

Tiber River, flood of, 253–57

Tidey, Mr., 151, 159n4

Tidey, Alfred, 151, 155, 159n4

Tidey boys, 151, 162

Tiffany, Mr. and Mrs. Dexter, 7, 9n13

Tilton, Theodore, 118, 122n25, 129

Titian, liii, 245, 249n13

Torquay, England, 169, 171n1

Tours, cathedral of, xlvi, 115

Tours, France, xlvi, 93, 96, 97, 105n2, 105n4, 106n14, 113, 125; Alcotts' arrival in, 92; letters from, 92–103, 108–12; LMA's description of, 102; location of, 95n1; May's description of, 108

Tremezzo, Italy, 243n9
Trentino, Italy, 196n5
Tribuna, the, 245, 248n8, 248n9, 248n10,
    249n14
Trowbridge, John Townsend, 264n17
Troyon, Constant, 110, 112n9
Tuckerman, Stephen Salisbury, xxii, xxiii
Tunis, 215, 221, 222n3
Turin, Italy, lx, lxi
Turner, J. M. W., lxi; May's copies of, lxiv,
    lxvi
Twain, Mark, 249n13
Tyrol, the, 195, 196n5

Uffizi, the, liii, 245, 247nn7–8, 248n10,
    249n11, 249n13
Under the Lilacs (LMA), lxvi

Vandal, 256, 263n11
Vatican, 255, 257
Vecelli, Tiziano. See Titian
Venice, Italy, lxi, 253
Venus (goddess), 104
Verdi, Giuseppe, lii, 238n10
Vernayaz, Switzerland, 169n6
Vevey, Switzerland, xlviii, lxvi, 1, 117,
    122n20; Alcotts' arrival in, 124; letters
    from, 117–18, 123–24, 179–232; LMA's
    first visit to, 122n19
Victor Emmanuel II (king), lviii, 189n7,
    267; acclaim for, 257, 258, 260, 261, 262;
    arrival of, in Rome, 258; departure of,
    from Rome, 261; opens free school in
    Rome, 255, 263n10; Pope's anger at,
    263n9; proposes peaceful settlement
    with Pope, 226n6; royal residence of,
    in Florence, 248n7
Victoria, Pension, 117, 122n19, 214, 216n1
Villars-sur-Ollon, Switzerland, 145, 145n5
Villeneuve, Switzerland, 115, 121n10

Vincent, Mrs., 269, 269n2
Vosages, the, 93, 96n8

Walpole, N.H., 192n1, 238n11
Warren, Angelina (Lena), 126, 129n2,
    137, 143, 227; accompanies LMA
    and May to Villeneuve, 214;
    accompanies May to Bex salt-mine,
    144; accompanies May to Geneva,
    144, 161; accompanies May to Grot
    des Fees, 139; accompanies May to
    Mount St. Bernard, 132–35, 138, 193,
    215; as companion for May, 141; LMA's
    opinion of, 185; pays Count's expenses,
    146; stepmother of, 229, 232n2; as
    thankful to be remembered by LMA's
    parents, 212
Warren, Angelina Greenwood, xlvii;
    121n11, 129n2, 232n2
Warren, Emma, 126, 130n2, 141, 147, 228;
    LMA's opinion of, 185
Warren, Henry Edward, xlvii, lxii, 130n2
Warren, Richard, xlvii, 121n11, 129n2,
    130n3, 232n2
Warren, Winslow (judge), 125, 130n3
Warren family, 115, 121n11, 125, 147, 158,
    183, 185, 221
Warren sisters, 168, 205; LMA's opinion
    of, 153
Warwick, Earl of (Richard Neville), 104,
    106n12
Webster, Daniel, lx
Weedy, Aunt, 32, 94, 158, 224, 269; as
    LMA's nickname, 32n5
Weissenburg, France (Wissemborg),
    184n1, 189n5
Weld, Anna, xxvi, xlvii, 2, 16n2, 126,
    130n9; engagement of, 126, 130n10; stay
    of, in Pension Victoria, 216n1
Weld, Elizabeth, 12n2

Weld, George, xxvi
Weld, William Fletcher, xxvi, 12n2
Weld family, 199
Wells, Miss, 116, 122n18
Wells, Clara, 136, 137n7
Wells, Eliza May, 224, 226n4
Wells, Elizabeth Sewall Willis (Lizzy),
    lvi, 68n5, 118, 122n24, 226n4; letter to,
    265–67
Wells, Thomas Goodwin, 118, 122n24
Westminster Abbey, 147, 150n6
Wheildon, Juliet Frances, 9n8
Wheildon, William Wilder, 9nn7–8
Wheildon family, 6, 9n7
Whipple, Charlotte Hastings, 115, 121n9,
    124
Whipple, Edwin Percy, 121n9
Whitman, Alfred, xxii, 181n4, 196n6
Wilbur, Dr. Hervey B., xxiv
Willard, Mrs., 206, 208n3, 210
Willis, Benjamin, 118, 122n24, 191n1; death
    of, 195

Willis, Elizabeth Sewall May, 122n24,
    191n1
Willis, Hamilton, 191, 191n1
Willis, Louisa, 191n1
Wilson, Mr., 182
Windsor Castle, 170
Winship, Charles W., 191n1
Winship, Martha Ruggles, 192n1
Wisniewski, Ladislas, xxvi, 216n1
Wissemborg, France, 184n1, 189n5
Woerth, France, 184n1, 189n5
Woman's Journal, 131n18, 178
Work (LMA), lxvi
Wörth, France (Woerth), 184n1, 189n5

Youth's Companion, 35, 36n10, 178n1

Zenobia, 141
Zermatt, Switzerland, 214, 217n5
Zermatt Valley, 237n3
Zoroaster, 141, 142n2
Zurich, Switzerland, 190n12